AMERICAN REVOLUTION

Selected titles in the Perspectives in American Social History series

PERSPECTIVES IN
AMERICAN SOCIAL HISTORY

American Revolution

People and Perspectives

Andrew K. Frank, Editor
Peter C. Mancall, Series Editor

A B C ⬗ C L I O

Santa Barbara, California · Denver, Colorado · Oxford, England

Cataloging-in-Publication Data is on file with the Library of Congress
ISBN: 978-1-85109-703-6   ebook: 978-1-85109-708-1

11 10 09 08   10 9 8 7 6 5 4 3 2 1

This book is also available on the World Wide Web as an eBook. Visit www.abc-clio.com for details.

ABC-CLIO, Inc.
130 Cremona Drive, P.O. Box 1911
Santa Barbara, California 93116–1911

Production Editor: Kristine Swift
Editorial Assistant: Sara Springer
Production Manager: Don Schmidt
Media Editor: Julie Dunbar
Media Resources Manager: Caroline Price
File Manager: Paula Gerard

This book is printed on acid-free paper ∞

Manufactured in the United States of America

Contents

Series Introduction

S ocial history is, simply put, the study of past societies. More specifically, social historians attempt to describe societies in their totality, and hence often eschew analysis of politics and ideas. Though many social historians argue that it is impossible to understand how societies functioned without some consideration of the ways that politics works on a daily basis or what ideas could be found circulating at any given time, they tend to pay little attention to the formal arenas of electoral politics or intellectual currents. In the United States, social historians have been engaged in describing components of the population which had earlier often escaped formal analysis, notably women, members of ethnic or cultural minorities, or those who had fewer economic opportunities than the elite.

Social history became a vibrant discipline in the United States after it had already gained enormous influence in Western Europe. In France, social history in its modern form emerged with the rising prominence of a group of scholars associated with the journal *Annales Economie, Societé, Civilisation* (or *Annales ESC* as it is known). In its pages and in a series of books from historians affiliated with the École des Hautes Études en Sciences Sociale in Paris, brilliant historians such as Marc Bloch, Jacques Le Goff, and Emanuel LeRoy Ladurie described seemingly every aspect of French society. Among the masterpieces of this historical reconstruction was Fernand Braudel's monumental study, *The Mediterranean and the Mediterranean World in the Age of Philip II*, published first in Paris in 1946 and in a revised edition in English in 1972. In this work Braudel argued that the only way to understand a place in its totality was to describe its environment, its social and economic structures, and its political systems. In Britain the emphasis of social historians has been less on questions of environment, per se, than in a description of human communities in all their complexities. For example, social historians there have taken advantage of that nation's remarkable local archives to reconstruct the history of the family and details of its rural past. Works such as Peter Laslett's *The World We Have Lost,* first printed in 1966, and the multi-authored *Agrarian History of England and Wales*, which began to appear in print in 1967, revealed that painstaking work could reveal the lives and habits of individuals who never previously attracted the interest of biographers, demographers, or most historians.

Social history in the United States gained a large following in the second half of the twentieth century, especially during the 1960s and 1970s. Its development sprang from political, technical, and intellectual impulses deeply embedded in the culture of the modern university. The politics of civil rights and social reform fueled the passions of historians who strove to tell the stories of the underclass. They benefited from the adoption by historians of statistical analysis, which allowed scholars to trace where individuals lived, how often they moved, what kinds of jobs they took, and whether their economic status declined, stagnated, or improved over time. As history departments expanded, many who emerged from graduate schools focused their attention on groups previously ignored or marginalized. Women's history became a central concern among American historians, as did the history of African Americans, Native Americans, Latinos, and others. These historians pushed historical study in the United States farther away from the study of formal politics and intellectual trends. Though few Americanists could achieve the technical brilliance of some social historians in Europe, collectively they have been engaged in a vast act of description, with the goal of describing seemingly every facet of life from 1492 to the present.

The sixteen volumes in this series together represent the continuing efforts of historians to describe American society. Most of the volumes focus on chronological areas, from the broad sweep of the colonial era to the more narrowly defined collections of essays on the eras of the Cold War, the Baby Boom, and America in the age of the Vietnam War. The series also includes entire volumes on the epochs that defined the nation, the American Revolution and the Civil War, as well as volumes dedicated to the process of westward expansion, women's rights, and African American history.

This social history series derives its strength from the talented editors of individual volumes. Each editor is an expert in his or her own field who selected and organized the contents of his or her volume. Editors solicited other experienced historians to write individual essays. Every volume contains first-rate analysis complemented by lively anecdotes designed to reveal the complex contours of specific historical moments. The many illustrations to be found in these volumes testify too to the recognition that any society can be understood not only by the texts that its participants produce but also by the images that they craft. Primary source documents in each volume will allow interested readers to pursue some specific topics in greater depth, and each volume contains a chronology to provide guidance to the flow of events over time. These tools—anecdotes, images, texts, and timelines—allow readers to gauge the inner workings of America in particular periods and yet also to glimpse connections between eras.

The articles in these volumes testify to the abundant strengths of historical scholarship in the United States in the early years of the twenty-first century. Despite the occasional academic contest that flares into public notice, or the self-serving cant of politicians who want to manipulate the nation's past for partisan ends—for example, in debates over the second amendment to the United States Constitution and what it means about potential limits to the rights of gun ownership—the articles here all reveal the vast increase in knowledge of the American past that has taken place over the last half century. Social historians do not dominate history faculties in American colleges and universities, but no one could deny them a seat at the intellectual table. Without their efforts, intellectual, cultural, and political historians would be hard-pressed to understand why certain ideas circulated when they did, why some religious movements prospered or foundered, how developments in fields such as medicine and engineering reflected larger concerns, and what shaped the world we inhabit.

Fernand Braudel and his colleagues envisioned entire laboratories of historians in which scholars working together would be able to produce histoire totale: total history. Historians today seek more humble goals for our collective enterprise. But as the richly textured essays in these volumes reveal, scholarly collaboration has in fact brought us much closer to that dream. These volumes do not and cannot include every aspect of American history. However, every page reveals something interesting or valuable about how American society functioned. Together, these books suggest the crucial necessity of stepping back to view the grand complexities of the past rather than pursuing narrower prospects and lesser goals.

Peter C. Mancall

Series Editor

Introduction

F ew events in U.S. history are more associated with a handful of elite white men than the American Revolution. Americans typically associate the late eighteenth-century movement for independence with privileged politicians and generals, the events in which they participated, and the documents they created. It is hard to imagine the Revolution without George Washington and his crossing of the Delaware River in 1776 or Thomas Jefferson and his writing of the Declaration of Independence. (For modern books that focus on the Founding Fathers, see Fischer, 2004; Fischer, 1994; Ellis, 2001; and Ellis, 2004.)

Traditionally, the story of the Revolution has followed these and other proverbial "dead white men on horses" along their paths to mythic immortality. The story of the experiences of the so-called Founding Fathers, though, is drastically incomplete, and the findings of social historians have led many recent scholars to interpret these individuals within their social contexts. The Revolution was fought and shaped by men and women of all walks of life—whether farmers, day laborers, Indians, Africans, enlisted soldiers, sailors, children, women, Loyalists, or recent immigrants. In cities, on farms, and in the backcountry, ordinary Americans were central actors in the unfolding drama. They understood the importance of the conflict and made choices according to their religious teachings, economic needs, political connections, personal ambitions, and local contexts. From their vantage points, the Revolution was an ideological, political, economic, military, and, perhaps most important, social event. This volume explores the Revolution as a social event and reveals how ordinary Americans of diverse interests and backgrounds understood and experienced the eighteenth-century movement for independence. (Other works have synthesized modern social history scholarship on the Revolution; see Raphael, 2001. For a more balanced view, see Countryman, 2003.)

Few observers at the time denied the broad participation of the masses during the War for Independence. The military struggle, itself only a part of the revolutionary experience, brought a new set of realities for soldiers and civilians. Families dealt with the injuries and deaths of loved ones, the absence of male relatives from their homes and daily lives, and an economy that struggled under the weight of blockades and the loss of labor to the militaries. Backyards turned into battlefields, houses became makeshift hospitals, and households up and down the eastern seaboard dealt with shortages of food, supplies, and labor. Soldiers similarly, though perhaps more overtly, found the war to be a transforming event. They dealt with the distance from their homes, a lack of food and other basic supplies, and the prospect of long marches and armed conflict. The intense fighting between the colonial and British armies lasted for more than six years and took place in each of the thirteen colonies. Of all of the American wars, only the Civil War resulted in a greater percentage of U.S. casualties and deaths (Higginbotham, 1988). For the civilians who lived through it and the soldiers who fought in it, the American Revolution was a defining experience.

The American Revolution was more than the military struggle we now call the War for Independence. It was also an attempt to rewrite the norms of daily life and to break away from the monarchical system that guided both personal and political behavior (this issue has been taken up most effectively in Wood, 1992; see also "How Revolutionary Was the Revolution," 1994; Young, 1976; Young, 1993). Patriot leader and U.S. president John Adams recognized that the Revolution was a popular movement. In an 1818 letter to Hezekiah Niles, he made it clear that the Revolution was not simply an event of the social elite or of the militaries. "What do we mean by the American Revolution?" he asked. "Do we mean the American war? The Revolution was effected before the war commenced. The Revolution was in the minds and hearts of the people. This radical change in the principles, opinions, sentiments, and affections of the people, was the real American Revolution" (quoted in Jensen, 1968). The Revolution, Adams contended, was as much an ideological transformation as it was a military event. The everyday experiences of common people led them to push for, join, shape, or resist the independence movement. In this manner, to paraphrase Abraham Lincoln's definition of American democracy, the Revolution became an event "of the people, by the people and for the people" (Abraham Lincoln, Gettysburg Address, November 19, 1863).

When the Revolution is expanded to include more than the military conflict, the chronological bookends that traditionally define the era dissipate. Between the confrontations at Lexington and Concord in 1775 and the 1781 Battle of Yorktown, most of the military struggle for independence was fought. Most scholars continue their examination through the official signing of the Treaty of Paris in 1783 (Higginbotham, 1971). Yet the American Revolution had a much longer history, constituting what many scholars have renamed the "revolutionary age." The social context that shaped the movement for independence had historical roots that predated the actual fighting. It is hard to understand the Revolution without an understanding of the new taxes and the enforcement of old taxes that occurred after the French and Indian War (known as the Seven Years' War in Europe). Americans took to the streets to protest the new taxes, and for more than a decade they signed petitions to claim their liberties as loyal English citizens (Maier, 1972). The struggles over western lands predated the Revolution by more than a century, and they shaped the participation of white settlers and

Native Americans during the war (Merritt, 2003). On the frontier, fighting occurred right up until the official peace was secured in 1783, as Natives and farmers continued to shape the meaning of the Revolution (Richards, 2002; Gross, 1993). The struggle of African Americans and women to obtain the equality promised in the Declaration of Independence and then later in the Constitution continued long after the war ceased (Nash, 1988; Frey, 1991; Olwell, 1998). As a result, the history of the Revolution predates 1775 and continues through the war's technical conclusion in 1783.

Despite the ambiguity of dates, most scholars begin their discussion of the American Revolution with the end of the French and Indian War (1754–1763) (Anderson, 2000; Fowler, 2005). The social implications of this event and its aftermath are hard to miss. Starting in 1763, the British Crown began to reassert control over its American colonies. Having just fought to protect the colonies from its French and Native enemies, it pursued policies of the kind embodied in the Proclamation of 1763 and the Quebec Act that gave Quebec the right to many Indian lands claimed by the American colonists to ensure future domestic tranquility. The British also began to institute new taxes and enforce old ones in order to pay for its wartime expenses. Great Britain, which had amassed tremendous debts in its war with France, turned to its colonies as an untapped source of revenue. The litany of resulting parliamentary acts is familiar—the Sugar Act, Currency Act, Stamp Act, Tea Act, Quartering Act, Intolerable Acts, Coercive Acts, and the rest. The responses of Americans to these actions varied. Many colonists accepted them as the inevitable inconveniences of a desirable condition—being part of the British Empire, while others declared that they were burdensome and arbitrary impositions of the Crown.

The Proclamation of 1763, the first of many imperial insults, frustrated many eastern and western farmers. In an attempt to secure peace with powerful Native American neighbors, Great Britain forbade settlement west of the Appalachian Mountains. Such actions cut off opportunities for land speculators and western farmers, many of whom were already coveting or squatting on these lands. In addition, from the vantage point of the colonists, the Crown seemed to be sacrificing the ambitions of the colonists in favor of the Indians. The colonists later expressed their outrage as one of their grievances in the Declaration of Independence. The king "has endeavoured to bring on the inhabitants of our frontiers, the merciless Indian Savages, whose known rule of warfare, is an undistinguished destruction of all ages, sexes and conditions."

Many colonists responded to the Proclamation of 1763 and the other new impositions of the Crown through the written word. They wrote petitions, public letters, sermons, and broadsides. They sang songs, wrote poetry, and otherwise voiced their displeasure with the Crown and their growing desire for independence. Thomas Paine's famous pamphlet *Common Sense* asserted, "Until an independence is declared the continent will feel itself like a man who continues putting off some unpleasant business from day to day, yet knows it must be done, hates to set about it, wishes it over, and is continually haunted with the thoughts of its necessity" (Paine, *Common Sense*, 1776). Paine's argument for independence was reprinted in each of the colonies and shaped discussions on South Carolina plantations, Connecticut farms, and Pennsylvania taverns (Foner, 1976). Other petitions were less supportive of political independence and instead pointed to the desire to claim personal liberties. African American slaves in Boston, for example, declared, "We have in common with all other men a naturel right to our freedoms without Being depriv'd of them by our fellow men as we are a freeborn Pepel" (*Collections of the Massachusetts Historical Society*, 1877). Their petition was denied, though by the end of the war all of the northern states had moved toward ending slavery within their borders. On the other hand, when the colonists' complaints resulted in the repeal of taxes, thousands of colonists celebrated and redeclared their loyalty to the Crown (Countryman, 2003, 42).

Many Loyalists, who accounted for as many as one-third of all residents in the colonies, similarly voiced their concerns. They urged their neighbors and communities to keep their faith in King and Crown, and tried to counter the prevailing "common sense" of independence. Some called for reforms, while others dismissed the revolutionary rhetoric as the unrefined ranting of the rabble. Alexander MaGee, writing from his small farm in Maryland, tried to convince his neighbors that the impulse for independence "is not calculated or designed for the defence of American liberty or property, but for the purpose of enslaving the poor people thereof" (quoted in Hoffman, 1974, 191). The colonists, he explained, should be seeking conciliation rather than fanning the flames of conflict.

Others sat on the sidelines, silently hoping that the disputes would dissipate and that the conflicts would not turn into war. This was the case for many Quakers, who professed neutrality in the dispute. This attitude led many Patriots to see neutrality as a counterrevolutionary decision. Samuel Adams declared, "If they would not *pull down Kings*, let them not support *tyrants*" (quoted in Brock, 1968, 146–147).

Other colonists formed organizations to discuss their interests and shape the public and private discussions. Some organized into voluntary associations such as the Sons of Liberty and Committees of Safety, while others organized local militias, such as the well-known minutemen in Massachusetts. Many colonists simply used preexisting organizations to resist the Crown. In the capital of South Carolina, for example, the Charleston Fire Company served as the cornerstone of radical resistance (Walsh, 1959, 38–39). Some forms of resistance, such as the various boycotts of British goods and the general nonimportation movements, began as small local signs of resistance before spreading across the colonies. By refusing to purchase imported goods, colonists sought ways to defy the new taxes and avoid violent confrontations. In this way, economic power could be used rather than physical coercion. "Let us not," one Rhode Islander urged in response to threats of violence against a merchant, "by offering any violence to him or his property, give a wound to liberty himself." Instead, many colonists concluded that a boycott of British goods would be effective by bringing about a "starving condition" for workers in England (Maier, 1972, 74–75). In a song urging women to join the nonimportation movement, the lyrics united politics and fashion: "Young ladies in town, and those that live 'round / Wear none but your own country linen; / Of economy boast, let your pride be the most / To show clothes of your own make and spinnin'" (*Boston Newsletter*, 1769; see also Holton, 1999). Sewing clothes and making sure that their families wore homespun became the duty of all Patriot women.

Those who would not support the boycotts often faced the wrath of their neighbors. Violent threats and economic coercion, the *New York Journal* reported, usually had "a more powerful Effect in reducing such Culprits to Reason than the most convincing Arguments that could be used" (Maier, 1972, 126). Ordinary Americans, often as faceless participants in so-called mobs and public protests, used their numbers to oppose the Crown. Many Loyalists suffered at the hands of the revolutionary forces, and in some places the struggle for independence turned to civil war. As Methodist leader John Wesley commented in a note on the back of a letter from Thomas Rankin, a Methodist preacher in America, "The Rebels in Scotland did not even hang or Shoot those who refused to Join with them. But if they had what mercy had that been compared to the death inflicted by the Rebels in America? Can Englishmen Still open their Mouth in favor of those worse than Indian savages?" (Thomas Rankin to John Wesley, September 17, 1777, Preachers Collection, Methodist Archives).

Colonial responses to the Stamp Act demonstrated the power of the masses. On August 14, 1765, several thousand Bostonians took to the streets to protest the new tax on stamps used for legal documents. The angry residents destroyed the personal property of the stamp distributor for the colony and then hanged and beheaded him in effigy. The outrage spread throughout the colonies, as indebted colonists now faced greater fees when they were taken to court. George Sims, a North Carolina farmer, explained that to pay court costs, a farmer often had to see his "living wrecked and tore to pieces . . . if he had but one horse to plow with, one bed to lie on, or one cow to give a little milk for his children, they must all go to raise money which is not to be had." When goods were not enough, "then his lands . . . must go the same way to satisfy these cursed hungry caterpillars. . . . It would be enough to make us turn rebels" (quoted in Kars, 2002, 71–72). During the next four months after Boston's riot, Sims and other frustrated colonists engaged in similar public protests in all of the other colonies. As a result, all but one of the thirteen stamp distributors resigned, and the Stamp Act was repealed. The protests had apparently made their intentions clear. Over the following eight years, colonists continued to voice their complaints through crowd actions that colonists called "rough music," tarring and feathering, and other forms of public protest. These events culminated in the Boston Tea Party, where once again, thousands of Bostonians watched or later applauded the colonists who dressed as Mohawk Indians, boarded three boats, and threw the tea overboard. Several months later, in December 1774, residents in Charleston, South Carolina, followed the example of Bostonians. Through their public actions, the Carolinian protestors demonstrated their opposition to the policy as well as their solidarity with Bostonians.

Small farmers and herders in the colonial backcountry similarly voiced their frustrations through various acts of civil unrest. The complaints varied, but western settlers complained about Native Americans, unscrupulous land speculators, a lack of law and order, unfair taxes, greedy creditors, and unjust tenant laws. In 1771 North Carolina, for example, men calling themselves Regulators organized an army to end the "abuses of Power" that had led to their economic troubles. They closed courts, freed their supporters from prison, disrupted travel, and stopped paying taxes. Whereas the Stamp Act protestors saw their grievances temporarily addressed, North Carolina's Regulators disbanded only after they were defeated in a battle with the British army. The Regulators in North Carolina were not the only agrarian protesters. Regulators also tried to bring "law and order" to South Carolina a few years earlier, while the Liberty Men in Maine and the Paxton Boys in Pennsylvania brought their own forms of order to the backcountry. For more than a decade, farmers used violence to protect their interests when the colonial elite or the Crown would not. The Paxton Boys, for example, attacked nearby Conestoga Indians in 1764. Although these were not the Indians who had done them injury, they were conveniently living in a nearby mission. The Paxton Boys then marched toward Philadelphia, where other Indians were being protected by the colony. Benjamin Franklin led the makeshift militia that pacified and dispersed the Paxton Boy leaders (Merritt, 2003, 285–289; Klein, 1990).

Just as the Paxton Boys sought to obtain their liberty at the expense of Indians, other Americans drew upon the rhetoric of liberty, freedom, and equality in ways that reveal the contradictions of the era. As white colonists repeatedly declared their desires for "freedom" and "liberty," many African slaves concluded that they too should enjoy this natural right. In 1773, for example, the *Virginia Gazette* ran an ad for two runaway slaves who were presumed to be heading to Great Britain. There, the paper explained, "they imagine they will be free (a Notion now too prevalent among the Negroes, greatly to the Vexation and Prejudice of their Masters)" (quoted in Mullin, 1972, 131). For others, obtaining "liberty" required colonial laws to go unenforced. For small farmers in New Jersey, frustrations over debt collection resulted in the forced closing of courts by various Liberty Boys (McConville, 1999, 240–241). In other instances, securing freedom required repressing others. Throughout the colonies, revolutionaries formed People's Courts, extralegal grand juries of local residents to charge known Tories for activities such as naming their children after the royal family or singing "God Save the King."

Soon after the colonists declared independence and the war began, everyone in eastern North America found themselves involved in an intercontinental struggle. Even those who wanted to be neutral often discovered that this was much more difficult than they had imagined it would be. The British, especially in the war's later years, based much of their military strategy on the expectation that African Americans, Native Americans, and white Loyalists would assist them in subduing the rebellion. In many instances, the British calls for assistance were heeded, and the results often terrorized the revolutionaries. Commander of the Continental Army George Washington, for example, believed that the outcome of the war might be determined by "which side can arm the Negroes faster" (General Washington to Colonel Henry Lee, December 20, 1775, in Rhodehamel, 1997).

In the backcountry, especially in the South, Native Americans also tried to turn the war into their own struggle for independence. At first, most Indians took the path of neutrality. The Oneidas, for example, asked the governor of Connecticut in 1775 to "let us Indians be all of one mind, and live in peace with one another; and you white people settle your disputes betwixt yourselves" ("A Speech of the Chiefs and Warriors," 1775, 601–602). Soon after, however, this position was no longer tenable, and Oneida warriors split among themselves, some making British and others American alliances.

Both the British and Continental Armies incorporated members from across the social spectrum from every region. General Washington could not help recognizing that the troops that fought under his command represented more than the privileged world of his upbringing. Instead, he described them as "an exceeding dirty and nasty people" (quoted in Fischer, 2004, 19–21). The Continental and British Armies both enlisted almost every imaginable European ethnic group—Germans, Poles, Italians, Scots, Irish, and others. Those enlisted were blacksmiths, small farmers, merchants, servants, ministers, and cobblers. Soldiers also came from all of the thirteen colonies, as well as some from Florida and Canada. Other assistance came from France in the form of advisers and Germany as mercenaries. There were even some women who pretended to be men in order to enlist in the Continental Army. African American slaves volunteered for the Continental and especially the British Army in return for promises of freedom, and Native Americans fought alongside and against both armies (Royster, 1979, 3–53).

The military campaigns affected far more than the men (and handful of women) who were enlisted in the respective armies (Young, 2005). Battles frequently took place on the fields of farmers, turning cornfields into battlefields. Troops (on both sides) stole food, burned fields, and destroyed houses. Soldiers frequently foraged as they marched, leading to shortages and general despair. The resulting destruction led an American general in 1782 to describe a trip in war-torn South Carolina as "the most dull, melancholy, dreary ride that anyone could possibly take." The rural landscape once filled with "live-stock and wild fowl of every kind, was now destitute of all. It had been so completely checquered by the different parties, that not one part of it had been left unexplored; consequently, not the vestiges of horses, cattle, hogs, or deer, &c. was to be found. The squirrels and birds of every kind were destroyed" (quoted in Weir, 1985, 76–77). With all of the battles fought on American soil, residents everywhere in the American countryside did not recover for years.

The destruction of fields and attacks on civilians and their property were central parts of the military policies of both Britons and Americans. This was especially true when it came to policy toward Native Americans, where soldiers waged what would be called during the American Civil War the "hard hand of war" (Grimsley, 1995). South Carolinian William H. Drayton, for example, ordered his Patriot soldiers to "make smooth work as you go—that is, you cut up every Indian corn-field, and burn every Indian town—and that every Indian taken shall be the slave and property of the taker; that the nation be extirpated, and the lands become the property of the public" (quoted in Raphael, 2001, 282). Native Americans had faced similar attacks prior to the Revolution, but during it they faced simultaneous assaults from the British and the Americans on many fronts. In 1779, as General John Sullivan's campaign devastated the Iroquois, the Continental Army attacked and destroyed villages in almost all thirteen colonies (Graymont, 1972).

Some of the disruptions caused by the war were more mundane than burned homes and razed fields. The war brought soldiers into homes, as both armies quartered their men in private homes. Even so, many women refused to leave their homes for safety. "If the two opposite Armys were to come here alternately ten times," one Pennsylvanian woman explained to John Adams, "she would stand by her Property until she should be kill'd. If she must be a Beggar, it should be where she is known" (quoted in Norton, 1996, 199–200). Other families moved to avoid the passing soldiers or to find comfort with their relatives. The war similarly transformed the lives of even the most privileged children. As many schoolteachers enlisted and wartime demands for labor increased, most white children stopped their formal schooling. In addition, families in all of the colonies dealt with shortages of every imaginable necessity. Nathaniel Goddard, for example, recalled, "We were extremely distressed for even the necessaries of life, and we had very few of its luxuries or conveniences. The women were obliged to use thorns instead of pins to fasten on their clothes" (Goddard, 1906).

Some residents turned the wartime disruptions into opportunities. Many Americans turned to smuggling or became privateers, occupations that proved to be very lucrative during the war. The war also provided opportunities for some slaves to claim their freedom. In April 1775, African slaves offered their services to Virginia governor Lord Dunmore in exchange for their freedom. By November, Dunmore agreed to the offer, and more than 800 enslaved men found their way to Dunmore's home. As many as 80,000 other slaves fled to British lines in order to emancipate themselves. Before the war ended, thousands had secured their freedom in Florida, Canada, and elsewhere (Holton, 1961, 29, 149).

The war brought challenges to religious leaders, who carefully balanced ethical and communal concerns with their loyalty to the Crown and their transatlantic connections. Some hoped for independence, and others wanted to preserve their ties to the Crown. Some, such as the minister John Murray, saw the fight as a religious one. "To shun the dangers of the field," he proclaimed, "is to desert the banner of Christ" (quoted in Royster, 1979, 16). Not all religious leaders believed that fighting for the Revolution was a holy endeavor. Methodist Charles Wesley urged ministers to be "like-minded with me. I am of neither side, and yet of both; on the side of New England and old. Private Christians are excused, exempted, privileged, to take no part in civil troubles" (quoted in John Wesley to Thomas Rankin, March 1, 1775, in Telford, 1931, 6:142–143). Even if they did not see neutrality as desirable, many Quakers similarly declared that religious principles mandated pacifist methods. As one Quaker leader explained, the devout "cannot . . . contend for liberty by any methods . . . contrary to the peaceable spirit and temper of the Gospel" (Mekeel, 1979, 47).

For Americans with ties across the Atlantic, the Revolution forced them to make careful and often complex decisions. Methodist leader Francis Asbury, for example, struggled between the British ties of his birth and his current local connections. He recognized that his English friends across the Atlantic might not understand his decision. As a result, he was "under some heaviness of mind. But no wonder: three thousand miles from home—my friends have left me—I am considered by some as an enemy of the country—every day liable to be seized by violence, and abused" (Clark, 1958, 1:263–264). Similarly merchants often found themselves cutting ties with their connections in the colonies or their connections overseas. Breaking with Great Britain, at least in the short term, required many to sever costly personal and professional ties as well.

The war had other rather ambiguous social results. Many of the inequalities that defined colonial life continued after independence was secured. Slavery remained in the southern colonies, where the majority of slaves lived, and a growing slave population faced ever more draconian slave codes. Similarly, Abigail Smith Adams could hardly declare victory when at the outset of the political struggle she had asked her husband, John Adams, to "Remember the Ladies." In 1776, she asked her husband, "Why should I not have liberty whilst you strive for liberty?" (Adams, 1848, 1:148). When the war ended, her husband believed he had obtained his liberty, but the position of women remained the same. Native Americans, most of whom supported Great Britain during the war, often found themselves punished for their support of the Crown and their lands and sovereignty under assault. Similarly, urban workers and small farmers discovered that the fight for their liberties would have to be waged in the decades that followed the Revolution.

At the same time, though, the Revolution created new political and social networks, the end of slavery in many colonies, the right to self-rule, and for many a new identity. Most white colonists stopped thinking of themselves as Britons or subjects of the king, and now began to see themselves as part of a new American Republic. By the end of the eighteenth century, these changes had transformed the United States. As historian Gordon Wood has explained, "In destroying monarchy and establishing republics they were changing their society as well as their governments, and they knew it. Only they did not know—they could scarcely have imagined—how much of their society they would change." The Revolution, from this vantage point, set in motion a vast range of social transformations. It "made possible the antislavery and women's rights movements of the nineteenth century and in fact all our current egalitarian thinking. The Revolution . . . also brought respectability and even dominance to ordinary people long held in contempt and gave dignity to their menial labor. . . . Most important, it made the interests and prosperity of ordinary people—their pursuits of happiness—the goal of society and government" (Wood, 1992, 5, 7–8).

In 1909, historian Carl Becker observed that the American Revolution was not only fought over "Home rule . . . but also who was to rule at home" (Becker, 1909, 5). Becker understood that winning the War of Independence was not the same as winning the American Revolution. With independence, the colonists may have obtained the ability to write a new future, but they were not compelled to share a single vision of that future. The Revolution, then, was also about the question of whose domestic vision would be pursued.

The chapters that follow examine, in far more detail, how Americans of varied backgrounds experienced and shaped the outcome of the American Revolution. Immediately following this introductory chapter, the volume discusses how the Revolution shaped the lives of ordinary farmers and non-British immigrants to the colonies. The next three chapters explore the social realities for African Americans, Native Americans, and settlers in the backcountry. The next two chapters explore children and soldiers in the Continental Army. The next two chapters examine the experiences of two religious communities—the Quakers and the Methodists. Subsequent chapters explore the war from the perspective of sailors, women, and Loyalists, those men and women who supported the Crown throughout the war. Although the chapters are neatly defined, they inevitably overlap. History does not lend itself to simple classification. African Americans were often Loyalists; immigrants were often laborers; and Native Americans obviously interacted with settlers in the backcountry. Taken together, these overlapping chapters reflect the braided narratives that form the story of the American Revolution as the people saw it.

Andrew K. Frank

References and Further Reading

Adams, Charles Francis, ed. *Letters of Mrs. Adams, the Wife of John Adams.* 4th ed. Boston: Wilkins, Carter, 1848.

Anderson, Fred. *The Crucible of War: The Seven Years' War and the Fate of Empire in British North America, 1754–1766.* New York: Knopf, 2000.

"A Speech of the Chiefs and Warriors of the *Oneida* Tribe of Indians, to the four New-England Provinces; directed immediately to Governor Trumbull, and by him to be communicated." *Pennsylvania Magazine; or, American Monthly Museum (1775–1776)* 1 (1775): 601–602.

Becker, Carl L. *The History of Political Parties in the Province of New York, 1760–1776.* Madison: University of Wisconsin Press, 1909.

Boston Newsletter.

Brock, Peter. *Pioneers of the Peaceable Kingdom.* Princeton, NJ: Princeton University Press, 1968.

Clark, Elmer T., ed. *Journal and Letters of Francis Asbury.* 3 vols. London: Hazell, Watson and Viney, 1958.

Collections of the Massachusetts Historical Society. 5th series, III. Boston: Massachusetts Historical Society, 1877.

Countryman, Edward. *The American Revolution.* Rev. ed. New York: Hill and Wang, 2003.

Ellis, Joseph J. *Founding Brothers: The Revolutionary Generation.* New York: Knopf, 2001.

Ellis, Joseph J. *George Washington*. New York: Knopf, 2004.

Fischer, David Hackett. *Paul Revere's Ride*. New York: Oxford University Press, 1994.

Fischer, David Hackett. *Washington's Crossing*. New York: Oxford University Press, 2004.

Foner, Eric. *Tom Paine and Revolutionary America*. New York: Oxford University Press, 1976.

Fowler, William M., Jr. *Empires at War: The French and Indian War and the Struggle for North America, 1754–1763*. New York: Walker, 2005.

Fox, Francis S. *Sweet Land of Liberty: The Ordeal of the American Revolution in Northampton County, Pennsylvania*. University Park: Pennsylvania State University Press, 2000.

Frey, Sylvia R. *Water from the Rock: Black Resistance in a Revolutionary Age*. Princeton, NJ: Princeton University Press, 1991.

Goddard, Nathaniel. *Nathaniel Goddard: A Boston Merchant, 1767–1853*. Cambridge, MA: Printed at the Riverside press for private distribution, 1906.

Graymont, Barbara. *The Iroquois in the American Revolution*. Syracuse, NY: Syracuse University Press, 1972.

Grimsley, Mark. *Hard Hand of War: Union Military Policy toward Southern Civilians, 1861–1865*. New York: Cambridge University Press, 1995.

Gross, Robert A., ed. *In Debt to Shays: The Bicentennial of an Agrarian Rebellion*. Charlottesville: University Press of Virginia, 1993.

Higginbotham, Don. *The War of American Independence: Military Attitudes, Policies, and Practice, 1763–1789*. Boston: Northeastern University Press, 1971.

Higginbotham, Don. *War and Society in Revolutionary America: The Wider Dimensions of Conflict*. Columbia: University of South Carolina Press, 1988.

Hoffman, Ronald. *A Spirit of Dissension: Economics, Politics and the Revolution in Maryland*. Baltimore: Johns Hopkins University Press, 1974.

Holton, Woody. *Forced Founders: Indians, Debtors, Slaves, and the Making of the American Revolution in Virginia*. Chapel Hill: University of North Carolina Press, 1999.

"How Revolutionary Was the Revolution: A Discussion of Gordon Wood's *The Radicalism of the American Revolution*." *William and Mary Quarterly*, 3rd ser., 51 (1994): 677–716.

Jensen, Merrill. *The Founding of a Nation: A History of the American Revolution, 1763–1776*. New York: Oxford University Press, 1968.

Kars, Marjoleine. *Breaking Loose Together: The Regulator Rebellion in Pre-Revolutionary North Carolina*. Chapel Hill: University of North Carolina Press, 2002.

Klein, Rachel N. *Unification of a Slave State: The Rise of the Planter Class in the South Carolina Backcountry, 1760–1808.* Chapel Hill: University of North Carolina Press, 1990.

Kulikoff, Allan. *From British Peasants to Colonial American Farmers.* Chapel Hill: University of North Carolina Press, 2000.

Maier, Pauline. *From Resistance to Revolution: Colonial Radicals and the Development of American Opposition to Britain, 1765–1776.* New York: Knopf, 1972.

McConville, Brendan. *These Daring Disturbers of the Public Peace: The Struggle for Property in Early New Jersey.* Ithaca, NY: Cornell University Press, 1999.

Mekeel, Arthur J. *The Relation of the Quakers to the American Revolution.* Washington, DC: University Press of America, 1979.

Merritt, Jane T. *At the Crossroads: Indians and Empires on a Mid-Atlantic Frontier, 1700–1763.* Chapel Hill: University of North Carolina Press, 2003.

Mullin, Gerald W. *Flight and Rebellion: Slave Resistance in Eighteenth-Century Virginia.* New York: Oxford University Press, 1972.

Nash, Gary B. *Forging Freedom: The Formation of Philadelphia's Black Community, 1720–1840.* Cambridge, MA: Harvard University Press, 1988.

Norton, Mary Beth. *Liberty's Daughters: The Revolutionary Experience of American Women, 1750–1800.* Ithaca, NY: Cornell University Press, 1996.

Olwell, Robert A. *Masters, Slaves and Subjects: The Culture of Power in the South Carolina Low Country, 1740–1790.* Ithaca, NY: Cornell University Press, 1998.

Paine, Thomas. *Common Sense,* in *Thomas Paine: Collected Writings,* ed. Eric Foner. New York: Library of America, 1995.

Preachers Collection, Methodist Archives, Manchester, England.

Raphael, Ray. *A People's History of the American Revolution: How Common People Shaped the Fight for Independence.* New York: New Press, 2001.

Rhodehamel, John, comp. *George Washington: Writings.* New York: Library of America, 1997.

Richards, Leonard. *Shays's Rebellion: The American Revolution's Final Battle.* Philadelphia: University of Pennsylvania Press, 2002.

Royster, Charles. *A Revolutionary People at War: The Continental Army and American Character, 1775–1783.* New York: Norton, 1979.

Telford, John, ed. *Letters of John Wesley.* 8 vols. London: Epworth, 1931.

Vickers, Daniel. *Farmers and Fishermen: Two Centuries of Work in Essex County, Massachusetts, 1630–1830.* Chapel Hill: University of North Carolina Press, 1994.

Walsh, Richard. *Charleston's Sons of Liberty.* Columbia: University of South Carolina Press, 1959.

Weir, Robert M. "'The Violent Spirit': The Reestablishment of Order, and the Continuity of Leadership in Post-Revolutionary South Carolina," in *An Uncivil War: The Southern Backcountry during the American Revolution,* ed. Ronald Hoffman, Thad W. Tate, and Peter J. Albert. Charlottesville: University Press of Virginia, 1985.

Wood, Gordon S. *Radicalism of the American Revolution*. New York: Knopf, 1992.

Young, Alfred F. *Beyond the American Revolution: Explorations in the History of American Radicalism*. De Kalb: Northern Illinois University Press, 1993.

Young, Alfred F. *Masquerade: The Life and Times of Deborah Sampson, Continental Soldier*. New York: Vintage, 2005.

Young, Alfred F., ed. *The American Revolution: Explorations in the History of American Radicalism*. De Kalb: Northern Illinois University Press, 1976.

About the Editor and Contributors

Terry Bouton is assistant professor at the University of Maryland, Baltimore County. He is author of "A Road Closed: Rural Insurgency in Post-Independence Pennsylvania," which was published in the *Journal of American History* (2000). He is currently completing a book entitled *Taming Democracy: Pennsylvania Farmers and the Betrayal of the American Revolution*.

A. Glenn Crothers is assistant professor of history at the University of Louisville and director of research at the Filson Historical Society. He has published numerous articles on early American history, including essays in the *Journal of American History, Business History Review, Journal of the Early Republic*, and *Agricultural History*. He is currently finishing *Quakers in Northern Virginia, 1750–1865: Negotiating Communities and Cultures*.

Lisa Ennis is a reference librarian at the University of Alabama at Birmingham's Lister Hill Health Sciences Library. She received her M.A. in history from Georgia College (1994) and an M.S. in information sciences from the University of Tennessee (1997). She has published several articles on women in sport and medical history.

Andrew K. Frank is assistant professor of history at Florida State University. He is author of *Creeks and Southerners: Biculturalism on the Early American Frontier* (University of Nebraska Press, 2005) and *The Routledge Historical Atlas of the American South* (Routledge, 1999). He is currently working on *The Second Conquest: Indians, Settlers and Slaves on the Florida Frontier*. He received his Ph.D. from the University of Florida in 1998.

Andrew C. Lannen is assistant professor of history at Stephen F. Austin State University. He received his Ph.D. from Louisiana State University. He has published numerous encyclopedia articles about early America and American military history. He is currently preparing a book-length manuscript on colonial Georgia.

Anna M. Lawrence is assistant professor of history at Florida Atlantic University. She received her Ph.D. from the University of Michigan in 2004. She is finishing a book-length manuscript on the transatlantic Methodist community during the American Revolution and has published several articles on religion in the Revolutionary era.

Robyn McMillan is currently a Ph.D. candidate in American history at the University of Oklahoma. McMillan is engaged in writing her dissertation on the cultures of science in eighteenth-century America, focusing in particular on the intellectual, cultural, and material realms of the physical sciences.

Daniel S. Murphree received a Ph.D. in history from Florida State University and is currently an assistant professor of history at the University of Texas at Tyler. He received the Arthur W. Thompson award for "Constructing Indians in the Colonial Floridas: Origins of European–Floridian Identity, 1513–1573," *Florida Historical Quarterly* (2002), and has recently published *Constructing Floridians: Natives and Europeans in the Colonial Floridas, 1513–1783* (University Press of Florida, 2006).

Doug Phinney received his M.A. in history at Florida Atlantic University.

Matthew Raffety is assistant professor of history at Gonzaga University. He received his Ph.D. from Columbia University in 2003 for his dissertation, "The Republic Afloat: Violence, Labor, Manhood, and the Law at Sea, 1789–1861." He is currently working on a book project focusing on the meanings of violent crimes at sea before the Civil War.

Margaret Sankey is assistant professor of history at Minnesota State University Moorhead. Her book, *Jacobite Prisoners of the 1715 Rebellion: Preventing and Punishing Insurrection in Early Hanoverian Britain* (Ashgate, 2005), and ongoing research deal with British government responses to insurgency in the eighteenth century.

Jon Sensbach is professor of history at the University of Florida. He is the author of *Rebecca's Revival: Creating Black Christianity in the Atlantic World* (Harvard University Press, 2005) and *A Separate Canaan: The Making of an Afro-Moravian World in North Carolina, 1763–1840* (University of North Carolina Press, 1998).

Steve Triana received his B.A. in history from Florida Atlantic University.

Elizabeth McKee Williams is a Ph.D. candidate in American culture at the University of Michigan. She is the author of several articles, including "Childhood, Memory, and the American Revolution" in *Children and War: A Historical Anthology*, edited by James Marten (New York University Press, 2002).

Chronology

June and July 1754 Delegates from seven colonies meet at the Albany Congress to discuss coordinating Indian affairs and other colonial issues. They issue an "Albany Plan of Union."

1754 to 1763 Great Britain, France, and many eastern Native Americans battle in the French and Indian War.

February 1763 Great Britain and France sign the Treaty of Paris.

May 1763 Pontiac's Rebellion begins in the Great Lakes Region as Native American warriors destroy eight British forts.

October 1763 King George III of England signs the Proclamation of 1763, which prohibits settlement west of the Appalachian Mountains and reserves them as Indian hunting grounds.

April 1764 Parliament passes the Sugar Act. It increases duties on imported sugar and other items such as textiles, coffee, and indigo.

July 1764 James Otis, a leader of the opposition to British policy in the colonies, publishes a pamphlet, "The Rights of the British Colonies Asserted and Proved."

August 1764 Boston merchants begin a boycott of British luxury goods.

March 1765 Parliament passes the Quartering Act, which requires American colonists to house British troops and supply them with food. On March 22, Parliament passes the Stamp Act, creating a tax on printed materials, including newspapers, pamphlets, legal documents, licenses, and almanacs.

May 1765 Stamp Act Resolves are passed in Virginia. Patrick Henry delivers "If This Be Treason" speech.

July 1765 Sons of Liberty form to oppose the Stamp Act.

August 1765 A mob in Boston attacks the home of Thomas Hutchinson, chief justice of Massachusetts.

October 1765   Representatives from nine colonies meet at a Stamp Act Congress in New York City. They petition for the repeal of the Stamp Act and the other acts of 1764.

November 1765   The Stamp Act goes into effect. Riots erupt in New York City, where a mob burns the royal governor in effigy.

December 1765   British General Thomas Gage asks the New York Assembly to make colonists comply with the Quartering Act. In Boston, more than 200 merchants join the American boycott of English imports.

January 1766   The New York Assembly refuses Gage's request to enforce the Quartering Act.

March 1766   Parliament repeals the Stamp Act and passes the Declaratory Act, which affirms the right of the British government to pass laws for the American colonies.

July 1766   Chief Pontiac surrenders, and the pan-Indian rebellion dissipates.

August 1766   Violence breaks out in New York between British soldiers and colonists, including Sons of Liberty members. The violence results from the refusal of colonists to comply with the Quartering Act.

December 1766   Great Britain suspends the New York legislature for its refusal to comply with the Quartering Act.

June 1767   Parliament passes the Townshend Revenue Acts, which create taxes on imported paper, tea, glass, lead, and paints. The acts also establish a colonial board of customs commissioners in Boston.

Summer 1767   The Regulator movement begins in the backcountry of South Carolina.

October 1767   The American Board of Customs Commissioners arrives in the Colonies.

November 1767   Bostonians reinstate the boycott of luxury items from England. Two weeks later the Townshend Revenue Act goes into effect.

February 1768   Samuel Adams writes a circular letter opposing taxation without representation and calling for the colonists to unite in their actions against the British government.

April 1768   A British warship armed with fifty cannons sails into Boston harbor after a call for help from customs commissioners who are being harassed by Boston agitators.

June 1768   British customs officials seize the *Liberty*, the boat of John Hancock, because of suspicion that it was involved in smuggling.

July 1768   The governor of Massachusetts dissolves the general court after the legislature defies his order to revoke Samuel Adams's circular letter.

August 1768 Merchants in Boston and New York agree to boycott most British goods until the Townshend Acts are repealed.

September 1768 Residents in Boston are urged to arm themselves.

October 1768 Two regiments of English infantry set up permanent residence in Massachuetts to keep order.

March 1769 Merchants in Philadelphia join the boycott of British trade goods.

May 1769 The Virginians agree to a boycott of British trade goods, luxury items, and slaves.

October 1769 New Jersey, Rhode Island, and North Carolina join the boycott of English goods.

January 1770 Violence erupts at Golden Hill in New York between the Sons of Liberty and forty British soldiers.

March 1770 British soldiers fire into a crowd that is harassing them. Crispus Attucks, a man of African American and Native American heritage, is the first casualty in the Boston Massacre.

April 1770 Parliament repeals the Townshend Acts and chooses not to renew the Quartering Act.

May 1771 The Regulator movement ends in North Carolina at the Battle of Alamance.

June 1772 Americans burn the customs ship HMS *Gaspee* in Narragansett Bay, Rhode Island.

November 1772 Committee of Correspondence forms in Boston.

March 1773 Virginia's House of Burgesses appoints a Committee of Correspondence to discuss complaints against Britain with other colonies. Virginia is followed a few months later by New Hampshire, Rhode Island, Connecticut, and South Carolina.

May 1773 Parliament passes the Tea Act.

October 1773 Colonists hold meetings in Philadelphia, New York, and Boston to protest the Tea Act and the monopoly of the British East India Company.

November 1773 The *Dartmouth* arrives in Boston, carrying the first shipment of tea to the colonies since the Tea Act. Bostonians hold two mass meetings and decide to send the *Dartmouth* back to England without paying any import duties.

December 1773 Disgruntled colonists and members of the Sons of Liberty of Boston disguise themselves as Indians, board the cargo ships, and dump 342 containers of tea into the harbor, an event known as the Boston Tea Party.

March 1774 Parliament passes the Boston Port Bill, which shuts down Boston harbor until the colonists pay the taxes owed on the dumped tea and reimburse the East India Company for its losses.

May 1774 After Bostonians call for a boycott of British imports, General Thomas Gage puts Massachusetts under military rule. Colonists in Providence, New York, and Philadelphia call for an intercolonial congress to discuss a common course of action against the British. Parliament enacts another round of Coercive Acts, which include the Massachusetts Regulating Act, the Government Act, the Administration of Justice Act, and the Quebec Act.

June 1774 Parliament enacts a new Quartering Act.

September 1774 British troops seize an arsenal of weapons from Charlestown, Massachusetts.

September 1774 The First Continental Congress meets in Philadelphia with fifty-six delegates on September 5 and remains in session until October 26. The Suffolk Resolves, which denounced the Intolerable Acts and called for a boycott of British goods, pass on May 9 and Congress declares its opposition to the Coercive Acts on May 17.

October 1774 Congress adopts the Continental Association, in which delegates agree to a boycott of English imports, initiate an embargo of exports to Britain, and discontinue the slave trade.

December 1774 British troops seize ordinance in Newport and then at Fort William and Mary in Portsmouth. On the twenty-second, the Charleston Tea Party occurs.

February 1775 Provincial Congress held in Cambridge, Massachusetts. John Hancock and Joseph Warren begin defensive preparations for a state of war. Parliament declares Massachusetts to be in a state of rebellion.

March 1775 Virginian Patrick Henry delivers a speech against British rule, declaring, "Give me liberty or give me death!"

April 1775 Massachusetts Governor Gage is secretly ordered by the British to enforce the Coercive Acts and suppress "open rebellion" among colonists. On April 18, Paul Revere and William Dawes are sent from Boston to warn colonists about General Gage's march toward Concord to destroy the colonists' weapons depot. The following day the British clash with colonists at the battles of Lexington and Concord. Four days later the Provincial Congress in Massachusetts orders mobilization of 13,600 American soldiers.

May 1775 The Second Continental Congress meets in Philadelphia on May 10; the same day Ethan Allen's Green Mountain Boys capture Fort Ticonderoga. Ten days later, the city of Mecklenburg, North Carolina, passes a Declaration of Independence.

June 1775 The Battle of Bunker Hill occurs outside of Boston.

July 1775   On July 3, Washington takes command of the Continental Army. Two days later the Continental Congress adopts the Olive Branch Petition to be sent to England. The following day, Congress issues a Declaration on the Causes and Necessity of Taking Up Arms. Later that month, they ask all colonies to establish units of minutemen.

November 1775   Loyalists besiege supporters in Ninety-Six, South Carolina, from the tenth through the twenty-first. On November 13, Montgomery captures Montreal for the Americans. The following day John Murray, Earl of Dunmore and royal governor of Virginia, offers freedom to slaves willing to fight for Great Britain.

December 1775   Ethiopian Brigade of 300 African Americans under British command sees action at the Battle of Great Bridge, Virginia.

January 1776   New Hampshire's Assembly adopts the first state constitution. Thomas Paine publishes *Common Sense*.

March 1776   Loyalists seize Savannah on March 7. Ten days later British forces evacuate Boston.

April 1776   Assembly of North Carolina empowers its delegates in the Continental Congress to vote for independence.

May 1776   France commits one million dollars in secret aid, in the form of arms and munitions, to the United States. Congress authorizes each colony to form a provincial government.

June 1776   A massive British war fleet arrives in New York Harbor with 30 battleships, 30,000 soldiers, 10,000 sailors, and 300 supply ships. On June 7, Virginian Richard Henry Lee presents a resolution for independence. On June 11, Congress appoints a committee to draft a declaration of independence, which is written by Thomas Jefferson and presented on June 28. That same day, colonists at Fort Moultrie, in Charleston, repel a British naval attack.

July 1776   On July 2, twelve colonial delegations vote for a resolution for independence. Congress endorses the Declaration of Independence on July 4. Eleven days later, Lyndley's Fort in South Carolina is attacked by Indians and Tories dressed as Indians.

August 1776   On the first of the month, Cherokee Indians attack Seneca, South Carolina. The following day, the Declaration of Independence is signed.

September 1776   British troops occupy New York City. On September 19, fire engulfs New York City. Four days later, Nathan Hale is caught spying on British troops on Long Island. He utters his famous last words, "I only regret that I have but one life to lose for my country."

December 1776   The British capture the naval base at Newport, Rhode Island, on December 6. On Christmas Day, General Washington crosses the Delaware River and launches a surprise attack on 1,500 British Hessian troops at Trenton, New Jersey.

January 1777   Washington wins the Battle of Princeton, New Jersey.

June 1777   Congress passes the Flag Resolution, which described in general terms the design of the first national flag.

July 1777   Major General Arthur St. Clair surrenders Fort Ticonderoga to the British on July 6. The Marquis de Lafayette arrives in Philadelphia to serve in the Continental Army.

September 1777   Congress leaves Philadelphia and relocates in Lancaster, Pennsylvania, on September 11. Fifteen days later British troops occupy Philadelphia.

October 1777   Americans achieve their first major victory at the Battle of Saratoga.

November 1777   Congress adopts the Articles of Confederation.

December 1777   Washington establishes his camp at Valley Forge, Pennsylvania, and remains there from December to June 1778.

February 1778   American and French representatives agree to a Treaty of Amity and Commerce and a Treaty of Alliance. Later, Baron von Steuben of Prussia begins to train Washington's troops.

May 1778   Iroquois Indians burn Cobleskill, New York, and initiate a campaign against American settlements in the backcountry.

July 1778   Congress returns to Philadelphia July 2. Days later, Washington sets up headquarters at West Point. France declares war against Britain on July 10.

August 1778   Americans and French launch an unsuccessful siege against Newport, Rhode Island.

September 1778   Benjamin Franklin becomes the American diplomatic representative in France.

November 1778   Loyalists and Native Americans kill over forty American settlers at Cherry Valley, New York.

December 1778   British troops occupy Savannah, Georgia.

April 1779   American troops from North Carolina and Virginia attack Chickamauga Indian villages in Tennessee.

May 1779   British burn Portsmouth and Norfolk, Virginia.

June 1779   Spain declares war on England.

July 1779   Loyalists raid coastal Connecticut, including Fairfield, Norwalk, and New Haven.

August 1779   Congress approves a peace plan that includes independence, the evacuation of the British, and the free navigation of the Mississippi River. American forces defeat the Indian and Loyalist forces at Elmira, New York, and they destroy nearly forty Cayuga and Seneca Indian villages.

October 1779 Revolutionaries fail to recapture Savannah. Washington sets up winter quarters at Morristown, New Jersey.

April 1780 The British attack Charleston, South Carolina.

May 1780 The British capture Fort Moultrie and neighboring Charleston, South Carolina. Washington faces near mutiny as regiments demand unpaid salaries.

June 1780 The new Massachusetts constitution states "all men are born free and equal." The clause extends to African American slaves. American forces defeat the British in the Battle of Springfield on June 23.

August 1780 Benedict Arnold is appointed commander of West Point. British troops rout Americans at Camden, South Carolina.

September 1780 Benedict Arnold's traitorous plans to cede West Point to the British are discovered.

October 1780 After Battle at King's Mountain, Washington appoints Nathaniel Greene the commander of the Southern Army.

January 1781 Unpaid soldiers from Pennsylvania stage a mutiny. Another mutiny occurs with American soldiers in New Jersey. Spirits improve when the Americans defeat the British at Cowpens, South Carolina. At the end of the month, another mutiny occurs in New Jersey.

March 1781 Americans adopt the Articles of Confederation. The British suffer heavy losses during their victory at Guilford Courthouse, North Carolina.

June 1781 Americans recapture Augusta, Georgia. Five days later, Congress appoints a Peace Commission to negotiate with the British. The commission includes Benjamin Franklin, John Jay, Thomas Jefferson, and Henry Laurens.

July 1781 Slave rebellion in Williamsburg, Virginia.

September 1781 The British and French fight a naval battle at Yorktown, Virginia. Benedict Arnold's troops loot and burn the port of New London, Connecticut. Washington's army begins the siege of Yorktown.

October 1781 British troops surrender at Yorktown on October 19.

January 1782 Loyalists begin fleeing the United States for Nova Scotia and New Brunswick, while the British withdraw from North Carolina.

February 1782 England's House of Commons votes against continuing the war in America.

March 1782 Parliament empowers King George III to negotiate peace with the United States. American militiamen retaliate for Indian raids in the region by murdering ninety-six Delaware Indians in Ohio. British prime minister Lord North resigns.

April 1782   Peace talks begin in Paris. The Dutch recognize the United States of America.

July 1782   British evacuate Savannah.

August 1782   Loyalists and Indians defeat American settlers near Lexington, Kentucky. The Mohawk Indian chief Joseph Brant raids settlements in Kentucky and Pennsylvania backcountries, while British and American troops fight each other for the last time during the war in South Carolina along the Combahee River.

November 1782   American troops attack a Shawnee village in the Ohio Territory, marking the final battle of the American Revolution. British and Americans sign a preliminary peace treaty in Paris at the end of the month.

December 1782   British evacuate Charleston, South Carolina.

April 1783   The Quock Walker Decision results in the abolishment of slavery in Massachusetts.

January 1783   England agrees to a preliminary peace treaty with France and Spain.

February 1783   Spain recognizes the United States on February 3. England declares an end to hostilities in America the next day.

April 1783   Congress declares an end to the war on April 11. Eight days later, Congress ratifies a preliminary peace treaty. More than 7,000 Loyalists flee New York for Canada.

June 1783   The Continental Army disbands, but protests by unpaid war veterans force Congress to relocate in Princeton, New Jersey. Later, the Supreme Court of Massachusetts abolishes slavery.

September 1783   The United States and Great Britain sign the Treaty of Paris.

October 1783   Virginia's House of Burgesses emancipates slaves who served in the Continental Army.

November 1783   George Washington delivers his Farewell Address to the army. On November 28, British troops evacuate New York.

December 1783   Washington resigns as commander of the Continental Army.

January 1784   Congress ratifies the Treaty of Paris.

Independence on the Land: Small Farmers and the American Revolution

Terry Bouton

1

The American Revolution would not have happened without ordinary farmers. Ordinary rural Americans composed the vast majority of the colonial population, and they did the bulk of the fighting. Without the support of farmers, the Revolution would have never gotten off the ground; the war with Britain would certainly have been lost. And yet, despite this obvious fact, most Americans know little about the role farmers played in the Revolution. Instead, the events of the 1760s and 1770s they know about are the ones that occurred in port cities, such as the Stamp Act protests, the Boston Massacre, and the Tea Parties of 1773 and 1774. When Americans think about the Revolutionary countryside, they are more likely to imagine genteel planters like George Washington than his small-farmer neighbors. Indeed, most Americans have little sense of what ordinary farmers wanted from the Revolution and whether they were pleased with the new government and society the Revolution created.

Part of the confusion is understandable: After all, farmers were a diverse group of people in early America. Many farmers did fit the standard definition of a yeoman, that is, a man who owns the land he works with the help of his wife, daughters, and sons—probably the kind of person who jumps to mind when most people think about the word *farmer*. In Revolutionary America, however, the category of farmer extended much more broadly. Wealthy slave owners in the South sometimes called themselves farmers, even though they never lifted a shovel, shoed a horse, or hauled a bale of tobacco. (Of course, white Americans did not consider black slaves farmers, even though they performed much of the actual farming in America.) A farmer might be a gentlemen landlord in New Jersey or New York who, like a slave owner, possessed thousands of acres of prime farmland that was worked by others. Farmers also included tenants and cottagers who paid rent to landlords for the privilege of scratching out a living on land they would never own. Other farmers survived by tramping across the countryside in

General Israel Putnam, a prosperous farmer, leaves his plow to go fight in the battles of Lexington and Concord at the start of the American Revolution. According to legend, upon hearing that fighting broke out between minutemen and British troops, Putnam raced 60 miles on horseback to the battlefield without changing his clothes. (*National Archives and Records Administration*)

search of work; still others were supplementing their income as craftsmen by growing crops or raising animals. In short, in Revolutionary America, "farmer" was a messy and complex category. This chapter primarily explores the men and women who worked in fields, sometimes as the owners of modest holdings of land and sometimes as renters.

The Agrarian Ideal

There is a tendency among Americans to think that the ideals of the Revolution were created by intellectuals like John Adams, Thomas Paine, and Thomas Jefferson. Such thinking obscures the reality that ordinary farmers acted upon their own ideas about life, liberty, and independence. These ideas often meshed with the thinking of the Revolutionary elite, but in some critical ways, they differed sharply. To understand what farmers wanted from the Revolution, we first have to appreciate their own unique idea of what freedom meant. As it turns out, this ideal begins with a single word: land.

As J. Hector St. John Crèvecoeur, a French immigrant who settled in New York's Hudson Valley, put it during the 1770s, land was everything. The prospect of owning land had "enticed so many Europeans who have never been able to say that such portion of land was theirs" to "cross the Atlantic to realize that happiness." Once in America, those immigrants discovered that land was their sustenance. "What should we American farmers be without the distinct possession of the soil? It feeds, it clothes us; from it we draw . . . our best meat, our richest drink, the very honey of our bees come from this privileged spot." And they discovered that owning land brought power and status denied them in Europe. The "pleasant farm" Crèvecoeur's father had built "has established all our rights; on it is founded our rank, our freedom, our power as citizens" (Crèvecoeur, 2000, 125).

Certainly, Crèvecoeur exaggerated the extent to which European immigrants prospered in America. Nevertheless, there was some truth to his rosy observations. Most white farm families—perhaps as many as two-thirds of colonial American farmers—owned the land they worked. This was in stark contrast to Europe, where the vast majority of those who farmed did so as landless peasants, tenant farmers, or itinerant laborers. American farmers also enjoyed a higher standard of living than their European counterparts. They tended to be wealthier and healthier than European peasants and tenants. They ate better and lived longer (Kulikoff, 2000, 3, 84).

American farmers also enjoyed more political rights than most rural Europeans, and the control of land was central to these rights. Every colony in America restricted voting to adult white men, and most colonies stipulated that voters be landowners, demanding that voters own fifty or one hundred acres of land. As a result, the percentage of adult white males who were eligible voters differed between colonies, Maryland and New York having among the lowest percentage and Virginia and the New England colonies among the highest. Overall, between 50 and 75 percent of adult white males in colonial America could vote—a number far higher than the estimated 15 percent who could vote in eighteenth-century Britain (Dinkin, 1977, 28–49).

This is not to say that colonial America was a paradise for ordinary farmers. Life was dirty and difficult. With limited sources of money and credit, most farmers were compelled to borrow from wealthy gentlemen who expected deference in exchange for their patronage—a factor that limited farmers' autonomy. Farmers enjoyed more political independence than in Europe, but there were clear limits. Most colonies had high property requirements for office holding that ruled out the majority of small farmers and ensured that most holders of political office were affluent gentlemen. In addition, farmers rarely had the right to elect the holders of the most powerful offices in the colony. Instead these positions were routinely appointed by the Crown or the proprietor of the colony.

Despite these limitations, the prewar experience of farmers created a powerful set of beliefs that American farmers brought with them into the 1760s and 1770s. Broadly speaking, they believed that ordinary farmers were only really free and independent when they owned the land they worked. As a result, farmers believed that ordinary people must be able to acquire good farmland at low cost and that their children must have access to a steady supply of new, cheap farmland. Farmers expected to hold onto their farms and to leave their land to their sons and daughters (women could own land, though it was quite rare for a woman to be the principal farmer of her own land). In the half century before the Revolution, many farmers in different colonies acted on their beliefs by pushing for reforms to government designed to enhance the position of ordinary farmers and limit the power of elites who wanted to accumulate large tracts of land. Farmers in various colonies called for laws that favored settlers over speculators; they pressured governments to provide farmers with access to paper money and low-cost credit; and they demanded revisions to expensive court systems that tended to side with creditors at the expense of debtors (Kulikoff, 2000, 125).

Most American farmers did not expect to become wealthy landlords or absentee planters who owned hundreds or thousands of slaves. Instead, they envisioned themselves earning what historians have called a competency, that is, making enough to buy land, pay off debts, provide for their families, and set their children on the path to their own independence. They expected to work hard, to be successful, and to prosper (Vickers, 1994). Indeed, to most rural Americans, large planters and landlords were not so much role models as they were potential threats to the independence of ordinary farmers. As one colonial explained, "Having land of their own and becoming independent of landlords is what chiefly induces people into America." Explaining why most farmers moved to the frontier rather than becoming tenants to the landlords of the great manors along the Hudson, one New Yorker observed that "people will not become their Vassals or Tenants for one great reason"—they wanted to own land that would "descend to their posterity that their children may reap the benefit of their labor and industry." Most farmers did not want to live in "dependence on landlords." Instead, most white colonists wanted to be able to repeat the words of one farmer who said: "We are all freeholders, the rent day does not trouble us" (quoted in Bushman, 1976, 100–101, 111).

The importance farmers placed on securing economic independence and the links they made between land ownership and political independence were reinforced by the ideology of republicanism that was in ascendance in the eighteenth century. In general, republicanism was a set of beliefs about how to protect freedom from domination by a powerful few. The ideals espoused by small farmers can be seen as a more popular version of the republicanism espoused by the educated elite, particularly in the ways they emphasized equality in terms of land ownership and access to the resources needed to maintain their farms and families. The way these ideals played out in action is best exemplified by the struggle in New Jersey between small farmers and large gentleman landholders that peaked in the 1740s. Challenging the colony's great proprietors who claimed thousands of acres, farmers stated that "no man is naturally intitled to a greater Proportion of the Earth, than another" and that land was "made for the equal Use of all." They said that land became "the property of that Man, who bestowed his labour on it," not of those who claimed it through wealth and connections (McConville, 1999, 168).

The religious beliefs of many farmers reinforced their conceptions of equality and disdain for the wealthy elite. Farmers often supported their appeals about land, tax, and economic policies by using biblical references about the right to enjoy the fruits of one's labor. Many farmers linked religion with their anti-elite policies as a result of their participation in the religious revivals of the Great Awakening, the evangelical religious movement that recently reinvigorated piety in the Atlantic world. Many of the evangelical

Baptist and Presbyterian ministers who spread the ideas of the awakening tapped into the agrarian ideals when they attacked materialism and greed as great sins. Crowds flocked to hear ministers condemn those who sought "too much worldly goods." "Go now, ye rich men, weep and howl for your miseries will come upon you" went the sermon of a leading revivalist. "Your gold and silver is cankered . . . and shall eat your flesh as if it were fire." Other ministers preached that "the great rock against which our society has dashed is the love of the world & the deceitfulness of riches, the desire of amassing wealth." Viewed through the prism of religion, many farmers perceived their personal struggles to acquire and maintain farms of their own in apocalyptic terms (McConville, 1999, 83; Kars, 2002, 118–119).

The Emerging Crisis

A convergence of distressing long-term trends and a series of British policies during the 1760s and 1770s came into conflict with their agrarian ideals about independence and land. The result was a sense that Great Britain and its agents in America were undermining the economic and political independence of ordinary farmers. That belief cut across a wide range of farmers, uniting those in the hinterlands surrounding port cities with farmers in the newest backcountry settlements. It brought together farmers from different regions, with different ethnicities, and of diverse religious beliefs. Farmers eventually disagreed over the best way to respond to the crisis, but during the 1760s and 1770s, American farmers agreed that their independence was under assault.

In some ways, the perception of being under assault had more to do with long-standing trends than it did with any specific British policy. In the older settlements, farmers put tremendous pressure on the land by trying to ensure that their grown children settled near them. As the population grew, available land was bought up, and farmers split their farms and pushed the soil toward exhaustion. In eastern Massachusetts, the land had been so parceled down into small plots and the soil so overused that many a town had to import food because its farmers could not produce an ample supply. Under these conditions, if children wanted to live near home, their only option was usually giving up the independence their parents had worked so hard to preserve. Adult children could farm someone else's land as tenants; they could roam the neighborhood as farm laborers; or they could abandon farming altogether and go into the trades. No matter whether children stayed or left, the results were troubling for many rural Americans. Although British policies played a small role in these dynamics, the heartbreak did little to make farmers love their rulers (Kulikoff, 2000, 125–163; Gross, 1976).

The movement to the frontier also ignited disenchantment with British rule in a more direct way, when many backcountry farmers began to feel that Britain did not do enough to protect them from their Indian neighbors. The recently completed French and Indian War had been devastating for both Indians and backcountry farmers alike, as they took turns attacking and visiting atrocities on one another. On the frontier, the end of that war spawned another, as farmers from Virginia, Pennsylvania, and New York battled with Native forces said to be under the leadership of an Ottowa Indian named Pontiac. Again whites and Indians traded in brutality, capped off by the infamous slaughter of peaceful Conestoga Indians by Pennsylvania's Paxton Boys in 1764. These farmers later marched to Philadelphia to complain about the lack of protection and about the practice of colonial leaders allowing Indian agents to arm the farmers' enemies by trading guns for animal skins. Those feelings were exacerbated during the 1760s and 1770s, when Britain tried to uphold the Proclamation Line of 1763—the imaginary line running down the Appalachian Mountains that white settlers were not supposed to cross. Britain's efforts here deepened the sense among many frontier farmers that Britain was more concerned with protecting the interests of Indians than it was those of its own colonial subjects (Calloway, 1995, 1–25).

Perhaps the most devastating policy was Britain's attempt to eliminate the supply of colonial paper money. On a continent that had long disappointed explorers and settlers with its lack of rich ores, Britain's colonies had been forced to print their own currencies to compensate for the lack of gold and silver. In rural parts of the colonies, where gold and silver seldom circulated, paper currency was perhaps the only form of money most farmers knew. The French and Indian War changed the minds of British officials about these currencies when colonial governments printed massive amounts of paper money to fund their share of the war effort, causing the value of the money to fall greatly. Fearing that this depreciated paper money would cut revenue from the colonies as well as the profits of British merchants, Parliament and its agents in America tried to ban these currencies. The Currency Act of 1764, for example, prohibited the colonies from printing new money that could be used as a legal tender for debts or taxes or to purchase goods. The colonies could still print money as long as they did not require anyone to accept it in payment, and several colonial legislatures passed laws to issue new money that was not legal tender. Time and again, however, colonial governors vetoed any new currency. As a result, the colonies faced an ever-dwindling supply of paper money. In effect, Britain left them to rely almost entirely on the scarce supply of gold and silver to meet the needs of trade (Ernst, 1973; McCusker and Menard, 1985, 338–339).

That forced reliance on gold and silver became an even bigger problem when Britain compelled colonists to trade only with England or its other colonies. The cutting off of foreign trade—the colonies' traditional source of gold and silver—made money even more scarce. Britain proceeded to make this difficult situation worse by enacting new taxes on the colonies that had to be paid in gold and silver. British officials claimed that the taxes did not harm the colonies because the amounts were relatively small. Colonists knew otherwise. They stated in petitions and pamphlets that even small taxes could be onerous burdens when money was extremely scarce. After all, what did it matter that the taxes were just a few shillings when one could only acquire a few pennies in hard money?

The whole problem was deftly summarized in 1765 by Revolutionary leader John Dickinson, who anonymously wrote *Letters from a Farmer.* "We had a paper currency which served as a medium of domestic commerce,"

Portrait of John Dickinson, Revolutionary leader, holding his *Letters from a Farmer*, ca. 1770. (*Library of Congress*)

Dickinson said of life before the new British policies. "We had a multitude of markets for our provisions, lumber and iron." But then Britain changed everything for the worse. The new policy enforcing mercantilism "sweeps off our silver and gold in a torrent to Great Britain." Now "drained" of hard money, "we are prohibited by new and stricter restraints being laid on our [foreign] trade, from procuring these coins as we used to; and from instituting among ourselves bills of credit [paper money]." And then came the new taxes. "In this exhausted condition," Dickinson wrote, "our languishing country is to strive to take up and to totter under the additional burthen of the Stamp Act." "From whence is the silver to come, with which the taxes imposed by this act, and the duties imposed by the other late acts, are to be paid?" he asked. "Or how will our *merchants* and the *lower ranks of people*, on whom the force of these regulations will fall first, and with the greatest violence, bear this additional load." To Dickinson, it was a question of survival: "What shall we expect, when the exhausted colonies shall feel the STAMP ACT drawing off, as it were, the last drops of their blood?" (Dickinson, 1895, 217–218, 228). In the minds of Dickinson and others, Britain's policies worked together to bring great distress to the colonies.

Dickinson scarcely exaggerated. British policies made the rural economy in most places a disaster. Across the colonies, farmers found themselves unable to pay debts; they were hauled into court; and, when they still could not pay, the courts foreclosed, taking away their livestock or land. Although the tide of lawsuits ebbed and flowed in the decade before 1776, courts in many rural counties processed enough debt cases to cover anywhere between 20 and 75 percent of the population (Bushman, 1976, 119). With the dire scarcity of money, most of these cases usually ended up in the hands of the county sheriff, who confiscated or auctioned property. For example, in the Pennsylvania countryside, lawsuits for unpaid debts generated enough court orders for sheriffs to confiscate property or hold an auction to reach anywhere between 20 and 50 percent of the taxable population. In Philadelphia County, between 1769 and 1771, the court issued 2,120 orders to foreclose property, enough to cover 20 percent of the taxable population of the city and county. Northwest of Philadelphia in Northampton County, between 1766 and 1775, the sheriff executed 1,170 orders to foreclose property—or enough to cover 42 percent of the taxable population (Philadelphia County Execution Docket, 1769–1771). (For estimates of taxable population, see *Hazard's Register of Pennsylvania*, 1829, 12–13; Northampton County Execution Dockets, 1766–1775; Berks County Execution Dockets, 1769–1775; Bedford County Execution Dockets, 1772–1775; Peter Schmuck and Stephen Collins, May 4, 1765, pers. comm.)

Since so little money was around, the prices farmers received for the property they sold tended to be low. In Virginia, property sold at about half of its worth, meaning that debtors had to "pay perhaps double what they owe," as one observer put it. The prices at Pennsylvania auctions were perhaps even worse, as storekeeper and farmer Peter Schmuck discovered. Although Schmuck had sued seventy-six of his customers, only four could pay under court order. So he had the sheriff foreclose the property of the seventy-two who could not come up with the money. The auctioned property, however, did not earn him enough to repay his creditor, a Philadelphia merchant. Consequently, the merchant sued Schmuck, forcing him to sell the remaining inventory in his store for less than half its value. Even this was not enough to repay the merchant, and he ultimately had to sell his farm. Years before Schmuck had purchased the farm for £300; now in 1767, amid the cash scarcity, he was forced to part with it for just £50—or less than 17 percent of what it had been worth (Holton, 1999, 63; Peter Schmuck and Stephen Collins, May 4, 1765 and September 23, 1767, pers. comm.).

For many farmers, the sheriff's auction was only the start of a new phase of the problem. All this litigation meant high court costs for the farmer. Nearly every piece of paper the court generated carried a fee. There were fees for the judges, lawyers, sheriffs, and constables, and for the mileage any of them had to travel to issue a warrant, assess property, or hold an auction. The 1765 Stamp Act made matters worse, as it put a new duty in gold and silver on every piece of paper the court generated. With all these fees and taxes, court costs often grew to more than the debt that had landed the farmer in court in the first place. A farmer named George Sims from North Carolina—where court fees of £3 on a debt of £5 were common—put it best in 1765. To pay court costs, a farmer often had to see his "living wrecked and tore to pieces. . . . If he had but one horse to plow with, one bed to lie on, or one cow to give a little milk for his children, they must all go to raise money which is not to be had." When goods were not enough, "then his lands . . . must go the same way to satisfy these cursed hungry caterpillars."

"It would be enough," Sims said, "to make us turn rebels" (quoted in Kars, 2002, 71–72).

As Sims's remarks suggest, farmers found all these developments deeply troubling on a number of levels. Most farmers were distressed that they or their neighbors were losing their property, but even if they were spared the worst of the hardship, many farmers were concerned that these developments were undermining their yeoman ideals. The same was true of those who lost the things needed to make their farms productive and their independence tolerable. One Virginia gentlemen explained that as farmers lost "Land, Negroes, Horses, Cows, Hoggs and Feather Beds or old Potts and Panns" to pay for debts or court costs, they found themselves deprived of the very means of enjoying their independence (Holton, 1999, 97; Bushman, 1976, 91).

In slaveholding colonies, British actions helped spur fears among ordinary farmers about slaves running away or rising in an insurrection against whites. Thousands of slaves saw the upheavals with Britain as a chance to make a bid for freedom. Many small farmers, slave owners and non–slave owners, perceived the loss of slaves who ran away and the potential for insurrections as direct threats to their own independence. All had reason to fear when in 1775 Virginia's royal governor, Lord Dunmore, issued a proclamation offering slaves of rebel masters freedom if they fled to join the British Army. Dunmore's Proclamation—made as a threat to compel loyalty among colonists—ended up backfiring by deepening the resentment many ordinary farmers felt against Britain (Holton, 1999, 133–163; Frey, 1991).

Petitions, Boycotts, and Rebellions

In response to these varied developments, farmers throughout the colonies openly expressed their fears about the distressed state of America by drafting petitions that challenged British policies. Many farmers signed petitions calling for Parliament and colonial governors and assemblies to end the ban on paper money. Most of these petitions demanded the opening of public loan offices that would allow farmers to use their land as collateral to borrow paper money—a way to bring both currency and low-cost credit to the cash-starved countryside. Many farmers called for Britain to rescind the gold and silver taxes. Others joined farmers in North Carolina in demanding that Parliament and their colonial governments refrain from collecting any taxes "until a currency is made." Some joined the chorus of those saying that Britain did not have the right to tax the colonies because the colonists were not represented in Parliament. Other challenged both British and colonial leaders by calling for progressive taxation, so as to make the wealthy pay a greater share than ordinary folk. Finally, there was a widespread call for reforming the courts to decrease fees and relieve debtors. In their petitions, farmers said that all these reforms were designed to save their independence (Kars, 2002, 172).

For many farmers, the growing crisis with Britain was tied as well to long-standing efforts at fundamental land reform. During the 1760s and

By his Excellency the Right Honourable JOHN Earl of DUNMORE, his Majesty's Lieutenant and Governour-General of the Colony and Dominion of Virginia, and Vice-Admiral of the same:

A PROCLAMATION.

AS I have ever entertained Hopes that an Accommodation might have taken Place between *Great Britain* and this Colony, without being compelled, by my Duty, to this most disagreeable, but now absolutely necessary Step, rendered so by a Body of armed Men, unlawfully assembled, firing on his Majesty's Tenders, and the Formation of an Army, and that Army now on their March to attack his Majesty's Troops, and destroy the well-disposed Subjects of this Colony: To defeat such treasonable Purposes, and that all such Traitors, and their Abetters, may be brought to Justice, and that the Peace and good Order of this Colony may be again restored, which the ordinary Course of the civil Law is unable to effect, I have thought fit to issue this my Proclamation, hereby declaring, that until the aforesaid good Purposes can be obtained, I do, in Virtue of the Power and Authority to me given, by his Majesty, determine to execute martial Law, and cause the same to be executed throughout this Colony; and to the End that Peace and good Order may the sooner be restored, I do require every Person capable of bearing Arms, to resort to his Majesty's S T A N-DARD, or be looked upon as Traitors to his Majesty's Crown and Government, and thereby become liable to the Penalty the Law inflicts upon such Offences, such as Forfeiture of Life, Confiscation of Lands, &c. &c. And I do hereby farther declare all indented Servants, Negroes, or others (appertaining to Rebels) free, that are able and willing to bear Arms, they joining his Majesty's Troops, as soon as may be, for the more speedily reducing this Colony to a proper Sense of their Duty, to his Majesty's Crown and Dignity. I do farther order, and require, all his Majesty's liege Subjects to retain their Quitrents, or any other Taxes due, or that may become due, in their own Custody, till such Time as Peace may be again restored to this at present most unhappy Country, or demanded of them for their former salutary Purposes, by Officers properly authorised to receive the same.

GIVEN under my Hand, on Board the Ship William, off Norfolk, the 7th Day of November, in the 16th Year of his Majesty's Reign.

D U N M O R E.

G O D SAVE THE K I N G.

Lord Dunmore's *Proclamation of November 1775*, offering freedom to Virginia slaves who were willing to take up arms for the British cause. (*Library of Congress*)

1770s, in New Jersey, New York, North Carolina, and Vermont, large groups of farmers—many of them tenants, squatters, or holders of uncertain land titles—pressed for laws that favored actual settlers and complained that land speculators threatened the independence of ordinary folk. For example, some North Carolina farmers complained that land speculators had engrossed "much of the most fertile lands in the Province" and left the "poor people . . . to toil in the cultivation of bad Lands whereon they can hardly subsist." These farmers were especially alarmed that members of government "as well as their friends and favorites" had acquired "large Quantities of Lands" by claiming rights to farms that ordinary folk had already carved out. They demanded a new land system that would prevent "Individuals in Power, and who has Money" from marking poor farmers "out for a Prey." In New York in 1766, many of the tenants living on Robert Livingston's estate called for an end to the manorial system altogether (Kars, 2002, 172–173; Countryman, 1981, 50).

Farmers did more than petition; they also protested. Many protests centered on courts and the legal system. The reasons were clear: Courts were where farmers experienced the problems of British rule, from the lawsuits for unpaid debts to the legal decisions that favored speculators and large landholders over settlers and tenant farmers. The most dramatic protests involved crowds of farmers who tried to close courts. For example, farmers in Worcester, Massachusetts, closed the courts from November 1765 to April 1766 to protest the Stamp Act and "the great Decay of the trade of the Province, the Scarcity of Money, the heavy Debts contracted in the late war, which still remains on the People, and the great Difficulties to which they are by these means reduced." New Jersey farmers blocked courts on several occasions in 1769 and 1770 to stop debt lawsuits and to protest lawyers whom they said "oppress'd them with exorbitant Costs, in bringing Suits for Debt." Calling themselves "Liberty Boys," these farmers marched to the court behind a pennant that read "Liberty and Property." These court closings, together with attacks on courts in other colonies, helped convince some colonial leaders such as those in Virginia and Maryland to close courts voluntarily, rather than face the angry farmers protesting debt lawsuits and court costs who would close them by force (Brooke, 1989, 139; McConville, 1999, 240–241).

Many farmers tried to boycott courts altogether; some even attempted to establish their own independent legal systems. In 1774, Worcester, Massachusetts, farmers who were angered by the "the machinations of some designing persons in this Province, who are grasping at power, and the property of their neighbors" pledged to "avoid all lawsuits with all men as much as possible." In 1764 a Virginia gentleman observed that "in some Countys, the People have agreed to defend one another against the officers" in an effort to protect themselves from a wave of debt lawsuits. Farmers in parts of New Jersey, Vermont, New York, and North Carolina actually established their own unofficial courts. Some New Jersey farmers went so far as to create their own extralegal governments, which passed laws and even issued their own paper money (Brooke, 1989, 140; Holton, 1999, 61).

Many landless farmers engaged in their own unique protests. Some, like tenant farmers in several Virginia counties in 1775, engaged in rent strikes. Amid the cash scarcity and closed markets, these farmers believed it was "Cruel in the Land Holders to expect their Rents when there is no market for the produce of the Land." In parts of upstate New York, tenants called themselves Sons of Liberty and tried to end the manorial system through force by taking possession of landlords' estates east of the Hudson River (Holton, 1999, 178–180; see also Countryman, 1981; Lynd, 1961, 330–359).

These protests revealed another dimension to rural rebellion: Many farmers were willing to resort to violence to express their discontent. Much of this violence fit within a tradition called "rough music" that had been brought to America from Europe. This ritualized violence had been used as a political tool by ordinary people who felt that the elite-dominated political system did not serve their interests. Rough music generally involved large crowds that used physical humiliation to punish those who violated community standards of right and wrong. Sometimes the violence involved attacks on people: beatings, tar and featherings, stripping of clothes, cropping of hair, or being made to "ride the rail"—a form of attack during which a man was bound to a sharp fence rail and bounced along in a painful parade. Just as often farmers went after the property of the offender: repossessing goods and livestock that had been sold at auction for unpaid debts or court costs, destroying wheat fields, pulling down homes and barns, or burning the tobacco warehouses of wealthy planters (Pencak, Dennis, and Newman, 2002).

In 1773, in what is now Vermont, Ethan Allen and the Green Mountain Boys used rough music to defend their farms against New York land speculators by targeting the farmers and officials who settled on lands the Vermonters had claimed. In February, the Green Mountain Boys formed militia companies to oppose the New Yorkers. In April, they pulled down one New Yorker's fences, ruined his fields, and took possession of his farm. In August, one hundred Vermonters sacked a New Yorker town, burning houses, destroying fields, and leveling the grist mill. In December, an extralegal court established by the Green Mountain Boys tried two justices of the peace from New York. They sentenced one to have his house burned and the other to have his roof removed and some of his corn crop destroyed. As Ethan Allen put it, all these actions were designed to protect "a poor people . . . fatigued in settling a wilderness country," from being dispossessed by "a number of Attorneys and other gentlemen, with all their tackle of ornaments, and compliments and French finesse" (quoted in Countryman, 1981, 44, 50).

Farmers and Political Allegiance

For many farmers, as their petitions were denied and their protests escalated, it was not a far walk to the break with Britain. Still, farmers greeted these frustrations and the discussions of independence differently. Given the diversity of responses by farmers to the Revolutionary War (and the scant evidence from farmers about why they made their decisions), it is impossible to give some overarching explanation of why some farmers sided with Britain, why more became Patriots, and why an even larger number tried to stay out of the conflict. Probably the best that can be done is to observe that farmers often saw different paths leading to the same goal of independence. And in many ways, those choices depended on the kinds of governments the new states created.

Some farmers, like the Green Mountain Boys of Vermont, became Patriots because they saw the conflict with Britain as an extension of their efforts to obtain landed independence. Allen and his followers said their struggles with the wealthy landlords of New York were an extension of the broader struggle against Britain's tyrannical empire. In both cases, the government and laws were stacked in favor of the wealthy and powerful. As Allen put it, he and his fellow Vermonters were sick of "diving after redress in a Legal way, & finding that the Law was only made use of for the Emolument of its Creatures & the immesaries of the British tyrant." To the Green Mountain Boys, the war was a fight to free themselves from rule by a powerful few who wanted to dominate the land and government. They tried to fulfill their ideals by creating one of the most democratic of the new state govern-

The Green Mountain
Boys harassed New
York settlers and even
dispossessed some
of their land in 1773
because they believed
the land had previously
been claimed by
Vermonters.
(*Library of Congress*)

ments: Vermont's constitution gave the vote to every adult male, removed property requirements for holding office, and allowed citizens to vote for every office; it contained a strong bill of rights that, among other things, outlawed slavery; and it established a unicameral assembly with few of the checks that the elite had traditionally placed on government. Vermont farmers responded to their new democratic government with great enthusiasm. Almost to a man, they took up arms in the Patriot cause (Bellesiles, 1993, 106–107, 137–141).

New Jersey followed a similar pattern, as the ordinary farmers who had struggled against the colony's proprietors for the right to own the land they farmed tended to side with the Patriots. In many ways, the Revolutionary War plunged the colony into a civil war over land rights—a civil war that many of these farmers would win, at least in the short run, when New Jersey's Revolutionary government rejected the claims of the Loyalist proprietors (McConville, 1999, 250–255).

Struggles over land did not always lead farmers to the Patriot cause, however. In New York, where the new government was not especially democratic, tenant farmers were divided in their loyalties. Some tenants of Patriot landlords became Loyalists after British officials promised to carve up the rebel landlords' estates and distribute them to tenants who fought for the Crown. Others opposed their Loyalist landlords when Patriot leaders promised that "when the Independency is established the Manors would be parceled out to such Tenants as were in Favor with the New established

Herman Husband

Herman Husband did not seem like the kind of person who would lead a farm uprising against North Carolina's colonial government. He was a prosperous farmer who owned 600 acres of rich farmland in the Piedmont of central North Carolina where he lived with his wife and young children. Husband was also a religious pacifist. Like many of his Piedmont neighbors, however, Husband thought the British government, North Carolina's colonial administrators, and local law enforcement were undermining the independence of ordinary farmers. That belief eventually transformed him into one of the leaders of the North Carolina Regulation—a movement that was aimed, as Piedmont farmers put it, at "Regulating publick Grievances & abuses of Power" (quoted in Kars, 2002, 138).

Like most of his neighbors, Husband was upset about a government that made it hard for ordinary farmers to own and maintain farms because it seemed preoccupied with catering to the interests of a wealthy few. Husband complained that much of the good farmland was owned, not by family farmers, but by large speculators who were either royal officials or "great men from Virginia and other southern governments" who wanted to populate the land "with their Tribes of Negroes" (quoted in Kars, 2002, 25). He was also angered by the ways these men used their control of the court system to kick small farmers off land they thought they owned. The speculators claimed the farmers had purchased the land illegally and threatened to evict them unless they paid the speculators high prices (that included value the farmers had added by clearing away trees and building houses).

The injustice Husband saw in the land system was doubled by problems Piedmont farmers faced from debts and taxes. The 1760s brought to the Piedmont the same array of British policies that brought hardship throughout the colonies: the Currency Act of 1764 that stripped North Carolina of paper money; trade restrictions that made it difficult for the colony to acquire new gold and silver; and the new taxes that siphoned off what little hard money remained. Like Americans everywhere, Piedmont farmers found it hard to pay debts or the new taxes. Many farmers were hauled into court and saddled with high legal fees. Worse yet, when farmers paid taxes, they often discovered that county sheriffs pocketed the money and told colonial administrators that the farmers had not paid. Topping it all off, the royal governor Lord Tryon enacted a new tax so that he could build a mansion for himself.

At first Husband and other Piedmont farmers tried to solve the problems through legal means. Husband wrote letters and organized his neighbors into an "Association" that drafted petitions calling for fundamental political and economic reform. A lay preacher, he published pamphlets that used Scripture to sermonize that farmers should band together against the great men who designed "the whole Train of our Laws" for "the Promotion of their [own] Wealth" (quoted in Kars, 2002, 170). Husband even won a seat in the colonial legislature. The rest of the assembly, however, refused to listen to Husband or acknowledge the petitions. In fact, the other legislators expelled Husband from the assembly on trumped-up libel charges for having exposed government corruption.

When legal means failed, many Piedmont farmers turned to protest and violence. Husband tried to restrain his neighbors and push

Government." Most tenants, however, tended to follow the political sympathies of their landlords. Many of these farmers probably did not believe that either side (both of which were dominated by wealthy landlords) would ever actually overthrow the manorial system (Lynd, 1961, 347).

Receipt given to Thomas Sitgreaves for assisting in Herman Husband's 1771 incarceration. (*Courtesy of the North Carolina Office of Archives and History, Raleigh, North Carolina*)

them toward a peaceful solution. Growing desperate, however, the Regulators—as the farmers now called themselves—decided that their only recourse was to refuse to pay taxes and to try to shut down the courts. In response, the royal governor order Husband arrested and in 1771 marched an army to the Piedmont that defeated the Regulators and hanged several of its leaders. The pacifist Husband, who had left the battlefield when the shooting started, fled the colony after the governor put a price on his head. The only victory the Regulators could claim was that Britain replaced Lord Tryon with a new governor who tried to clean up the worst of the corruption.

When the Revolution came, most Regulators tried to stay out of the conflict altogether, not trusting either Britain or the Patriot elite. In fact, given the choice, many sided with Britain, largely because they saw the new governor as a better protector of farmers' interests than Patriot leaders, who had participated in the corruption and had heartily approved of using the army to crush the Regulation.

Husband fled with his family to Pennsylvania and became a supporter of the Revolution. Indeed, Husband saw the democratic changes in Pennsylvania as a sign that foretold the imminent return of Jesus. For Husband, the final battle of the millennium, however, was not between Britain and the colonies. Instead, he saw it as an internal conflict within Pennsylvania during the 1780s and 1790s, a conflict between ordinary farmers and the colony's elite leaders over the issues that had defined the North Carolina Regulation—land, debts, taxes, and the definition of good government. This conflict ended with another "regulation" (the so-called Whiskey Rebellion) and another army marching to crush the farmers' movement. As before, Husband was arrested. This time, however, he did not make it back home: Husband died trying to get back to his family after he was released from prison.

Elsewhere farmers sided with the Patriots when they believed Revolutionary leaders would look out for the interests of ordinary farmers. For example, the Revolution enjoyed strong support among ordinary farmers in Pennsylvania, due in large part to the new state government that was nearly as democratic as Vermont's (except for the ban on slavery). Still, not every Pennsylvania farmer sided with the Revolution. Many Quaker farmers in the counties surrounding Philadelphia either became Loyalists or tried to remain out of the conflict due to their pacifist beliefs. These farmers experienced widespread persecution by Patriot farmers, sometimes for their openly Loyalist views, and sometimes merely because of the suspicion that they supported Britain (Fox, 2000, 76–77).

The strong presence of the British Army in Massachusetts made most farmers there into Revolutionaries, despite the fact that the new government was not as democratic as many of them had hoped. Many Massachusetts farmers felt that the new government did not go far enough, since it lacked many central tenets: universal voting rights for men (or at least property holders), the right to elect their militia officers and justices of the peace, laws for debt relief, limited powers for the state governor, and a bill of rights. Some even wanted the new constitution to emancipate slaves. Farmers in one Massachusetts county complained that the property requirements in the 1778 constitution made "Honest Poverty a Crime" because they denied the vote to "a large Number of the true and faithful Subjects of the State who perhaps fought and bled in their Countrys Cause." Other Massachusetts farmers wanted the new constitution to prevent the wealthy from accumulating large tracts of land, so as to preclude "landed estates manners or lordships, as has been practiced in other parts of the world" (quoted in Kulikoff, 1992, 138–139; Bushman, 1976, 124).

Similar misgivings about Virginia's new gentry-led government caused many Virginia farmers to douse their Revolutionary ardor. Like colonial leaders everywhere, most Virginia gentleman worried that ordinary farmers would try to democratize power and undermine the gentry's economic and social authority. As planter Landon Carter put it in May 1776, most farmers wanted "a form of Government that by being independ[en]t of the rich men eve[r]y man would then be able to do as he pleasd." They would establish an "independence" of their own "in which no Gentleman should have the least share." When Virginia leaders tried to preserve their authority, many ordinary farmers began to doubt their leaders' willingness to uphold popular revolutionary ideals. These farmers came to believe that, in Virginia, "The Rich wanted the Poor to fight for them, to defend there property, whilst they refuse to fight for themselves." Farmers also complained that the "men of Fortune" who were willing to fight would only serve if they could be officers. "The Gentlemen have more at stake and ought to fight to protect it," many farmers said, "but that none enter the service but as officers" because they were "fond of officer's places" and the money, perks, and authority that went with them. This kind of resentment led to a waning of support for the militia and the complete failure of the Virginia gentry's plan to establish a corps of minutemen organized in a rigid top-down hierarchy. In 1782, Virginia farmers pressed their vision of the Revolution by petitioning for a variety of reforms, including disestablishing the Anglican Church, legally reducing the prices that speculators charged for land, enacting laws that allowed debtors to pay debts in paper money rather than gold and silver, and confirming title to land held by squatters (McDonnell, 1998, 968–969, 978).

The War Comes Home

In North Carolina, South Carolina, and Georgia, the Revolutionary War set farmer against farmer in a particularly brutal civil war. Here ordinary farmers were as likely to support the Crown as they were the Revolutionary governments. And here, probably more than anywhere else, most people tried to sit out the war or else switched their allegiance depending on which side seemed to be winning. It was not that these farmers lacked conviction. Rather it is probably more accurate to say that they did not trust either side to serve the interests of ordinary farmers (Hoffman, 1985, 273–318).

No matter which side farmers chose, whether they joined the army or remained at home, their experiences during the war tended to be difficult. The idea that most farmers somehow sat out the war in ease and plenty or that they were merely wartime profiteers—an idea shared by much of the Revolutionary elite at the time—badly distorts the actual experiences of rural life during the War for Independence. Certainly there were farmers who profited from the war; many American farmers undermined the American cause by selling grain to British troops. But these were the exceptions rather than the rule. By and large, the war brought hardship to ordinary farm families regardless of their choice of sides in the conflict (Kulikoff, 2000, 255–288).

In many cases, there was little separation between the war and the home front for farmers, as the conflict transformed their corn and tobacco fields into battlefields. Troops tramped over growing crops and sometimes burned fields and farmhouses. In the backcountry, where fighting between farmers and Indians descended into total war, with each side trying to destroy as many people, homesteads, and villages as they could, it was extremely difficult to grow anything. In fact, farmers often had to plant or harvest with armed militia keeping lookout for attack. In the southern colonies, where civil war had broken out, one's crops were just as likely to be burned by a neighbor. The sum total of army and vigilante violence turned many fertile fields into wastelands. For example, a Scottish minister in South Carolina reported that "all was desolation" in his neighborhood: "Every field, every plantation, showed marks of ruin and devastation." This devastation spread as well to livestock and the game animals that farmers depended on for meat. In 1782, an American general called the hundred-mile trek through war-torn rural South Carolina "the most dull, melancholy, dreary ride that anyone could possibly take." The landscape once filled with "live-stock and wild fowl of every kind, was now destitute of all. It had been so completely checquered by the different parties, that not one part of it had been left unexplored; consequently, not the vestiges of horses, cattle, hogs, or deer, &c. was to be found. The squirrels and birds of every kind were destroyed" (quoted in Weir, 1985, 76–77).

When crops and livestock survived combat, they often fell before foraging armies. British, French, and Patriot armies impressed horses and wagons and demanded grain and meat. Tenant farmers in New York who supported the Revolution said that they were suffering from demands to supply the Continental Army that was "constantly Cantoned & encamped around us, notwithstanding our willingness at all times to supply their reasonable wants but how inadequate was our little property to the Support of an Army often hungry, Naked and distressed for the necessary Comforts of life, which consequently, at times, by living so contiguous to them Reduced us to the same predicament" (quoted in Lynd, 1961, 344).

Selling crops to either army often proved hazardous. Those who sold to the British sometimes found themselves facing arrest or receiving a beating from their Patriot neighbors. Those who sold to the Continental Army often had to accept payment in depreciated paper money or in IOUs that were never worth more than a fraction of the amount printed on the face. In these cases, farmers paid a steep price to show their patriotism by essentially giving away their livestock and crops for worthless slips of paper. Even before the war ended, many farmers found themselves facing lawsuits because they had no money to pay their debts or taxes—a problem that only increased in the postwar years.

Farmers who hoped to sell their crops at market rather than to armies were often sorely disappointed. Even if they could avoid looting soldiers or civilians, the war disrupted local markets, making it difficult to sell at all. It was even harder to trade overseas. The British Navy and Loyalist privateers patrolled the Atlantic and were all too happy to capture U.S. merchant vessels and take their cargoes as booty. This blockade drastically cut overseas trade, and it was especially hard on southern farmers who needed foreign markets for their tobacco. The blockade also stopped farmers from importing tools and other necessities. As a result, farmers faced serious shortages of necessities like salt (something farmers needed for livestock and food preservation). In many places, these shortages caused farmers to protest or even riot over what many of them saw as scarcities produced by the hoarding of merchants, whom some New York farmers called "a vile set of Men whose God is their Gain"(quoted in Lynd, 1961, 345).

For many farm families, the problem wasn't selling their crops, it was finding the labor to plant and harvest them. Even before the war began, tens of thousands of slaves in the southern colonies ran away, and by claiming freedom, dealt a blow to the plantation economy built on their labor. When the fighting started, the farm economy faced a severe labor shortage, as many fathers and sons left the fields to fight. The shortage sometimes included farmwomen, who left to nurse, cook, and sew for the contending armies. As the war dragged on, the labor shortage grew to include the farm laborers who left the fields for the land, cash, and sometimes slave bounties offered by the Continental Army. Some northern farmers, desperate to escape military service, freed their own slaves to fight in their place. Due to this labor shortage, many farmers had a difficult time producing enough to feed their families, let alone harvesting a surplus crop to sell.

These kinds of difficulties made many farmers reluctant soldiers: Put simply, many farmers worried that signing up for long tours of duty with the Continental Army or the militia would lead their families to ruin. For example, many Virginia farmers complained that long-term service undermined their independence. "We generally procure a sustenance for our Selves and families by the labour of our own hands," these farmers stated, "and one

The American colonies began circulating their own currency prior to their independence. States issued their own, with Continental dollars coming a few months later. The issuances were initially unregulated, which caused a loss of market value and extreme inflation. (*National Archives and Records Administration*)

days Labour is Necessary for the Next days support." They said that those most hurt by service were "the poorer sort who have not a slave to labour for them." Other Virginia farmers worried that if they were forced "to leave our Farms" for military service, their families would be thrown into poverty and "that if ever we Shou'd return again Wou'd find our Wives & Children dispers'd up & down the Country abeging, or at home aSlaving." In Dutchess County, New York, many farmers said they "would not serve [because] the People were wore out last year. Those in the Army lost the opportunity of seeding their Ground and were now starving for Bread" (McDonnell, 1998, 966–967; Lynd, 1961, 339).

Conclusion

In these ways, the war put both Patriot and Loyalist farmers in difficult positions. Whether they sided with Britain or the Revolution, the demands of war meant that farmers risked losing their livelihoods in their quest for independence. Given the stakes involved, it is no wonder that most farmers—no matter their political sympathies—tried to stay on the sidelines or joined the war effort only when the fighting came into their neighborhoods. By the end of the war, though, the Revolution belonged to ordinary farmers. They shaped the ideological debate over the importance and meaning of independence prior to the war, and when the fighting began, thousands became soldiers in the Patriot or British causes. When the fighting ended, they continued to believe that the war belonged to ordinary farmers.

References and Further Reading

Bedford County Execution Dockets, 1772–1775. Bedford County Courthouse, Bedford, PA.

Bellesiles, Michael. *Revolutionary Outlaws: Ethan Allen and the Struggle for Independence on the Early American Frontier.* Charlottesville: University Press of Virginia, 1993.

Berks County Execution Dockets, 1769–1775. Berks County Courthouse, Reading, PA.

Brock, Peter. *Pioneers of the Peaceable Kingdom.* Princeton, NJ: Princeton University Press, 1968.

Brooke, John L. *The Heart of the Commonwealth: Society and Political Culture in Worcester County, Massachusetts.* New York: Cambridge University Press, 1989.

Bushman, Richard L. "Massachusetts Farmers and the Revolution." In *Society, Freedom, and Conscience: The American Revolution in Virginia, Massachusetts, and New York*, ed. Richard L. Jellison. New York: Norton, 1976.

Calloway, Colin G. *The American Revolution in Indian Country: Crisis and Diversity in Native American Communities.* New York: Cambridge University Press, 1995.

Countryman, Edward. *A People in Revolution: The American Revolution and Political Society in New York, 1760–1790.* Baltimore: Johns Hopkins University Press, 1981.

Countryman, Edward. *The American Revolution.* Rev. ed. New York: Hill and Wang, 2003.

Crèvecoeur, J. Hector St. John. *Letters from an American Farmer.* In *From British Peasants to Colonial American Farmers*, ed. Allan Kulikoff. Chapel Hill: University of North Carolina Press, 2000.

Dickinson, John. "The Late Regulations Respecting the British Colonies on the Continent of America Considered," Vol. 14, *Memoirs of the Historical Society of Pennsylvania.* Philadelphia: Pennsylvania Historical Society, 1895.

Dinkin, Robert J. *Voting in Provincial America: A Study of Elections in the Thirteen Colonies, 1689–1776.* Westport, CT: Greenwood, 1977.

Ernst, Joseph. *Money and Politics in America, 1755–1775: A Study in the Currency Act of 1764 and the Political Economy of Revolution.* Chapel Hill: University of North Carolina Press, 1973.

Fox, Francis S. *Sweet Land of Liberty: The Ordeal of the American Revolution in Northampton County, Pennsylvania.* University Park: Pennsylvania State University Press, 2000.

Frey, Sylvia R. *Water from the Rock: Black Resistance in a Revolutionary Age.* Princeton, NJ: Princeton University Press, 1991.

Gross, Robert A. *The Minutemen and Their World.* New York: Hill and Wang, 1976.

Gross, Robert A., ed. *In Debt to Shays: The Bicentennial of an Agrarian Rebellion.* Charlottesville: University Press of Virginia, 1993.

Hazard's Register of Pennsylvania 4: July 1829.

Higginbotham, Don. *The War of American Independence: Military Attitudes, Policies, and Practice, 1763–1789.* Boston: Northeastern University Press, 1971.

Hoffman, Ronald. *A Spirit of Dissension: Economics, Politics and the Revolution in Maryland.* Baltimore: Johns Hopkins University Press, 1974.

Hoffman, Ronald. "The 'Disaffected' in the Revolutionary South." In *The American Revolution: Explorations in the History of American Radicalism.* De Kalb: Northern Illinois University Press, 1976.

Holton, Woody. *Forced Founders: Indians, Debtors, Slaves, and the Making of the American Revolution in Virginia.* Chapel Hill: University of North Carolina Press, 1999.

Kars, Marjoleine. *Breaking Loose Together: The Regulator Rebellion in Pre-Revolutionary North Carolina.* Chapel Hill: University of North Carolina Press, 2002.

Klein, Rachel N. *Unification of a Slave State: The Rise of the Planter Class in the South Carolina Backcountry, 1760–1808.* Chapel Hill: University of North Carolina Press, 1990.

Kulikoff, Allan. *From British Peasants to Colonial American Farmers.* Chapel Hill: University of North Carolina Press, 2000.

Lynd, Staughton. "Who Should Rule at Home? Dutchess County, New York, in the American Revolution." *William and Mary Quarterly*, 3rd ser., 18 (1961): 330–359.

McConville, Brendan. *These Daring Disturbers of the Public Peace: The Struggle for Property in Early New Jersey.* Ithaca, NY: Cornell University Press, 1999.

McCusker, John J., and Russell R. Menard. *The Economy of British America, 1607–1789.* Chapel Hill: University of North Carolina Press, 1985.

McDonnell, Michael. "Popular Mobilization and Political Culture in Revolutionary Virginia: The Failure of the Minutemen and the Revolution from Below." *Journal of American History* 85 (1998): 968–978.

Northampton County Execution Dockets, 1766–1775. County Archives, Northampton County Courthouse, Easton, PA.

Pencak, William, Matthew Dennis, and Simon P. Newman, eds. *Riot and Revelry in Early America.* University Park: Pennsylvania State University Press, 2002.

Philadelphia County Execution Docket, 1769–1771. City Archives, Philadelphia, PA.

Richards, Leonard. *Shays's Rebellion: The American Revolution's Final Battle.* Philadelphia: University of Pennsylvania Press, 2002.

Vickers, Daniel. *Farmers and Fishermen: Two Centuries of Work in Essex County, Massachusetts, 1630–1830.* Chapel Hill: University of North Carolina Press, 1994.

Weir, Robert M. "'The Violent Spirit': The Reestablishment of Order, and the Continuity of Leadership in Post-Revolutionary South Carolina." In *An Uncivil War: The Southern Backcountry during the American Revolution,* ed. Ronald Hoffman, Thad W. Tate, and Peter J. Albert. Charlottesville: University Press of Virginia, 1985.

Young, Alfred F. "English Plebeian Culture and Eighteenth-Century American Radicalism." In Margaret C. Jacob and James R. Jacob, eds., *The Origins of Anglo-American Radicalism.* London: Allen and Unwin, 1984.

An "Epidemical Fury of Emigration": The Flight of the Non-English into the Colonies on the Eve of the American Revolutionary War

2

Robyn McMillan

Great Britain is generally understood to have been the primary source for European migration to the North American mainland colonies in the two centuries prior to the American Revolutionary War. Did not the "British"—itself a designation calling for some distinctions—form the majority of settlers to those New World outposts whose very names resonate with Englishness? Virginia, Plymouth Rock, Charles Town, New York: Yes, it was the English who swarmed across the Atlantic. Adventurers and seekers of fortune flocked to Jamestown; Utopian dreamers sailed en masse to New England and Pennsylvania; and Barbadian sugar planters originated Carolina. American colonists for the most part spoke English, consumed large quantities of English goods, and everywhere followed the English common law. Indeed, the Revolutionary War was fought in part to free the mainland colonies from British rule. When we think of colonial America, we picture an offshoot of Britain. This is entirely understandable, and during the seventeenth century the English certainly made up the bulk of European emigration to America. Yet for all those tens of thousands of British transplants, on the eve of the American Revolutionary War, perhaps fewer than half of all American colonists could trace their ancestry to England.

"A Strange Mixture of Blood"

A close look at eighteenth-century colonial society immediately moves us past our expectations of an Anglicized America. We find instead that cultural diversity had existed in North America from the earliest days of English settlement and that the constitution of colonial societies grew increasingly varied over time. The eighteenth century saw exceptionally heavy migration into the colonies, and non-English people came in such large numbers that they altered the ethnic composition of virtually every colony. When

J. Hector St. John de Crèvecoeur penned an interpretation of his adopted homeland then in revolution, he acknowledged and applauded this multiformity, pronouncing America the "most perfect society now existing in the world." Speaking to a European audience in his *Letters*, he asked "what, then, is the American, this new man?" (*Letters from an American Farmer*, 1782, 42). Crèvecoeur posed a prescient and timeless question, and he provided an equally timeless and durable answer: Europeans from many nations met in America and "melted into a new race of men."

Ah, but where did Americans really come from? In surveying his adopted countrymen, Crèvecoeur found them to be a motley bunch. A Revolutionary-era American was "either an European, or a descendant of an European . . . a mixture of English, Scotch, Irish, French, Dutch, Germans, and Swedes . . . a promiscuous breed." Such was the rootstock that produced the American. Though Crèvecoeur spoke to the influence of environment on shaping America's national character—one suited for the creation of his "perfect society"—he was also at pains to demonstrate that American society emerged from an almost infinitely varied assortment of different nationalities. (Of course we recognize the limitations of his diversity: Africans, African Americans, and American Indians were excluded.) Perhaps some of the cross-ethnic alliances that Crèvecoeur extolled to drive home his point about this novel American race were a bit fanciful. But his attention to the variety, the dizzying array of the population, reflected a wider truth about the composition of pre-Revolutionary American society.

Always excepting the more homogeneous New England colonies, which admittedly loom large in U.S. collective colonial memories, diversity had long been the rule in America. The colonies attracted not only the English, but Poles, Greeks, Italians, French Huguenots, Swiss Protestants, English Catholics, Welsh Baptists, and Jews, among others, to say nothing of the largest voluntary migrant groups—Scots, Irish, and Germans. This multiplicity held especially true for the eighteenth century in the mid-Atlantic region of New York, New Jersey, Delaware, and Pennsylvania, where the population grew tenfold from 1700 to 1775. That boom owed much to the influx of European migrants, as Dutch, Swedish, Danish, Jewish, French, Germanic, Scottish, and Irish immigrants poured into the region. Indeed, such was the explosive population growth in Pennsylvania—a Restoration colony founded in 1681—that on the eve of the Revolution, Philadelphia was the second-largest city within the British Empire. Only London had a larger population. And Philadelphia's was an ethnically mixed populace. Well before 1800, barely one-third of the mid-Atlantic population traced its ancestry to England.

Notwithstanding this extended influx of newcomers over the course of the eighteenth century, it is a mistake to imagine this migration as a steadily increasing groundswell of people. Instead, the character of eighteenth-century migration more accurately can be described as intermittent waves of people, rushing across the Atlantic during the interstices of imperial wars. The dozen years of peace between the end of the Seven Years' War and the outbreak of the American Revolutionary War saw perhaps the greatest mass migration of people to America up to that time, as tens upon tens of thousands of northern Irish, Germans, and Lowland and Highland Scots flooded into the colonies.

Salzburgers arrive at Frankfort to settle in colonial Georgia, 1733. (*North Wind Picture Archives*)

Meticulous accountings of this resettlement are almost certainly unattainable. With few exceptions, colonial officials kept no tallies at the points of emigrant disembarkation. Nonetheless, the most recent and careful assessments of available evidence have determined more precisely the shape and texture of the mass migration that took place on the eve of the American Revolution. These analyses allow historians to challenge some of the received wisdom and long-standing assumptions about European migration to the colonies. It is now clear that many fewer Irish migrated to the colonies in the dozen years preceding the Revolution than previously. German migration into the colonies also tapered off from previous highs in the years immediately prior to the Revolution. However, Scottish emigration from the Highlands, which had been negligible in previous decades, soared in the fifteen years before the onset of the Revolution. Whole families and even entire Scottish towns removed across the ocean. The outbreak of the war in 1775 understandably brought to a sudden halt this traffic in people.

The first federal census of the American population, called for by the newly ratified Constitution and conducted in 1790, confirmed part of Crèvecoeur's appraisal of America's "strange mixture of blood," one unknown elsewhere. As part of the compromise over representation, the constitutionally mandated census required "actual enumeration" for the purpose of allocating seats in the House of Representatives and direct taxes. The Constitution divided the population into three broad groups: the free, the enslaved, and Indians not taxed. Native Americans, as domestic dependent nations, were not considered to be a part of an emerging American nationality, nor were they enumerated in this census, since they were excluded from the population base for purposes of taxation and representation (Calloway, 1997, 40). Thus that first census did not probe the population deeply. It merely separated the population into white males below and above sixteen—seeking at a minimum to know the total number of adult men, those most likely to be involved in the political life of the new country—white females, and free blacks. Slaves were counted with no distinctions based on age or sex. Out of an enumerated population of nearly 4 million (though probably undercounting the population by at least 5 percent), that first census found just under half were of English origin. African Americans, the vast majority of them enslaved, made up 20 percent of the population and were the second-largest specified group. Unfortunately, ethnic and regional differences within that cohort were unaccounted for. People from other European nations made up the last third of the population; they were primarily Scottish, Irish, and Germanic, demonstrating a more limited variety than Crèvecoeur put forward, but one that is supported by the most current demographic studies of pre-Revolutionary migration.

Regrettably, to establish an authoritative accounting of the numbers of emigrants who entered eighteenth-century America remains an impossible task. The only records that were kept over any length of time were ship manifests maintained in Philadelphia for German-speaking travelers arriving in Philadelphia. These ship lists, covering most of the eighteenth century, have survived, and they allow historians to determine with greater precision than elsewhere how many German immigrants arrived in Pennsylvania. These records are relatively complete, and compared to extant records for other immigrant groups, the German passenger manifests represent the broadest and most comprehensive accounts collected at the point of arrival for any immigrant group. Though the Naturalization Act of 1790 expressed national policy on immigration and made explicit the process by which an emigrant could become a citizen, not until 1819 did the federal government require ships' captains to report the number of disembarking passengers. Even with these limitations, enough data exist to allow some cautious estimates as to the numbers of immigrants who entered the colonies on the eve of the American Revolution. Conservative estimates find that for the generation before the war, 35,000 Protestant Irish, 40,000 Scots, and 60,000 German-speakers entered the Philadelphia port alone. (Thirty thousand Englishmen also traveled through the port of Philadelphia in the twenty-five years prior to 1775.) In the dozen or so years between the end of the Seven Years' War and the commencement of the Revolutionary War, approximately 12,000 Irish and 12,000 Germans migrated to the colonies, as did 25,000 Scots (Wokeck, 1999; Fogelman, 1992, 691–709).

It seems clear, however, that a significant majority of European migrants before the Revolution came from Great Britain and northwestern Europe. One of the largest European groups to migrate to what became the United States came from northern Ireland, the Ulster-Scots (frequently called the Scotch-Irish and in the eighteenth century, as in this essay, simply "the Irish"). These were migrants who had already crossed in the previous century from lowland Scotland into Ulster, encouraged by the English, who wished to

Page from a 1773 mustering book, showing some of the *Britannia* passengers that arrived in Philadelphia from Rotterdam. The list shows their signatures, as well as the freight and head charges. (*Historical Society of Pennsylvania (HSP)*, #553, *Mustering Book, 1773, Am 209*)

introduce a Protestant presence into Catholic Ireland. Over the course of the eighteenth century, the Presbyterian population of Ireland declined by one-half, as "the Irish" left for America. Because of obstacles facing Roman Catholics, the eighteenth century had no mass movement from southern Ireland, though Maryland and Pennsylvania certainly had their share of Celtic Irish. German speakers made up the largest non-British European group to arrive in the eighteenth century, and they came from many parts of the Holy Roman Empire, and from Swiss cantons, Alsace, and Lorraine, as well as from the western German states. The majority of these migrants left the Rhenish lands that extended from Cologne to Basel, and most particularly those in the Palatinate, Hesse, and Württemberg. But the dozen years between the end of the Seven Years' War (known in the colonies as the French and Indian War) and the onset of the American Revolution saw Highland Scots fairly depopulate their countryside in a massive and concentrated migration to America. This exodus brought more than 25,000 Highlanders to America in the years after 1763. These fellow travelers—the Germans, the Irish, and the Scots—entered America primarily through Philadelphia, the colonies' main port for immigrants.

Improvement in material circumstances being a primary factor for this population shift, these immigrants streamed to where land was affordable and labor in demand. These two factors frequently determined where free families chose to settle, and where indentured labor was sent. By the 1760s, neither New England nor the Chesapeake tidewater region nor lowland South Carolina could provide newcomers with either of these inducements. Choice land in New England had long been settled by the descendants of the earliest settlers; indeed their young people were forced to migrate further and further west in the quest for self-sufficiency. The Chesapeake as well provided little incentive to those seeking land, as it too was a well-developed area. Those Scots who did migrate into the Chesapeake area did so almost exclusively because of connections to the tobacco trade. The vast majority of the Scottish settlers to the region in the 1760s and 1770s—merchants, storekeepers, and factors—were directly involved in the tobacco trade, or provided services, as clergymen, doctors, and teachers, to those in the community who were so engaged. Furthermore, the slave societies of the Chesapeake and the Lower South had little need for free or only temporarily bound labor.

The foothills of the Appalachian mountain chain drew these immigrants. They poured into the southwestern Pennsylvania backcountry, spreading north and south, establishing communities in western Pennsylvania, upper New York, and the Carolina Piedmont as well. Ultimately, these new colonists settled predominantly in the mid-Atlantic region because of the opportunities they perceived existed for them in what came to be called the "best poor Man's Country in the World" (Lemon, 2002).

Coming to the Colonies

Establishing the reasons for transatlantic migration is confoundingly difficult, though primary push factors frequently were economic want and religious persecution at home. Conversely, economic opportunity, in the form of available land and the ever-increasing demand for labor in the colonies, as well as freedom from religious persecution were principal pull factors. In the end, multiple issues contributed to all aggregate migrations. The German migration to the American colonies was not an exception. Chief reasons for the exodus were the diverse conditions of southwestern Germany that encouraged migration: the devastations of war and famine, oppressive government practices, abusive credit policies, religious persecution. Indeed, push factors in eighteenth-century Germany were manifold, and it is important to realize that German migration to places other than the American colonies reached three-quarters of a million persons during the eighteenth century. America offered a variety of pull factors, primarily the economic and religious opportunities that settlement in the colonies provided. The networks of recruiters and shippers who made possible, and easy, the transport of those tens of thousands of hopeful migrants must also be accounted for. These factors were intricately related and constant neither over time nor in their influence. Indeed, not only did the tide of German immigration change over time, from its peak at midcentury to a standstill during the Revolution, but the composition of it changed over time as well. As the transportation networks grew stronger, the numbers of those who could pay their own way decreased, and the percentage of those who relied on some form of indentured servitude to pay for the costs of their relocation increased.

Emigration from northern Ireland and from Scotland was stimulated not merely by religious maltreatment of Presbyterians, but more importantly by discontent with the land system. Absentee landlords, high rents, and short leases were an Irish bane. The Highland Scot artisans struggled with underemployment, weavers especially. Farmers suffered from the insecurity of tenure and exorbitant rents, with rents doubling or even tripling, expressly to clear tenants from land to be consolidated and modernized by landholders. Many of these Irish and Scottish migrants were agriculturalists, traveling in family groups. Since colonial land speculators needed families to settle on their land, this provided a significant and important alignment of push and pull factors in this migration. Until the early 1760s, Highland Scots had formed an insignificant part of the European migration to the colonies. But in the years after 1763, their migration gained in momentum and volume. These emigrants traveled mostly as members of organized groups. Led by intermediate landlords known as tacksmen, Highlanders flooded into the colonies after the Peace of Paris. Many decommissioned Highlander soldiers chose to remain in the colonies after their regiments disbanded at the end of the French and Indian War. These former soldiers settled in frontier areas such as the Mohawk and Hudson valleys of upper New York. They prevailed upon relatives and friends to join them, and their favorable reports home enticed many to migrate. Thousands of other Scots were lured to North Carolina by the liberality of the legislature; they settled Cape Fear.

Scottish emigration was encouraged also by letters that appeared in the newspapers or as pamphlets. William Smith, a prominent New York lawyer, published in Glasgow in 1773 *Information to Emigrants*. The pamphlet sold for two pence and promised to provide "A full and particular Account of the Terms on which Settlers may procure Lands in North-America." But enticements to migrate were not limited to farmers: Tradesmen and laborers would also find "Encouragement . . . by going there to Settle." Indeed, Smith had published a broadsheet the previous year in the middle colonies promoting his lands in upstate New York, addressing himself to "All Farmers and Tradesmen, Who want good Settlements for themselves and Families, especially those lately arrived, or that may yet come, from Scotland or Ireland." A series of five pamphlets appeared in Scotland between 1770 and 1774, and declared the service of the Scottish soldiers in the French and Indian War "providential," in that it made known to so many the blessings of residence in America.

Financial hardships gave a strong impetus to Scottish migration, both in the Lowlands and the Highlands. The men of entire towns indentured themselves; small farmers joined together in associations and companies in order to finance and organize their wholesale removal to the colonies. The *Virginia Gazette* in 1774 printed a letter from a Glaswegian, describing unimaginable distress in the region: "There is an almost total stagnation in our manufactures, and grain is dear; many hundreds of labourers and mechanics, especially weavers in this neighbourhood, have lately indented and gone to America." A farmer from the Shetland Isles who sailed to America in 1774 put forward an overabundance of reasons for his resettlement. He had two sons already in Carolina, and they pleaded with him to bring the rest of the family over; he wished to improve the lot of his remaining children; recent harsh winters had killed his livestock; and his rents continued to rise. James Boswell and Dr. Samuel Johnson, on a tour of the Hebrides, noted that "whole neighborhoods formed parties for removal; so that departure from their native country is no longer exile." They continued,

> We had again a good dinner, and in the evening a great dance . . . a dance which I suppose the emigration from Skye has occasioned. They call it "America" . . . it goes on till all are set a-going, setting and wheeling round each other. . . . It shows how emigration catches till all are set afloat. Mrs. Mackinnon told me that last year when the ship sailed from Portree for America, the people on shore were almost distracted. . . . This year there was not a tear shed. The people on shore seemed to think that they would soon follow. (Boswell, 1961, 242–243)

This massive migration provoked serious panic in Britain. Its sheer volume—in some cases so significant that regions faced depopulation—led Parliament to discuss proposals to prevent emigration. Hoping to stem the depopulation of the northern isles, the British government in 1772 rejected a petition from several men of Skye for 40,000 acres of land in North Carolina. The possibility of cheap land in America threatened the large landholders, who worried about the leases held by their tenant farmers. The *Edinburgh Courant* in 1773 published details about the ways in which this substantial transatlantic resettlement was reshaping, in unfavorable ways, life in Scotland:

> 1500 People have emigrated from the Shire of Sutherland within these two Years, and carried with them £7500 Sterling; which exceeds a Year's Rent of the whole County; and that the single Consideration of the *Misery* which most of those People *must suffer* in America, independent of the Loss of Men and Money to the Mother Country, should engage the Attention not only of the *landed Interest, but of Administration*. (Lemay, 1987, 705)

Benjamin Franklin mocked the author of that lament as disingenuous in his concern for the misery of the migrants. In a published response, Franklin offered as consolation "the Reflection, that perhaps the apprehended future Sufferings of those Emigrants will never exist: for it was probably the authentic Accounts that they had received from Friends already settled there, of the Felicity to be enjoyed in that Country, with a thorough Knowledge of their own Misery at home, which induced their Removal. And . . . if they meet with greater Misery in America, their future Letters lamenting it, . . . [will] effectually without a Law put a Stop to the Emigration" (Lemay, 1987, 705).

Unlike enslaved Africans, of whom it is safe to say that none migrated voluntarily to America, even those German, Irish, and Scottish migrants who were forced to contract their labor did so with the understanding that theirs was not a lifelong obligation. For perhaps half of German migrants and a smaller percentage of Irish and Scottish migrants before the Revolution,

Eighteenth-century indentured servitude contract. Indentured servitude was a form of serfdom people entered into in order to pay their way to the English colonies in North America. (*Library of Congress*)

transplantation to the colonies involved the likelihood of servitude. Those who sailed from Britain entered into their indentures before they sailed from Europe, whereas poorer German migrants promised to redeem the costs of their passage upon arrival in America. Often, these families could pay part of the costs of their passage before sailing, though the rates to travel from inland were prohibitive and exploitative experiences on the journey to the port cities might rob them of their remaining funds. By midcentury, shippers and ships' captains had had decades in which to develop this method of "redemption" by which German immigrants were transported to North America. If upon arrival in America they were not able to raise the costs of their passage, they could be sold into servitude by the ship captain to recoup those expenses. The length of their service might run from one to four or more years and depended on how much they still owed.

The Immigration Debate

The American colonies had need of immigrants: laborers, who could supply growing colonial industries with the manpower they required, and families, who could settle on backcountry land and pay rents to the wealthy land speculators. Nonetheless, by the middle of the eighteenth century, this ever-increasing immigration aroused considerable anxiety among long-established colonial settlers. Benjamin Franklin, early to recognize the market these German speakers represented, in 1732 began publishing America's first German-language newspaper, the *Philadelphische Zeitung*. It soon failed, though the market in German speakers that he identified only grew larger, and by 1751 Franklin spoke for many of those alarmed by the huge influx of newcomers when he maintained that if the flood of migrants were not curbed, his beloved Pennsylvania would grow unrecognizably foreign. "Why should *Pennsylvania*, founded by the *English*, become a Colony of *Aliens*, who will shortly be so numerous as to Germanize us instead of our Anglifying them, and will never adopt our Language or Customs?" (Lemay, 1987, 374). Franklin, opposing the migration of non-English into the colonies, argued that the general "Observation concerning the Importation of *Germans* in too great Numbers into *Pennsylvania*, is, I believe, a very just one." Again, he fretted about the ethnic composition of the colony, fearing that Pennsylvania "in a few Years become a *German* Colony. . . . Already the *English* begin to quit particular Neighbourhoods surrounded by *Dutch*, being made uneasy by the Disagreeableness of dissonant Manners, and in Time, Numbers will probably quit the Province for the same Reason." These Germans spoke the wrong language, displayed the wrong manners, were burdened by a "swarthy Complexion," and probably could not be counted on to be good subjects, "faithful to the *British* Interest." Though the British Parliament had in 1740 enacted the Naturalization Act, conferring British citizenship on alien immigrants to the colonies, German allegiance to the British Crown was clearly suspect. These untrustworthy, and possibly treacherous, outsiders appeared to be taking over the colony (Lemay, 1987, 445).

In fact, in the half-dozen years before 1754 and the outbreak of hostilities leading to the French and Indian War, more than 30,000 Germans did come to Pennsylvania. By the time German migration began anew, after the 1763 Peace of Paris, Pennsylvanians with German ancestry accounted for somewhere between one-half and two-thirds of the population. In the twelve years before the Revolution, perhaps another 15,000 migrated to the colonies, until a 1768 imperial decree forbidding emigration slowed the depletion of the countryside, and the outbreak of hostilities during the American War for Independence halted it completely. That ending, in combination with the very large post-1763 influx of other European migrants into the middle colonies, diluted the German concentration. The 1790 census found that those of German ancestry represented only a third of the population as a whole.

It was not only in Pennsylvania that objections to the large German migration could be heard. Gottlieb Mittelberger, an organist and schoolmaster, sailed with 500 countrymen and arrived in Philadelphia in 1750. Disenchanted with American colonial life, he soon returned home and immortalized egregious examples of brutality in the redemptioner trade with his 1754 pamphlet warning against immigration, *A Journey to Pennsylvania*. Threatening potential émigrés with an ocean passage of up to twelve weeks, after many months of travel from the interior, Mittelberger promised in any event "pitiful signs of distress—smells, fumes, horrors, vomiting" during the crossing, and any number of diseases, including dysentery, boils, scurvy, cancer, and mouth-rot. The provisions would be poor, with the stale food and putrid water auguring hunger and thirst, to add to the discomforts brought about by "frost, heat, dampness, fear, misery, vexation, and lamentations as well as other troubles." But the duke of Württemberg, whose lands were being depopulated, almost certainly arranged for this diatribe to be written as a deterrent against continued emigration from his lands. He may even have written it himself (Mittelberger, 1960, 12).

Others experienced a far more favorable crossing and found that the time spent on board the ship was an adventure. Still, this was not the norm, especially in the years prior to the Revolution. The worst oceanic crossings that German emigrants suffered through took place in the boom years of the early 1750s, when it was most difficult to avoid the reach of calculating promoters and others intent on maximizing profits at the expense of the health and well-being of the passengers. Another German writer deplored the migration, but raised no alarms about the perils of the voyage itself. He called for wiser policies and economic administration in order to preclude the need for emigration to America, without resorting to frightening tales. In the end, unable to foresee such a reworking of the social contract, he resigned himself instead to the hope that the large migration might be the work of divine intervention, creating a moral and enlightened area in remote America. In any event, Mittelberger decried the trade to little effect. The years of peace following the final defeat of France in the Seven Years' War saw the greatest of all the colonial migrations, until the Declaration of Independence and the onset of hostilities profoundly discouraged European immigration.

But on the eve of the Revolution, and in the face of European and British restrictions on emigration to America, some Americans found that they were unwilling to do without the flow of migrants from overseas; indeed it appeared American progress depended in part on them. Philip Freneau's *Stanzas on the Emigration to America, and peopling the Western Country*, published in 1772, made just such a claim, asserting that America's bright future relied in part on European refugees: "From Europe's proud, despotic shores / Hither the stranger takes his way, / And in our new found world explores / A happier soil." These expatriates would "tame the soil, and plant the arts" in America. But Benjamin Franklin was more discriminating in the kind of migration he wished to see. Publishing a long and carefully reasoned response to a proposed Parliamentary act to restrict British emigration to the colonies, Franklin argued against both its inhumanity toward British subjects and the harm such restrictions might bring to the colonies.

> The proposed Law would forbid increasing, and confine Britons to their present Numbers, keeping half that Number too, in wretchedness. The Common People of Britain and of Ireland, contributed . . . to the success of that War, which brought into our Hands the vast unpeopled Territories of North America; a Country favoured by Heaven with all the Advantages of Soil and Climate; Germans are now pouring into it, to take Possession of it, and fill it with their Posterity; and shall Britons, and Irelanders, who have a much better Right to it, be forbidden a Share of it? (Lemay, 1987)

When Thomas Paine in 1775 published *Common Sense*, perhaps the most incendiary of all the political pamphlets to appear in the colonies during the imperial crisis leading up the Revolutionary War, he had it issued both in English and in German. How much this fact speaks to the political passions of the German-speaking population is not clear. More than likely it reflected the demographic realities of Pennsylvania rather than any deep revolutionary fervor on the part of the German population. In it, Paine did assert that "Europe, and not England, is the parent country of America." The following year, the German press published a defense of the War for Independence, eulogizing the freedoms Germans enjoyed in America and compared their conditions in the old country to slavery. "Remember—and remind your families—,that you came to America, suffering many hardships, in order to escape servitude and enjoy liberty. Remember, in Germany, serfs may not marry without the consent of their master . . . they are regarded as little better than black slaves." The German press catalogued a long list of injustices and abuses suffered at home and assured their readers that the British government had every intention of treating the colonists "the same way, or worse."

The Imperial Crisis

How did the recent settlers, or more established ethnic migrants, respond to the political pressures of the imperial crisis? American conditions, not ethnic ties, generally determined the settlers' responses to the Revolution. In Pennsylvania, nearly all the Irish supported the war, with many becoming quite ardent Patriots. (The majority of the men and officers of the Pennsylvania Line were Irish—it was named the Line of Ireland by General Henry "Light Horse Harry" Lee.) But of course, settlers elsewhere did not form a solid block of ethnic support. In the Carolina backcountry, the Irish were sharply divided and infrequently joined the rebels. Efforts at winning them over to the Patriot cause produced fairly insipid responses. Even when the Continental Congress sent two Presbyterian ministers into the Carolina backcountry to convince them of the rightness of the independence movement, the Irish remained largely noncompliant. They were not quite Loyalists, and certainly not hostile, but they remained unresponsive to the revolutionary cause. Of course, many of those who did remain loyal or took positions of neutrality were recent immigrants who had received land grants from the British government that they were loath to jeopardize by joining the rebellion.

German settlers also took political decisions during the Revolution more because of personal situations than by bonds of common ethnic ties. The controversy with Great Britain took a definite backseat to local issues. Germans in the western and central counties of Pennsylvania frequently sided with the revolutionaries because of antagonism toward those they perceived as eastern political elites. Actually, and further underscoring their motives, many Pennsylvania Germans deserted the Continental Army once the political leadership in the colony had been overthrown. Independence from the Crown, for these Pennsylvanians, was less important than ridding the colony of its local political leaders. On the other hand, German frontier settlers in the lower south tended to side with the Loyalists so as not to lose British protection against Indian raids. At times, religious differences trumped the exigencies of localism or geography. Each of the many German churches and sects took action in the Revolution in its own distinct way. Some had ties to Hanover and were thus doubly allied to George III. Sect peoples scrupled at the use of force in general. Some felt gratitude to Britain, which had provided them with a religious haven and the freedom from persecution they enjoyed in the colonies. However, the vast majority of German settlers remained relatively uncommitted to either side. Most German settlers before the war had been politically indifferent and uninvolved, and so most remained. Conservative habits, language barriers, and the universal desire to live peaceable lives all played a role in keeping Germans neutral as long as circumstances permitted.

The patriarch of German Lutheranism in America, the Reverend Henry Melchior Muhlenberg, best exemplified that watchful neutrality. Disinclined to "change my oath of allegiance nor yet to be a sacrifice to *Anarchie* at the hands of an angry mob," at the outbreak of the war Muhlenberg chose not to choose. He retired into the countryside rather than take sides. Muhlenberg later became a general in the Continental Army, and both his sons retired from the ministry and fought on the side of the revolutionaries. But what his political convictions might have been at the outset of the war is still a matter

Henry Melchior Muhlenberg, ordained minister and brigadier general in the American Revolutionary War (1746–1807). (*Finck, William J. 1913.* Lutheran Landmarks and Pioneers in America. *Philadelphia: General Council Publication House*)

George Taylor

George Taylor of Pennsylvania might well be considered among the least representative of those fifty-six Founders who signed their names to the treasonous Declaration of Independence in the summer of 1775. On the one hand, much like the other delegates deliberating at the Continental Congress, Taylor was a propertied man, substantial and well-off, politically engaged, and a moderate radical. On the other, he was also an Irish-born emigrant and a former indentured servant who had traveled to the colonies to seek his fortune, and he had risen to his prominent position through a fortuitous combination of hard work and serendipity. Taylor was not the only emigrant to sign the Declaration of Independence. Other foreign-born signatories were James Smith of Pennsylvania and Matthew Thornton of New Hampshire, both Irish. James Wilson of Pennsylvania and James Witherspoon of New Jersey were Scottish immigrants. Francis Lewis of New York was born in Wales. Though Taylor does not easily fit the traditional image of the American aristocrats who were engineering the mainland colonies' split from the British Empire, it is in him that we recognize the classic American rags-to-riches story.

Born in 1716 to an Irish clergyman, as a young man Taylor was too poor to pay for his passage to the colonies. At twenty, like countless other impoverished Europeans, Taylor indentured himself in order to make the

George Taylor immigrated to North America nearly destitute but worked successfully enough to become a delegate to the Continental Congress and a signer of the Declaration of Independence. His impoverished background made him perhaps the most unlikely signer of the Declaration of Independence. (*Cirker, Hayward, and Blanche Cirker, eds. 1967.* Dictionary of American Portraits. *New York: Dover Publications, Inc.*)

crossing to America. A Mr. Savage, owner of the Warwick Furnace and Coventry Forge just outside Philadelphia, bought his indenture and

of some uncertainty. In 1777, having learned of a Hessian plot to hang him, Muhlenberg assured General William Howe that he had remained loyal to the king as long as circumstances had allowed.

Several Scottish émigrés inserted themselves prominently into the revolutionary cause. The signatories to the Declaration of Independence included the Reverend John Witherspoon, educated at Edinburgh, who arrived in 1768 to head the College of New-Jersey (later Princeton), and James Wilson, who had arrived in Philadelphia only in 1766. Arthur St. Clair, from Thurso, arrived in the colonies in 1758 as an imperial officer. He remained in the colonies as a civil servant and was among the earliest of revolution-

put him to physical labor in the iron foundry. Learning in time that Taylor had received some education, Savage promoted him to clerk; Taylor eventually advanced to become the foundry's manager. Six years after his arrival in the colonies, George Taylor was able to marry his former master's widow, Anne Savage. Upon his marriage, he took control of the ironworks and managed it profitably. Anne Savage Taylor bore her husband two children, both of whom survived infancy. For years, however, Taylor conducted an extramarital affair with his housekeeper, Naomi Smith, and had five more children with her. Regrettably, we know too few details about Taylor's surprisingly dramatic life.

At the conclusion of the Seven Years' War, in 1763, Taylor removed to Easton, in Northampton County, from which he was elected the following year to the provincial legislature. He evidently served his constituency well, as they returned him to the Pennsylvania legislature annually for the next five years. At the time, Pennsylvania politics were roiled by divisions between those who wished the colony to remain a proprietary colony and those who hoped to have it made into a royal colony. Taylor, bitterly opposed to a royal government, was in the minority in wishing the colony to remain a proprietary colony. His position put him in heated and vocal conflict with the chief proponent of the royal colony scheme, Benjamin Franklin. Taylor was a daring political thinker and found himself at odds with

Franklin once again when the imperial crisis heated up. Taylor openly criticized Franklin, by far the most famous man in the colonies, for not opposing Britain with enough vigor at the start of the troubles with Britain.

Though a man of substantial wealth—wealth earned outside the channels of imperial trade—Taylor was strongly in favor of independence. Early on in the crisis, he sat on the committee that drew up instructions for delegates to the Stamp Act congress. Indeed he was appointed a delegate to the second Continental Congress as part of the radicalized Pennsylvania delegation. Taylor took the place of one of several Pennsylvanians who refused to sign the Declaration of Independence, to which Taylor readily appended his signature in August 1776.

Unfortunately, ill health prevented Taylor from serving in the Congress for very long. Prior to his retirement, Congress deployed him to negotiate a treaty with the Indians at Easton, on the Susquehanna border. Once out of the Congress, he was almost immediately elected to the new Supreme Executive Council of Pennsylvania, but resigned from all active public affairs soon after due to continued infirmity. Taylor died in February 1781. He did not live to see Cornwallis surrender later that year on the Yorktown peninsula, not far from where the English colonial experiment had begun at Jamestown in 1607.

aries. He fought victoriously at the Battle of Princeton and in consequence was appointed as a major general of the Continental Army. He later served as governor of the western Ohio territory, where he may have used his Scot connections to help populate the region.

Those Scots in the tobacco trade and otherwise associated with the imperial mercantile economy performed a reverse migration with the outbreak of the American Revolution. The loyalism of the Scots was strong and a matter of received wisdom among the revolutionaries. Many denounced the Scottish antagonism to the rebellion. Thomas Jefferson's first draft of the Declaration of Independence lamented that George III had unleashed

"Scotch and foreign mercenaries" to rain destruction on the colonists. Other Patriots promised widespread and continued resistance to the "tyrannical Acts of Parliament" always excepting "a few tattered Scotch Highlanders," recently emigrated and totally ignorant. Indeed, Tory and Scot were often used as synonyms. How many of these recent migrants returned to Britain in the Loyalist exodus after 1775 cannot be known. Though several ships with Highlanders attempted to arrive in the colonies after Parliament forbade further emigration to America in 1775, a larger and unknown number of others left.

On the eve of the American Revolution, nearly one-half of Scottish emigrants to America were indentured servants, and more than one-half of the German migrants arriving in Philadelphia in those years were as well. The years after the establishment of the republic saw a significant decline in such indentures for all ethnic groups except the Germans. Immigration to America, when it resumed in 1783, still included many indentured servants, but that portion of the trade swiftly declined. The ideology of the war, and the strains that American independence placed on the British Empire, took a toll on the servant system that had thrived until just a few years before. All those involved, including prospective migrants, were forced to reconsider their participation in such a system. While large-scale migration among European ethnic groups resumed after 1783, those migrants came less and less frequently as servants. Emigrants less often bound themselves to terms of labor; shippers and ship captains involved in the trade grew increasingly more skeptical that American courts would uphold their contracts. Thus American independence rewrote the terms of the American trade in people and the parameters under which people moved between Europe and the new United States. While pockets of this servant trade continued into the nineteenth century, for the most part the impact of the American Revolution on immigration was profound. More than half of migrants to America in the eighteenth century were indentured servants or redemptioners. (When African slaves and convicts are included, the number jumps to three-quarters of all immigrants.) But in the generation immediately after the war, fewer than 5 percent of immigrants entered the new nation as bound servants.

The ideology of the Revolution and the formation of the United States forced a reevaluation of the nature of citizenship. As Americans articulated a civic tie between citizens and nation that was a contractual choice, instead of a natural and permanent condition—they were monarchical subjects no longer—they were forced to consider as well who could and should be a citizen. Not long before assuming the presidency, George Washington wrote about Scottish migration into the new nation in a private letter to Richard Henderson, operator of an ironworks near Antietam Creek. Washington "conceded" that "America, under an efficient government, will be the most favorable Country of any in the world for persons of industry and frugality, possessed of a moderate capital, to inhabit. It is also believed, that it will not be less advantageous to the happiness of the lowest class of people because of the equal distribution of property, the great plenty of unoccupied lands, and the facility of procuring the means of subsistence. The scheme of purchasing a good tract of freehold estate and bringing out a number of able-bodied men, indented for a certain time appears to be indisputably a rational one" (George Washington to Richard Henderson, June 19, 1788, in Rhodehamel, 1997, 686).

Washington promoted Scottish migration into the western lands, assuring Henderson that were he "a young man, just preparing to begin the world or if advanced in life, and had a family to make a provision for," Washington would settle those lands west of the Ohio River. Washington directed Henderson's correspondents, who were themselves seeking information about emigrating to America, and indeed all potential emigrants, to Benjamin Franklin's 1784 pamphlet on European migration, which Franklin had written from Passy (Lemay, 1987, 975–983). Washington was convinced that it "contains almost every thing, that needs to be known on the subject

Notice for sale or leasing of land in Northampton County, Pennsylvania. The advertisement, printed in 1788, appears in both German and English. (*Library of Congress*)

Es ist zu Verkaufen,

oder auf Anbauungs-Bedingungen zu Verlehnen,

Ein Strich sehr köstlich Bauland, in Northampton Caunty, in Pennsylvanien, fünf oder sechs Meilen von der Neuyorker Linie; es fängt an an den Haupt-Gewässern der Schobocking Krieck, etwan vier Meilen von der Rivier Delaware, und erstreckt sich Südwestlich etwan drey Meilen, da der Lauf des Landes sich von Süden drehet, und nach Westen gehet. Die Nördlichsten Gewässern der Equinunc berühren die Südlichsten Lotten. Jedes Stück ist mit einer hinreichenden Quantität Gras- und Wiesengrund versehen, wie auch mit Bauholz, als Büchen, Zucker-Mapel, Birtsch, Aeschen-Holz, rc. Die Eigenschaft dieses Landes ist in maachen Faden vortrefflich, und wird überhaupt gute Plantaschen machen. Die Producten werden in kurzer Zeit auf leichte Bedingungen zu Markte können gebracht werden, wegen der Verbesserung der Schiffahrt auf der Delaware und der Susquehanna, ein Strohm davon entstehet in dem Westlichen Theil des Landes, und läuft gegen Norden in selbige Rivier bey der Grossen Krümmung. Es liegt etwan 80 Meilen von Easton, nicht über 60 Meilen von der Jersey, und eben so weit von Poughkeepsie, an der Nord-Rivier. Dieses Land hat den Vorzug vor den meisten unangebauten Länderyen, welche zum Verkauf oder Verlehnung feil geboten werden, indem es nahe bey volkreichen Anbauungen gegen Osten und Süden liegt, und die Anbauungen auf der Susquehanna in Neuyork und Pensylvanien, nebst besagter Rivier, zur Nachbarschaft hat, um es gegen die Indianer zu vertheidigen, im Fall einige Unruhen entstehen solten. Die 23 Taunschips, welche Neuyork neulich an Massachusetts abgetreten, liegen gegen Nord-Westen, und laufen in einer beträchtlichen Entfernung gegen Westen an diesem Lande; und da man jede Ursach zu vermuthen hat, daß diese Taunschips in dem Lauf des Jahrs 1788 mit etlichen 100 Familien werden besetzt werden, so werden sie zur Vertheidigung dieses Landes dienen. Wegen den Bedingungen kan man sich melden bey Georg Palmer, in Moore Taunschip, in Northampton Caunty, bey Capitain William Craig, in Easton, (welche wirkliche Abmessungen von dem Lande haben) oder in Philadelphia, bey   Tench Coxe,
Chestnut-strasse, den 8ten Jenner, 1788.   N. Frazier.

Philadelphia: Gedruckt bey Melchior Steiner, in der Race-strasse, zwischen der Zweyten und Dritten-strasse.

TO BE SOLD,

Or Let on Improving Leases,

A BODY of very valuable Farming LANDS in Northampton County, Pennsylvania, five or six Miles from the New-York Line, beginning on the Head Waters of Shohocking Creek, about four Miles from the River Delaware, and extending southwesterly about three Miles, when the Course of the Lands turns from the South, and runs nearly due West. The northernmost Waters of the Equinunc touch two of the southernmost Lots. There is an ample Quantity of Grass and Meadow-Ground to each Tract, and they are well timbered with Beech, Sugar, Maple, Birch, Ash, &c. The Quality of these Lands is in many Instances very fine, and they will all make very good Farms. Their Produce will in a short Time be got to Market on easy Terms, from the Improvement of the Navigation of the Delaware, and of the Susquehannah, a Stream of which rises in the western Part of the Tracts, and runs northerly into that River at the Great Bend. The Distance from Easton is about 80 Miles, from Jersey does not exceed 60 Miles, and from Poughkeepsie, on the North River, is the same. They have the Advantage of most of the unimproved Lands now offering for Sale or Lease, in being very near to thick Settlements, that lie Eastward and southward of them, and in having the Settlements on the Susquehannah, in New-York and Pennsylvania, with that River itself, to defend them from the Indians, if any Disturbances should take Place. The twenty-three Townships granted lately by New-York to Massachusetts lie on the North-west, and run nearly West of them to a great Distance. As there is every Reason to expect those Townships will have several hundred Families on them in the Course of 1788, they will form a Frontier for the Lands now offered. For Terms apply to GEORGE PALMER, Esq; Moore Township, Northampton County, Capt. WILLIAM CRAIG, Easton, (who have actual Surveys of the Lands) or in Philadelphia, to

TENCH COXE,
Chesnut-street, January the 8th, 1788.   N. FRAZIER.

Philadelphia: Printed by MELCHIOR STEINER, in Race-street, between Second- and Third-streets.

of migrating to this County." Joyful at the expanse of vast and "uninhabited" western lands, Franklin no longer argued in favor of limiting migration to the British, as he had a generation earlier. (Of course, after the Revolution, the British government discouraged migration to the new United States, at one point going so far as to prohibit the emigration of craftsmen and manufacturers, temporarily drying up that stream of newcomers.) Neither did Washington feel that migration should be limited to any specific ethnic group: He wished to see the pamphlet republished not only in Scotland, but in "every other part of Europe." Any person who could ply a useful trade was welcome. Should he someday earn enough in wages to purchase land on the western frontier, so much the better. Indeed, in an effort to restrict the western lands to honest and industrious farmers, Congress offered large 640-acre plots at $1 dollar per acre, payable in hard currency. Heeding in part Thomas Paine's advice in *Common Sense* to "prepare in time an asylum for mankind," America continued to welcome migrants, enthusiastic laborers in particular—but the republic was getting choosier about the strangers admitted into its sanctuary. The indolent and the idle would find a cold reception.

Long before Paine's call for asylum, the American colonies promised to Europe the comforts of refuge and the prospects of opportunity to emigrants. It went through what one observer called an "epidemical fury of emigration" (Johnson, 1985, 99). Freedom from persecution, religious toleration, accessible land, economic advancement—America pledged all this and more. The American Revolution in many ways expanded those promises. In its aftermath, as well as during the war, many recent immigrants were determined to defend and define their future in the new nation. In the aftermath of independence, the United States resolved that the future of liberty and the strength of their republican experiment demanded that they grant asylum and citizenship to those seeking it. The tensions of the 1790s would test these convictions. Especially in the wake of the French and Haitian Revolutions, when the security of the United States was invidiously linked to the presence of aliens within society, diverse political thinkers in the United States found they could agree on the appropriateness and timeliness of retooling the nation's naturalization processes. At the heart of this periodically modified ruling was one core principle: A prolonged residence in the republic was the surest way of guaranteeing that an immigrant would grow genuinely attached to the country. Only thus, by spending time imbibing and adopting the country's particular ways, could Crèvecoeur's new race of men truly be realized.

References and Further Reading

Bailyn, Bernard. *The Peopling of British North America: An Introduction.* New York: Knopf, 1986.

Boswell, James. *Journal of a Tour to the Hebrides with Samuel Johnson, LL.D.,* ed. Frederick A. Pottle. New York: McGraw-Hill, 1961.

Calloway, Colin G. *New Worlds for All: Indians, Europeans, and the Remaking of Early America*. Baltimore: Johns Hopkins University Press, 1997.

Dickson, R. J. *Ulster Emigration to Colonial America, 1718–1775*. London: Routledge, 1966.

Fogelman, Aaron. "Migrations to the Thirteen British North American Colonies, 1700–1775: New Estimates." *Journal of Interdisciplinary History* 22 (1991): 691–709.

Johnson, Samuel. *A Journey to the Western Islands of Scotland*. 1798. Reprint, New York: Oxford University Press, 1985.

Jones, Maldwyn Allen. *American Immigration*. 2nd edition. Chicago: University of Chicago Press, 1992.

Landsman, Ned C. *Scotland and Its First American Colony, 1683–1765*. Princeton, NJ: Princeton University Press, 1985.

Lemay, J. A. Leo, ed. *Writings: Benjamin Franklin*. New York: Library of America, 1987, 705.

Lemon, James T. *The Best Poor Man's Country; Early Southeastern Pennsylvania*. Baltimore: Johns Hopkins University Press, 2002.

Letters from an American Farmer. London: Davies and Davis, 1782.

Mittelberger, Gottlieb. *Journey to Pennsylvania*, ed. Oscar Handlin and John Clive. Cambridge, MA: Belknap Press, 1960.

Rhodehamel, John. ed. *George Washington: Writings*. New York: Library of America, 1997.

Wokeck, Marianne S. *Trade in Strangers: The Beginnings of Mass Migration to North America*. University Park: Pennsylvania State University Press, 1999.

"Self-Evident Truths" on Trial: African Americans in the American Revolution

3

Jon Sensbach

"Liberty," cried the protestors in Charleston, South Carolina. "Liberty!"

It was December, 1765, and for months angry crowds had rallied in towns up and down the Atlantic seaboard against the hated Stamp Act. In August, a crowd sacked the lieutenant governor's home in Boston, and in October, Charleston's Sons of Liberty organization surged through the streets shouting "Liberty, liberty." But the demonstrators who echoed that cry in Charleston two months later were not the Sons of Liberty, nor were they protesting the Stamp Act. They were enslaved African Americans, who made up two-thirds of the town's population. In the middle of the colonies' quarrel with Britain, they were using white colonists' own words and tactics to call for a more fundamental kind of freedom—the freedom of their own bodies (Wood, 1978, 277). Nothing came of the protest—armed patrols made sure of that—but the slaves' call for justice was a pointed reminder of one of the enduring paradoxes of the American Revolution. The struggle for independence from Britain took place while slavery was deeply embedded in American society. As white American patriots clamored for dignity and the rights of man—espousing what the Declaration of Independence called "self-evident truths"—Americans of African heritage strove to achieve those revolutionary ideals for themselves. Would white America heed their appeal?

Some black Americans were optimistic. After all, as the dispute with Britain grew more bitter, white colonists repeatedly accused Parliament of trying to make them "slaves," no idle rhetorical flourish since many of them were slave owners and knew all about servitude and mastery. African Americans, however, reasoned that no one understood more about slavery than they, and that surely whites would recognize an appeal to empathy, a shared sense of struggle against injustice. So in 1774 a group of enslaved Bostonians submitted a petition on behalf of "A Grate Number of Blackes of the Province" to the governor and general court of Massachusetts. "We have in common with all other men a naturel right to our freedoms without Being depriv'd of them by our fellow men as we are a freeborn Pepel and have never forfeited this Blessing by aney compact or agreement whatever," the petitioners declared. "We were unjustly dragged [from Africa] by the cruel hand of power . . . to be made slaves for Life in a Christian land" (*Massachusetts Historical Society Collections*, 1877, 3:432–433). We are just like you, they were saying—we have rights, too. We want freedom.

The governor and court ignored their plea.

Slavery, Resistance, and Liberty

Who were these Americans, the Boston petitioners and Charleston protestors, who asked only for what white colonists took for granted? Perhaps they were anonymous bit players on the margins of liberty's grand stage, a small group of disaffected, and unpatriotic, outsiders trying to spoil America's independence party. Maybe they were too naive, and should have recognized that the primary concerns of white colonists lay elsewhere and waited to press their case. Or perhaps they had something more profound to say about the nature of American liberty.

One thing is certain—the advocates for black freedom represented a larger segment of colonial British America than we generally realize. On the eve of revolution, 20 percent of the population—half a million of the thirteen colonies' 2.5 million people—were of African descent, the highest proportion in American history. Of those, 90 percent were held in bondage, while about 50,000 were free. Slavery had been entrenched in British North America since the early seventeenth century, and unfree black laborers lived in every colony from New England to the British Floridas. New York, Philadelphia, Boston, and Providence all had black populations of 10 to 20 percent. Rhode Island merchants became rich transporting slaves from Africa.

It was in the South, however, that most African Americans lived, working in the tobacco fields of the Chesapeake and North Carolina, the rice plantations of South Carolina and Georgia, in domestic service, maritime trades, crafts, and many other occupations. In Virginia, the largest colony, 40 percent of the population was black. In South Carolina, African Americans were actually a majority, outnumbering white colonists two to one. Colonial society, in other words, was based on the denial of freedom to a large group of people—an irony the British were quick to pick up on. "How is it that we hear the loudest yelps for liberty from the drivers of Negroes?" asked the British satirist Samuel Johnson as the American push for independence gathered force. "If there be an object truly ridiculous in nature," noted another Englishman, "it is an American patriot, signing resolutions of independency with the one hand, and with the other brandishing a whip over his frightened slaves" (Horton and Horton, 1977, 58).

Some whites did sympathize with the cause of black freedom. Bostonian James Otis, an early critic of the Stamp Act, argued in 1765 that "all men . . . white or black" were "by the law of nature free born," and that the colonists, "black and white, born here, are free born British subjects, and entitled to all the essential civil rights of such." Evangelicals such as John Wesley and

A notice from the 1780s advertising slaves for sale. Slavery in British North America began in the early seventeenth century and ended with the adoption of the Thirteenth Amendment in 1865. (*Library of Congress*)

Granville Sharp in Britain, as well as Quakers such as Anthony Benezet and John Woolman in America, contended that slavery violated God's law. A group of Scots immigrants in Darien, Georgia, declared in 1775 that slavery was "an unnatural practice" based on "injustice and cruelty." Other proponents of American independence acknowledged the hypocrisy of doing nothing to end slavery. But through the mid-1770s, most white colonists, including many prominent revolutionary leaders, either had too much capital invested in plantations and slaves, found it difficult to acknowledge the humanity of African Americans, or thought the issue too peripheral to the political dispute with Britain. No colonial legislature condemned slavery or linked it to the cause of independence. If anything, legislators and slaveholders clamped down even harder to keep black aspirations in check (Horton and Horton, 1977, 56–58).

Despite petitions and protests, most African Americans realized it was fruitless to count on the good intentions of white colonists. Instead, many set out to seize freedom without asking permission. In itself, that determination was nothing new. Africans had resisted enslavement since their earliest days in America, by running away, by subtle acts of daily subterfuge, by occasionally killing overseers and even planters, and by organizing larger insurrections. The image of contented, loyal slaves that masters sometimes liked to project had no basis in reality. A major revolt broke out along the Stono River just south of Charleston in 1739; two plots were discovered and foiled in New York in 1712 and 1741; and slaves took part in dozens of smaller rebellions during the colonial period. All of these uprisings were violently suppressed. Still, the political unrest of the 1760s and 1770s, as many blacks perceived it, offered an ideal—even unprecedented—opportunity to win liberty. They understood that the biggest impediment to freedom was unified white resolve to keep them enslaved. Now, that unity was splintering. The time to act had arrived.

Between 1765 and 1775, the records of colonial officials and planters tell an unmistakable story of increasing African American unrest and resistance. Individually and in small groups, greater numbers of slaves escaped their plantations for refuge in the western mountains or in the network of isolated low-country swamps and creeks along the coast. Some even tried to find passage to England in the wake of the Somerset decision of 1772, which, though it did not end slavery in Britain, gave slaves some protection by ruling that masters could not send them back to America. Again and again, small uprisings broke out through the colonies, particularly in the South, where slaves poisoned overseers, murdered planters, and set fire to buildings. White retribution intensified in turn. Black rebels, or suspected rebels, were whipped, hanged, shot, broken on the wheel, and burned alive. The cycle of revolt and retaliation was an essential element of the American revolutionary movement of the early 1770s. As Patriot leaders directed the resistance against Britain, they sought to crush the rebellion against themselves by their own slaves (Wood, 1983, 169–172; Holton, 2000, 139–140).

Looming over this inner struggle, and fueling its intensity, was the specter of the British. Since the early 1770s, when signs pointed increasingly toward a colonial demand for independence, the British had discussed the possibility of using enslaved African Americans as a deterrent. British military and political planners understood well that the high proportion of slaves in the southern colonies made whites fearful of rebellion, and they argued that a British threat to emancipate the slaves would intimidate the American Patriot movement. Patriot leaders knew the threat was part of British strategy; as James Madison wrote in 1774: "If America & Britain come to a hostile rupture I am afraid an Insurrection among the slaves may and will be promoted" (Kaplan, 1976, 254). Black Americans too were well aware of the idea, and by 1775 rumors that the British would issue an emancipation order drove tensions even higher. In the spring, as British and Patriot forces fired at each other for the first time in Massachusetts, a new wave of slave revolts, possibly coordinated, rippled across Virginia, foreshadowing a dramatic move by Lord Dunmore, the royal governor of the colony.

Dunmore Lights a Fuse

On April 21, 1775, Dunmore ordered the removal of fifteen kegs of gunpowder from the munitions storehouse in the colonial capital, Williamsburg. Outraged white Virginians, accusing the governor of trying to weaken their defenses against slave rebellion, vowed to march on Williamsburg and demand the return of the powder. Dunmore in turn threatened to free and arm the slaves, making explicit what was once rumor, filling Patriots with

Boston King

In the waning days of the American Revolution, as the British prepared to evacuate New York, their last remaining outpost in the former thirteen colonies, they faced a question: what to do about thousands of runaway slaves they had sheltered during the war?

American general and slave owner George Washington pressed the British to return the escapees, but the British general, Guy Carleton, argued that to do so would be a grave injustice to those promised their freedom. Washington reluctantly agreed to a compromise—refugees who had joined the British before a provisional 1782 treaty could leave, and everyone else would be returned. Carleton ordered a list drawn up, and three thousand names were entered into a *Book of Negroes*—a partial, but representative, inventory of black Americans determined to win liberty. In April 1783, those on the list boarded British ships and evacuated New York as free people. Among them were a thirty-three-year-old South Carolinian named Boston King and his wife, Violet.

Loyalist, prophet, Atlantic sojourner—Boston King was all these and more. Caught in the maelstrom of revolution, like thousands of African Americans he saw the chaos as equal parts opportunity and risk. We are fortunate that, unlike most people in the *Book of Negroes*, King wrote an autobiography in 1796 describing his life and his harrowing journey to freedom. He was born in about 1760 near Charles Town, South Carolina, the son of an African-born father, a plantation driver, and a mother who was a healer and seamstress. As a youth, King endured harsh treatment at the hands of a craftsman to whom he was apprenticed, and in about 1780, fearing another beating, he escaped to Charles Town, where the British harbored several thousand runaway slaves. His dramatic adventures had just begun. Surviving a smallpox epidemic, he was abducted by a deserter but escaped back to British lines,

then sailed to New York on a British ship. There he married and settled into the black refugee community. But while serving on a pilot boat he was captured by the Americans and became "fairly distressed at the thought of again being reduced to slavery" (Brooks and Saillant, 2002, 215). Again he managed to escape by crossing the river in a boat from New Jersey to Staten Island. He stayed in New York till the end of the war.

As the British negotiated their departure, a rumor spread among the black Loyalists that they would be returned to their former owners, filling them with "inexpressible anguish and terror, especially when we saw our old masters coming from Virginia, North Carolina, and other parts, and seizing upon their slaves in the streets of New York, or even dragging them out of their beds." Their fear turned to "joy and gratitude" when they received certificates of freedom and were allowed to evacuate with the British. Buoyed by hopes for a new life, three thousand formerly enslaved people from all over the eastern seaboard sailed to Birchtown, Nova Scotia, in August 1783, in time to build homes before the onset of winter (Brooks and Saillant, 2002, 217).

A Christian religious revival soon surged through the black community, perhaps an emotional response to the dislocation its members had endured. King and Violet were swept up in it, both experiencing long periods of spiritual torment before God "removed every doubt and fear and reestablished me in his peace and favor." The black Nova Scotians thus shared in the increasingly popular embrace of evangelical religion by people of African descent throughout the Atlantic world. King became a preacher and religious leader and began to long for the opportunity to take the Christian message to his "poor brethren in Africa" who

(continued)

Page from the *Book of Negroes*, a ledger of black Americans who evacuated the country after the American Revolution. (*The National Archives of England, Wales, and the United Kingdom / PRO30-55-100*)

Where Bound	Negros Names	Age	Description	Claimants Names	Places of Residence
St Johns River	Jack Hyde	50	Almost past his Labour		
	Dick	43	Stout Fellow		
St Johns River	Corn. Moss	30	Do likely		
	Tho. Brinkerhoof	34	Very short bodina. man		
	Peter Bean	32	likely fellow		
	Smith. Gillman	46	Stout short fellow		
	George Black	40	Stout fellow		
	Betsy Black	35	Ordinary Wench		
	Wm. Black	11	fine boy		
	Sam	30	Stout fellow		
	Luke Spencer	25	Do		
	Abigail his Wife	26	Stout Wench, small Child		
	Bill Pigott	23	Stout fellow		
	Pompey Chase	28	Do	Reuben Chase	River St. Johns
	John Doree	36	Do B		
	Dean	20	Stout squat Wh. small Child		
Port Roseway	Peter Johnson	25	Stout Fellow		
	Judith Johnson	27	Ordinary Wench		
	Tho. Danvers	45	Do Fellow		
	Sariah Cross	34	Stout squat Wench M.		
	Harry Spencell	33	Slender fellow		
	Jn. Dunham	25	Do		
	Jack Smith	25	Do		
	Venus	28	Do Wench		
	Sam: Drayton	40	Stout Fellow		
	Cath. Drayton	40	Ordinary Wench		
	Dinah Edmonds	34	Do		
	Tho. Edmonds	5	small Boy		
	John Rogers	29	Stout fellow		
	Henry Masfield	33	Do		
	Hannah his Wife	23	Stout Wench 2 small Child.		
	Bell Browne	24	Stout Fellow		

Names of the Persons in whose Possession they now are.		Remarks.
John Ketchum	"	Formerly Slave to Joseph Hyde, Fairfield New England left him 6 Years past G.B.C
Capt. Peacock	Do	to Jno. Jones Savannah left him 5 Y. past, Indented for 7 Years with s.d Capt.
Capt. Col. Ellison	Do	to Dan.l Moore Woodbridge N. Jersey left him 7 Years ago G.B.C
James Potten	Do	to Corn.l Boggard near Hackinsack N. Jersey left him 5 Years past G.B.C
James Graves	Do	to Dav.d Davis White Plains left him 2 Years past say he has since been Sold by his Mis. to s.d Graves
Gilliard	Do	to Major Gillman Plast. N. England left him ab.t 3 Years past
Jone.h Ketchum	Do	to Jos.h Portress, Peterburg Virg.a left him 4 Years past G.B.C
Do	Do	to Do Do
Do	Do	to Do Do
James Sayre	Do	to Henry Bray, Great Bridge Virg.a left him ab.t 2 Years ago G.B.C
Dr. Stevens	Do	to Oliver Spencer, Elizabeth Town N. Jersey left him 5 Years ago Do
Do		Served her time out with Jos: Graham of Boston
Geo: Harding		Formerly Slave to Gabriel Jones, Augusta Co. Virginia left him 8 Years ago
Reuben Chase		Property of Reuben Chase as p.r Bill of Sale from Jacob Sharp of Boston
Capt. Stewart, St Soverg.		Free born at Venta Bell Barbadoes
Geo: Harding		Formerly Slave to Jno. Scull Philadelphia left him 4 Years ago
Jos.h Shakespeare		Says he got his freedom from Solo.n Brindly, Quaker N. Jersey that he has liv'd in New York y.e 6 Years past G.B.C
Do		Formerly Slave to Garret Langston, Shrewsbury left him 3 Years past G.B.C
Arch.d Clarke	Do	to Tho.s Brown Savannah left him 5 Years past G.B.C
Do		Says she was born free, at Saffcore, serv'd her time to Ja.s Prickman N. York Island
Jos.h Cienan		Formerly Slave to R. Benson N. York Isl.d that Benson left him on y.e Surrendry of y.e Troops on N. York Island
Nath.l Hannah	Do	to Ja.s Dunham of Augusta left him 5 Years past G.B.C
Edw.d Hannah	Do	to W.m Smith Charles Town left him ab.t 5 Years past
Do	Do	to Do Do
Do	Do	to W.m Drayton near Charles Town left her before y.e Siege of Charles Town
Do	Do	to Do Do
Jos.h Shakespeare	Do	to W.m Edmonds Charles Town left him 5 Years past
Do	Do	to Do
And.w Gibson	Do	to Capt. Rogers, Brig Dispatch who went to England & left him free
Alex. Watson		Free born in M. Philipse's House of Philipse Manor G.B.C.P
Do	Do	in Jno. Gloster N. Jersey
Nich.l Brown		Formerly Slave to Jacob Arnold Morris Town N. Jersey left him 3 Years ago

Boston King (continued)

he believed were "involved in gross darkness and wickedness" (Brooks and Saillant, 2002, 221–222). His immediate concern, however, as with everyone else in his community, was survival. When British aid to the settlement ended in 1786, many had no means of livelihood, and as famine set in, they sold their possessions or indentured themselves as servants to white Canadians. King scratched out a living with his carpentry skills.

In 1792 King finally gained his chance to take the Christian mission to Africa when he and Violet accompanied some twelve hundred black settlers to the new colony of Sierra Leone on the west coast of Africa. The colony had been founded by British antislavery advocates who believed that Christian education would improve and "civilize" Africans, thus undercutting the argument that they could be enslaved because they were a barbarous people. King endorsed this idealistic mission to stamp out what he called the "evil traits" inherent in African religions. He became a schoolteacher in the new colony, though he did not speak the local language. The project met indigenous resistance as well; not all Africans in the region welcomed the African Americans who came to "improve" them, and King complained that parents "showed no great inclination to send their children" to the school (Brooks and Saillant, 2002, 230).

The colony also struggled as dozens of settlers, including Violet, died of tropical fevers. In 1793 King accepted an offer from benefactors of the Sierra Leone Company to travel to England for more religious education. The experi-

ence of worshiping with white co-religionists changed his outlook. "I have great cause to be thankful that I came to England," he wrote, "for I am now fully convinced that many of the White People, instead of being enemies and oppressors of us poor Blacks, are our friends, and deliverers from slavery, as far as their ability and circumstances will admit." King returned to Sierra Leone in 1796 and resumed his teaching post, though, with about forty pupils in the school, his mission achieved only modest gains (Brooks and Saillant, 2002, 232).

The story of Boston King embodies several interrelated themes. Enslaved African Americans were hungry for the "self-evident" freedom and equality that white revolutionaries were unwilling to give them. Not content to wait while someone else decided their fate, many eagerly attached themselves to the British cause—and were even willing to leave America—to win their rights. King and his fellow emigrants in the *Book of Negroes* also participated in the spread of black Christianity—a faith that would fuel the antislavery movement and provide spiritual nourishment to millions for generations to come. And King was enmeshed in an emerging pan-African social and philosophical movement that linked the fortunes of people of African descent to each other across the Atlantic. The reverse migration of black Americans to Africa (even as the slave trade to America continued to drain Africa of people) laid the foundations of the modern nations of Sierra Leone and Liberia. The cause of black freedom in the age of Revolution reverberated far from American shores.

fear and anger. The governor hadn't actually proclaimed freedom for the slaves, but his threat to do so gave black Virginians hope. Several runaway slaves made their way to the governor's palace in Williamsburg to offer their service, and anxious whites reinforced their slave patrols. By June, wary of a Patriot attack, Dunmore withdrew to British warships in the Chesapeake Bay. Through the summer and into the fall of 1775, as British marines raided coastal towns and skirmished with Patriot militias, enslaved African Americans ran to join them.

Word of the governor's threat rapidly spread through the colonies, further inspiring African American dreams of freedom and putting white authorities on high alert that summer. In North Carolina, an uprising along the Tar River was discovered before it could unfold; in Wilmington and elsewhere, patrols searched slaves' houses and tightly enforced curfews. In the town of Salem, the Moravians, a supposedly pacifist, but slaveholding, German religious group, quietly stockpiled arms and powder in case of insurrection. In Charleston, South Carolina, a free black pilot named Thomas Jeremiah was accused of planning a revolt with the aid of the British, proclaiming: "The War was come to help the poor Negroes." He was hanged and burned. A slave preacher named George was executed for exhorting slaves with the incendiary prophecy that "the Young King, meaning our Present One, came up with the Book, and was about to alter the world, and set the Negroes Free." The message was clear: whereas white revolutionaries regarded the British as oppressors, enslaved Americans saw them as liberators. And the colonies had not even declared their independence yet (Wood, 1983, 174–176; Holton, 2000, 137–154; Frey, 1991, 55–58; Quarles, 1961; Crow, 1980, 79–102; Olwell, 1989, 21–48; Sensbach, 1998, 85–91).

Lord Dunmore finally played his ace card on November 15, 1775, when he issued a proclamation declaring "all indented Servants, Negroes, or others, (appertaining to Rebels,) free, that are able and willing to bear Arms, they Joining HIS MAJESTY'S Troops as soon as may be" to help suppress the American Patriot uprising. Dunmore's decree must be understood for what it was, and was not. Like Lincoln's Emancipation Proclamation of 1863, it did *not* proclaim all enslaved workers free. In fact, it was directed only at the slaves of American revolutionaries, while not liberating those held by British or Loyalist sympathizers. Dunmore did not base his declaration on a high-minded belief in human rights or universal freedom. His was a political and military calculation intended to stun the Patriots into submission through fear. When it finally came, the announcement electrified the colonies.

Despite the Patriots' best efforts to contain the news, word of Dunmore's action quickly spread through the slaves' clandestine interplantation communication network. Patriot leaders tried cajolery and threats. "Be not then, ye negroes, tempted by his proclamation to ruin your selves," urged the *Virginia Gazette*. But from Maryland, Virginia, Delaware, and North Carolina, hundreds, perhaps thousands, of African Americans ran away, or tried to run away, to join the governor, inspired by the chance to fire a gun at their masters. "Numbers of Negroes and Cowardly Scoundrels flock to his Standard," reported one planter nine days after the proclamation was issued. On one plantation, all eighty-seven slaves escaped. Ignoring the fine points of the declaration, many slaves of Loyalist planters tried to flee, only to be returned to slavery by the British. The fugitives took terrible risks to slip through the restrictive curtains of a heavily armed police state, traveling at night or through the woods, or trying to find a boat to go downriver. Many never made it. Slave owners regularly checked slave cabins, scoured the roads for runaways, and executed those they caught, sent them off to work in lead mines, or returned them to their plantations for punishment. Dunmore's proclamation, far from intimidating the revolutionaries, galvanized them all the more to resist the governor. Deriding him as "King of the Blacks," they regarded his attempt to arm the slaves as a "diabolical scheme," in George Washington's words, a ghastly betrayal of white racial unity, "fatal to the publick Safety," as Patrick Henry called it. Patriots effectively used the decree as a recruiting tool to argue that a war for independence was the only effective response to Dunmore's treachery. Militia enlistment soared (Raphael, 2001, 254–257; Kaplan and Kaplan, 1973, 60).

Overcoming great odds, by early December several hundred black escapees made their way to Dunmore in eastern Virginia, where they received uniforms and arms "as fast as they came in." The governor formed the new recruits into an all-black unit of the British Army called the Ethiopian Regiment, whose soldiers wore sashes proclaiming "Liberty to Slaves." It must have been thrilling for these former bondsmen to bear arms as free men, to feel a sense of control over their own destiny, to come alive with the chance to respond to generations of indignity and servitude. Most, however, had little military training or experience. In a sharp engagement with Patriot forces at Great Bridge near Norfolk on December 9, the Ethiopian Regiment and British troops were defeated, and thirty-two black soldiers were captured. The rest evacuated to British ships in the Chesapeake Bay, but in

SIR,

*A*S *the Committee of Safety is not fitting, I take the Liberty to enclose you a Copy of the Proclamation issued by Lord* **Dunmore***; the Design and Tendency of which, you will observe, is fatal to the publick Safety. An early and unremitting Attention to the Government of the* **SLAVES** *may, I hope, counteract this dangerous Attempt. Constant, and well directed Patrols, seem indispensably necessary. I doubt not of every possible Exertion, in your Power, for the publick Good; and have the Honour to be, Sir,*

Your most obedient and very humble Servant,

P. HENRY.

HEAD QUARTERS, WILLIAMSBURG,
November 20, 1775.

Letter by Patrick Henry warning of Lord Dunmore's action to arm slaves, November 20, 1775. (*Library of Congress*)

March 1776, the crowded vessels became floating death traps when small-pox, typhus, and dysentery ravaged the black troops. Dunmore tried to quarantine the sick men on Gwynn's Island and contain the epidemic through smallpox vaccination, but when Patriot forces invaded the island in June, they found hundreds of dead and dying African American soldiers. Dunmore could only lament that his plan to "penetrate into the heart of this Colony" with 2,000 or more black troops had been foiled by an invisible enemy. He eventually evacuated the Virginia coast with about 300 black soldiers who lived to fight another day (Quarles, 1961, 29–32; Fenn, 2001, 46, 59–61).

Similar episodes unfolded farther south when black refugees flocked to British commanders. Patriot militias raided a community of runaways on Sullivan's Island outside of Charleston, killing or capturing hundreds. In March, 1776, Patriots raided Tybee Island near Savannah, where 200 escaped slaves had sought haven. According to plan, those who could not be recaptured would be hunted and shot by Creek Indians, "as it may deter other negroes from deserting, and will establish a hatred or aversion between the Indians and negroes" (Wood, 1983, 178–180).

To many Patriot leaders, these events provided the final convincing piece of evidence that a complete break from Britain was necessary, and they were not afraid to say so in their eloquent testament to human freedom, the Declaration of Independence. The limitations on those Thomas Jefferson had in mind with his immortal phrase "all men are created equal" are obvious. But a lesser-known passage further down in the Declaration is more revealing. In his long catalogue of accusations against George III, Jefferson said the king had "excited domestic insurrections amongst us." Though the phrase might puzzle modern readers, his intended audience understood it perfectly well: "Domestic insurrections" meant slave revolts. The desire of African Americans to be free, in other words, had helped drive the revolutionaries to declare independence. The founding document of the United States *defends* the enslavement of one group of Americans to argue that another group should be free (Holton, 2000, 133–163; Olwell, 1989, Wood, 1983; Kaplan, 1976, 243–255).

Choosing Sides

Blacks, like all Americans, now had to choose which side to support by asking themselves, were they more likely to gain their freedom from the British or the Patriots? For many, the answer was clear. In 1777, an eavesdropper in Philadelphia overheard a conversation between two black servants: "They secretly wished that the British army might win, for then all Negro slaves will gain their freedom. It is said that this sentiment is almost universal among the Negroes in America." The British continued to encourage slaves of rebel masters to escape to British lines, though they were sometimes equivocal on whether the runaways would actually be freed. Still, the lure of liberty did not necessarily make for easy choices among the enslaved population. Escaping through the Patriot security net was perilous business; many people, rooted to home by family, simply could not attempt to flee and remained on their plantations. And what were the enslaved workers of Loyalist owners to do with the ambiguous message that the British might emancipate some slaves, but not them? Many chose to wait cautiously (Kaplan and Kaplan, 1973, 65–66; Frey, 1991, 113–114).

To the smaller number of free black Americans, on the other hand, the American independence movement often seemed a better bet to preserve their liberty. Many identified with the ideals of the Revolution and had nothing to gain from siding with the British. Indeed, several free blacks had already lost their lives in the early independence struggle. One, Crispus Attucks, was among the five civilians killed by British troops in the Boston Massacre of March 1770; his death, in fact, helped inspire the enslaved Bostonians who petitioned unsuccessfully for their freedom several years later. (Attucks was venerated by black abolitionists in the 1850s as one of the nation's original freedom fighters.) Free blacks, along with several slaves, fought with the minutemen in Lexington and Concord and with the militia at Bunker Hill. A free black named Salem Poor shot a British officer in that battle, went on to serve at Valley Forge and White Plains, and earned a commendation as a "Brave and gallant soldier." Artist John Trumbull commemorated the participation of black Patriots in these early battles in his famous painting *The Battle of Bunker Hill*, which shows a slave soldier named Peter Salem wielding a musket on the edge of the fray (Kaplan and Kaplan, 1973, 7–20; Raphael, 2001, 281–282).

But it was the image of armed black men, in fact, that greatly troubled revolutionary leaders. Most of these leaders saw the Revolution as a white man's fight. Many of them, including Washington, Jefferson, and Patrick Henry, were slaveholders and shared a general disdain for blacks; the idea of giving guns to African American soldiers—even free blacks—raised the threatening possibility that those guns could be pointed at *them*. As a result, in June 1775 Washington and his military advisers forbade black soldiers from enlisting in the new Continental Army. Faced with a shortage of manpower by the end of the year, Washington reluctantly eased his rules somewhat, but restrictions by all the northern states kept black recruitment down. In New Hampshire, "lunatics, idiots, and Negroes" were exempted from a requirement to bear arms for the revolutionary cause (Bell, 1888, 91).

By 1777, however, Washington and his officers could no longer afford to shun the potentially valuable source of African American manpower. The problem of finding enough soldiers to fill his army became acute in 1777 when the states struggled to meet troop quotas imposed by Congress, particularly as three-year terms expired and soldiers returned home. Disturbed by the British tactic of recruiting blacks, Washington concluded that victory would depend on "which side can arm the Negroes faster" (Blackburn, 1988, 113–114). Free black volunteers increasingly stepped in to fill the army's empty ranks. Wealthy Patriots summoned to service often paid men of lesser means to take their place, and blacks entered the army in this way as well. Sometimes a slave owner promised freedom to a bondsman who would agree to replace him, giving perhaps several thousand slaves an opportunity to gain their freedom by the war's end. One state, Rhode Island, even guaranteed freedom to all slaves enlisting in the Continental Army.

Battle of Bunker Hill. In the first and bloodiest battle of the Revolutionary War, British troops crossed Boston Harbor to confront a force of New England militia entrenched on a small peninsula opposite the city. General Howe's men only drove off the defenders after three frontal assaults in which they suffered horrific casualties—almost 40 percent of their force. (*National Archives and Records Administration*)

All told, an estimated 5,000 African American soldiers, enslaved and free, served in the American forces during the Revolution. Many fought in scores of battles alongside white soldiers in integrated units; as a Hessian officer observed in 1777: "One sees no regiment in which there are not negroes in abundance, and among them are able-bodied, sturdy fellows." Several hundred black sailors served in the American Navy, many of them experienced seamen who had worked as river pilots and transatlantic mariners before the war. Several states, such as Rhode Island and Connecticut, also organized all-black infantry units under the command of white officers. Almost all black soldiers who served the United States during the war came from the North; southern planters refused to allow slaves to enlist, and southern regiments included few free blacks. Having bowed to expediency, Washington himself seems to have appreciated the contributions of black soldiers, though he is not known to have left much recorded praise of their efforts. Fighting to earn, or preserve, their own freedom, these soldiers greatly helped the cause of independence for a nation that did not fully embrace them (Hirschfeld, 1997, 141; Raphael, 2001, 368–369).

During the course of the war, however, far more African Americans flocked to support the British whenever they could, in British-held areas like New York and, especially, in the South, after the British campaign moved there in late 1778. The presence of a huge slave population, several hundred thousand strong, between Virginia and Georgia, in fact, became a crucial strategic factor in the British decision to shift the fight southward away from the stalemate in the North. British military planners figured that either the fear of losing their slave property would convince white southerners to remain loyal, or, if not, their slaves would gladly help the British suppress the rebellion. On the latter point, they reckoned well. When a British naval force sailed south to lay siege to Savannah in late 1778, they were hailed as liberators by thousands of Patriot-owned slaves. One of them, in fact, played a crucial role in the capture of Savannah by leading British forces on a secret path through a swamp behind the town to attack its undefended rear, surprising the Americans and forcing them to capitulate on January 1, 1779. The British policy of courting black support paid early dividends (Frey, 1991, 79–84).

The British capture of Georgia plunged the Deep South into turmoil, even as it raised hopes and expectations for African Americans. A fierce civil war raged between Loyalist and Whig militias contesting large areas left unoccupied by the British Army between the Savannah River and the frontier with British East Florida. Partisans on both sides raided plantations, plundered and burned homes, and stole slaves. As thousands of people on all sides became refugees, the chaos represented both opportunity and peril for enslaved blacks. Many Patriots fleeing the British occupation took their slaves with them; others simply left their workers behind on plantations. Thousands of these slaves made their way to British lines to volunteer their services, and were put to work digging trenches, strengthening fortifications, and performing domestic duties for the British. This African American shadow army became the loyal support group propping up the British occupation. Others escaped to communities of runaways in the swamps and forests of coastal Georgia, often emerging to pillage local plantations. At the same time, any slaves who tried to escape from Loyalist owners were captured and returned; the British even sent troops to occupy the plantations of absentee owners to restore discipline and prevent slaves from fleeing. Many slaves from these plantations were pressed into service by the British when a combined force of Americans, French, and free blacks from St. Domingue attacked Savannah in the fall of 1779. Several hundred armed blacks helped repulse the assault and preserve the city for the British (Frey, 1991, 84–98).

When the British sought to extend their successes in Georgia by invading South Carolina in early 1780, African Americans were likewise central to the campaign. The British general, Henry Clinton, had issued a proclamation in June 1779 in Philipsburg, New York, declaring that captured slaves belonging to revolutionaries would be regarded as war contraband and sold. The proclamation also guaranteed "full security" to slaves of rebels who escaped to join the British, though it stopped short of promising them freedom. As with Dunmore's proclamation before it, many African Americans apparently interpreted the Philipsburg decree as the general emancipation order it was not, and British forces marching north from Georgia to encircle Charleston in the spring of 1780 were joined by thousands of escapees who viewed them as liberators. When the city fell in May, an occupation force of British soldiers and their African American allies moved in. And when General Cornwallis took the war into the South Carolina backcountry in pursuit of the Continental Army in the summer of 1780, his army was accompanied by a marching flotilla of black soldiers, guides, laborers, and camp followers.

Again reminiscent of Dunmore's experience, however, the British strategy of courting the slaves to help suppress the white American insurgency backfired. It stiffened the resolve of slave-owning revolutionaries in the Deep South, who regarded the British ploy as the ultimate perfidy and vowed never to surrender. This sense of betrayal helps explain the vicious desperation of the guerrilla warfare in South Carolina, as combatants on both sides burned homes and plantations, slaughtered civilians, bayoneted wounded soldiers, and executed prisoners. The strength of the Whig partisans helped blunt the military superiority of the British Army, which, after several easy victories, bogged down as it chased the Continental Army through the backcountry into North Carolina in late 1780 and early 1781, unable to deliver the coup de grace.

Still, black Loyalists remained true to the British cause, accompanying or running to join Cornwallis when he abandoned North Carolina and took the fight to Virginia in the summer of 1781. The gambit proved disastrous for the redcoats and their African American allies. When American and French forces trapped Cornwallis at Yorktown in October, smallpox broke out among hundreds of blacks huddling behind fortifications with the British. Unable to feed or care for them, and terrified the epidemic would spread, the British simply evicted them; evidence suggests they even intended these infected carriers to spread the disease to Washington's army. Whatever the circumstances, African Americans were now betrayed by the army in whom they had put such trust. Many were recaptured or shot by Continental forces, while hundreds more perished from the pox. "During the siege," remembered one American soldier, "we saw in the woods herds of Negroes which Lord Cornwallis . . . in love and pity to them, had turned adrift, with no other recompense for their confidence in his humanity than the smallpox for their bounty and starvation and death for their wages." Another Patriot recalled: "An immense number of Negroes" perished "in the most miserable Manner in York[town]." For those victims, as well as for the great majority of enslaved blacks elsewhere, the dream of liberation that held such promise during the war died as well on the bluffs of the York River. The British surrender, and the victory celebration of Washington's soldiers on fields strewn with black corpses, drove home a sobering conclusion. The *American* victory brought disaster for one large group of *Americans*—those who did not win the prize of freedom (Fenn, 2001, 129–133).

Slavery and the Contradictions of Freedom

Though another two years passed before the formal end of the war, triumphant revolutionary forces, who now controlled most of the United States, began reclaiming black Loyalists as war booty to be sent back to their former masters for reenslavement. New York, Charleston, Savannah, and St. Augustine, meanwhile, remained in British hands, their populations swollen by thousands of black and white refugees. By 1782, British ships began evacuating planters and slaves to Caribbean colonies such as Jamaica, Antigua, and the Bahamas, as well as to England. Perhaps tens of thousands of blacks left North America this way. Many African Americans who had run away to join the British were victimized in this evacuation when the redcoats, who had always considered their legal status ambiguous, simply reenslaved them and sent them away. A major exception took place when several thousand black refugees claiming free status were able to leave the Atlantic port towns and resettle in Nova Scotia under British protection. From there they worked with antislavery advocates in Britain to emigrate to the new colony of Sierra Leone in West Africa in the late 1780s. Thus did the African American freedom struggle during the American Revolution generate far-reaching repercussions for people of African descent on both sides of the Atlantic (Wilson, 1976, 21, 37; Quarles, 1961, 163, 173).

In the United States, the nation's political independence could not conceal, and in fact, underscored more starkly than ever, the social unfreedom gnawing from within. While some European intellectuals applauded the nation's break from imperial bondage, others derided its failings and pretensions. Aware of the contradiction, and responding to continued pressure by African American activists, some white Americans began taking tentative steps to curtail or end slavery, planting the seeds of the early antislavery movement. In the early 1780s, even as the war was still being contested, northern states such as Pennsylvania, Connecticut, Rhode Island, New Hampshire, and others passed so-called gradual emancipation bills, which, while freeing no slaves outright, generally provided for the eventual manumission of the children of enslaved people. In many cases, years passed before these lukewarm measures took effect; though slavery was on the wane in the North by the early nineteenth century, it persisted in many states until well into the 1840s and 1850s. The Northwest Ordinance of 1787 prohibited slavery in new territories north of the Ohio River. In parts of the South, slavery came under challenge as well in the war's aftermath. Virginia—along

Black loyalist refugees settle in Nova Scotia. (*Robert Petley / Library and Archives of Canada / [C-115424]*)

with several northern states—banned slave imports from Africa. Bowing to the rhetoric of liberty and equality, some conscience-stricken slave owners, mostly in Virginia and Maryland, began freeing slaves, though legislators later restricted manumission and required freed persons to leave the state. Evangelical Christian churches, too, particularly the Baptists and Methodists, incubated antislavery sentiment by equating the ideal of spiritual freedom with social freedom. In the 1780s and 1790s, white evangelicals preached against slavery; congregations welcomed black men and women as brothers and sisters in the service of Christ; and some churches barred slave owners from membership. The long-held assumption that blackness signaled unalterable difference, justifying slavery, came under fire from many sides (Melish, 1998; White, 1991; Nash and Soderlund, 1991; Frey and Wood, 1998).

Together, these measures fell short of a sustained, critical assault on slavery before the turn of the century, but they did signal that the age of Revolution had opened up new ways to challenge the institution and new ways for enslaved African Americans to gain their freedom. Indeed, between the disruptions of war, increased possibilities for escape, private emancipations, and manumissions through military service, the free black population increased dramatically in the last quarter of the eighteenth century. Northern cities such as Boston, New York, Philadelphia, and Newport, and southern towns such as Savannah, Charleston, Petersburg, and Williamsburg became centers of free black life, where churches, fraternal organizations, and schools provided self-help and protection. From these bastions of freedom, African Americans strove to make good on the promise of revolution and called on the nation to do likewise (Horton and Horton, 1997; Nash, 1998).

The reality was that the nation as a whole was unwilling to do so. The nation's independence was in part a victory for property rights, and thousands of slave owners insisted on their right to own property in human beings. The end of the war gave new life to slavery in many parts of the Deep South. Southern plantations, their workforces restocked with slaves recaptured or confiscated from the British, resumed production of rice, tobacco, and other crops. New England shipping companies, eager to cash in on the opportunity, resumed the transatlantic slave trade to South Carolina and Georgia, which had been disrupted by war. "The Negro business is a great object with us," noted a Georgia merchant, Joseph Clay, in 1784. "It is to the Trade of this Country, as the Soul to the body" (*Documents Illustrative of the Slave Trade to America*, 1935, 4:630).

Many of the country's Founding Fathers were wealthy planters and slave owners, men like James Madison, George Washington, and Thomas Jefferson, who, by and large, were unable to reconcile their slaveholding with their belief in human freedom. Most famously, perhaps, in his *Notes on the State of Virginia* of 1787, Jefferson professed an aversion to slavery while issuing one of the most racist condemnations of African Americans ever written. He never freed a single slave. Some planters eventually did—such as Washington, who emancipated his slaves in his will upon his death in 1799—but most convinced themselves that economic necessity trumped idealism. For these leaders, political union and social stability were the most important objectives. They were unwilling to give up slavery or to see the nation's large black population, free and enslaved, as inheritors of the revolutionary promise or participants in the new republican society (Miller, 1977; Wiencek, 2003; Finkelman, 1993, 181–224).

Nothing captured the troubled relationship of the new nation with slavery better than the constitutional debates of 1787. All of the fifty-five delegates to the Philadelphia convention were well-to-do white men, including many southern planters as well as a few northern delegates on record as opposing slavery. After initial pro- and antislavery exchanges among the delegates went nowhere, it became clear that the central issue was not the fate of slavery itself but its role in determining political representation in the new government. Northern states, with far fewer slaves, wanted only a state's free population counted in apportioning representatives, while southern states wanted slaves counted, though, as the northerners pointed out, they were not citizens and held no political power. Fearful that delegates from Georgia and South Carolina would scuttle the entire constitutional document over the issue, thereby spoiling national unity, northern delegates agreed to a compromise by which three-fifths of a state's enslaved population would count in a representative tally.

Another contentious issue was the importation of slaves from Africa, which some delegates wanted to outlaw. "While there remained one acre of swampland uncleared in South Carolina, I would raise my voice against restricting the importation of negroes," vowed delegate Charles Pinckney. "The nature of our climate, and the flat, swampy situation of our country, obliges us to cultivate our lands with negroes, and . . . without them South Carolina would soon be a desert waste." In another compromise, the importation of slaves was safeguarded for at least twenty years. A fugitive-slave clause also required Americans to return "any person bound to service or labor" in one state who escaped to another. Thus, the nation's new blueprint became a proslavery document, a "covenant with death," in the words of nineteenth-century abolitionist William Lloyd Garrison, though, in a squeamish bow to the delicacy of the issue, the word *slave* was never used in the final version. If the constitutional moment ever represented a chance to sound a death knell for American slavery, the founders squandered the opportunity, committing the nation to a divisive policy that only civil war could erase (Farrand, 1937, 3:254; Finkelman, 1987, 188–225; Rakove, 1996, 70–77, 85–88).

If, in some ways, the American Revolution heralded on one hand a possible opening up of society for black Americans, a potential gap in the wall of slavery, the response to it by much of white America represented a conservative counterrevolution, a backlash against that possibility. In part that reaction stemmed from a fear of losing property, and in part it stemmed from fear of what that property might do. The Revolution had given impetus to enslaved people throughout the hemisphere to claim the fruits of freedom for themselves. The response of African Americans during the war can be considered an enormous slave rebellion, which spawned a rolling series of subsequent revolts in North America and the Caribbean. In fact, an important reason that British West Indian colonies like Jamaica and Antigua did not join the mainland colonies' uprising against the British was that they

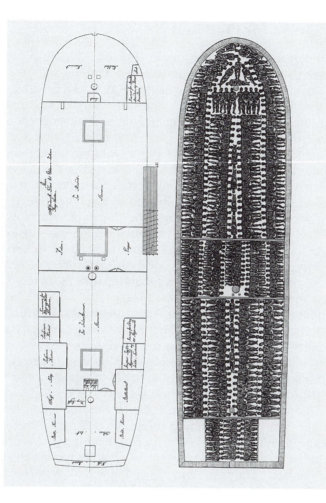

Deck plan of a slave ship, showing how captured Africans were arranged as cargo, 1700s. (*North Wind Picture Archives*)

depended on British military force to keep their enormous slave populations in check. For the most part, they did so. In the French colony of St. Domingue, however, nearly half a million slaves rose in rebellion in 1791, overthrew their masters, and won their independence by 1804, creating the nation of Haiti, the second republic in the Western Hemisphere (Geggus, 2001; Geggus, 2002; Geggus and Gaspar, 1997).

The example of so many slaves emancipating themselves through armed struggle filled African Americans in the United States with inspiration, and slaveholders with terror, just as Dunmore's Ethiopian Regiment had done years before. Along the Atlantic seaboard, vigilant planters and officials tightened security on slave workforces and intensified punishments for insubordination. In 1800, a rebel named Gabriel organized hundreds of slaves outside Richmond in a plan to capture the city's armory, distribute its weapons, and ignite a massive revolt. The plot was betrayed from within, its leaders executed. As one of them mounted the gallows, he told his executioners that in striking a blow for freedom, he had done only what George Washington had done (Egerton, 1993).

The Continuing Quest for Freedom

In the early nineteenth century, the quest for black liberty continued, as more plots were uncovered and suppressed from Virginia and the Carolinas to Louisiana. But slavery became more deeply entrenched in the South than ever, as the opening of rich upcountry lands in Georgia, Alabama, Mississippi, and Louisiana for cotton planting created vast new opportunities for profits and a resurgent demand for slaves. Correspondingly, planters and other apologists for slavery refurbished pre-Revolutionary arguments that blacks were inherently fit for enslavement and that they (the slaveholders) were doing their workers a favor by holding them in captivity. White evangelical Christians who had previously spoken out against slavery were co-opted by the planting class and now joined the chorus of voices arguing that the institution was God's will. Planters recruited evangelical missionaries to preach to their slaves, emphasizing a Christian message of subservience to worldly authority. It was all part of the backlash against black freedom. The slave states committed themselves to the maintenance of slavery as fundamental to their survival (Frey, 1991, 243–283).

"Liberty, liberty!" cried the African American protestors who marched through the streets of Charlteston in 1765. No mere gate crashers at America's freedom party, they, and those who followed in their footsteps, were at the very heart of the American Revolution. The African American freedom struggle underscored the extent and the limits of the nation's war for independence. Black Americans had as much invested in the struggle with Britain as other Americans—indeed, even more, because they felt the absence of freedom more acutely. In claiming the same rights as white colonists, they pressed the revolutionaries to clarify the meaning of freedom—who should get it, what its limits were, what responsibilities it entailed. Too often the answer came back: Only white men need apply. Slavery remained the great cancer at the core of the American Revolution. Still, African Americans saw the Revolution as the best opportunity they might ever have to seize freedom rather than wait for whites to act. Some succeeded; many others lost their lives, and more still emerged from years of turmoil and high expectations with only disappointment. Rare was the black family that did not endure chaos, dislocation, or retribution during those years. But in calling on the nation to make good on the words "all men are created equal," African Americans were the true radicals of the struggle. They were the real American revolutionaries.

References and Further Reading

Bell, Charles H. *History of Exter, New Hampshire*. Boston: J. E. Farwell, 1888.

Berlin, Ira, and Ronald Hoffman, eds. *Slavery and Freedom in the Age of the American Revolution*. Charlottesville: University Press of Virginia, 1983.

Blackburn, Robin. *The Overthrow of Colonial Slavery, 1776–1848*. New York: Verson, 1988.

Brooks, Joanna, and John Saillant, eds. *"Face Zion Forward": First Writers of the Black Atlantic*. Boston: Northeastern University Press, 2002.

Crow, Jeffrey J. "Slave Rebelliousness and Social Conflict in North Carolina, 1775–1802." *William and Mary Quarterly*, 3rd series, 37 (1980): 79–102.

Documents Illustrative of the Slave Trade to America. Washington, DC: Carnegie Institution, 1935.

Egerton, Douglas R. *Gabriel's Rebellion: The Virginia Slave Conspiracies of 1800 and 1802*. Chapel Hill: University of North Carolina Press, 1993.

Farrand, Max, ed. *The Records of the Federal Convention of 1787*. 4 vols. New Haven, CT: Yale University Press, 1937.

Fenn, Elizabeth. *Pox Americana: The Great Smallpox Epidemic of 1775–1783*. New York: Hill and Wang, 2001.

Finkelman, Paul. "Slavery and the Constitutional Convention: Making a Covenant with Death," in *Origins of the Constitution and American National Identity*, ed. Richard Beeman, Stephen Botein, and Edward C. Carter II. Chapel Hill: University of North Carolina Press, 1987, 188–225.

Finkelman, Paul. "Treason against the Hopes of the World," in *Jeffersonian Legacies*, ed. Peter Onuf. Charlottesville: University Press of Virginia, 1993, 181–224.

Frey, Sylvia R. *Water from the Rock: Black Resistance in a Revolutionary Age*. Princeton, NJ: Princeton University Press, 1991.

Frey, Sylvia R., and Betty Wood. *Come Shouting to Zion: African American Christianity in the American South and British Caribbean to 1830*. Chapel Hill: University of North Carolina Press, 1998.

Geggus, David P. *The Impact of the Haitian Revolution in the Atlantic World*. Columbia: University of South Carolina Press, 2001.

Geggus, David P. *Haitian Revolutionary Studies*. Bloomington: Indiana University Press, 2002.

Geggus, David P., and David Barry Gaspar, eds. *A Turbulent Time: The French Revolution and the Greater Caribbean*. Bloomington: Indiana University Press, 1997.

Hirschfeld, Fritz. *George Washington and Slavery: A Documentary Portrayal*. Columbia: University of Missouri Press, 1997.

Holton, Woody. *Forced Founders: Indians, Debtors, Slaves, and the Making of the American Revolution in Virginia*. Chapel Hill: University of North Carolina Press, 2000.

Horton, James Oliver, and Lois E. Horton. *In Hope of Liberty: Culture, Community and Protest among Northern Free Blacks, 1700–1860*. New York: Oxford University Press, 1997.

Kaplan, Sidney. "The 'Domestic Insurrections' of the Declaration of Independence." *Journal of Negro History* 61 (1976): 243–255.

Kaplan, Sidney, and Emma Nogrady Kaplan. *The Black Presence in the Era of the American Revolution*. Washington, DC: New York Graphic Society and Smithsonian Institution Press, 1973.

Melish, Joanne Pope. *Disowning Slavery: Gradual Emancipation and "Race" in New England, 1780–1860.* Ithaca, NY: Cornell University Press, 1998.

Miller, John C. *The Wolf By the Ears: Thomas Jefferson and Slavery.* New York: Free Press, 1977.

Nash, Gary B. *Forging Freedom: The Formation of Philadelphia's Black Community, 1720–1840.* Cambridge, MA: Harvard University Press, 1988.

Nash, Gary B., and Jean B. Soderlund. *Freedom by Degrees: Emancipation in Pennsylvania and Its Aftermath.* New York: Oxford University Press, 1991.

Olwell, Robert A. "'Domestick Enemies': Slavery and Political Independence in South Carolina, May 1775–March 1776." *Journal of Southern History* 55 (1989): 21–48.

Pybus, Cassandra. *Epic Journeys of Freedom: Runaway Slaves of the American Revolution and Their Global Quest for Liberty.* Boston: Beacon Press, 2006.

Quarles, Benjamin. *The Negro in the American Revolution.* Chapel Hill: University of North Carolina Press, 1961.

Rakove, Jack N. *Original Meanings: Politics and Ideas in the Making of the Constitution.* New York: Random House, 1996.

Raphael, Ray. *A People's History of the American Revolution.* New York: New Press, 2001.

Sensbach, Jon. *A Separate Canaan: The Making of an Afro-Moravian World in North Carolina, 1763–1840.* Chapel Hill: University of North Carolina Press, 1998.

Slave Petition to the Governor, Council and House of Representatives of the Province of Massachusetts, May 25, 1774, *Massachusetts Historical Society Collections*, 5th ser. Boston: Massachusetts Historical Society, 1877, 3:432–433.

White, Shane. *Somewhat More Independent: The End of Slavery in New York City, 1770–1810.* Athens: University of Georgia Press, 1991.

Wiencek, Henry. *An Imperfect God: George Washington, His Slaves, and the Creation of America.* New York: Farrar, Strauss and Giroux, 2003.

Wilson, Ellen Gibson. *The Loyal Blacks.* New York: Capricorn, 1976.

Wood, Peter H. "'Taking Care of Business' in Revolutionary South Carolina: Republicanism and the Slave Society," in *The Southern Experience in the American Revolution*, ed. Jeffrey J. Crow and Larry E. Tise. Chapel Hill: University of North Carolina Press, 1978.

Wood, Peter H. "'The Dream Deferred': Black Freedom Struggles on the Eve of White Independence," in *In Resistance: Studies in African, Caribbean, and Afro-American History*, ed. Gary Okihiro. Amherst: University of Massachusetts Press, 1983, 169–172.

"The Times Have Turned Everything Topside Down": Native Americans and the American Revolution

4

Andrew K. Frank

American Indians appear in the background in virtually every narrative of the conflict known as the War of Independence. Some are described as allies of the British and others appear as friends to the colonists. Yet, the social perspectives of Native Americans are frequently ignored. Few if any Natives chose sides because of their concerns about the proper relationship between Crown and colony or about issues of representation or taxation. Instead, they found themselves participating in the imperial struggle as part of their own attempts to define their futures as independent sovereign nations or as individuals in pursuit of personal interests. When the war began, these interests led most Indians to conclude that pursuing a policy of neutrality was best. Nonetheless, by the time the War of Independence was over, nearly all Indians east of the Mississippi River were affected and concerned by the political and military struggle that formed the United States. Not only did the war transform diplomatic relations on the continent, but on a personal level, thousands of Native warriors and civilians lost their lives, some villages moved while others were razed, and many Indian families struggled to survive the wartime shortages of food and other essential supplies. The war was "the greatest blow that could have been dealt us" (Kinnaird, 1946, 3:117; Calloway, 26–64).

A New World for Natives

Before Great Britain and the American colonists came to blows in the Revolution, many Native Americans had already undergone revolutionary changes in their daily lives, their cultural outlooks, and the geopolitical contexts in which they lived. These transformations—demographic, cultural, economic, religious, and political—set the Native stage for their participation in the American Revolution. In the preceding century, the Indian populations in

North America had been devastated by the ravages of new diseases and warfare. Many Indians survived by forming new nations and organizing into various new confederacies, such as the Creek and Iroquois. Other changes transformed how Natives lived. In the eighteenth century, Native Americans became fundamentally dependent on trade with European Americans to obtain necessary goods such as guns, hoes, and knives. The arrival of thousands of new European settlers further threatened their control over their lands, as Indians struggled to repel squatters and herders. Throughout the seventeenth and first half of the eighteenth centuries, Indians had ceded much of their easternmost land in various treaties and continued to feel pressured to cede more. They had moved their villages away from intrusive settlers, and they traveled further from their homes in order to find new hunting grounds. In addition, Native warriors had fought in all of the major wars between the colonial powers. From almost every vantage point, prior to the American Revolution the Native Americans' world had already undergone revolutionary changes (Calloway, 1997; Merrell, 1989).

In this "new world," all of the Native groups in the eastern part of North America struggled with the tensions created by the conflicting forces that propelled them toward coexistence with and physically resisting their intrusive neighbors. Although some areas enjoyed sustained periods of mutual understanding and interdependence, the North American frontier in the decades preceding the Revolution was typically marked by both intercultural tensions and cooperation. In some places, the search for "accommodation and common meaning" led Indians and Europeans to construct "a common, mutually comprehensible world" with "new systems of meaning and exchange" (White, 1991, ix–x). Throughout much of North America, trading networks connected Natives and colonists, as did relationships forged by diplomacy, travel, and even intermarriage. At the same time, local tensions frequently erupted over trade disputes, free-range livestock, and runaway slaves. As a result, Native leaders engaged in frontier diplomacy in order to obtain compromises and concessions their peoples could endure (Piker, 2004).

Resistance on the Frontier

By the middle of the eighteenth century, diplomacy could not prevent tensions within Native communities from bubbling over. Native Americans increasingly concluded that their sovereignty and lives were at risk. The westward migration of European Americans who were intent on obtaining Indian lands, rather than Indian skins or furs, made this increasingly apparent. The British government, especially overseas in London but also in the form of their representatives in the colonies, recognized that these migrants threatened the peace and sought to restrain them. Stemming the flood of westward migration, though, was more difficult than British officials often imagined. Despite a series of proclamations, the unrestrained colonial masses squatted on Indian lands, bringing livestock and crops onto Indian hunting grounds and farms, and even into villages. The result was more frequent violence between Native Americans and Euro-American settlers (Jennings, 1978, 319–382; Holton, 1994, 453–478).

The acts of violence and increased tensions of the frontier in many ways shaped the French and Indian War that lasted from 1754 to 1763. As in previous wars between European empires, the war had a way of incorporating Natives. Most Native Americans sided with the French in the conflict; others supported the British or tried to remain neutral. Some Indian nations split their loyalties and provided warriors and other assistance to both the British and the French. In most instances, Native Americans acted out of their own national concerns. They used the tensions between Britain and France to obtain guns and even European soldiers to use against Indian enemies. They used the conflict to redraw geopolitical boundaries and to rid themselves of troublesome traders (Fowler, 2005; Anderson, 2000).

When the French and Indian War ended and France removed most of its presence from North America, Native Americans lost their ability to play European nations off against one another. Now many Indians had no choice but to negotiate with the British and deal with the increasing flood of English settlers. In addition they had little choice but to deal with British traders, who were often "not the honestest or Soberest People" (James Wright to the Board of Trade, quoted in Snapp, 1996, 35). Before the war even ended, many Natives appealed to the British Crown to curb the assaults on their liberties and freedoms. They called on Great Britain to regulate traders, control the

Ottawa chief Pontiac and Major Robert Rogers meet in 1763 to agree on peace terms after the siege of Detroit during the French and Indian Wars. (*Library of Congress*)

actions of Christian missionaries, and otherwise end the land grab through-out the colonies. The British began building forts to guard the frontier, which of course led to the indignity of bringing soldiers into and near In-dian lands. They also created a new system of laws to regulate the Indian trade, the source of many disputes. Despite the presence of forts and new Indian policies, English settlers continued to move onto eastern Native lands (Countryman, 2003, 16–19; Snapp, 1996, 33–54).

Determined to prevent another pan-Indian attack, the British Crown recognized the need to restrict the expansion of colonial settlements. They addressed this issue through the Proclamation of 1763. Issued by George III, it reserved the lands west of the Appalachian Mountains as Indian hunting grounds. Colonists were forbidden from settling on the lands or negotiating to settle on the lands. Only the Crown could negotiate for the lands. This policy outraged many western settlers and eastern speculators. Some squat-ters continued to move onto Indian lands even though they could not legally obtain title, but most land speculators and planters were prevented from turning Indian lands into financial rewards. Between 1763 and 1775, many American colonists blamed the Proclamation of 1763 and then the Quebec Act for their financial problems and pressured Great Britain to change its frontier policies. Others increasingly recognized that independence from the Crown would solve this particular problem (Holton, 1999, 35–38; Snapp, 1996, 158). Not surprisingly, then, in the Declaration of Independence, Americans expressed outrage that the king "has endeavoured to bring on the inhabitants of our frontiers, the merciless Indian Savages, whose known rule of warfare, is an undistinguished destruction of all ages, sexes and con-ditions." Given this background, the Indian in eastern North America had everything to fear from warfare returning to the continent.

In the northern colonies, many Natives expressed outrage when Brit-ish traders replaced Frenchmen and Spaniards in the fur and skin trades. French traders were often men who were married into Indian communi-ties, whereas British traders followed the dictates of the marketplace and ignored the concerns of Indian communities. British traders faced accusa-tions of using false weights, intoxicating warriors before negotiating, and other unscrupulous tactics. British officials also deviated from trading norms that had created amicable relationships between the French and Indians. For example, Jeffrey Amherst, who was charged with overseeing Indian af-fairs in the Northeast, stopped the French tradition of giving annual gifts to Indian allies. In addition, he decided that it would be best not to sell or trade guns to Indian hunters in the region. Native dependence on European trade goods left Indians with few choices but to acquiesce (White, 1991, 263–265; Countryman, 2003, 33).

In this context, a new Native religious movement emerged among the Ohio and Great Lakes Indians. Neolin, known as the Delaware Prophet, called upon Indians to unite and reject all of their ties to European society and culture. This path, he preached, was the only one that could lead toward political autonomy and cultural well-being. Pontiac, an Ottawa chief and prophet, drew upon Neolin's ideas as well as his own anti-British sentiments and emerged with a narrower message for fellow Indians in the Great Lakes region. He advocated the rejection of the British—their trade goods, culture, and political ties. The region's warriors, who were angry with Amherst's decisions and the loss of their French allies, responded to Pontiac's call. Warfare erupted in the Ohio Valley, as Chippewas, Delawares, Senecas, Miamis, Potawotomis, Hurons, and other Indians united against their British neighbors. The Natives attacked all twelve of the British forts on the Great Lakes and captured eight of them. In the process, Pontiac announced that he hoped that his French "father" would resume control over the region. His overture to the French fell on deaf ears, and French troops never arrived to reinforce the Indian forces. When many of the Indians fell sick from smallpox (some argue spread by a British "gift" of infested blankets to the Delaware), Pontiac's forces were forced to retreat. Ravaged by disease and a lack of supplies, the Natives could not overcome the English military power. By 1765, although the preconditions that had motivated the war remained unchanged, most of the fighting had ended (Dowd, 2002; White, 1991, 269–314).

As the War Approached

The treaties that Great Britain negotiated after the Proclamation of 1763 did not soothe Native American fears that the settlers would continue their land grab. Nevertheless, many Indians had little choice but to negotiate with the British. As a result, Indians creatively tried to preserve their own national interests. In 1768, for example, the Iroquois ceded Cherokee lands to Sir William Johnson at the Treaty of Fort Stanwix. The Cherokees, watching the Iroquois cede their land while settlers increasingly squatted on other parts of their territory, responded by establishing a clear geographic division with South Carolina in the Treaty of Hard Labor. The line, which was marked by burning marks on a strip of trees, only lasted a couple of years. In 1770, the Treaty of Lochaber further restricted the Cherokee lands, and in 1772, Virginians demanded the cession of all lands east of the Kentucky River. The Cherokees complained to little avail. By now they could "see the smoke of the Virginians from their doors" (Calloway, 1995, 189). For many Cherokees, the fear of the land grab was impossible to overstate.

When warfare erupted between the colonies and Great Britain, both British and American officials kept careful watch on their Native American neighbors. For the fledgling United States, a prime consideration was given to what the Continental Congress referred to as "securing and preserving the friendship of the Indians Nations" (*Journal of the Continental Congress*, 2:93; Prucha, 1984; 36–37). Keeping the Native Americans neutral seemed to be the best policy for the young nation. As a result, Congress authorized a series of meetings with various Indian groups to explain that "this is a family quarrel between us and Old England. You Indians are not concerned in it. We don't wish you to take up the hatchet against the king's troops. We desire you to remain at home, and not join either side, but keep the hatchet buried deep" (O'Donnell III, 1973, 23).

Many Native Americans also had a desire to maintain their neutrality. On June 19, 1775, in the immediate aftermath of the Battle of Bunker Hill,

Eighteenth-century depiction of an Iroquois warrior. (*Library and Archives Canada / Bibilothèque et Archives Canada [R9266-3492] Peter Winkworth Collection of Canadiana*)

the "Chiefs and Warriors of the *Oneida* Tribe of Indians" sent a speech to Governor Jonathan Trumbull of Connecticut. "*Brothers*," the Oneidas explained through an interpreter, "we have heard of the unhappy differences, and great contention betwixt you and Old England; we wonder greatly, and are troubled in our minds." Their consternation about the growing tensions between the colonists and the Crown should not surprise us. In the years prior to the speech, British colonists particularly in New England seemed on the edge of a continental war, one that threatened to envelop all of the inhabitants of the region. The Boston Massacre, unrest over the Stamp Act, and then the military confrontations at Concord and Lexington revealed tensions between mother country and colony that neighboring Indians could hardly ignore. This would not be the first time that European colonists had fought each other, and the Oneida representatives declared that they would not repeat the mistake of getting caught up in European American politics and diplomacy. Instead, the Oneidas declared, "Respecting us Indians, we cannot intermeddle in this dispute between two brothers, the quarrel seems to be unnatural; you are two brothers of one blood; we are unwilling to join on either side in such a contest; for we bear an equal affection to both of you, Old England and New England." The message of neutrality could not be clearer: "Let us Indians be all of one mind, and live in peace with one another; and you white people settle your disputes betwixt yourselves" (*Pennsylvania Magazine; or, American Monthly Museum [1775–1776]* 1 [1775]: 601–602).

British and American officials tried their best to shape the diplomatic paths of the Indians. As the war progressed, several Indian agents and traders tried to sway particular leaders and villages to support the Patriot cause, but in general, representatives of the United States understood that the best they could usually hope for was neutrality (Calloway, 1995, 29). The British, on the other hand, were more optimistic about their ability to control the Indians and even obtain Native allies. At first, the British tried to keep the Indians on the sidelines of the dispute, perhaps not wanting to turn the dispute into an Indian war and thus help the Revolutionaries attract support for the cause. In a January 1775 speech to the Iroquois, British official Guy Johnson dismissed the events stemming from the Boston Tea Party as simply being the logical response to "some people, who notwithstanding a law of the King and his wise Men, would not let some Tea land, but destroyed it." The king "was angry, and sent some Troops with the General [Thomas Gage], whom you have long known, to see the Laws executed and bring the people to their sences . . . I expect it will soon be over." As it became clear that the rebellion would not end quickly, the British changed strategies. Armed with gifts and a history of cracking down on unruly settlers, the British tried to obtain allegiances throughout the continent. With rhetorical flair, the British invited the Indians "to feast on a Bostonian and drink his Blood" (Graymont, 1972, 57, 68). They pointed, with occasional success, to the Proclamation of 1763 and the colonial violations of it, and they used trade goods to obtain allegiances.

Choosing Diplomatic Paths

Despite the efforts of both the British and the Americans, Native Americans made their decisions to participate in the war on terms of their own. Their previous experiences with colonists and the British government shaped some of their decisions, but so did the tensions between Indian nations, long-standing relationships, and recent diplomatic events. The result was a mosaic of choices and a cacophony of voices from Native communities. Some nations split into warring camps; others changed diplomatic paths as their options changed. In most of these instances, Natives fought for their own freedom. In the months and years after the Oneidas announced their desire to remain neutral in the affairs between the Crown and colonies, they discovered that neutrality was easily declared but much more difficult and often undesirable to maintain. By the time the War of Independence was over, the Oneidas and nearly all Indians east of the Mississippi River were affected and concerned by the political and military struggle that formed the United States. Few if any Natives chose sides because of their concerns about the proper relationship between Crown and colony or about issues of representation or taxation. Instead, they found themselves participating in the imperial struggle as part of their own attempts to define their futures as independent sovereign nations or as individuals in pursuit of personal interests. Protecting their homelands, many Natives concluded, required that they participate in the war between Great Britain and the United States. For the Oneidas, the calls for neutrality eventually ceased, as many of their warriors and chiefs sided with the Revolutionaries. The Oneidas, however, did not act in unity, and members of the nation and the Iroquois League of which they were a part often pursued contradictory diplomatic paths. The Oneidas were not the only Native allies of the Revolutionaries. The majority of Catawbas, for example, found themselves fighting alongside the recently formed United States. For others, like the Creeks, Shawnees, and most of the Iroquois Confederacy, the path of neutrality was abandoned when they decided that supporting the British offered their best option (Calloway, 1995, 29–31).

Some Indians, especially in New England, fought as individuals within the colonial armies and militias. In this region, many Native Americans lived as semi-integrated members of the region's towns and villages. Some were considered free blacks, and most kept their Indian identities secret. When the fighting began, they fought alongside their black and white neighbors. In 1770, for example, Crispus Attucks became the first casualty of the American Revolution when he was shot and killed in what later became known as the Boston Massacre. Attucks, who is often remembered as a black sailor, was the son of a Native American mother and African American father. Like many Natives in New England, his racial identity as a mulatto man merely hid his Indian background (Mandell, 1996, 1, 204–205). Attucks was not the only Indian to respond to the war as an individual within the colonial context. Some drew on the era's rhetoric of freedom and equality as part of their strategy for resisting the assault on their culture and land. Some moved to port cities and American villages or enlisted in the Continental Army to pursue economic opportunities opened by the war. For others, the war meant enlisting in colonial armies or more likely engaging in warfare in the pursuit of individual tribal ambitions. Some Indians in New England served as "Indian Rangers" on behalf of the Patriot cause (Mandell, 1996, 168, 204–205).

Unlike Attucks, most Native Americans lived as members of sovereign Indian nations outside of the confines of American colonies and towns. Like Attucks, though, when hostilities broke out, most Native Americans could not or chose not to remain neutral throughout the war. The Choctaw Indians found the Revolution to be a divisive moment. The United States, which tried vigorously to get this southeastern nation to help them in their revolutionary struggle, could never obtain the allegiance of more than a handful of Choctaws. Instead, a majority of the Choctaws supported Britain during the war, while some residents of the Sixtowns Division helped Spain capture Mobile and Pensacola from the British (O'Brien, 2002, 10).

The Choctaws' decision to support either the Crown or the Revolutionaries resulted from indigenous rather than imperial concerns. On one

Crispus Attucks, of both African and Native heritage, was the first man killed at the Boston Massacre and became a symbol of the American struggle for independence. (*Library of Congress*)

expedition, for example, the Choctaws demonstrated their loyalty to the Crown as well as their own tribal ambitions. In 1778, Choctaw chief Franchimastabé led a British-Choctaw war party down the Mississippi, in hopes of attacking a relatively small group of rebels who had plundered British settlements along the Mississippi River. When the Choctaws arrived at Natchez, James Willing, who had led the group of about thirty Americans on a series of raids in the region, had already retreated to the safety of Spanish New Orleans. Franchimastabé and his men were not frustrated by their lack of a battle and their inability to fight those who plundered the British settlements. Instead, the Choctaw force remained at the British fort for about a month. There, they served on guard duty, declared their resolution to resist any future attack, and received lucrative presents and trade goods for their loyalty. As they left, Franchimastabé made the Choctaws' position clear: "In case you are threatened with an attack from the rebels, remember we are behind you. Write to our beloved men who will acquaint us and we will always be ready to follow him out to your assistance and protection. But, on the other hand, should you offer to take the rebels by the hand or enter into any treaty with them, remember also that we are behind you and that we will look on to you as Virginians and treat you as our enemies." Although they had not fought, Franchimastabé's war party returned home victorious. Franchimastabé returned with the honor accorded to warriors who were

Alexander McGillivray

Born in the Little Tallassee village around 1750, McGillivray was the Creek child of Sehoy, an Indian woman of the prominent wind clan, and a Loyalist Scotsman named Lachlan McGillivray. During and after the Revolution, he used his influence in both societies to secure Creek economic and political interests.

McGillivray spent most of his childhood under the careful watch of his mother and her Creek family. Since Creek society was matrilineal, McGillivray was embraced as a full member of society. When he was a teenager, his father brought him into colonial society, where he soon became equally comfortable. By the time the Revolution began, McGillivray had lived in Little Tallassee as well as in Augusta, Georgia. He was an eloquent speaker in Muskogee, and he had received a European-style education in Charleston. He also spent time in a business apprenticeship in Savannah.

For McGillivray, the onset of hostilities threatened both of the worlds in which he lived. His father, whose Loyalist leanings were well known in South Carolina, suffered at the hands of revolutionaries, who confiscated his property and threatened his life. In 1777, McGillivray escaped the chaos in South Carolina by moving back into his mother's village, where many other Creeks similarly saw the emergence of the independence movement as a threat to their security. As a result, McGillivray discovered that his personal inclination to seek retribution was supported by similar anticolonial sentiments in Creek villages.

The British, recognizing McGillivray's peculiar position as both the child of a Loyalist and a potentially influential Indian, commissioned him and paid him as a colonel in order to further secure his loyalty to the Crown. Although McGillivray never led substantial groups of warriors into battle against the United States, he used his influence to urge fellow Creeks to fight against Georgia rather early in the war as well as to defend Pensacola against the Spanish in 1780 and 1781.

The victory by the United States had tremendous ramifications for McGillivray. His father, who had returned to Scotland, would

willing to fight, the satisfaction of having none of his warriors wounded or killed, and the prestige that accompanied the lucrative trade goods that were given to him by the British (O'Brien, 2002, 40–41).

Indians became central components in the British war policy in the 1779 Southern Strategy. Many Creek and Cherokee warriors became active fighters when they joined British general Augustine Prevost's attack on Savannah. Some Creeks remained neutral or fought against the British, especially those with connections to the influential chiefs known as the Tame King and the Fat King or ties to trader George Galphin. Throughout the war, however, the Creeks were also concerned with their own war with neighboring Choctaws. Nevertheless, for the next three years, southeastern Indian warriors helped keep Georgia under British control. They attacked frontier settlements and otherwise occupied the Revolutionary forces. When U.S. general Anthony Wayne surrounded Savannah in 1783, Emistesigo and other Creek warriors unsuccessfully tried to assist their British allies. Emistesigo died during the battle, leaving Alexander McGillivray as one of the Creek's leading pro-British chiefs. Despite the assistance of the Creeks,

not return to South Carolina. As a result, McGillivray's Creek connections became even more important.

In the postwar years, McGillivray used his understanding of both societies to protect the interests of the Creek Nation, which were increasingly under assault by Georgian settlers, Indian traders, and land speculators. This postwar reality became clear in the 1783 Treaty of Paris, when Great Britain ceded land belonging to the Creeks to the United States. In this context, McGillivray emerged as a Creek spokesperson, explaining that the Creeks had never surrendered and were the rightful owners of the territory. In order to protect the sovereignty of the Creeks, McGillivray sought to centralize power within Creek society. A national council, for example, allowed the Creeks to negotiate as a single entity and from a position of strength, rather than as a loose collection of villages.

Through his actions, he helped the Creeks prevent Georgia from confiscating 3 million acres of hunting grounds. In addition, in order to restrain the actions of the United States, he negotiated treaties with Spain and tried to coordinate the behavior of Indians elsewhere in eastern North America. In 1784 he negotiated the Treaty of Pensacola with Spain, which protected Creek territorial rights in Florida and guaranteed access to the British trading firm of Panton, Leslie, and Company. "For the good of my Country I have Sacrificed my all," he explained. "It is a duty incumbent on me in this Critical Situation to exert myself for their Interest. The protection of a great Monarch is to be preferrd to that of a distracted Republic" (Caughey, 1938, 22). Afterward he relied on his alliance with Spain to help convince officials of Georgia and the United States to respect Creek boundaries.

In 1790, McGillivray arranged the Treaty of New York with the United States. He used his position among the Creeks and the uncertainty within the United States to define Creek borders, preserve sovereignty, and obtain control over the trade between the United States and the Creek Indians. McGillivray did not live to see the results of his efforts. He died on February 17, 1793.

the British were ordered to withdraw from the city on June 1, 1783 (Edgar, 2001).

The Cherokees similarly pursued their self-interest in the war. In their case, their participation in the war stemmed from the problems that resulted from a 1775 treaty with North Carolinians. In March 1775 Richard Henderson, along with eight other North Carolinian land speculators, negotiated a deal with Cherokees. In the Overhill Cherokee Treaty, Little Carpenter, Oconostota, and the Raven of Chota sold more than 20 million acres of territory between the Cumberland River and the Kentucky River. The 2,000 pounds sterling and 8,000 pounds of trade goods that the Cherokees received in return for the territory hardly satisfied many younger Cherokee warriors. An outraged Dragging Canoe, for example, refused to agree to the cession and warned Henderson that he would make the lands "dark and bloody." His fears could not be understated. "Whole Indian Nations have melted away like snowballs in the sun before the white man's advance. They leave scarcely a name of our people except those wrongly recorded by their destroyers" (Palmer, 1960, 1:283–286). This treaty, he explained, promised to do the same for the Cherokees. Even those who signed the deal later complained that they had been tricked into signing away their lands. Opposition to the treaty also came from the British side. Royal governors Lord Dunmore of Virginia and Josiah Martin of North Carolina declared that the transaction violated the Royal Proclamation of 1763 and thus was illegal. In 1778 the Virginia House of Delegates voided the entire transaction. Nevertheless, white settlers with their African American slaves flooded the region, and tensions between Cherokees and colonists reached a feverish pitch (Hatley, 1995).

As a result of the controversial treaty, many Cherokees fought alongside the British in an effort to remove the unwanted settlers on their land and to reclaim the lands that they felt were unjustly "sold" away. Thus they quickly abandoned their stance of neutrality, as several Cherokee villages almost immediately sided with Great Britain and attacked neighboring frontier settlements. Even before independence was formally declared, some Cherokee warriors conducted deadly raids into Virginia and the Carolinas. These attacks resulted in terror on the southern frontier, where, according to one 1776 account, "plantations lie desolate, and hopeful crops are going to ruin" (Hatley, 1995, 192). The result was cries in the South to destroy the Cherokees uttered by many of the same voices that called for the breaking of the ties between Great Britain and the colonies. The ensuing Cherokee war helped South Carolinians create a unified agenda that combined Indian and imperial affairs. Although some younger Cherokees remained wary of opposing the local rebels, the Cherokees' support of Great Britain remained steadfast throughout most of the war.

Some Indians began the war as supporters of the Patriots but, as time passed, switched allegiances. Many Indians in New England, for example, helped Revolutionary soldiers defend the St. John Valley against the British in 1777. The Micmacs and Abenakis, however, did not assist the Americans for long. British military successes in the region convinced them that neutrality or a pro-British stance would be more advantageous in the long run. In the Southeast, many pro-American Indians became less supportive when American and Spanish trade goods failed to materialize. On the other hand, when the economic ties that connected some Indian villages with the British disappeared, so too did diplomatic ties (Salisbury, 1996, 1:452).

In the Ohio Territory, several Indian leaders tried to keep their nations neutral. The Shawnee chief Cornstalk, for example, tried to limit hostilities with the English at a time when most of his fellow Shawnees saw the war as an opportunity to eliminate the intrusive American settlers and settlements. While many Shawnees attacked frontier settlements at the start of the war, Cornstalk sought to preserve a peace that he had helped create after the French and Indian War. On October 6, 1777, Cornstalk and his son traveled to Fort Randolph to assure Revolutionary leaders of the neutrality of the Shawnee people and to figure out why two Shawnees who had professed friendship were taken hostage. Upon their arrival, they too were detained. About a month later, members of the Revolutionary militia killed Cornstalk and the other hostages. Apparently, the soldiers were retaliating for an American soldier who had recently been killed by Shawnee warriors.

The cold-blooded murder of unarmed hostages outraged Revolutionary sup-porter Patrick Henry, who was then governor of Virginia, and he tried to keep the peace by offering a reward for the apprehension of the militiamen responsible. It was to little avail. After the attack, most of the Indians in the region fought against the Patriot cause, and their opposition continued even after Cornwallis surrendered (Calloway, 1992, 39–52).

Native Americans abandoning neutrality and choosing to participate in the Revolutionary War had ramifications across the continent. One of the earliest repercussions was the destruction of the Iroquois Confederacy. Es-tablished during the sixteenth century in response to the challenges brought by European colonialism, this confederacy of six Indian nations could not withstand the pressures unleashed by the War of Independence. The league was originally formed as an alliance of the Cayuga, Mohawk, Oneida, Onon-daga, and Seneca nations, and it later incorporated Tuscaroras. It was never intended to have a coercive centralized polity. As a result, the outbreak of war meant that each participating nation and even each village had to de-cide for itself a political and diplomatic path. When the fighting began at Lexington and Concord, the Six Nations for the most part tried to remain on the sidelines. The fighting between their primarily white neighbors seemed tangential to their central concerns. As the fighting continued, both Great Britain and the United States pressured the Iroquois to choose sides. Their stances of neutrality slowly disintegrated, as some Mohawk warriors united with the Loyalists and some Oneidas allied themselves with the revolutionar-ies. Matters worsened when in January 1777, three peace chiefs and various other Onondagas died during an epidemic. The crisis that ensued resulted in the extinguishing of the ceremonial council fire, the very symbol of the unity of the Iroquois League, and the emergence of powerful and often unopposed war chiefs (Wallace, 1972, 125–148; Graymont, 1972, 104–128).

Some of the war chiefs, such as Joseph Brant (Thayendanegea), feared that an American victory would lead to further invasions of their territory. As a result, by 1776 Brant with mostly Mohawk supporters and a handful of Tory Rangers had repeatedly attacked the frontier regions of New York and Pennsylvania. The revolutionaries retaliated, and for nearly three years the Iroquois fought in western New York and the Susquehanna. In 1779, leader-ship in this campaign passed to U.S. general John Sullivan. After his invasion of Burgoyne in 1779, the Iroquois lost any thought of remaining neutral or united. Although all of the members of the Iroquois League divided their loyalties, the Mohawks and Senecas remained under the anti-Patriot leader-ship of Joseph Brant. Similarly, most Cayugas, Mohawks, Onondagas, and Senecas fought alongside the British. The Oneidas, largely because of the influence of Christian missionary Samuel Kirkland, and the Tuscaroras for the most part supported the Americans. During Sullivan's invasion, Brant and his Mohawk allies welcomed other displaced Iroquois at the British fort at Niagara, where his Mohawk allies had already taken refuge. By November 1779, approximately 3,300 Indians were obtaining rations from the British at this fort. From this outpost, the Indians launched repeated raids on the American frontier (Graymont, 1972, 220).

Mohawk chief Joseph Brant, also known as Thayendanegea, was perhaps the most significant Native American leader during the American Revolution. Brant allied himself with the British against the American colonists. (*National Archives and Records Administration*)

The War and Its Aftermath

When the Revolutionary War ended, the divisions within the Iroquois nation remained. The league did not officially disband until the Second Treaty of Fort Stanwix in 1784, but the actions of the Six Nations revealed the reemergence of local village and national pursuits. Some scholars have suggested that the Revolution became a civil war within the Iroquois Confederacy, as villages and nations divided their loyalties and fought on competing sides. Yet, in most instances, Native warriors tried to avoid directly fighting each other, instead directing their attention to the British regulars and American soldiers who entered the territory. In the 1780s, New York confiscated most of the Iroquois land, even though it was largely inhabited by those who had supported the revolutionaries during the war. While many refugees tried to return to their homes, others chose exile in Canada or moved west of American control. As a result, the Iroquois League established separate council fires representing separate political entities at the Six Nations Reserve in Ontario and at Onondaga, New York (Calloway, 1997, 149; Jennings, 1985, 57–59).

While the Revolutionary War tore the diplomatic entity known as the Iroquois Confederacy apart, Natives across America dealt with the physical violence unleashed by the war. Villages were burned, warriors were killed, and communities split apart (Salisbury, 1996. 1:453). Few Indian nations were able to avoid suffering from the physical destruction of war. At the start of the war, South Carolinian William H. Drayton ordered his soldiers to "make smooth work as you go—that is, you cut up every Indian corn-field, and burn every Indian town—and that every Indian taken shall be the slave and property of the taker; that the nation be extirpated, and the lands become the property of the public" (Raphael, 2001, 282). In 1779 alone, American troops razed villages in almost all of the thirteen colonies. In addition to the destruction caused by Sullivan's forces among the Iroquois Confederacy, Indians suffered at the hands of several other American forces. For example, months earlier, John Bowman and soldiers from Kentucky destroyed most of the Shawnee Indian villages along the Ohio River. Throughout the year, Patriot soldiers from Virginia burned neighboring Chickamauga towns, and Daniel Brodhead burned Delaware and Seneca villages (Salisbury, 1996, 1:453; Fenn, 2001).

Even Natives who lived far from the fighting found themselves affected by the war. In Texas, the war led to inflated prices, shortages of trade goods, and the flight of many traders out of Indian villages. The result was often devastating for Natives. The Wichitas, for example, discovered that the war prevented French traders from living up to long-established trading obligations. One Taovayas chief protested these broken promises and proclaimed, "We find ourselves with half of what we need. The few fusils, hatchets, and powder that we have, we find them all in ruin." As a result, many Wichitas became used to seasonal migrations to hunt buffalo and trade with the Spanish. In other cases, the lack of trade led many warriors to confiscate goods from the handful of traders and mail carriers who traveled through the region. By 1782, postal and trade routes were completely shut down (Anderson, 1999, 173).

Near the end of the war, and especially as the news of the British surrender came to the countryside, all Indians had to adjust to a new diplomatic reality. Some Shawnees had left Ohio for Missouri, the Seminoles had moved further southward into northern Florida, and separate Iroquois Leagues existed in Ontario and in New York. Similarly, many Cherokees became increasingly migratory during the war, preferring to move their villages west, rather than accept the terms of peace demanded by the United States (Calloway, 1997, xii–xiv, 149).

When the war ended, many Native communities continued efforts to secure their sovereignty. Some, like the Creeks and Chickasaws in the Southeast, pursued the diplomatic path of creating treaties with the United States. Before the Treaty of Paris was even signed in 1783, several nations had signed treaties with the United States. Excluded from the privileges of citizenship within the new republic, other Natives struggled to accept the reality that the English Crown had granted their lands to the United States in the 1783 Treaty of Paris. As a result, many Indians refused to recognize the legitimacy of the treaty and of the United States itself, and many, in both the North and the South, met to discuss forming a pan-Indian alliance to oppose the United States (Calloway, 1995, 173).

Across the eastern part of North America, the end of the war forced Indians to create and recreate trade relations with the United States and Spain. Playing European nations off of one another became increasingly difficult with the centralization of power in the United States and the elimination of the British from the region. Still, the Choctaws tried to capitalize on their proximity to both Spanish Florida and the United States. In 1784, for example, the Choctaws simultaneously sent leading men to Spanish Mobile and Savannah in order to secure a trading agreement and diplomatic alliance. When, in 1787, Tobaca led a group of Choctaw chiefs to negotiate with the United States in Philadelphia and New York, Franchimastabé stayed at home in order to chastise the Spanish for the rapidly declining value of deerskins (O'Brien, 2002, 51–52, 85).

Those who supported the United States did not always fare so well in the aftermath of the war. Several Mashpee Indians in Massachusetts enlisted in the Continental Army, only to return to villages that had been ravaged by disease or largely abandoned. Other Mashpees did not return at all, as at least thirty-five enlisted Mashpee men died on the battlefield. Most of the Natick Indians supported the United States. In a petition to the young government, the Natick Indians proclaimed that "almost all that were able did go into the Service of the United States and either died in the service or soon after their return home. We your petitioners are their widows, there not being one male left now that was then of age to go to war." They were now forced to be migratory. Their meeting house had been destroyed. Their minister died. For the Hassanamiscos, the Revolution was disruptive but not as devastating. They, too, opposed the Crown and emerged from the war in shambles. With the exception of one family, the entire nation sold their land and moved to nearby towns like Worcester to find work as laborers and domestics (Mandell, 1996, 167–168, 181).

Conclusion

The war between the forming United States and Great Britain created new opportunities, challenges, and pressures for Native peoples. In the end, it proved disastrous for most. Political confederacies collapsed, Native warriors were killed, and countless villages were destroyed. Few Native Americans remained neutral in the conflict, and when the war ended, the United States punished all supporters of the British cause harshly. Even Natives who sided with the Americans, though, frequently found themselves marginalized in the aftermath of the war. The postwar settlement left "Indian country" under the control of the United States, and it opened the floodgates to an invasion of surveyors and settlers. Just as independence revolutionized life for the colonists, it also transformed the Native world. In the years following the war, American settlers were virtually unchecked by other European powers in their attempts to dispossess the Natives. Indians could no longer turn to traditional methods of playing European powers off of one another to stem the tide, and as a result the balance of power between the Americans and the Natives dramatically turned. In 1789, a petition from the Mohegan Indians expressed this transformation quite distinctly: "[T]he times are exceedingly altered, yea the Times have turned everything topside down" (Mohegan petition to the Connecticut Assembly, May 14, 1789, Connecticut Indian Records, vol. 2, 1st ser., document no. 330).

References and Further Reading

"A Speech of the Chiefs and Warriors of the *Oneida* Tribe of Indians, to the four New-England Provinces; directed immediately to Governor Trumbull, and by him to be communicated." *Pennsylvania Magazine; or, American Monthly Museum (1775–1776)* 1 (1775).

Anderson, Fred. *The Crucible of War: The Seven Years' War and the Fate of Empire in British North America, 1754–1766.* New York: Knopf, 2000.

Anderson, Gary Clayton. *The Indian Southwest, 1580–1830: Ethnogenesis and Reinvention.* Norman: University of Oklahoma Press, 1999.

Calloway, Colin G. *The American Revolution in Indian Country: Crisis and Diversity in Native American Communities.* New York: Cambridge University Press, 1995.

Calloway, Colin G. *New Worlds for All: Indians, Europeans, and the Remaking of Early America.* Baltimore: Johns Hopkins University Press, 1997.

Calloway, Colin G. "'We Have Always Been the Frontier': The American Revolution in Shawnee Country." *American Indian Quarterly* 16 (1992): 39–52.

Caughey, John Walton. *McGillivray of the Creeks.* Norman: University of Oklahoma Press, 1938.

Countryman, Edward. *The American Revolution.* New York: Hill and Wang, 2003.

Dowd, Gregory Evans. *A Spirited Resistance: The North American Indian Struggle for Unity, 1745–1815.* Baltimore: Johns Hopkins University Press, 1992.

Dowd, Gregory Evans. *War under Heaven: Pontiac, the Indian Nations, and the British Empire.* Baltimore: Johns Hopkins University Press, 2002.

Edgar, Walter. *Partisans and Redcoats: The Southern Conflict That Turned the Tide of the American Revolution.* New York: Morrow, 2001.

Fenn, Elizabeth. *Pox Americana: The Great Smallpox Epidemic of 1775–1782.* New York: Hill and Wang, 2001.

Fowler, William M., Jr. *Empires at War: The French and Indian War and the Struggle for North America, 1754–1763.* New York: Walker, 2005.

Graymont, Barbara. *The Iroquois in the American Revolution.* Syracuse, NY: Syracuse University Press, 1972.

Hatley, Tom. *The Dividing Paths: Cherokees and South Carolinians through the Revolutionary Era*. New York: Oxford University Press, 1995.

Holton, Woody. *Forced Founders: Indians, Debtors, Slaves and the Making of the American Revolution in Virginia*. Chapel Hill: University of North Carolina Press, 1999.

Holton, Woody. "The Ohio Indians and the Coming of the American Revolution in Virginia." *Journal of Southern History* 60 (1994): 453–478.

Jennings, Francis. "Indians' Revolution," in *The American Revolution: Explorations in the History of American Radicalism*, ed. Alfred Young. De Kalb: University of Northern Illinois Press, 1978, 319–382.

Jennings, Francis. "Iroquois Alliances in American History," in *The History and Culture of Iroquois Diplomacy: An Interdisciplinary Guide to the Treaties of the Six Nation and Their League*, ed. Francis Jennings. Syracuse, NY: Syracuse University Press, 1985.

Journal of the Continental Congress, 1774–1789. ed. Worthington Chauncey Ford. Washington, DC: Government Printing Office, 1904–1937.

Kinnaird, Lawrence, ed. *Spain in the Mississippi Valley, 1765–1794*. 3 vols. Washington, DC: Government Printing Office, 1946.

Mandell, Daniel R. *Behind the Frontier: Indians in Eighteenth-Century Eastern Massachusetts*. Lincoln: University of Nebraska Press, 1996.

Merrell, James H. *The Indians' New World: Catawbas and Their Neighbors from European Contact through the Era of Removal*. Chapel Hill: University of North Carolina Press, 1989.

O'Brien, Greg. *The Choctaws in a Revolutionary Age*. Lincoln: University of Nebraska Press, 2002.

O'Donnell, James H., III. *The Southern Indians in the American Revolution*. Knoxville: University of Tennessee Press, 1973.

Palmer, William P., ed. *Calendar of Virginia State Papers*. New York: Kraus Reprint Corp., 1960–1969.

Piker, Joshua. *Okfuskee: A Creek Indian Town in Colonial America*. Cambridge, MA: Harvard University Press, 2004.

Prucha, Francis Paul. *The Great Father: The United States Government and the American Indians*. Lincoln: University of Nebraska Press, 1984.

Raphael, Ray. *A People's History of the American Revolution: How Common People Shaped the Fight for Independence*. New York: New Press, 2001.

Salisbury, Neal. "Native People and European Settlers in Eastern North America, 1600–1783," in *The Cambridge History of the Native Peoples of the Americas*, ed. Bruce G. Trigger and Wilcomb E. Washburn. New York: Cambridge University Press, 1996.

Snapp, J. Russell. *John Stuart and the Struggle for Empire on the Southern Frontier*. Baton Rouge: Louisiana State University Press, 1996.

Wallace, Anthony. *Death and Rebirth of the Seneca*. New York: Vintage, 1972.

White, Richard. *The Middle Ground: Indians, Empires, and Republics in the Great Lakes Region, 1650–1815*. New York: Cambridge University Press, 1991.

Redcoats, Regulators, and the *Rattletrap*: The Backcountry Experience during the American Revolution

Daniel S. Murphree

T he American Revolution meant both continuity and change for inhabitants of the backcountry. Violence, economic upheaval, and community diversity persisted during the war much as it had during the previous two centuries. The day-to-day lives of residents remained precarious, marked by famine, fortune, danger, and delight. In some locales, backcountry residents never realized that a revolution was even taking place, and those who did notice often cared very little. In another sense, a great deal changed for backcountry residents during the Revolution. Symbols and structures of authority that had shaped their lives disappeared, and new peoples and entities emerged to take their place. In some parts of the backcountry, populations expanded during the war, while in others the human presence diminished. Means of subsistence transformed, and the backcountry economy became more interconnected with the larger Atlantic world. Territorial claims and boundaries shifted; new ethnic groups appeared, and others receded in numbers; and all peoples adapted to changing local and geopolitical realities. In the end, many aspects of backcountry life in 1783 hardly resembled those of 1763.

Defining the Backcountry

Between 1763 and 1783, the backcountry generally consisted of lands bordering the Appalachian Mountains, the Ohio River valley, the southern Great Lakes region, and the interior hinterlands near the Gulf of Mexico. No single population group or collective entity dominated these regions, which were often characterized by their distance from densely populated settlements. Instead, the backcountry existed where political, military, economic, and cultural hegemony did not. As a result, contemporaries who wrote about the backcountry used rather ambiguous descriptions. Some characterized it

Settlers dance with Native Americans (perhaps Shawnee) in Vincennes, Indiana, during a period of pleasant relations in the 1700s. (*Library of Congress*)

as those lands to the west, in the "woods," or inhabited primarily by Indians. Others took more legalistic approaches, referring to unsurveyed or poorly mapped regions as the backcountry. Royal officials in England, France, and Spain saw as backcountry areas on the edges of their imperial possessions, which did not clearly belong to one country, and therefore were constantly contested through warfare and diplomacy. Although areas that fit the basic definition of the backcountry tended to lie west of populous settlements, this was not always the case. Multiple backcountry enclaves remained east of long-established towns until long after the Revolution. Control of these enclaves became an important objective of both rebels and redcoats once fighting broke out in 1775.

The residents of the backcountry represented American diversity in its most comprehensive form during the war years. Although its constantly shifting setting prevents an accurate population count, tens of thousands of Americans lived in the backcountry during the Revolution. In the opinion of some observers, inhabitants of the region consisted of "a laborious hardy set of people" deemed "formidable" due to their numbers (Smith, 1983, 1:576–577). These residents represented every background imaginable. By 1783, European immigrants shared the region with long-established and recently arrived Native Americans and lesser numbers of free and enslaved African Americans. But such generalized descriptions obscure the pluralism of the region. Depending on locale, one would encounter English governmental officials, French fur traders, Spanish soldiers, German religious pilgrims, Scots-Irish political exiles, or Dutch merchants, and frequently all could be found in the same place. In addition, one would commonly meet Iroquois diplomats, Delaware guides, Shawnee hunters, Creek spiritual leaders, Chickasaw translators, and Mingo farmers. More than likely, while interacting with these populations, visitors would also see African Americans, most of whom worked and lived among Europeans, Indians, or both groups. The fastest-growing population in the region reflected the true integration of backcountry residents: those people of mixed origins, heritage, ethnicity, and cultures. Variously labeled by scholars as *métis*, *mestizos*, *castas*, half-breeds, and go-betweens, these individuals transcended traditional categories of description and identity.

Regardless of heritage or ethnicity, many backcountry residents challenged the colonial governing structure long before seaboard colonists protested against the Stamp Act or dumped tea into Boston harbor. In large part, these challenges to authority resulted from a collectively held fear of outside persecution, a fear that began in the seventeenth century, when white settlers first arrived in the region. Communities supported leaders and laws that guarded against external influences deemed restrictive or tyrannical. Typically, these alien forces took the form of Indians or opposing imperial powers like Spain and France, but by the late eighteenth century royal authorities in England and colonial officials along the seaboard increasingly fell into this category. Residents especially resented the more established, wealthy, and powerful coastal elites, who they believed, often accurately, attempted to diminish the influence of backcountry peoples by limiting their representation in colonial assemblies. The tendency of colonial officials to appoint easterners as tax collectors, justices of the peace, and sheriffs increased anxiety in the backcountry. Making matters worse, settlers often believed that taxes tended to fall more heavily on backcountry residents, while government-sponsored improvements appeared less common in the region. Perceptions of unfairness in British taxes and policies helped create a bond between backcountry rebels and revolutionaries of other regions.

Protests on the Hinterlands

Some of the earliest revolutionary outbreaks took place in the backcountry. In late 1763, a group of Scots-Irish settlers inhabiting the community of Paxton in western Pennsylvania rebelled against perceived inadequacies of colonial rule. Angered by threats to their homes from the recent pan-Indian uprising nominally led by Pontiac, these backcountry inhabitants requested greater military support from colonial authorities. In a "Declaration of the Injured Frontier Inhabitants," a proclamation written to defend their actions, they claimed that colonial policies toward Indians "have long been oppressive Grievances we have groaned under" (Greene, 1975, 96). When the government did not respond to their requests as desired, the "Paxton Boys" violently took matters into their own hands. Unable to confront the actual Indians representing threats to their community, dozens of settlers attacked a nearby missionary settlement that served as the home to Christianized Conestoga Indians. There they killed and scalped six natives before local officials intervened and placed the remaining Conestogas in the community's jail for their own protection. Two weeks later, however, a larger group of Paxton rebels attacked the building and killed the fourteen Conestogas they found inside, despite the pleas of the local sheriff. Still unsatisfied with government responses, a group of 250 Paxton settlers began to march to the provincial capital of Philadelphia in February 1764, hoping to kill more Christian Indians housed there and force colonial officials to redress their grievances. In the words of the participants, this march was necessary to correct abuses committed by government leaders who "have got the Political Reins in their hands, and tamely tyrannize over the other good Subjects of the Province" (Greene, 1975, 97). Only after a hastily assembled army led by Benjamin Franklin confronted and pacified the leaders on the outskirts of the city did the rebels disperse and return to their homes (Merritt, 2003, 285–289). The incident led to few backcountry concerns with the government being resolved, but indicated the frustration of many residents over perceived outside threats. Backcountry rebels conducted similar attacks on Indian allies of the British after 1775.

Backcountry protests against colonial government also surfaced in the Revolutionary South. In 1767, subsistence farmers and fur traders in western South Carolina rebelled against officials in Charleston whom they deemed to be lax in regard to maintaining law and order in their region. Forming vigilante committees to patrol the countryside and establish their own court systems, these "Regulators," as they called themselves, asserted self-government where they believed colonial officials had been deficient. Defending their actions, the colonists claimed that "unrelieved by Government, many among Us have been obliged to punish some of these Banditti and their Accomplices . . . compelling them to Do, what was expected that the Executive Branch of the Legislature would *long ago*, have Done" (Greene, 1975, 100). Unnerved by their audacity and often violent measures, officials in the capital subsequently responded to the demands of the unruly settlers by creating additional courts and appointing more sheriffs to cut down on criminal activity in the region. This gesture hardly resolved the tensions between the east and west in South Carolina, and conflict endured into the Revolution.

In North Carolina, a similar revolt took place between 1768 and 1772, though for significantly different reasons. There the tensions were most felt by predominantly Scottish, German, and Scots-Irish setters in the western Granville district, ethnic groups that had long-standing grievances against the mostly English holders of government power in the east. Grumbling about these grievances transformed into violent rebellion when the colonial assembly imposed a poll tax on residents to help fund the construction of a new mansion for the colony's royal governor, William Tryon. Outraged, backcountry settlers protested that "the poor Inhabitants in general are much oppress'd by reason of disproportionate Taxes, and those of the western Counties in particular; as they are generally in mean circumstances" (Greene, 1975, 105). In April 1768, residents of Granville adopted the name Regulators from their South Carolina counterparts, drew up a manifesto of grievances that was delivered to the governor, and began interfering with regional courts that they believed unfairly targeted backcountry settlers for unpaid debts. Alarmed by the perceived anarchy developing in the western

William Tryon, British governor of North Carolina, confronts an angry mob of Regulators in 1771. (*Library of Congress*)

part of the colony, Governor Tryon created a militia army of 1,100 to disperse the protesters and reassert royal control. At the Little Alamance River this force encountered a 2,000-man Regulator army. The ensuing battle ended in the fragmentation of rebel opposition and capture of most Regulator leaders. Tyron executed six settlers for their roles but pardoned the rest. Following the battle, many Regulators immigrated west, while others joined the growing independence movement against British rule (Risjord, 2002, 97–99). Regardless of outcomes, both Regulator movements challenged colonial authority in the southern backcountry.

The events involving the Paxton Boys and the Regulators revealed that political leadership in the backcountry tended to be less structured and ideologically based than in the more settled East. In the years that immediately preceded the Revolution, positions of authority were seldom clearly defined and laws were seldom rigorously enforced in America's backcountry. Due to the frequent absence of strong royal or colonial authority, and sometimes in spite of such a presence, backcountry settlers preferred to handle their politics and issues concerning authority in their own way. In the backcountry, far more than on the eastern seaboard, personality, pragmatism, and consensus opinion generally played large roles in governing.

Backcountry Life

The economy of the backcountry replicated patterns seen elsewhere in Revolutionary America, though the scale of activity tended to be much smaller, as did the scope of practices pursued. In addition, the items produced through farming, trade, and manufacturing in the backcountry differed from those most commonly generated in seaboard settlements. Time and resources tended to be the primary factors differentiating economic endeavors in the backcountry and other areas of early America. Since most backcountry areas had only recently been settled, colonist agriculture, exchange networks, and industry generally existed only in their initial, formative stages. Any deficiencies in these regards were frequently overcome by relying on preexisting Native economic systems. In no other region did Native American economic practices remain as vital to settler economies.

Hunting and the fur trade provided the bulk of economic growth in the backcountry, more so than in any other region of Revolutionary America. According to one observer of the Ohio River valley, "No country is better stocked with wild game of every kind" (Morse, 1794, 459). In the North, colonists typically bought and sold beaver pelts, in the South, deerskins. Rather than harvest animal coats themselves, traders generally arranged informal contracts with local Indians who often hunted, killed, and cleaned animals in exchange for tools, weapons, alcohol, and money. Surviving records indicate that these exchanges sometimes promoted friendship, harmony, and understanding between participants, sometimes animosity, distrust, and violence. Some settlers amassed enormous fortunes via the fur trade, using their profits to erect mansions, diversify into other businesses, and enjoy lives of luxury. Most, however, earned enough from the trade only to survive on a day-to-day basis. Throughout the eighteenth century, the quest for animal-skin-related profits bound backcountry residents together on a variety of levels. Once fighting between the British and rebellious colonists broke out in the 1770s, relationships formed through the fur trade sometimes determined loyalties and allies. Gaining greater access to pelts and resolving trade-related grievances motivated many backcountry residents to participate in the conflict.

For obvious reasons, the sea trade played little direct role in the frontier exchange economy, and despite the large number of rivers, transportation of goods via internal waterways was similarly limited. As a result, little plantation agriculture existed in the region until the late eighteenth century, and most farming remained at a subsistence level. A British officer visiting the lands north of the Ohio River provided additional insight into this situation when he wrote, "The price of labour in general is very high, as most of the young men rather chuse to hunt and trade amongst the Indians, than apply to agriculture" (Pittman, 1973, 55). Nevertheless, the transatlantic trade played a significant role in backcountry society, because most manufactured goods used in the region came from European ports. Additionally, many of the commercial crops produced on seaboard plantations contributed to complicated exchange networks involving backcountry furs and Old World materials. Frequently, pelts provided the capital for North American consumption of European muskets, Caribbean rum, and African slaves, regardless of how infrequently these items appeared in settlement outposts. Consequently, British naval blockades of the colonies after 1775 and seizure of trade goods ultimately affected the majority of backcountry residents.

Land speculation gained in intensity throughout the period. People of all classes and backgrounds often claimed hundreds of acres, not for development, but in hopes of selling parcels to other settlers at a later date for profit. During the war, many speculators stepped up their land acquisitions, believing that removal of British authority would make prices soar. This system led to wealth for some, but it also often fostered violence due to disputed land claims and uncertain boundaries. A good example of such a situation involved a longtime backcountry resident, George Croghan. After negotiations with Iroquois representatives, Croghan obtained a grant of nearly 200,000 acres near the headwaters of the Ohio River in 1740. Despite the grant's unclear boundaries, its repudiation by natives living in the exchanged area, and the British government's failure to acknowledge its legitimacy, Croghan set up an office and began selling tracts to anyone who could pay for them. Other speculators and individual settlers bought portions ranging in size from a few hundred to 20,000 acres. Almost instantly, colonial officials in both Virginia and Pennsylvania challenged these purchases, since they too claimed the lands, as did another speculative company that wanted to sell the tracts themselves. All groups resorted to legal and violent challenges to assert their rights; many of Croghan's customers lost their holdings; and much confusion still existed over land titles well into the nineteenth century (Hinderaker, 1997, 172–173). By the end of the American Revolution, few backcountry disputes sparked violence as much as land deals gone awry and subsequent quests for justice or revenge.

Significantly, due to the survival-oriented economic structure of the eighteenth-century backcountry, the region promoted equality of sexes to a greater extent than any other region. Survival demanded that men accept and promote the participation of women in the economy, which in turn fostered more female autonomy and societal influence. Enhancing this situation was the gendered division of labor exhibited by backcountry Native societies. Adopting indigenous patterns, females in backcountry communities tended to supervise agricultural production, determine settlement food needs and allocations, and orchestrate the day-to-day business affairs when males were absent on hunting or fur-trading expeditions. The end result was a backcountry economy that floundered or collapsed on occasions when females could not carry out their customary subsistence duties. Battles and accompanying dislocations associated with revolutionary activity tended to cultivate such situations.

Backcountry Beliefs

Due to the previously mentioned population diversity, no single spiritual belief system or philosophy of life dominated the backcountry. Syncretism, the merging of two or more belief systems, characterized the religion of many of the region's residents, at least to judge from their words and actions. Individualistic spiritual practices appeared more frequently than in the eastern colonies, and mainstream philosophies gained influence only after significant adaptations to local realities. Backcountry residents did not lack religion or complex worldviews in comparison to their seaboard counterparts. The environment they lived in had, however, far more influence over the way they held their beliefs than in the eastern and more urbanized settings. Most did, however, understand such things through an environment-oriented perspective less significant in more urbanized settings.

Organized religion in the backcountry was haphazard in terms of influence and membership, primarily due to population density and geographic obstacles. In addition, Revolutionary-era fighting strained ties between churches in England and North America. Nevertheless, most of the Christian denominations present in the seaboard colonies also had adherents in the region. Methodists, Presbyterians, and nascent Baptists predominated in the South; Moravians, Mennonites, and Lutheran sects played prominent roles in northern areas. Unusually for British America, Catholic influence was also great, inspired in part by Spanish and French missionaries inhabiting the same area or neighboring imperial possessions. The primary form of religious instruction took place in the form of circuit riders, usually Protestant preachers who constantly traveled throughout the backcountry spreading their message to whoever would listen. Because they often represented the only source of religious instruction and never stayed in one place for long, circuit riders tended to intensify the fluid religious belief systems among many backcountry inhabitants.

One such circuit rider left extensive writings of his experiences: Charles Woodmason, an Anglican missionary. Traveling extensively in the backcountry areas of the Carolinas in the late 1760s, Woodmason noted that missionaries intensely competed for settler souls. He claimed that the region was "eaten up by Itinerant Teachers, Preachers, and Impostors from New England and Pennsylvania—Baptists, New Lights, Presbyterians, Independents,

Methodist circuit riders traveled the countryside and preached wherever they could draw an audience. (*Hyde, A. B. 1887*. The Story of Methodism throughout the World. *Chicago: Johns Publishing House*)

and an [*sic*] hundred other Sects" (Breen and Hall, 2004, 314). Woodmason lamented the presence of competitors and attributed his inability to convert those settlers he encountered in the backcountry partially to their efforts. But he placed most of the blame on the settlers themselves. Though they often enthusiastically listened to his sermons, many in his audiences were people "of abandon'd Morals, and profligate Principles—Rude—Ignorant—Void of Manners, Education or Good Breeding." Moreover, they "delight in their present low, lazy, sluttish, heathenish, hellish Life, and seem not desirous of changing it" (Hinderaker and Mancall, 2003, 171).

Equally disturbing to Woodmason and those with similar views was the fact that traditional Native belief systems greatly influenced many settlers. When these belief systems merged with Christian ideals, as frequently occurred, new spiritual hybrids emerged. Such syncretism encouraged a greater reverence in the backcountry for nature in a nonhuman form (animals, plants) and less dogmatic interpretations of natural events. Though it is impossible to determine the number of backcountry residents who embraced hybrid beliefs, anecdotal evidence from the era provides clues. Many hunters participated in elaborate ceremonies celebrating the enduring spirit of animals recently killed for food or furs. Members of all communities interpreted storms and droughts as natural responses to disruptions in environmental harmony. Strategists planned battles and hunting expeditions based on the menstrual patterns of women and their impact on living conditions. Though they were far from identical to modern-day environmentalists in terms of their goals, settlers who engaged in these practices tended to respect and protect their natural surroundings as much for spiritual considerations as for practical, subsistence-related reasons. Both rebels and Loyalists often attributed their successes or failures in military campaigns to the spirituality of participants.

More secular-minded inhabitants of the backcountry also constructed their worldviews based on the setting in which they lived. This is not to say that popular philosophies had no impact in the region. Once fighting began in the 1770s, the revolutionary ideas of John Adams, Thomas Jefferson, and Thomas Paine gradually filtered into the region and influenced the loyalties of residents. Many grizzled and sometimes illiterate traders, trappers, and farmers understood and could recite the viewpoints of philosophers such as Locke and Voltaire. But ideas dealing with topics such as natural rights and republican virtues had practical impact only if melded with daily concerns. Most settlers struggled to survive on a daily basis and held somewhat fatalistic views of the world, regardless of their knowledge of Enlightenment or pre-Enlightenment thinkers. Self-preservation had to be the main concern, and pragmatism dominated day-to-day activities. Thus in 1775, when a backcountry traveler "entered into discourse on politics" with a resident "which ended in high words," concerns for survival determined the outcome. The prudent traveler eventually decided to withdraw from the debate when his adversary "threatened to tar and feather" him (Cresswell, 1928, 74). The same person might hold diametrically opposite beliefs at the same time, or change beliefs radically and quickly, and the same was true of whole communities. Foreign ideas, items, and people could be warmly embraced one evening, only to be violently rejected the next morning. King George III's policies could be wholeheartedly supported at the beginning of a community meeting and then roundly booed at the end, even if he or his government had not been a primary topic of conversation. Rather than illustrating mindless confusion, such changes in attitude reflected the constantly changing needs, desires, and realities of backcountry life, even during times of warfare.

Cultural Ties

Although backcountry cultures constantly evolved, certain themes can be detected. Relative to other colonial sections, the backcountry before and during the Revolution probably had less disparity in terms of economic and social classes than any other region. Material wealth such as expensive clothing, fine-crafted furniture, or fancy houses seldom appeared and represented an aberration. Those who possessed much land, goods, or currency typically dressed like those who possessed little and lived in dwellings almost identical to those inhabited by the poorest in the community. Often labeled "English wigwams," these structures usually had dirt floors and little furniture, though many were enclosed by crude wooden forts or barricades for protection (Hoffer, 2000, 378). Ostentation involved efforts that detracted from subsistence patterns or profit making and seemed unnecessary to most colonists. In a letter to friends on the East Coast, a settler arriving in modern-day Kentucky just after the war wrote, "Believe me my dear friends the sight of a log house on these Mountains after a fatiguing days Journey affords more real pleasure that all the magnificent buildings your city contains" (Mary Dewees's journal). During the fighting, both rebels and loyalists at times selected their enemies based on displays of wealth. The few that amassed riches and wanted to display their material success usually departed backcountry settings for seaboard communities that seemed much more appreciative of such displays. Nonetheless, wealth and social status did have a significant impact. Leadership standing in the community often depended on family background, amount of capital, and manifestations of knowledge. For the most part though, recent accomplishments in the community proved much more important, and consensus prestige lasted only briefly. A person's standing generally changed based on what he contributed to urgent needs in terms of words, actions, or items. These standards frequently determined military leadership roles in the region during the war years.

As for family structure, the backcountry tended toward extremes. Families either had one or no children or consisted of extended kin groups with multiple offspring and generations inhabiting the same household. Survival needs led to the incorporation of children into various types of labor at an early age. Frequent migration and mortality ensured little continuity in terms of household duties and membership, though in some areas, dozens of family members inhabited the same locale. Kinship networks could also extend over great distances, and they maintained connections between backcountry settlements and seaboard towns. Late eighteenth-century immigrants from Europe often disembarked on the coast and then traveled inland to the backcountry, in the process, maintaining kinship ties that bound peoples together in the Old World. Long-term, transatlantic bonds often suffered, however, as a result of the fighting and interruptions of communication associated with the American Revolution.

The life of Rebecca Ryan Boone illustrates the complexity of family life in the Revolution-era backcountry. Upon marrying the soon-to-be-famous Daniel in 1756, Rebecca instantly became matriarch for a diverse assortment of family relations located in western North Carolina. Within two years and before she turned the age of twenty, Rebecca had two sons of her own and took responsibility for the two young sons of Daniel's dead brother. Over the next two decades, she had a total of ten children. Many of her offspring married young, had babies of their own, and continued to live in Rebecca's home. When she reached her forties, Rebecca adopted six motherless nieces and nephews of her widowed brother and by this time supervised several African American slaves of varying ages as well. Most of the time, Rebecca looked after her boarders and kin alone, Daniel being away on hunting or military expeditions. She also managed this household as it moved from North Carolina to present-day Kentucky on two different occasions. Even in the last years of her life, Rebecca continued to welcome visitors to her household. In this regard, the Revolution seemed to have limited effect (Faragher, 1992, 43, 47, 236–237, 313).

Formal education and literacy were generally limited in the eighteenth-century backcountry, though in some places, learned skills appeared at proportionally greater rates than in other regions of colonial America. In the words of one observer of settlers in Georgia's western lands, "I found these people, contrary to what a traveler might . . . reasonably expect from their occupation and remote situation from the capital or any commercial town, to be civil and courteous: and though educated as it were in the woods, no strangers to sensibility" (Van Doren, 1955, 255). No public school system existed in the colonies at this time, and the primary purveyors of organized education, religious organizations, had few resources for such endeavors in the backcountry. But many residents still obtained needed skills from family, friends, or business associates out of necessity. This occurred because some talents associated with schooling—reading, writing, and basic mathematics—became necessary for those involved in trade or cross-cultural interaction. Moreover, a greater percentage of multilingual people lived in the backcountry than elsewhere, due to the ongoing necessity of understanding various European and Native peoples and interpreting vital legal or imperial documents. For the most part, however, reading material of all types was limited, as was the flow of foreign news and information. Paradoxically, during the American Revolution, formal educational opportunities declined, but the availability of reading materials increased.

Overall, standards and morals in the region were very flexible, and rigid codes of right and wrong did not endure. The diverse nature of society on all levels prohibited consensus on such matters, and most members of backcountry communities preferred not to provoke disharmony by asserting minority viewpoints. Consequently, attitudes and standards deemed conservative or progressive by today's measures alternately dictated community behavior and expectations with no rhyme or reason. The most important values that

Daniel Boone

Few individuals illustrate the backcountry experience and its complexities during the American Revolution better than Daniel Boone. Despite the multiple myths characterizing his existence that were prevalent during his lifetime and still linger today, Boone's activities during this period reflect the dynamics of the society in which he lived.

Born along the unsettled fringes of western Pennsylvania in 1734, the son of an English Quaker developed into a skilled and avid hunter as a youth and thus became familiar with the largely unsettled areas where game, Euro-American hunters, and Native American travelers frequently intermingled. Possessing great disdain for farming, as a teenager Boone embarked on several "long hunts," expeditions lasting over several months for the purpose of amassing enough animal pelts to be sold for profit upon return home. Though he achieved modest economic success as a result, the hunter increasingly felt crowded by newly arriving settlers and relocated to the Carolina backcountry in the 1750s, where he subsequently married and started a family. Even in this locale, however, Boone constantly moved his home in attempts to be closer to hunting grounds and farther away from colonial obstructions. During a "long hunt" in 1769, he became one of the first Anglo-Americans to visit and map the future state of Kentucky. Impressed by his discovery, Boone persuaded about fifty of his Carolina neighbors to build a settlement in the region, despite the fact that he had no legal

Daniel Boone was a pioneer who established a route through the Appalachians and helped establish Kentucky's first white settlement. (*Library of Congress*)

title to the lands or governmental permission to settle them. These factors proved significant, as the expedition failed due to attacks by Shawnee, Delaware, and Cherokee Indians fearing settler incursion into their traditional hunting lands. In 1775, Boone made another settlement attempt in Kentucky, this time with more promising results. By the end of the year, the

guided social relationships were respect, justice, and compensation. Those seeking redress for wrongs almost always cited desire for satisfaction of at least one of these principles and could not be pacified until their expectations were fulfilled. All backcountry inhabitants held these ideals dear, though their interpretations of what they meant often differed. For these reasons, rights and grievances proclaimed by colonists on the seaboard typically had different connotations and impacts among residents in the backcountry.

hunter had established the outpost of Boonesborough, hundreds of settlers had migrated to the region, and land surveyors had begun marking the lands for future purchase and settlement. Boone's ongoing quest for open lands appeared to have concluded successfully (Hinderaker and Mancall, 2003, 161–163).

Yet when the American Revolution began, life remained precarious for the pioneer and his fellow settlers in the Kentucky backcountry. A series of raids and reprisals by local Shawnees (sometimes affiliated with the British, sometimes not) initiated an ongoing guerilla conflict between Indians and settlers that involved mutual attacks, kidnappings, murders, and destruction of property. Consequently, hundreds of colonists streamed back east across the Appalachians and some of the settlements became ghost towns. Boone himself almost died due to wounds received through combat and in 1778 was captured by the Shawnees. Upon his escape and return to Boonesborough, many of his fellow settlers, most of whom supported the Independence movement, questioned his loyalties and never valued his leadership again. According to his own words, Boone proclaimed neutrality in the conflict, preferring pragmatism and survival over ideological affiliation. Unnerved by the situation, the wanderer devoted his next efforts to economic ventures. As the war raged, he became a recruiter of settlers for Kentucky and was employed by land speculators hoping to prosper in the region upon the conflict's conclusion. In this capacity, he regained the trust of

enough Kentuckians to be elected as a representative in the Virginia Assembly (Virginia was the colony that claimed control of Kentucky). Briefly captured by British forces during his journey to the capital, upon his release Boone's political career proved less than praiseworthy. Most of his time in Virginia was spent hunting and socializing with friends, leading state officials on at least one occasion to order his arrest so that he might be present for legislative business.

Boone could never fully escape the war's violence, however. Even as fighting diminished in other colonial regions, it intensified in Kentucky, highlighted by the Battle of Blue Licks in August 1782. In the skirmish between British-allied Indians and rebel colonists, dozens of Boone's neighbors were killed along with one of his sons, Israel. Though this was the last major battle of the war in the backcountry, sporadic violence between settlers and Indians continued into the 1790s. As with most backcountry residents, Boone's life had been changed forever due to the conflict. In addition to the physical suffering of his family and destruction of personal property, he lost much of the prestige he had once enjoyed among his fellow settlers. At the same time, the fighting enabled him to expand his economic opportunities and become a political figure in the fledgling state. Combined, Boone's experiences typified the overall backcountry experience in the American Revolution. Loyalties and conditions shifted, but the local setting continued to determine one's activities (Faragher, 1992, 131–223).

Wartime Disruptions

When fighting broke out between British soldiers and rebellious colonists in 1775, the backcountry quickly became a setting for each side to assert its perceived rights and resolve its ongoing grievances. At times this involved traditional combat, though for the most part, the conflict manifested itself in other ways. Neither group orchestrated major campaigns, troop movements, or territorial acquisitions in the region with any consistency during the war. Compared to the seaboard colonies, the backcountry experienced few significant battles or destruction of communities. Nevertheless, many indirect effects of the war could be felt in all backcountry locations. Customary trade systems faltered, Native-settler interaction took on different forms, and local, regional, and international loyalties shifted. Diplomats from both sides constantly traveled through the region trying to enlist support, alternately through bribery and threats. Scavenging expeditions suddenly arrived to seize goods or demand various types of labor. Veterans of the fighting appeared in many settlements spreading news of their experiences and at times emphasizing the conflict's brutality through fresh scars and missing limbs. By the time the war officially ended in 1783, its impact could be seen or felt in most backcountry communities, even if the residents failed to appreciate the changes.

For the most part, violence associated with the Revolution arose from previously existing local disputes. In western New York and Pennsylvania, historic disagreements between settlers and Iroquois Indians over boundaries and trade resulted in the settlers joining the Revolution and most Iroquois Indians joining the British and devoting much of their efforts to destroying one another's homes and economic resources. A similar situation emerged in the western Carolinas and what later became eastern Tennessee, as Cherokee Indians and local settlers used the fighting to attack one another and seek revenge for mutual atrocities dating back to the Seven Years' War of the 1750s and 1760s. In the end, these conflicts resulted in little advantages for either the British or rebels, but did strengthen settler claims to more western lands once the war ended and the new nation came into being.

Certain specific incidents merit attention due to their immediate impact on backcountry society and cultural interaction. One of the more colorful, though less well-known, campaigns centered on an expedition led by James Willing. A supporter of the Revolution with connections to the Continental Congress in Philadelphia, Willing devised a plan to secure the Ohio and lower Mississippi rivers. After receiving arms and supplies from the Continental Army at Fort Pitt (Pittsburgh) in January 1778, the adventurer embarked on his voyage with thirty volunteers in a boat named *Rattletrap*. Along the way, the force grew to over 100 men before landing at the settlement of Walnut Hills (present-day Vicksburg, Mississippi). After seizing control of the outpost from British agents, Willing's group proceeded down the river to the larger town of Natchez, where all inhabitants were rounded up and forced to sign loyalty oaths to the "United States of America." The contingent continued south along the river repeating the process until they finally arrived at Spanish-held New Orleans in March. After a short stay, during which his presence provoked heated diplomatic exchanges and near bloodshed between Spanish garrisons in Louisiana and British outposts in Florida, Willing with some of his followers departed New Orleans in November with intentions of acquiring parts of the Gulf Coast for rebel use. Soon thereafter, however, he was captured by British soldiers, transferred to New York, and held as a prisoner of war until just prior to the Revolution's conclusion (Starr, 1976, 83–121).

Though Willing's excursion resulted in the death of few British soldiers or subjects and no long-term territorial exchanges, it did disrupt society along the southern Mississippi River. Willing's followers seized cattle and food during the campaign as well as numerous slaves of Loyalist inhabitants. Some residents' houses were burned in addition, though in at least one instance, such destruction resulted from a prewar feud between Willing and the building's owner, and thus reflected backcountry notions of justice. By the time the campaign reached New Orleans, local residents had deemed Willing a scoundrel and his supporters banditti. Stories of the band's atrocities reached as far east as British-held Pensacola within days and heightened hysteria among regional inhabitants. One Loyalist resident near New Orleans exaggerated when he wrote that Willing's men had "cleared all the English side of the river of its inhabitants, and nothing [is] to be seen but destruction and desolation." In reality, Willing's efforts often reflected typical notions of backcountry fairness. On one occasion, his forces came upon a settlement jointly owned by a Loyalist and a rebel. Rather than destroy everything on the site, the commander ordered that only half the slaves and goods of the plantation be seized, taking great care not to unjustly punish the patriotic partner (Starr, 1976, 83–121).

More well known and indicative of cross-cultural relationships in the backcountry are the actions taken by George Rogers Clark, a relative of the famous explorer, William, who later participated in the famed Lewis and Clark expedition. In 1778, rebel leaders in Virginia sent George and a contingent of hunters and traders into what are today Kentucky, Illinois, and Missouri to dislodge British forces, pacify hostile Indians, and assert American claims to the region. Clark and his companions built forts near the ancient Native trading city of Cahokia on the Mississippi River, as well as in the neighboring former French outposts of Kaskaskia and Vincennes. Hoping to impede these efforts, an army of British soldiers, Indian warriors, and French trappers from Detroit journeyed to the area and engaged the rebels throughout the latter months of the year, at one point seizing control of Vincennes. By early 1779, however, a lack of supplies and declining morale slowly debilitated the British-led force, allowing Clark to regain control of Vincennes and conduct further military operations in the southern Great Lakes hinterlands. Unfortunately for the rebellious colonists, Clark's contingent failed to make substantial territorial gains and by the end of the war still had not secured this section of the backcountry for the Patriot cause (Nobles, 1997, 90–91).

As these events unfolded, backcountry standards of propriety manifested themselves, along with some of the most savage atrocities recorded during the American Revolution. Upon being surrounded at Vincennes by Clark and his men, the British commander, known by the telling name of Henry "the Hair Buyer" Hamilton, extended a flag of truce indicating his force's surrender. Before acknowledging the overture, Clark decided to seek retribution for the many settler scalps he believed that Hamilton and his Native allies had played a part in obtaining. In full view of the British soldiers remaining in the fort, Clark executed four Indians who had previously assisted Hamilton. According to eyewitness accounts, Clark had the natives held down, hacked to death, and thrown into the nearby river. Only after the

British colonel Henry Hamilton surrenders Fort Sackville, near the village of Vincennes, to George Rogers Clark. (*National Archives and Records Administration*)

executions did the rebel commander accept Hamilton's surrender, reportedly "with his hands and face still reeking from the human sacrifice in which he had acted as chief priest" (Barnhart, 1951, 248).

Such grisly examples of the American Revolution's impact in the back-country tell only part of the story. Much more common were the day-to-day hardships endured by the region's families as indirect results of the conflict. In this regard, the experiences of Elizabeth Jackson, mother of the future U.S. president Andrew Jackson, reveal a great deal. At the time the war began, Elizabeth lived in the Waxhaws, an ill-defined settlement about 160 miles northwest of Charleston located along the border of North and South Carolina. She was a long-term inhabitant of the region, and her life up to this point had mirrored that of many female settlers in similar situations. Two years after the family immigrated to the region from Ireland, Elizabeth's husband died, leaving her pregnant and with sole responsibility for her two young sons. Subsequently taking up residence in her physically disabled sister's home, she assumed management of the household as well as supervision over numerous other relatives and boarders. In this position, Elizabeth worked to keep her extended family together while instilling in her sons values common to backcountry settings. According to Andrew, she insisted that he should never steal, tell a lie, hurt the feelings of those around him, or suffer injustice in any form. Above all, he should not rely on others to provide solutions to his problems and must "settle them cases yourself!" (Remini, 1969, 15).

Like many of her neighbors, Elizabeth's day-to-day existence was transformed as a result of the war. When British and rebel forces clashed in the Waxhaws during the spring of 1780, she joined other females in converting the local meetinghouse into a hospital and then assumed duties as a nurse and provider for hundreds of debilitated soldiers. Elizabeth's new routine proved short-lived after she discovered that two of her sons, Andrew and Robert, had been captured by British troops for supporting rebel armies and imprisoned forty miles from their home. Obtaining two horses under difficult conditions, she journeyed alone to the prison camp, where she was able to obtain the release of her sons. Upon returning home, she successfully nursed Andrew back to health from both injuries and smallpox, though Robert soon died. Rather than mourn her son's loss, Elizabeth then joined two other women from the community and journeyed by foot and horseback to Charleston in order to care for other relatives being held there in prison ships. A short time after arriving on the coast, the Jackson matriarch visited another relative in the area and while there became sick with cholera. Her subsequent death in Charleston proved to be a devastating and perhaps ironic tragedy for the dozens of dependents she had cared for in the Carolina borderlands (Remini, 1969, 17–19).

The experiences of Willing, Clark, Jackson, and others symbolize the varied impact of the American Revolution on backcountry communities. Organized campaigns and sporadic engagements, with their consequences, led to many deaths, even in locales far removed from the major theaters of the war. At the same time, effects of the Revolution that had nothing to do with military confrontations also made their mark and disrupted economies, lifestyles, family relationships, and intercultural contact. In addition to these effects, the war played a major factor in determining future backcountry settler identities. Memories of the conflict shaped understandings of the region and its peoples well into the nineteenth century.

Conclusion

Seen from the perspective of backcountry residents, the American Revolution takes on a different meaning. Protests commonly heard in seaboard colonies such as "no taxation without representation" and "independence at any price" resonated quite differently among settlers on the colonial margins. Though many in the backcountry shared these sentiments, their actions almost always reflected the realities of the setting in which they lived and thus depended on different dynamics. Supporters and opponents of the independence movement characterized key issues based on the unique modes of interaction common to their communities. Population diversity, standards of leadership and dissent, work and economic conditions, spiritual and philosophical norms, as well as societal and cultural mores influenced backcountry settler perceptions of independence and related warfare in distinctive ways. The experiences of the Paxton Rebels, the Carolina Regulators, James Willing, George Rogers Clark, Elizabeth Jackson, and others represent the impact of these variables on backcountry participation in the revolutionary conflict. As a result, peoples of the region experienced and remembered the War for American Independence in ways quite distinct from most other colonists. Nevertheless, certain experiences and themes transcended geographical locales and participant experiences. Much like residents in other colonial regions, inhabitants of the backcountry endured hardship, loss, and disillusionment while severing ties to a once revered homeland and celebrating new ideologies and freedoms. These shared experiences in many ways eroded regional barriers and fostered the growth of a new American identity shaped as much by seaboard sensibilities as backcountry realities. In this sense, the backcountry's impact on the revolutionary conflict and later societal development in the future United States offers important alternate perspectives that must be taken into account.

References and Further Reading

Barnhart, John D., ed. *Henry Hamilton and George Rogers Clark in the American Revolution with the Unpublished Journal of Lieut. Gov. Henry Hamilton*. Crawfordsville, IN: R. E. Banta, 1951.

Bellesiles, Michael. *Revolutionary Outlaws: Ethan Allen and the Struggle for Independence on the Early American Frontier*. Charlottesville: University Press of Virginia, 1993.

Breen, T. H., and Timothy Hall. *Colonial America in an Atlantic World*. New York: Pearson-Longman, 2004.

Calloway, Colin G. *New Worlds for All: Indians, Europeans, and the Remaking of Early America*. Baltimore: Johns Hopkins University Press, 1997.

Cayton, Andrew R. L., and Fredrika J. Teute, eds. *Contact Points: American Frontiers from the Mohawk Valley to the Mississippi, 1750–1830*. Chapel Hill: University of North Carolina Press, 1998.

Cresswell, Nicholas. *The Journal of Nicholas Cresswell, 1774–1777*. Edited by Lincoln MacVeagh. New York: Dial, 1928.

Faragher, John Mack. *Daniel Boone: The Life and Legend of an American Pioneer*. New Haven, CT: Yale University Press, 1992.

Greene, Jack P., ed. *Colonies to Nation: A Documentary History of the American Revolution, 1763–1789*. New York: Norton, 1975.

Hinderaker, Eric. *Elusive Empires: Constructing Colonialism in the Ohio Valley, 1673–1800*. New York: Cambridge University Press, 1997.

Hinderaker, Eric, and Peter C. Mancall. *At the Edge of Empire: The Backcountry in British North America*. Baltimore: Johns Hopkins University Press, 2003.

Hoffer, Peter C. *The Brave New World: A History of Early America*. New York: Houghton Mifflin, 2000.

"Mary Dewees's journal describing her journey from Philadelphia to Lexington, Kentucky," Reuben T. Durrett Collection on Kentucky and the Ohio River Valley, Durrett Codex Collection, Special Collections Research Center, University of Chicago Library, American Memory Collection, online collection of Library of Congress. http://memory.loc.gov/ammem/index. html (accessed December 14, 2006).

Merritt, Jane T. *At the Crossroads: Indians and Empires on a Mid-Atlantic Frontier, 1700–1763*. Chapel Hill: University of North Carolina Press, 2003.

Morse, Jedidiah. *The American geography, or, a view of the present situation of the United States of America: containing astronomical geography; geographical definitions, discovery, and general description . . . a particular description of Kentucky, the western territory south of Ohio, and Vermont . . . with a view of the British, Spanish, French, Portuguese, and Dutch dominions, on the continent, and in the West Indies*. London: Stockdale, 1794.

Nobles, Gregory H. "Breaking into the Backcountry: New Approaches to the Early American Frontier." *William and Mary Quarterly*, 3rd ser., 46 (1989): 641–670.

Nobles, Gregory H. *American Frontiers: Cultural Encounters and Continental Conquest*. New York: Hill and Wang, 1997.

Pittman, Philip. *The Present State of the European Settlements of the Mississippi* [1770]. Edited by Robert Rea. Gainesville: University Press of Florida, 1973.

Remini, Robert V. *Andrew Jackson*. New York: Harper and Row, 1969.

Risjord, Norman K. *Jefferson's America*. Boston: Rowman and Littlefield, 2002.

Rohrbough, Malcolm J. *The Trans-Appalachian Frontier: People, Societies, and Institutions, 1775–1850*. New York: Oxford University Press, 1978.

Smith, Paul H., ed. *Letters of Delegates to Congress, 1774–1789*. Washington, DC: Library of Congress, 1983.

Starr, J. Barton. *Tories, Dons, and Rebels: The American Revolution in British West Florida*. Gainesville: University Press of Florida, 1976.

Van Doren, Mark, ed. *Travels of William Bartram*. New York: Dover, 1955.

"Born in the Midst of Bloodshed and Battles": Children during the American Revolution

6

Elizabeth McKee Williams

Revolutionary America was a nation of young people. According to the first national census in 1790, almost half the U.S. population was under age sixteen (U.S. Census Bureau, 1975, 10). Sixteen was the age the census used to divide child from adult for the purpose of counting. Age sixteen marked adult status for some purposes, such as military service, but not for others, such as voting or signing contracts, and sons and daughters remained under varying degrees of parental control well into adulthood. (The concept of adolescence as a distinct period of life did not arise for another century.) Even if sixteen-year-olds are classified as adults, almost half the people who lived through the Revolution were children. This chapter will explore their experiences.

The Challenges of Family in Early America

American birthrates were high during this era, with women marrying relatively young and often bearing six, eight, or ten children. Benjamin Franklin wrote that America's abundant land allowed men and women to marry earlier. "By these early Marriages, we are blest with more Children, and, from the Mode among us—founded in Nature—of every mother suckling and nursing her own Child, more of them are raised. Thence, the swift Progress of Population, among us—unparallel'd in Europe" (Franklin, 1987, 836). The average birthrate varied by race and region, and statistical evidence is scattered and incomplete, but Franklin's observation fits the known facts. Women who married in their late teens had time to bear many children. Attempts to limit childbearing did not become significant until the nineteenth century (Gemery, 2000, 143–190).

Birthrates were high. Infant and child mortality rates were also high, but lower in America than in Europe. Childbirth was dangerous for both mother

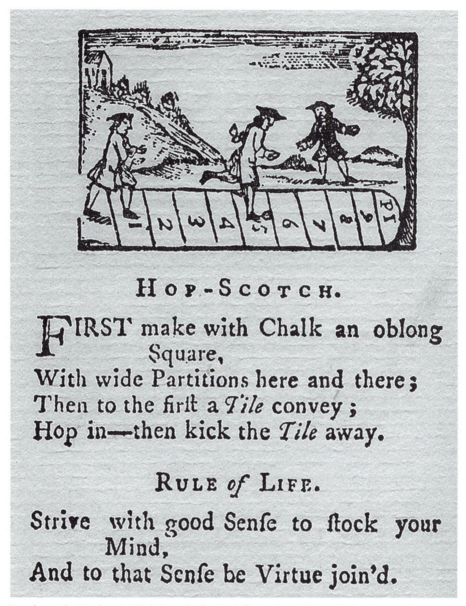

Page from John Newbery's *A Little Pretty Pocket-Book*, illustrating children playing hopscotch.
(*Newbery, John. 1744.* A Little Pretty Pocket-Book)

and baby. Historical records are incomplete, but we do know that mortality rates were lowest in New England and highest in the South. While most women did not die as a result of childbirth, they all would have known women who did, and people generally believed that, in giving birth, women risked death. For Americans of African descent, "historical records are scantier, but it seems clear that birthrates were somewhat lower than for white Americans, mortality rates higher" (Gemery, 2000, 143–190; Walsh, 2000, 191–240).

Most infants were born at home. The mother was typically attended by older women: family members and, in larger communities, experienced midwives. Diaries frequently record a woman's mother coming to assist with the childbirth, and with the management of the household and other children. Men were not involved in the birth process until shortly before the Revolution, when William Shippen of Philadelphia was one of the first American men to work as a "male-midwife," claiming to provide superior medical care at this dangerous event and starting the transition from female midwives to male physicians (Scholten, 1985; Schultz, 1985, 57–109).

As Franklin had noted, most American women chose to nurse their infants rather than send them out to nurse. Exceptions did occur when a woman was ill after childbirth. Elizabeth Drinker's journal records her reluctant decision in 1771 to follow her doctor's advice and have a neighbor woman nurse one of her sons. The baby was sent to the neighbor's home. But Drinker visited her son often, sometimes more than once a day, and finally instructed the woman to wean him so that he could come back home. Women knew that by breastfeeding they provided for the infant's health while increasing the interval between births, decreasing risks to their children and to themselves (Drinker, 1991).

Birth was only the first hazard the child faced, nor did threats to the child end after the first year of life. The period of teething was considered a time of danger, so much so that parents were often advised to hasten the process by lancing the child's gums. But the real health threat was weaning, rather than teething, as the young child moved to foods which might be less nutritious and faced high risk of contamination or spoilage.

Children who survived birth and weaning faced accident and disease. Drowning, accidents, and fire injured or killed many children. Joel Adams remembered his childhood primarily as a series of accidents. "When I was about three years old, I fell and hit my head, which injured me very much, and almost killed me; and when I was in my fifth year, I had my elbow put out of joint, by being pushed out the door at school, by one of the scholars; when I was about nine years old, I fell on the ice, which cut a hole in my head, and came very near killing me, and the next summer, by being thrown from a horse, I was badly hurt." Fire may have been the most frequent cause of serious injury to children. Chloe Willey recalled that, "At about the age of ten months, I was severely burnt, by being left alone in the house, while my mother was gone a little distance for water; during which time the house took fire, and I was taken from the flames by the vigilance of the neighbors. This disaster was so great to me, and the marks so visible, that I shall go down to the grave disfigured both in my face and hands. From this event my life was not expected for many weeks; but it pleased God to restore me." Her experience, unfortunately, was far from unique (Andrews, 1850; Willey, 1810).

Disease also took many young lives. Most children caught measles and other infectious diseases. Periodic outbreaks of diphtheria killed many children, and epidemics like the yellow fever epidemic of 1793 killed children along with their parents. In 1769 Martha and Ephraim Ballard lost three of their six children to diphtheria in just ten days. The girls were two, four, and eight years old when they died. The Ballards later had three more children. Their loss was dwarfed by that of Martha's aunt, who lost eight of her eleven children to disease (Ulrich, 1990, 12–13). But the most dreaded disease was smallpox. Until vaccination became widespread in the early nineteenth century, using the related and relatively benign cowpox virus, many people died of smallpox. Some eighteenth-century Americans had a chance to undergo inoculation, a controversial and dangerous procedure that involved injecting the patient with cells from an infected person. But inoculation was not always available and, at some times and places, it was illegal. The letters of Abigail Adams from fall 1775 describe her family's bout with dysentery and smallpox while John Adams was in Philadelphia with the Continental Congress. Their younger daughter Patty was ill for five weeks, while her siblings fell ill and recovered. Abigail's mother came to help nurse the sick, took ill, and died. Patty finally died one week after her grandmother's death. John Adams had been inoculated before their marriage, but Abigail's parents had forbidden her to undergo inoculation. While death rates from inoculation were much lower than from "natural" smallpox, the risk remained very real. The noted minister and theologian Jonathan Edwards was one of many who had died in previous years from smallpox inoculation (*Adams Papers,* 1963; Fenn, 2001).

Childbirth, accidents, and illness all took many young lives. These high mortality rates meant that every child would have grown up familiar with the experience of death: death of a parent, brother or sister, or a friend. They would also have grown up fully aware of the possibility of their own early death. And they would have understood that possibility within the context of their religious beliefs.

Religious Upbringings

Most Americans, both black and white, were Protestant Christians, with more northerners attending Congregational or Presbyterian churches, in the Calvinist tradition, more southerners worshipping as Anglicans or Episcopalians, and Quakers found primarily in the middle states. By the time of the Revolution, church membership had declined somewhat, and people were seldom required by law to attend public worship. Many families did attend church regularly, particularly those who lived in towns. Mary Palmer Tyler, who would become the wife of a Vermont Superior Court justice, recalled in 1818 that the children in her family took turns attending church, as the ladies had room in their carriage for one child.

Children who attended worship services stayed with their parents the entire time. Church buildings were seldom heated. In New England, large churches sometimes had walled compartments for families to sit in. A family was assigned a section or pew, with seating frequently based on social status, and could bring their own bench or chairs, and perhaps a small stove. Children sometimes sat on the floor. They were expected to behave and listen in church, as well as to study the Bible at home and to profit from that study. Colonial Americans had always had at least a few religious books written for children,

A father leads his son to church. The illustration, from *A Little Pretty Pocket-Book*, accompanies a chapter titled, "Rules for Behaviour." (*Library of Congress*)

starting with John Cotton's *Spiritual Milk for Boston Babes* (1646) and increasing in number during the eighteenth century. But most religious writing for children appeared in the decades after the Revolution, about the same time that the American Sunday School movement developed. During the Revolutionary era, children heard the same religious messages as did their parents.

Not all children attended public worship. Some had parents disinclined to take them; others lived in places that lacked regular worship. And children did not always understand what they saw and heard. James Jenkins, who later became a minister in South Carolina recalled, "We seldom heard preaching in those days. There was but one church in the Neck, and it was only occasionally supplied by a Presbyterian minister. I used to ride on the same horse with my father to meeting, but all that was said was as a sealed book to me, for I understood not the things that were spoken" (Jenkins, 1958, 10). Elias Smith, also a future minister from South Carolina, recalled being frightened by a public baptism: "Next the minister took another, younger than the first. This alarmed me, as I feared he might take me next, not knowing but he took some by force." Smith hid so that he would not be taken next (Smith, 1816, 30).

Many religious traditions emphasized a literal belief in heaven and hell, in original sin, and in the supreme importance of personal salvation. Believers reported intense emotional experiences of their own guilt and of God's mercy, and understood those conversion experiences as evidence of their own salvation. Children were taught that "In Adam's Fall, We Sinned All" and that they were doomed to hell unless saved by Christ, and they were encouraged to be open to conversion. Some young children reported conversion experiences, while others remembered seeking such experiences, or worrying at their absence. Abner Jones, raised in a farming family in Royalton, Massachusetts, recalled "thinking on death, judgment, and eternity. Although I was only 8 or 9 years old, the pride of my heart was so great, that I was ashamed to let anyone know that I felt concerned about my soul; neither could I bear to have any one see my crying; and so quenched the spirit of the Lord. I now felt the need of religion more than ever I had done before, I was fully convinced that I must be born again or be damned." Jones found a special rock at which he prayed regularly, seeking the conversion experience that he was to find at age ten (*New England Primer*; Jones, 1807).

Quaker children were not raised with this intense emphasis on original sin. Their theology affirmed the innocence of infants and young children, and that a child's sinful nature arose together with the ability to reason. Quaker parents strove to shelter their children from evil and to teach what was right. Quaker children attended public worship with their parents, starting as young as four, and sitting in silence. John Comly, who was born in 1773 and worked as a Quaker minister and schoolteacher remembered, "First-day afternoon meetings were held at Byberry meeting-house twice a month. These meetings furnished opportunities for children and young people to attend, and for parents to take their little ones to meeting. I also, among others, was taken by my concerned mother, who placed me by her side, and taught me to sit still." Comly wrote a lot about the value of silence and of children learning stillness. His narrative, like other Quaker ones, describes religious growth, including remorse at childhood bad behavior, but lacks the intense emotion of Calvinist religious narratives. He, like other Quaker children, was striving for purity and spiritual growth rather than salvation (Frost, 1973; Comly, 1853).

Parenting in Early America

Protestant religious tradition was one major source of authority that parents and community followed when shaping child-rearing practices. That tradition emphasized obedience, especially to the father, and involved breaking the child's will. Physical discipline was widely used: As the proverb stated, "Spare the rod and spoil the child." The other important child-rearing authority was John Locke. In 1693 Locke published *Some Thoughts Concerning Education*, and this work became increasingly influential in America after about 1750. Locke viewed childhood as an important developmental stage and assured parents that much natural development could be trusted rather than combated. For example, seventeenth-century parents had been advised to tightly swaddle infants, in order to keep their limbs straight and to keep them warm, and to prevent them from crawling on all fours like animals. Locke encouraged parents to dispense with tight swaddling and to permit infants to crawl. He assured parents that the children would progress to walking like adults, unharmed by having once crawled.

But Locke, with other Enlightenment writers like William Buchan, still advised parents to break the child's will. Discipline was to start in infancy. Parents were told to deny requests and to refuse to indulge a child's appetites in order to promote the virtues of self-control and self-denial. This discipline was to be enforced, not with physical force, but with emotional control through the giving or withholding of affection. Locke also recommended fresh air, simple diet, cold-water baths, and cold feet. He believed this regimen would harden the child, resulting in robust physical health. Buchan and other Europeans wrote advice manuals which, like Locke's, were sold in America.

Historians know approximately how many advice manuals were published and purchased, and what these manuals said. It is much harder to know how often or how fully the advice in those manuals was followed. Diaries and memoirs show that some parents did implement Locke's advice, occasionally creating lasting resentment in their children. Mary Palmer Tyler remembered her mother following Locke's advice on bare feet. "My parents, especially my mother, had just been reading Locke's celebrated work upon education, wherein he advocates the odious theory of letting children go barefoot, and, having become warm advocates of this cold doctrine, began that winter by letting us all run out upon the first snow and ice without shoes or stockings, intending to make us hardy and proof against the cold" (Tyler, 1925, 51). She reacted against this piece of Locke's advice in her memoir and in her own parenting. But, like her contemporaries, she found other suggestions of Locke's far more palatable.

By the Revolutionary era, in keeping with the advice of the Enlightenment writers, most parents had dispensed with swaddling and dressed infants and young children in simple, loose-fitting clothes. Young boys and girls dressed alike until age four or five, in loose frocks made of muslin, homespun, or coarse cloth, depending on the family's economic status. Diaries describe boys being "breeched" around age four or five, discarding the frocks for long trousers and jackets. These outfits were often modeled after the uniforms of soldiers or sailors. Girls often kept the simple frocks a little longer. Hairstyles were simpler too than in earlier decades. Boys and girls no longer wore miniature versions of adult styles; instead, both sexes wore their hair loose, shoulder length with bangs. Historians have understood this simple dress of childhood as one piece of evidence that late eighteenth-century Americans saw childhood as a distinct developmental period and did not view children simply as miniature adults (Reinier, 1996; Calvert, 1992).

Schooling the Revolutionary Generation

Literacy was much more widespread in America than in England. Most white children learned to read, either at home or at school. At home, children were often taught by parents or by older siblings. A few black children were taught to read at home, a practice which had not yet been made illegal. Literacy in past centuries is hard to measure. Historians have studied documents to see how many people could write their name, using the ability to write as a way to guess at people's ability to read. But some people

Mary Hunt Palmer

Mary Hunt Palmer was born in 1775, to an affluent Boston family. She was the second of nine children. Her family actively supported the Revolution, with her father and uncles participating in the Boston Tea Party before she was born and the Battle of Lexington when she was an infant. Mary remembered being frightened by a large group of army officers, until she learned that they were not British troops, but French allies, come to help. She was too young to remember the disruptions and violence of the war, but remembered the adults dancing for joy in 1783 when peace was declared.

Education was not taken for granted in Mary's family. Her maternal grandfather had believed that boys should be educated for the good of the country, but that girls need not learn to read or write; if they could make a shirt and a pudding, that was enough. Mary's aunt never learned to read, and her mother learned in her late teens, taught by the young man she later married. Mary's grandmother lectured her for "wasting time" by reading rather than sewing while she tended her baby brothers and sisters. Fortunately, Mary's parents did not share her grandparents' attitude. Mary did not go to school, but was taught at home by her mother and father, and by an unusual houseguest. A French army officer spent weeks with her family while recovering from his wounds, and he offered to teach the older children penmanship.

The Palmer children enjoyed playing outdoors, exploring an abandoned farmhouse, and wading on the tidal flats, collecting shells at low tide. Once they went too far, wading out to an island and being trapped there by the rising tide until her father rescued them.

Wartime inflation and currency devaluation destroyed the Hunt family fortunes. Mr. Hunt's business ventures failed, and he needed cash to repay his debts. He sold much of his land, but the paper money fell so quickly in value that his creditors refused it as worthless.

Mary was sharply confronted with her family's changed status. Her father's friend Elbridge Gerry invited her to go with his family for a year to New York City. She was to help tend the baby and to be inoculated against smallpox along with the Gerry family. The Hunts thought

who could read well never learned to write. They are harder to find in the historical record, but their numbers may have been very high (Spufford, 1979, 407–435).

By the time of the Revolution, formal schooling was becoming more widespread. Some towns were required to provide a school, but children were not required to attend. Schools often held separate sessions in winter and summer, with both boys and girls of all ages attending. Most schools taught only reading, writing, and arithmetic, the three Rs. Some schools taught only one subject, perhaps reading or writing. Formal schooling was almost entirely limited to white children and was rarely available on the Western frontier.

School attendance was often sporadic, and some people measured their attendance in days rather than in terms or years. Elias Smith's experience was not unusual. He lived in New England, and his formal schooling was limited to two short segments. When he was fifteen, his uncle taught a school and invited Elias to attend.

she would be treated as part of the family, but instead she found that she was treated as a servant. She never ate with the family, but ate in the kitchen with the servants or in the nursery. When company came, including guests who had been friends of her parents, she would bring the baby in to be admired and stand gazing at the floor until she was asked to take him back to the nursery. When she could, she eagerly returned to her family.

In 1790, shortly after Mary returned from New York, her family left Boston for the Vermont frontier, where they tried to adjust to life as poor farmers. Farm work was hard for her parents, and the family missed city foods and pastimes, but the children enjoyed playing and working outdoors. They learned to milk cows, make butter and cheese, and spin flax, wool, and cotton. Mary spent many happy hours picking berries with her brothers and sisters, almost always taking along a book. But rural life could be hazardous for children. One night the kitchen fire went out. Rather than struggle with the tinderbox, Mary's mother sent George, age five or six, to fetch a live coal from a neigh-

bor. A piece of it fell down his clothes, burning him badly as he ran home screaming. He suffered for weeks; his mother held him in her lap day and night, using both home remedies and doctors' advice. They managed to avoid infection, and George finally recovered, but he was lame for months afterward.

Even though Mary had never attended school herself, at age eighteen she taught school for three months in Vermont. She lived with a farmer's family and taught her dozen small students well, but was eager to return home when the three months were over. Not long after, she married family friend Royall Tyler, who was eighteen years her senior. Mary went on to have eleven healthy children. Years later, she drew on her successful experience raising those children to write a child-care book, *The Maternal Physician, by an American Matron*, which was published anonymously, one of the first child-care books written by an American woman.

S O U R C E : *Grandmother Tyler's Book: The Recollections of Mary Palmer Tyler, 1775–1866.*

My desire being very great to go, my father consented that I should attend one month. This I considered a great privilege indeed; and the first Monday in January 1785, I was, to my great joy, received as a member of the school, where I expected in one month to acquire much useful information. My uncle examined me as to the knowledge of letters . . . and said "you must learn grammar."—This was new business to me. . . .

On my return home, I informed my father of the study I had entered upon. He was not at all pleased with it; and told me, arithmetic was much more useful, as I could read some, and was entirely ignorant of the use of figures. This greatly dampened my zeal, as he almost forbid my pursuing the study of grammar. (Smith, 1816, 49–50, 89–91)

Elias's uncle persuaded his father to allow him to study grammar. Three years later, in "the winter of my eighteenth year, my father allowed me ten days to attend school to learn arithmetic, in which time I obtained some knowledge of the science. This was the last time of my attending school, and all attained to that time was but little" (Smith, 1816, 49–50, 89–91).

Memoirs written by people who were children during the Revolutionary era described school days filled with various forms of reading aloud, memorization, and recitation. Beginning readers and advanced students learned in the same room. Physical punishment was used regularly, often administered using the strap or the rod, and often more harshly to older boys than to younger boys or to girls. Most students said they studied reading and writing, and most boys—but not girls—mentioned learning arithmetic, often to the rule of three. Those boys headed for college mentioned having studied Latin.

Of course, not all children lived in towns large enough to provide a school. Children in rural areas might live for a time with relatives who lived near a school. But many areas of the South or along the frontier simply lacked schools. Children there were taught by parents or other available adults, or were not taught at all. Many of them educated themselves, in later childhood or as adults, following in the footsteps of Benjamin Franklin and sometimes using his *Autobiography* as their model.

Wealthy families who lived far from schools sometimes hired a tutor to live in their home and teach their children. The children of relatives or of neighbors might also be included. Philip Vickers Fithian, a recent graduate of Princeton College, worked for one year in eastern Virginia as a tutor for the many children of Robert Carter III of Nomini Hall. Fithian kept a journal of his life as a tutor. He described teaching eight children lessons that ranged from learning to write to Latin lessons. Fithian, who was studying for the Anglican ministry, was very well equipped to teach the sons and daughters of the Virginia gentry (Farish, 1943). But some tutors and teachers, like Elias Smith or young Mary Palmer, were not so well prepared.

Smith taught school at age seventeen despite the fact that he "had no learning. . . . I could write but poorly, and did not understand the rules of writing, and, to save my life, could not enumerate three figures." Smith managed, reading *Fenner's Grammar* at night to keep ahead of his pupils. Only after his first term as a teacher did he gain his father's permission and return to school for ten days to learn arithmetic (Smith, 1816, 89). For American children in the late eighteenth century, access to schools was uneven, school attendance was sporadic, and the teachers and lessons varied wildly. Yet American children of this era had unprecedented opportunities to achieve education, and many of them did so.

In 1770 the United States had nine colleges, which only a very few boys were able to attend. Boys started college young, often around age fourteen. The college curriculum was mostly classical, emphasizing Greek and Latin. To enter college, boys needed to pass tests in subjects like math and Latin. Girls had no opportunity to attend college, though a very few studied subjects like Latin at home. Nabby Adams, oldest child of John and Abigail, learned Latin alongside her younger brothers. Learning at the college level at home, with or without parental encouragement, was the only option for many girls and boys.

The Revolutionary War interrupted or ended formal schooling for some children. Fighting in the neighborhood would of course have disrupted school schedules. Colleges were also disrupted; Princeton closed entirely for months, its main building used variously as a stable, barracks, and hospital. Children of all ages sometimes left school if their father went to war. And some boys left school to go to war.

The eighteenth century saw a major expansion of English language books written specifically for children. Those books might be religious, educational or, increasingly, intended to be read for enjoyment. Englishman John Newbery was the first large-scale author and publisher of children's books, launching an industry that was to expand greatly in the nineteenth century. He published books on manners and morals, books of science and of stories, and those books were sold and read in both England and America. During the colonial era, English books had sometimes been adapted and reprinted for American audiences. Fully American texts emerged slowly in the years after the Revolution. One of the first was Noah Webster's *American Spelling Book*, first published in 1785. This book prescribed standardized American spelling of words and incorporated into the lessons American history and republican virtues (Murray, 1998; Kiefer, 1948).

Diaries and memoirs can offer evidence of what books children used in school as well as of what they read for fun. Some described, and lamented, an almost total lack of books. Some boys and girls calmly listed the novels and plays they read, while others described novels as sinful. And some children read books written for adults, ranging from controversial novels to works like *Pilgrim's Progress*.

Throughout the eighteenth century, children were economic assets to their families. Expenses specific to each additional child were minimal, and even young children contributed to the family's economic well-being. Children from all but the wealthiest families worked at a wide variety of often age- and gender-specific tasks. They worked within their own households and sometimes outside of their home.

A Life of Labor

Children started work at a very early age. One of their earliest tasks, sometimes assigned to boys and girls as young as four or five, was to watch younger children. Boys and girls of all ages often worked together at outdoor tasks like gathering berries, and they often found ways to make those tasks fun. Gender often influenced a child's work, with girls taking on their mother's household chores and boys working with the men. Class and race also shaped a child's work. Children of the elites were given work that might rather be considered part of their education, tasks like studying or needlework. Enslaved children often watched young white children as their first task, and they were assigned cleaning chores or field work at early ages.

A child's work could be physically dangerous. Both the kitchen and the farm were filled with hazards. Toddlers, supervised by siblings only a couple of years older, too often fell into kettles and buckets, fell on the stove, or fell into the fire. Children were scalded by boiling water for cooking or laundry, or were cut by knives in the kitchen and by axes out of doors. Philander Chase (a deacon and farmer from New Hampshire who always wrote of himself in the third person) described two "painful accidents . . . which totally changed the course of his future life." At Bethel, when visiting his sister, he cut with an axe his foot transversely nearly through in the middle. When in the course of a year and more this was healed, he had the misfortune, as it was called, while in the pursuit of his duty in preparing a field for wheat, in Cornish, to break his leg, and otherwise "bruise his limb." In his memoir he described how his father led him to see those injuries as signs that he should give up his plan to be a farmer, and instead study, attend Dartmouth College, and become a minister, which he did (Chase, 1848, 1:15).

Boys were sometimes formally apprenticed, though less often after independence was declared than in the colonial period. An apprentice was bound to serve for a period of years, during which time he was to be housed, fed, educated, and taught a trade. Ideally, a boy would agree to the apprenticeship and be interested in learning that trade, but of course many individual situations fell far short of that ideal. The Revolutionary War gave dissatisfied apprentices another place to run away to, further bringing the apprentice system to an end.

Continuing the colonial tradition, if a father could not support his family, the children could be "bound out" by the town authorities. They were then required to live with and work for another man in town, and were to receive in exchange basic support and, at least in theory, a basic education. On occasion, children were bound out because their fathers were in the army or had died in the war. Arial Bragg, who eventually became a shoemaker and colonel in the army, tells a pathetic story in his memoir of how he and his siblings were dispersed to different households, to spend miserable years as servants and apprentices after his father died of disease while in the army (Bragg, 1846).

Apprenticeship, both voluntary and involuntary, became less common over the course of the eighteenth century, particularly for native-born boys, and declined further after the Revolution. Some teenaged girls did continue to serve in the households of others. Girls sometimes stayed with relatives for short periods to help with specific tasks like weaving or preserving food, perhaps moving from one household to another in turn. Girls of lower social standing tended to stay longer with their masters, working for a family as household help. Martha Ballard's diary recounted her continued difficulties with her hired girls in Maine during the years after the Revolution (Ulrich, 1990). Of course the American Revolution was followed by the Industrial Revolution, which brought to northern cities in particular a new form of child labor.

Playtime in the Revolutionary World

Revolutionary-era children generally did, however, have opportunities to play and enjoyed a wide variety of games and toys. Some games involved physical activity, ranging from simple races or contests of strength or skill to organized ball games with teams and rules. In 1742, Englishman John Newbery published *A Little Pretty Pocket-Book,* a book for children which explained how to play over forty different games. Parents could even buy gender-specific toys packaged with the *Pocket-Book*: either a ball or a pincushion (Mergen, 1982; Plumb, 1975, 64–95).

Late eighteenth-century children had few toys, but they did have toys, and they used them. Some toys were educational, such as alphabet blocks, which were recommended by Locke and mentioned in numerous memoirs. Other toys were child-sized versions of the tools of adulthood. Sometimes

FISHING.

THE artful Angler baits his Hook,
    and throws it gently in the Brook;
Which the Fish view with greedy Eyes,
And soon are taken by Surprise.

RULE *of* LIFE.

Learn well the Motions of the Mind;
Why you are made, for what design'd.

Page from John Newbery's *A Little Pretty Pocket-Book*, showing children fishing and a short poem. (*Newbery, John. 1744.* A Little Pretty Pocket-Book)

children played games like checkers or backgammon; games involving cards or dice were not encouraged. But more often, play was improvised, often outdoors. Diaries and memoirs mention pastimes such as playing ball, seeking birds' nests, and fishing. Fishing could of course be considered both work and recreation. Children's play sometimes echoed and anticipated adult responsibilities (Mergen, 1982).

The Revolution inspired much martial play, especially among boys in larger towns or cities. When the militia drilled, the boys echoed the soldiers' training in a nearby field, emulating the adults and preparing for adult roles. In New Hampshire, "Lads from seven years old and upwards were formed into companies and being properly officered, armed with wooden guns and adorned with plumes, they would go through the manual exercise with as much regularity as the men. If two or three boys met, their martial ardor showed itself in exercising with sticks, instead of muskets." In New Jersey, Ashbel Green, the eighth president of Princeton University, remembered companies of boys aged ten to fifteen, "training, drilling and marching . . . encouraged and cheered on by our parents." Green did not consider this drill as play, but as preparation for joining the militia at age sixteen (Sherburne, 1828, 17; Green, 1849, 55). For many boys, it was only a short step from playing at war to war itself.

Children at War

The age for required military service was sixteen, but some boys served at much younger ages. Some ran away to sea or to join the army, often to escape a parent or master. Other boys enlisted with the consent of their father or guardian, sometimes accompanying their father or another adult, who might be an officer. Soldiers received a bounty for enlisting, which could be a strong incentive for a boy from a poor family. The military draft brought some boys (age sixteen or older) into the army involuntarily. Other boys enlisted as paid substitutes for men who had been drafted. Some young boys served as waiters to officers or as musicians, playing the fife or drum to transmit instructions to the soldiers. Hezekiah Packard was born in 1761 in North Bridgewater, Massachusetts, and when the war came, he served as a fifer, enlisting at the age of thirteen under a captain who was a friend of his father (Packard, 1850, 7).

Other young boys served as soldiers. In an age without birth certificates, a younger boy could claim to be sixteen, and many boys did so. One such boy later wrote: "At this period it was not an uncommon thing for lads to come out of the country, step on board a privateer, make a cruise and return home, their friends remaining in entire ignorance of their fate until they heard it from themselves. Others would pack up their clothes, take a cheese and a loaf of bread and steer off for the army. There was a disposition in commanders of privateers and recruiting officers to encourage this spirit of enterprise in young men and boys" (Sherburne, 1828, 19). And recruiters with a quota to meet would not have turned underage boys away. Boys often enlisted for short periods of time. Soldiers of all ages often enlisted for a specified number of weeks or months, or for a single campaign, perhaps enlisting several times during the war. In their memoirs, men who served as young boys mention serving as musicians, waiters, or guards more often than they mention shooting guns in battle.

Boys too young for the army sometimes served as cabin boys on navy ships or privateers. The latter were privately owned ships that attacked enemy vessels in order to aid the war effort, at the same time seeking personal profit for investors, officers, and crew. Andrew Sherburne had said for years that he wanted to run away to sea to serve on a privateer. In 1779, when Sherburne was thirteen, his father finally allowed him to go as cabin boy on the continental ship of war *Ranger*. His father "preferred the service of congress to privateering," and two of his uncles served on the *Ranger*, so, in theory, they could look out for him. Sherburne served as waiter to the boatswain; his other duties included reefing the topsails, and, when the ship was engaged in battle, "a boy was quartered to each gun to carry cartridges" (Sherburne, 1828, 16–25).

Boys serving in the military were sometimes captured along with their adult counterparts and incarcerated as prisoners of war. Their age did not seem a factor in deciding their treatment. Both boys and men who were captured from American ships were sometimes forced to serve in the British Navy. Prisoners of war, both boys and men, were imprisoned in land prisons and on prison ships, places notorious for bad food, filth, disease, and death. Andrew Sherburne was imprisoned twice, in 1781 in Britain's Old Mill Prison and a year later on the infamous *Jersey* prison ship. Both times he became extremely ill, was hospitalized, and saw others die.

Sherburne was just fifteen when his ship the *Greyhound* was captured off the coast of Newfoundland. He was imprisoned on land for some time and then was forced to serve on a British vessel that took him to England. Once there, he successfully pleaded his case to be treated as an American prisoner of war rather than impressed as a British sailor. He was sent to the Old Mill Prison, where he found some men from his hometown of Portsmouth, New Hampshire. He remained imprisoned with them until they were exchanged several months later. Sherburne returned to the sea, and in November 1782, he was captured a second time, along with his ship, and imprisoned on the *Jersey*, which was moored off the coast of New York. This was long after Cornwallis's surrender, but the British Army still occupied New York and still held Americans on overcrowded prison ships. While there, Sherburne became ill enough to be sent to the hospital ship, a place from which many did not return. Prisoners slept two to a bed, and Sherburne's bedmate "died, stretched across me. . . . After Mr. Wills, my bed-fellow was dead, I called to the nurses to take him away, as he lay partly across me . . . but they gave me very hard words, and let the dead man lay upon me half an hour before they removed him; and it was a great favor to me that they did not take away the blankets that was under us." Sherburne remained imprisoned on the *Jersey* and on hospital ships until after word came of the peace treaty in 1783 (Sherburne, 1828, 16–25).

Christopher Hawkins was also imprisoned on the *Jersey*, though at a much younger age than Sherburne and for a much shorter time. In some ways, the two boys' stories are similar. But where Sherburne sought adult permission or assistance, Hawkins took the initiative. Hawkins ran away from a Rhode Island apprenticeship in 1777 and, at age twelve, enlisted on a privateer. His ship was captured, and he too was forced to serve as a cabin boy on a British ship. After eighteen months, he escaped and, with many adventures, made his way home. He spent over two years at farm work and then quit abruptly one day in a fit of temper. While haying with two men, he could not keep up. "This provoked me to such a degree that I threw my scythe into a bush heap." As he stormed off, the men asked what he was doing, and "I answered that I was not pleased with my scythe, and that I was going to sea." They laughed, and he left. On the fifth day at sea, his ship was captured and the crew sent to the *Jersey* (Hawkins, 1968).

Hawkins's memoir, written decades later, included graphic descriptions of the ship: of hunger and filth, prisoners beaten to death, and prisoners reduced to eating their own lice. "Ev'ry prisoner was infested with vermin on his body and wearing apparel. I one day observed a prisoner on the forecastle of the ship, with his shirt in his hands, having stripped it from his body and deliberately picking the vermin from the plaits of said shirt, and putting them into his mouth." The man could not remember how long he had been on board the prison ship, replying "two years and a half or eighteen months" when Hawkins asked. Hawkins escaped the *Jersey* after only three days on board by swimming the two and a half miles to shore. He survived the icy water and reached land, naked, in Tory country. After more adventures, he returned safely home (Hawkins, 1968). The prison experiences of Sherburne and Hawkins were far from unique. Official records and the memoirs of many other men and boys describe similar experiences, but most prisoners of war were older.

The British were not the only ones to imprison boys as prisoners of war, though they probably held far more underage prisoners than did the Americans. Public records from New York include the story of Gabriel Valentine, who was captured in January 1777 with a group of thirty-six suspected Loyalists while allegedly traveling to join the British Army. The Committee and First Commission for Detecting and Defeating Conspiracies in the State of New York promptly imprisoned the entire group in the local guardhouse. On February 25, almost eight weeks later, Valentine came before the committee seeking to enlist in the Revolutionary forces. The committee resolved to permit his enlistment, which would serve as his route out of jail. The traditional next step was for a man to take the oath of allegiance to the American government and leave for the military. But Gabriel Valentine was under age sixteen, so the committee was "doubtful of the Propriety of tendering to him the Oath of Allegiance." The committee minutes make no mention of his age before this date. The committee had no qualms about imprisoning a boy of fifteen (or younger) for eight weeks with a group of men they defined as undesirable and perhaps dangerous, or about allowing him to risk life and limb in the army, but they could not accept his oath. Valentine's experience illustrates both the importance that late eighteenth-century society placed on oaths and the legal limitations faced by youths: The oath of a boy was not legally binding, so it meant nothing (Barch, 1924–1925, 70, 155).

The War At Home

Most children did not go to war, yet the war affected most of their lives. Men went to war, soldiers came to town, and daily routines were disrupted. Fathers went to war, and some did not return. In their absence, families struggled to manage farms, businesses, and all areas of life. Abigail Adams's letters record her struggle to keep the family farm productive while her husband was in Philadelphia and in Europe, and the military need for men made hired help hard to find. Children often had to step into adult roles, just as their mothers stepped into more traditionally male roles. And all the while, the family feared for the life and safety of the absent man.

For some, fear pervaded much of their childhood. Those fears were sometimes based on experience, sometimes based on imagination, and sometimes fueled by adults. Mary Palmer Tyler remembered being panicked by French soldiers in Boston. Her aunt had threatened her with the Regulars "to frighten us children after we were in bed, if we were noisy. We now thought they were surely come and began an outcry, some running up garret and some clinging to mother in great terror," until Mary's mother reassured her that these soldiers were friends. And Dan Huntington of Connecticut recalled living in constant awareness of war and constant fear that his father would die. He wrote, "I was born in the midst of [the country's] bloodshed and battles; and I know not if I thought it would ever be otherwise. Carnage and slaughter made the common news of the day. The first questions among neighbors, as they met in the streets and in each others' houses, were, 'What news from head-quarters? Has there been fighting of late? How

A minuteman says goodbye to his family as he leaves for battle. (*Grafton, John, ed. 1975*. The American Revolution. *New York: Dover Publications, Inc.*)

many were killed? Who were they? On which side was the victory?' Such was the dreadful routine from day to day, from month to month, and from year to year" (Tyler, 1925, 58; Huntington, 1857, 5–6).

For some children, these fears were realized when they learned of their father's death, in battle or of disease. In a father's absence, the children of a poor family might be dispersed; if the father died, that dispersal might be permanent. Arial Bragg was about five years old when his father left for the war. His mother was unable to feed her children and applied to the town selectmen, who bound out the four oldest to different masters. Bragg's father, an army barber, died of smallpox, and the children remained poor and apart (Bragg, 1846).

Battles ranged from New England to Georgia, from the coast to the backcountry, approaching the homes of many Americans. When soldiers were in the area, daily life was often disrupted. Soldiers were quartered in local homes. Some children, like Mary Palmer Tyler, remembered friendly officers living in their homes, while others remembered their parents being forced to house enemy troops or forced to abandon their homes to the enemy.

Children, like adults, were affected by shortages of goods caused by boycotts and blockades, and disruption of wartime shipping. Nathaniel Goddard, who would later become a Boston merchant, recalled that "we were extremely distressed for even the necessaries of life, and we had very few of its luxuries or conveniences. The women were obliged to use thorns instead of pins to fasten on their clothes." Abigail Adams's letters echo this shortage, as she repeatedly asked John to buy pins from Philadelphia. But children usually did not care much about objects like pins, and their narratives suggest that they were much less troubled by shortages than were their parents (Goddard, 1906).

Nevertheless, many people who were children during the American Revolution considered the Revolution to have been a major factor in shaping the course of their lives. They felt this way whether or not they had served in the war. It had been the major public event of their young lives and often had made a difference in their lives.

Many families moved during the war to flee the enemy or the fighting. Others moved after the war, some from economic necessity and others to pursue new opportunities. Many children of Loyalists, with their parents, left the country entirely. In some cases, a Loyalist father left, while his wife and children remained in America; this behavior could be either desertion or an attempt to keep land and property within the family. But not all Loyalists left the new United States, and the children of those who remained were usually able to craft lives as full-fledged American citizens.

Some people, especially those whose fathers had died, believed that the war caused them lasting harm: curtailing their schooling, destroying their family's prosperity, and limiting opportunities. Men who had served as young soldiers or sailors sometimes attributed their later ill health to the war. Andrew Sherburne did. In his application for a federal military pension, he stated that smallpox, illnesses while a prisoner of war, and "many other hardships endured in the revolution, such as compulsion to serve on board a british man of war, ship wreck starvation etc. has so wrecked my constitution, that I have been able to perform but little manual labour since" (File of Andrew Sherburne, National Archives and Records Service). Loss of parents, of health, of social standing and of opportunity, all could be blamed on the war.

On the other hand, many young veterans reaped practical benefits from their service. Soldiers were paid in cash and in land, and many veterans eventually were granted pensions. Some boys had used the army to escape from unpleasant situations, and military service gave many their only opportunity to travel or to learn. These benefits aside, many men looked back at their wartime service as a major influence or turning point in their lives. Sherburne learned to write while in the Old Mill Prison. If his adult companions had not decided to make sure that he learned, he might never have been able to record his experiences. Others, who had not fought, also felt that the war expanded their horizons, both material and mental.

In his old age, John Quincy Adams recalled the Battle of Bunker Hill. He was seven years old when his mother took him to watch the fighting. She had not expected that their family friend Dr. Joseph Warren would die in the battle they watched. Adams wrote to a friend in 1846:

> My father was separated from his family, on his way to attend the same continental Congress, and there my mother, with her children lived in unintermitted danger of being consumed with them all in a conflagration kindled by a torch in the same hands which on the 17th. of June lighted the fires of Charlestown—I saw with my own eyes those fires, and heard Britannia's thunders in the Battle of Bunker's hill and witnessed the tears of my mother and mingled with them my own, at the fall of Warren a dear friend of my father, and a beloved Physician to me. He had been our family physician and surgeon, and had saved my fore finger from amputation under a very bad fracture—Even in the days of heathen and conquering Rome the Laureate of Augustus Caesar tells us that wars were detested by Mothers—Even by Roman mothers.

He went on to describe how his mother had him intersperse reciting lines about heroes of English liberty with his childhood prayers (John Quincy Adams to Joseph Sturge, March [?] 1846. Adams Papers, Massachusetts Historical Society).

For John Quincy Adams and his contemporaries, their childhoods were defined by memories of the Revolution, of watching battles, of managing daily life while fathers were at war, and sometimes of going to war themselves. The Revolutionary War shaped their childhoods and helped to shape their adult lives. Politicians of Adams's generation very often spoke of their Revolutionary War experiences, just as he did. The war that shaped their childhoods influenced how they, as adults, shaped the nation.

References and Further Reading

Adams Papers. Series II: Family Correspondence, vol. 1, December 1761–May 1776. Edited by L. H. Butterfield, Wendell D. Garrett, and Marjorie E. Sprague. Cambridge, MA: Harvard University Press, 1963.

Andrews, Joel. *Sketch of the Life of Joel Andrews of Bethany, written by himself.* New Haven, CT: Storer and Storer, 1850.

Barch, Dorothy C., ed. *Minutes of the Committee and First Commission for Detecting and Defeating Conspiracies in the State of New York.* New York: Printed for the New York Historical Society, 1924–1925.

Bragg, Arial. *Memoirs of Col. Arial Bragg.* Milford, CT: Stacy, 1846.

Calvert, Karin. *Children in the House: The Material Culture of Early Childhood, 1600–1900.* Boston: Northeastern University Press, 1992.

Chase, Philander. *Bishop Chase's Reminiscences: An Autobiography.* 2 vols. Boston: Dow, 1848.

Comly, John. *Journal of the Life and Religious Labours of John Comly, late of Byberry, Pennsylvania. Published by his Children.* Philadelphia: Chapman, 1853.

Drinker, Elizabeth Sandwith. *The Diary of Elizabeth Drinker.* Edited by Elaine Forman Crane. Boston: Northeastern University Press, 1991.

Farish, Hunter Dickinson, ed. *Journal and Letters of Philip Vickers Fithian, 1773–1774: A Plantation Tutor of the Old Dominion.* Williamsburg, VA: Colonial Williamsburg, 1943.

Fenn, Elizabeth. *Pox Americana: The Great Smallpox Epidemic of 1775–1782.* New York: Hill and Wang, 2001.

Franklin, Benjamin. *Writings.* Edited by J. A. Leo Lemay. New York: Library of America, 1987.

Frost, J. William. *The Quaker Family in Colonial America: A Portrait of the Society of Friends.* New York: St. Martins, 1973.

Gemery, Henry A. "The White Population of the Colonial United States, 1607–1790," in *A Population History of North America*, ed. Michael R. Haines and Richard H. Steckel. Cambridge: Cambridge University Press 2000, 143–190.

Goddard, Nathaniel. *Nathaniel Goddard: A Boston Merchant, 1767–1853.* Cambridge, MA: Riverside, 1906.

Green, Ashbel. *The Life of Ashbel Green, V.D.M.* New York: Carter, 1849.

Hawkins, Christopher. *The Adventures of Christopher Hawkins* [1864]. New York: Arno, 1968.

Huntington, Dan. *Memories, Counsels and Reflections by an Octagenary.* Cambridge, 1857.

Jenkins, James. *Experience, Labours and Sufferings of Rev. James Jenkins of the South Carolina Conference* [1842]. Columbia: State Commercial, 1958.

Jones, Abner. *Memoirs of the Life and Experience, Travels and Preaching of Abner Jones.* Exter, NH: Norris and Sawyer, 1807.

Kiefer, Monica. *American Children through Their Books.* Philadelphia: University of Pennsylvania Press, 1948.

Mergen, Bernard. *Play and Playthings: A Reference Guide.* Westport, CT: Greenwood, 1982.

Murray, Gail Schmunk. *American Children's Literature and the Construction of Childhood*. New York: Twayne, 1998.

Packard, Hezekiah. *Memoir of Rev. Hezekiah Packard, D.D.* Brunswick: Griffin, 1850.

Plumb, J. H. "Children in Eighteenth Century England." *Past and Present* 67 (1975): 64–95.

Reinier, Jacqueline S. *From Virtue to Character: American Childhood, 1775–1850*. New York: Twayne, 1996.

Scholten, Catherine M. *Childbearing in American Society: 1650–1850*. New York: New York University Press, 1985.

Schultz, Constance B. "Children and Childhood in the Eighteenth Century," in *American Childhood: A Research Guide and Historical Handbook*, ed. Joseph M. Hawes and N. Ray Hiner. Westport, CT: Greenwood, 1985, 57–109.

Sherburne, Andrew. *Memoirs of Andrew Sherburne: A Pensioner of the Navy of the Revolution*. Utica, NY: Williams, 1828.

Smith, Elias. *The Life, Conversion, Preaching, Travels and Suffering of Elias Smith*. Portsmouth, NH: Beck and Foster, 1816.

Spufford, Margaret. "First Steps in Literacy: The Reading and Writing Experiences of the Humblest Seventeenth-Century Spiritual Autobiographers." *Social History* 4 (1979): 407–435.

Tyler, Mary Hunt Palmer. *Grandmother Tyler's Book: The Recollections of Mary Palmer Tyler (Mrs Royall Tyler) 1775–1866*. Edited by Frederick Tupper and Helen Tyler Brown. New York: Putnam, 1925.

Ulrich, Laurel Thatcher. *A Midwife's Tale: The Life of Martha Ballard, Based on Her Diary, 1785–1812*. New York: Knopf, 1990.

U.S. Census Bureau. *Historical Statistics of the United States, Colonial Times to 1970*. Washington, DC: Government Printing Office, 1975.

Walsh, Lorena S. "The African American Population of the Colonial United States," in *A Population History of North America*, ed. Michael R. Haines and Richard H. Steckel. New York: Cambridge University Press, 2000, 191–240.

Willey, Chloe. *Short Account of the Life and Remarkable View of Mrs. Chloe Willey of Goshen N.H.* New York: Totten, 1810.

"An Exceeding Dirty and Nasty People": Enlisted Men in the Continental Army

7

Andrew C. Lannen

O n Christmas night, 1776, the Continental Army gathered on the Pennsylvania side of the Delaware River to prepare for a dangerous crossing. The ice clogging the river could easily capsize or sink the small ferryboats. The army was launching its last campaign of the year. The target was the British garrison at Trenton. Tensions rode high, reflecting the stakes in this unusual winter offensive. Defeats in recent months weighed heavily on the enlisted soldiers. For a large number of them, their terms of service would expire in just a few days, and as things stood, few would reenlist. The chances of new men like them volunteering in the spring looked bleak.

The year had started off well for these soldiers. After a long siege, British troops evacuated Boston in the spring. Shortly thereafter, Congress approved the Declaration of Independence, transforming a rebellion into a struggle for sovereignty. Autumn, though, ushered in a series of reverses for the new nation. The British captured New York and drove the Continental Army into headlong retreat. Losing faith in America's army, the Congress in Philadelphia packed up and fled. Thomas Paine's famous words, written in *The Crisis* just two days before the Christmas Eve river crossing, probably expressed the shared sentiments of the common soldiers: "These are the times that try men's souls."

Overseeing the crossing from shore was Commander in Chief George Washington, whose stern and seemingly humorless demeanor was fast becoming legend. Mindful that morale could win or lose battles, Washington understood that someone or something needed to ease the tension in the ranks. He climbed into a boat beside Henry "Ox" Knox, a rotund 280-pound general. Prodding Knox with a toe, Washington said much too loudly, "Shift that fat ass, Harry—but slowly, or you'll swamp the damned boat!" (Fast, 1992, 6). Nearby men broke into laughter, and word of the episode spread like lightning. If their commander could crack a joke, perhaps the situation was not quite so grim.

Memorialized in this famous painting by Emanuel Leutze, George Washington crossed the Delaware River to attack the British in Trenton, New Jersey, in December 1776. (*National Archives and Records Administration*)

The crossing took hours longer than expected, but ended without the loss of a single man. The unexpected attack caught the Hessian mercenaries at Trenton by total surprise. The British lost over 1,000 men who were killed or captured; the Americans had only 4 wounded. After Washington's off-color wisecrack, the fortunes of both the Continental Army and the nation had turned for the better. When enlistments expired, many still left, but some stayed. Most important, more would come in the spring, buoyed by the belief that the war was still winnable. (For a discussion of the campaign as a whole, see Fischer, 2004, 19–21.)

In the Beginning

In the first year of the war, 1775, the country experienced a *rage militaire*—a sudden, burning passion for armed conflict. Anger, anxiety, and patriotism converged into impressive grassroots support for military action against the British government. Thousands of volunteers rushed toward Boston, where rebel forces had bottled up the main British force (Royster, 1979, 3–53). During this early period, most soldiers came from respectable backgrounds: small farmers, merchants, tradesmen. In short, they were men of means. Preachers bombarded their parishioners with the message that God favored the colonial side, and urged men to take up arms. As minister John Murray warned, "To shun the dangers of the field is to desert the banner of Christ" (Royster, 1979, 16). Thousands of volunteers enthusiastically and chaotically supported the army, showing up at random and then leaving as they pleased.

Those who bothered to enlist officially did so for short periods of time rang-ing from six months to a year. They were convinced that the war would not last long, that the superior virtue of American citizen-soldiers would bring swift victory. American simplicity and piety would overwhelm the vain and ungodly British opposition.

That same year Congress adopted the forces around Boston and ap-pointed George Washington as their commander. Though consisting at first almost entirely of New Englanders and New Yorkers, the army was dip-lomatically dubbed "Continental" to emphasize the unity of all American regions. Throughout 1775, Continental Army recruiters had no trouble at-tracting volunteers to fight the British. Officers paraded through city streets accompanied by drummers "beating out" the call for soldiers. Curious on-lookers would be treated to liberal servings of beer and rum, and then re-galed with tales of battlefield heroism that fired the imagination (Martin and Lender, 1982, 88). Men caught up in the moment enlisted—some for noble reasons, others not—and went off to war, certain of its swift resolution and positive outcome.

Flush with confidence, few Americans paused to consider how they might carry on the fight in future years if necessary. One option—a per-manent standing army—faced open hostility. Contemporary public opinion equated standing armies with tyranny and repression, and many revolu-tionaries were disinclined to reconstruct such a controversial feature of the Old World. Only the realization that the war would drag on into 1776 (and possibly beyond) led to the reluctant creation of a more permanent force. By then, however, the task had become considerably more difficult. By mid-1776, the *rage militaire* had faded into memory, taking with it the impas-sioned volunteer spirit. Men with families to feed could ill afford extended absences from home, and thousands of them declined to enlist once again.

Creating a Professional Army

The first step in building a permanent, professional army was to establish a stable core of veterans. Short enlistments created too much turnover and bred chaos in the ranks. The stream of soldiers flowing in and out of camp disrupted unit cohesion and frequently left commanders blindly guessing at their own unit's numerical strength. Congress preferred that soldiers join for "the duration," whether that meant a single year or ten. However, many otherwise willing recruits hesitated to sign up for military terms with no clear end. A rough compromise emerged, with "three years or the duration" be-coming standard, though the vague phrasing left questions as to what would happen if the fighting lasted more than three years. The lengthier commit-ments gave the army continuity, but were limited enough to preserve the illusion that the army as a whole was still temporary (Higginbotham, 1971, 390–391).

Despite this enlistment change, the army struggled to maintain steady numbers. After 1775, middle-class tradesmen and farmers stopped serving in large numbers. The new recruits instead came from the poorest classes:

the unemployed, unskilled, indentured, or even enslaved. Joining the Continental Army gave them financial benefits that eluded them in civilian life. In the first months of fighting, Congress instituted cash bounties for enlistees. Each man signing up for the duration of the fight would receive $20 and the promise of 100 acres of land when the war ended. A three-year stint brought the lesser reward of $10 (Martin and Lender, 1982, 77). Some men became "bounty jumpers," signing up to collect the cash bonus, deserting, enlisting someplace else for another payment, and then repeating the process.

To supplement the Continental Army's direct recruiting efforts, Congress assigned each state a quota of troops to fill, leaving recruitment methods entirely up to state and local authorities. Preferring volunteers, state governments established their own bounties, often higher than those promised by the army. Faced with a resulting drop-off in national volunteers in 1779, Congress countered by dramatically raising their signing bonus to $200. This drew more enlistments, but created murmurs of discontent from existing soldiers who had joined for only $10 or $20, and who resented the appearance that their lives were worth less than those of new recruits. To head off serious problems in the ranks, Congress ended up giving the $200 bonus to every enlisted man in the army (Martin and Lender, 1982, 89; Higginbotham, 1971, 391).

States that could not muster enough volunteers to reach mandatory quotas turned to military conscription. Each militia unit was asked to put forward a percentage of its men for short-term national armed service, whether the men came voluntarily or not. Concord, Massachusetts, pulled names randomly from a hat, a method accounting for nearly 75 percent of the town's soldiers from 1776 to 1778 (Gross, 1976, 147). Military drafts solved short-term manpower crises, but also created entirely new difficulties. Soldiers chosen in this fashion typically served only until December in the year of their selection. Many of them even insisted on leaving the ranks early so that they would already be home on the day their term expired. Conscription also bred disagreement between men of different social ranks. Drafted militiamen could legally avoid military service by paying a cash fine or, alternatively, providing a hired substitute. Both options to escape conscription required a certain degree of wealth. Southern slave owners sometimes provided one of their slaves to serve in their place. To the drafted poor who could not take advantage of these outs, the system appeared unfairly to favor the rich (Higginbotham, 1971, 393).

Despite all efforts, manpower levels continued to fluctuate wildly. During the peak of campaign season, the army's strength could swell to 15,000 or more. In midwinter, it might dwindle to a few thousand sturdy veterans. To flesh out the ranks, officers frequently had to turn a blind eye to the source of enlistees. Vagrants and beggars found themselves rounded up, handed muskets, and pushed toward the front lines. Runaway indentured servants, too, found refuge in the army. After initially refusing to allow African Americans to enlist, the army later accepted black soldiers, both free and slave alike, in large numbers—some scattered amidst the lines with white soldiers, others serving in segregated all-black units. Only South Carolina and Georgia (the two states with the highest percentage of slaves in their populations) stubbornly refused to arm blacks (Frey, 1991). Orders banned indentured ser-

Continental officers drill recruits within a fort of rough-hewn logs during the American Revolution. Forts in the American colonies, orginally designed to thwart Indian raids, were often simple structures, a circle or square of tall fence with towers at the corners surrounding a village or military garrison. (*Library of Congress*)

vants or slaves from enlisting without specific permission from their masters, but few officers looked deeply into the backgrounds of new recruits. In times of desperation, the army even convinced prisoners of war to fight against their former comrades. German mercenaries hired by the British government proved particularly susceptible to changing sides since they had no real stake in the war's outcome, only its income. Such dubious recruiting practices dismayed some American leaders, but the needs of the Continental Army took precedence over personal reservations (Mayer, 1996, 44, 58).

The Continental Army consisted of soldiers from a variety of races, ethnicities, occupations, and regions. Rough Pennsylvania frontiersmen mingled with New York dockworkers; Virginia tobacco farmers rubbed elbows with Massachusetts shopkeepers, slave owners with former or current slaves. Hundreds of Germans recently arrived from Europe took up arms in favor of their newly adopted country. Thousands of newly immigrated Irishmen, whose native isle had long suffered at the hands of England, proved willing to fight. The Continental Army contained so many foreigners that one royalist estimated, with only slight exaggeration, that "about one-half the Rebel Army was Irish and only a quarter of it American." Enlisted soldiers spoke a bewildering array of languages and dialects, held conflicting religious doctrines, and came from vastly different cultural settings. Most soldiers experienced culture shock. At times, it seemed like the only thing that unified them was that they all made the same decision to enlist (Neimeyer, 1996, 42). When he arrived to take command of this chaotic jumble, Washington felt disgusted. "They are an exceeding dirty and nasty people," he wrote. At the time, he had as yet encountered only New Englanders, collectively the most educated in the bunch (Fischer, 2004, 19).

The component parts of the Continental Line often looked like they belonged to entirely different armies. Until late in the war, Congress could not afford to provide standard uniforms. States and private individuals outfitted their troops according to their own liking. Backcountry settlers favored simple black or brown hunting shirts. Southern regiments from rich plantation areas could be seen in white frocks fringed with ruffles and lace. New Englanders often wore simple neutral jackets and "fisher's trousers." Individuality in uniform choices could lead to severe battlefield confusion. Smallwood's Maryland regiment, for example, favored bright scarlet coats until someone pointed out that they looked like British soldiers. Soldiers who otherwise could not find adequate clothing stripped uniforms off British casualties and wore them on the American side. Wearing captured uniforms became widespread enough that the army had to specifically forbid the practice in 1781 (Fischer, 2004, 22–29; Higginbotham, 1971, 398).

The combination of unfamiliarity and close contact could cause serious trouble. In 1778, a Virginia regiment bumped into one from Massachusetts. Many of the Virginians owned slaves, which, coincidentally, some of the New England soldiers had formerly been. The tense encounter between the groups began with a series of spoken insults. Pushing and shoving followed, then a rapid escalation into a violent brawl complete with "biting and gouging." Within minutes, more than a thousand men joined the fray, with more jumping in as word spread to other nearby regiments. The fighting threatened to engulf the entire camp until Washington took matters literally into his own hands. The commanding general rode into the thick of the fighting, leaped to the ground, and began grabbing the largest rioters by the throat and shaking them until the men took notice. Knowing that Washington was a stern disciplinarian, the rest of the combatants scattered, preferring a minor act of cowardice (running away) to facing down their commander's wrath (Fischer, 2004, 25).

This chaotic hodgepodge somehow had to transform into an organized, professional fighting force. Revolutionary rhetoric preached opposition to British authority, and defiance toward American authority ran rampant among the enlisted men as well. Soldiers showed scant respect for their officers—many of whom were untrained and inexperienced—and little inclination to follow unpopular orders. Men on the march regularly tossed their muskets into wagons to lighten their loads and then ran off from the column to drink in local taverns or plunder nearby farms. In camp, units scattered everywhere, with little concern for securing perimeters or establishing sanitary conditions. Outbreaks of dysentery, diarrhea, cholera, smallpox, and yellow fever were alarming, but routine. Farmhands who always had grown beards needed constant reminders to shave lest lice and other vermin take root. Merchants, prostitutes, and thieves came and went without inspection or challenge. Armies, though, needed order, discipline, and regimentation. The only way officers saw to accomplish these things was to punish the common soldier into obedience.

Physical punishments were the norm in the Continental Army, with flogging the most frequently employed. Prevailing military theory in both America and Britain held that withholding the whip encouraged idleness and disorder. To serve as a deterrent, penalties were administered frequently and publicly. The guilty party was stripped to the waist in front of witnesses, tied to a post, and beaten by a drummer (one of their nonmusical duties) across the back. After 50 lashes, a man's back looked like jelly, and the leather straps of the whip became caked with blood and ineffectual. A new, dry whip would then be substituted for the next 50. If the soldier received 100 or more lashes, sessions at the post might be spread over a period of several days to allow enough recovery time for the man to survive the experience.

Initial military regulations allowed a maximum of 39 lashes, a number derived from biblical law. Washington successfully lobbied to increase the limit to 100 swings, arguing that 39 might as well be zero for all the effect it had on insubordinate troops. A later bid to raise the upper range to 500 failed. A few contemporary observers considered the American commander too soft and lenient, though the average soldier might have strongly disagreed. In one case, a unit sent a very sick soldier out to stand guard, and he predictably fell asleep on duty. Obviously guilty, he received a whipping as punishment. However, Washington felt that the soldier's illness reduced the seriousness of the offense, so he stepped in and dropped the number of lashes to just 25. Compared to the brutality of the British Army, such a penalty was light, but not every witness drew the same conclusion. French officers expressed shock at the frequency of whippings and beatings in the Continental Army (Higginbotham, 1971, 413; Royster, 1979, 77–79). "The gauntlet" served as the main alternative to the whip. The convicted man marched between two long lines of soldiers armed with sticks. As he walked, men on either side of him rained blows down upon every part of his body. To prevent the walker from rushing through the gauntlet, a soldier walked slowly backward in front of him while holding a bayonet point against the guilty man's chest.

The ultimate sanction against a misbehaving soldier was the death penalty, levied typically for mutiny, plundering, or desertion. Possible methods of execution included the firing squad, hanging, or—in rare instances—beheading. Enlisted men might look up one morning to see a deserter's head impaled on a pike in plain view, delivering a gruesome reminder not to break the law. Though death sentences were handed down in hundreds of cases during the Revolution, comparatively few soldiers met their end in this way. Instead, officers used mock executions to instill fear in the soldiers witnessing the event. A condemned man would parade through the assembled ranks accompanied by drummers playing a death march. When the man was brought to the gallows or before the firing squad, a designated official would read out the crime and sentence. A chaplain would address the assembled crowd and then recite a prayer for the man about to die. Depending on the execution method, orders would be given to either take aim or prepare the trap door. At the climactic moment, the presiding officer would then order a halt and read the general's pardon, closing the drama with a stern warning to the men not to disobey in the future. This final act of mercy was omitted just frequently enough to sow doubt and dread in eyewitnesses.

In time, enlisted men accepted physical punishment as a routine part of life. As a practical matter, officers had little alternative. Imprisonment required moving needed men off the front lines for use as prison guards. Employment at hard labor did not terrify anyone, since it was not much different from normal military duties. So officers were left trying to beat respect and obedience into their subordinates, and enlisted men resigned themselves to it. Inconsistently or randomly applied discipline, though, could spark resentment. To the average soldier, pardons seemed to arrive with no rhyme or reason other than pure chance. Two men guilty of the same crime might receive vastly different sentences: death for one, whipping for the other. In one instance, three condemned prisoners drew straws to see which one would die and which two would receive pardons. Another example of disparity came in 1780, when orders came down that all men currently under death sentences would be executed on the same day. As happened many times before, eyewitnesses saw eleven men paraded to the place of execution. Firing squads faced off opposite three of them, nooses snaked around the necks of the other eight. At the pivotal moment, the presiding officer stepped forward and read an important message from the commander in chief. Washington had pardoned ten of the men. The eleventh, though, was hanged as an example to maintain soldiers' fear of the death penalty and of their superiors (Neimeyer, 1996, 143–144).

Continental officers expected military discipline to extend far beyond the performance of routine duties. Even simple vices were seen as signs of impending disorder and disarray, and had to be stamped out. Dice and card games were frowned upon and actively discouraged. Though soldiers could sometimes receive visits in camp from wives or sweethearts, officers struggled to keep prostitutes at bay. Surgeons considered alcohol a healthy alternative to drinking the often-polluted water that surrounded army camps, and every soldier's normal ration included sizeable amounts of rum or whiskey. Outright drunkenness, however, was punishable by whipping. Profanity, too, disturbed American officers, and they repeatedly ordered Continental soldiers to stop swearing. Profane language, though, proved impossible to stamp out, since even Washington was known to unleash an impressive stream of obscenities when he lost his temper (Royster, 1979, 76–77, 79–82).

Over time, enlisted men in the Continental Army found ways to assert partial control of the disciplinary process, if only on the delivery end. If the men considered a particular sentence unjust, they could act to subtly disrupt the punishment. Soldiers manning a gauntlet, for example, could deflect or soften their blows. Before whippings, men might pull aside the drummer assigned to wield the whip and threaten him with a beating unless he eased back on the blows (Neimeyer, 1996, 140). Even guilty soldiers eventually discovered ways to benefit from their punishments. Men whipped severely would recount the story as a source of pride, touting their courage in the face of pain. Surviving a brutal beating became a badge of honor rather than a mark of shame, elevating them in the eyes of their comrades. Still, the average private would much rather avoid punishment than brag about it afterward.

The Daily Life of a Soldier

The Continental soldier's basic experience was much like that of men in any war—long periods of boredom punctuated by short periods of sheer terror. Every day men dug latrines, cleaned, trained, cooked, gathered firewood, and stood watch. With the day's tasks finished, some turned to playing card games, drinking, or holding shooting contests to keep themselves occupied. Periodic holidays like Christmas and Easter also helped relieve the tedium. Two major holidays—the king's birthday and coronation day—did not survive the Revolution, but a new celebration emerged after 1776. Soldiers celebrated the Fourth of July as Independence Day, holding parades, firing thirteen-piece artillery salutes, shouting cheers, and imbibing extra rations of liquor. As mundane as these special events might seem, they kept the army going and improved morale. When the men's spirits flagged, so too did their performance in basic routines and everyday tasks.

The three most common sources of complaint along the Continental Line were clothing, food, and pay. The army fought a continuous battle to properly clothe its men. States occasionally stepped forward to provide attire for home-state troops, but did little for the rest of the army. Congress had no steady income to purchase uniforms for thousands of men each year. Though men were often promised new sets of clothing, the vagaries of war made such pledges a low priority. Men patched tattered clothing as best they could, borrowing scrap cloth or sometimes even snatching laundry from nearby farms as it dried in the sun. When new pairs of shoes ran out, some enterprising types tried to fashion their own footwear using bits of clothing or shreds of leather. With no training in shoemaking, such efforts usually yielded painful results. During warm weather months, the army could withstand some limited clothing shortages. When winter fell, shortfalls could prove fatal to the men. According to one veteran, as soldiers marched toward winter quarters in 1777, so many lacked shoes that anyone could track the army by following the trail of blood (Martin and Lender, 1982, 100).

At first glance, the officially established food ration appeared generous. Each man was to receive one pound of meat (usually corned beef or pork) and one pound of flour on a daily basis. Four times a week, the army passed out a liquor ration of one gill (half a cup) of whiskey or rum. Adding a touch of variety, each soldier was supposed to receive three pints of vegetables every week—usually peas or beans, sometimes onions, tomatoes, or turnips—and a small amount of rice. Under these guidelines, a force of 30,000 would consume 40 million pounds of meat and 200,000 barrels of flour per year. Rarely, though, did the Continental Army provide food at promised levels. Fresh beef proved difficult to come by for much of the year, as did fresh vegetables. Enlisted men constantly complained about trying to choke down rotten, spoiled meat. "Firecakes" became the most reliable staple of the military

The American army, dressed in tatters, marches toward Valley Forge to camp for the winter of 1777–1778. (*Grafton, John, ed. 1975*. The American Revolution. *New York: Dover Publications, Inc.*)

diet. Men mixed their flour ration with water, threw the combination onto a campfire's ashes until blackened, then devoured the bland bread soot and all. Even during the first year of the war, food shortages caused outbursts of anger. During the 1775 siege of Boston, a soldier sat down to eat what was to become a rare treat in the years ahead: a bowl of bread and milk. While eating, a British cannonball crashed into the ground right next to him, throwing dirt into the air and into the bowl. The man cursed the British—not for trying to kill him, but for ruining his supper (Bolton, 1902, 78–81).

Army wages caused serious discontent in the ranks. Apart from the enlistment bonus, military pay was far below the norm for most civilian occupations. A private in the Continental Army theoretically received $6.67 per month. On the outside, common laborers could earn $9 or more per month, and those with skilled trades saw an even greater disparity in potential income. Enlisted men also faced regular deductions from their $80 yearly income. If clothing or weapons were damaged or lost, replacements were charged against the soldier's wage. After various deductions, many men received only about $1 per month for their service. Officers levied small fines against individuals for breaking minor regulations, and these could chip away any remaining money at surprising rates. Some soldiers such as Private Elijah Fisher felt certain that officers abused this power to deprive common soldiers of their rightful wages. "[Officers] will promise them so and so," he complained, "and after they have got them to Enlist they are Cheated" (Neimeyer, 1996, 125).

When paydays did arrive, they frequently came weeks or months late. Soldiers fortunate enough to collect the wages owed them discovered that runaway inflation devoured the value of their meager incomes. With no steady source of gold or silver to prop up the currency it issued, Congress paid its bills with unsupported paper money that rapidly lost value. Congress tried compensating for inflation by tinkering with official exchange rates between paper and hard currency, but these adjustments lagged far behind the pace of inflation. In September 1777, a Continental dollar was still worth $1. By January 1778, the value of the same paper dollar was $0.68, by the beginning of 1781 less than a penny, and by 1782, no one at all would accept Continental money. For the last few years of the war, soldiers served essentially without any pay. The situation became so hopeless that in 1780 Congress gave up the task and charged each state with paying the Continental soldiers from their state. Since states also faced serious financial difficulties, they instead issued notes merely promising to pay the men after the war ended. Desperately poor soldiers looked for alternative ways of supplementing their rations. Private Joseph Plumb Martin recounted one such incident during a British siege of an American fort. His unit had a 32-pound cannon, but no ammunition. Noting that the enemy fired exactly the same type of artillery at American lines, officers offered extra rum rations for the retrieval of used British shells. Dozens of men stood in the open acting as targets so that they could collect the shots fired at them and cash them in for liquor. They tried to catch cannon balls before they stopped moving so that nearby collectors could not snatch away the prize, though catching could prove dangerous if the soldier radically underestimated a shell's speed (Neimeyer, 1996, 125–127).

The plundering of civilians was common during the war. Though the activity was illegal, enlisted men did not consider it shameful. Soldiers deprived of necessities often stole whatever they needed from homes along a march route or in the vicinity of a camp, at times even setting the houses on fire to hide the theft. Washington strongly condemned such incidents, since they damaged the army's reputation and turned the civilian population against the war. The army made plundering a hanging offense, but the threat of execution could not dissuade soldiers facing death by starvation. Soldiers considered domestic livestock to be fair candidates for the cooking pot, the same as wild animals. A sergeant in 1776 described how his company "liberated" some geese being held captive in a local pen and no doubt found them a very warm place indeed to rest. Next, he recounted how a sheep and two turkeys approached his hungry men. A sentry challenged them, but the advancing trio could not "give the countersign." Therefore they were arrested and given a "trial by fire," which having failed, the unfortunate defendants were pulled out of the flames and eaten (Martin, 1984, 131–132).

The worst time of year for enlisted men came in winter quarters, when harsh weather worsened the material shortfalls. The most famous of these winters was at Valley Forge, Pennsylvania, where the army rested from December 1777 until June 1778. It was not the worst winter camp in the Revolutionary War—that dubious distinction goes to the Morristown encampment of 1779–1780, which experienced the worst weather in forty years. Valley Forge, though, was the first horrific and traumatic experience of its type and took the army by surprise. Nothing went right so far as the

Joseph Plumb Martin

Joseph Plumb Martin was too young to understand most of the political and constitutional debates that divided England and its American colonies before the Revolution. He had no burning reason to oppose the British government until the *rage militaire* swept the colonies in 1775. Fascinated by the sight of marching troops, he would follow them until they left the boundaries of his Connecticut town. Yet he hesitated to enlist. He feared his family's reaction and balked at making an entire year's commitment. What if he disliked military life?

In 1776, Martin saw a more attractive opportunity—Connecticut called for six-month enlistments to help defend New York City. If the experience proved unbearable, he could be back home by the end of the year. At the age of fifteen, he headed off to battle (Martin 2001, 16). In the military, he soon encountered problems that plagued American forces throughout the conflict. Though promised ample provisions, troops received scant clothing and little food. To compensate, Martin scrounged or stole occasional scraps from local farmers. He referred to the soldiers' cooking utensils as "the most useless things in the army." Second

in uselessness to him were the officers. They hurried the men into battle, then mysteriously vanished, reappearing again only at night after the shooting ceased. On Christmas Day, 1776, Martin departed the army, having learned enough, he said, "to keep me home for the future" (Martin 2001, 19–20, 28, 37, 46, 50).

Despite this sentiment, 1777 saw Martin join the Continental Army for the war's duration, this time as a hired draft substitute. During his term, he never felt completely alone. Wherever he went, three "constant companions" followed: fatigue, hunger, and cold. He shivered through harsh winter camps at Valley Forge and Morristown, sometimes going three or four days without eating. Lacking shoes, he fashioned a crude and ill-fitting pair out of scrap leather, suffering as they rubbed his ankles raw. He bitterly recalled how, on Thanksgiving in 1777, the country "opened her sympathizing heart" to thank and reward the valiant defenders of liberty. For the special holiday meal, the United States gave them each a quarter cup of rice and a tablespoon of vinegar (Martin 2001, 52, 85, 87–88).

During the latter stages of the war, he transferred to a unit of sappers and miners and

average trooper could tell. They had not been paid a penny in the previous four months. Promised clothing supplies had not been delivered, so nearly 20 percent of the men had no shoes and walked with bare feet exposed to the cold, damp, and snow. They carried few provisions with them into camp, which fitted in a way, since they had no utensils to cook with. Pots and pans had been lost or discarded, but not replaced. They had only green wood for their fires, which belched burning smoke into their eyes and lungs. So they sat, froze, starved, and waited for spring. Local farmers had enough food to take care of the army, but did not want to take Continental paper money in payment. As a result, most chose to take their crops to the British camped in Philadelphia, who paid in gold and silver. Some desperate American soldiers roasted shoe or belt leather to fill their bellies, and a pet dog that used to wander through camp mysteriously disappeared. The winter proved disastrous for the American Army. Between December and June, some 2,500 men (nearly 25 percent of the army) died of exposure, disease, or malnutrition (Bodle, 2002, 102–243).

received a promotion to sergeant. He made it quite clear, though, that the higher non-commissioned rank did not make him an "officer." Martin and his fellow soldiers liked few of the officers they served under, tolerating them as a necessary evil. One hated captain even spurred the men to extreme action. A group of soldiers filled a canteen with gunpowder and planned to blow up the offending officer, but Martin exposed the plot. However, Martin did not stop the men from rigging a musket (primed with powder only) to fire at the unfortunate officer when he triggered the trap. "I did not wish him to receive any personal injury from their roguery," he explained, "but I cared very little how much they frightened him" (Martin 2001, 167, 226).

Martin participated in the Connecticut Line mutiny of 1780. The soldiers had had no choice, he later argued. They could either quietly starve to death or take action. The men rose up and refused to obey any orders until their basic needs were met. He did express regret over the treatment given one of the rare good officers in the army. During the incident, Colonel Return Meigs—"truly an excellent man"—received a bayonet wound. The mutiny ended quickly and

peacefully, but the men claimed partial victory, since rations arrived immediately afterward (Martin 2001, 157–162).

After the peace of 1783, the Continental Army dispersed. Martin accepted his final settlement certificates, then immediately sold some for pennies to investors to raise needed cash. He had had only one brush with death, catching yellow fever in 1782, though a nasty bout of green-apple-induced diarrhea once made him wish he was dead. He had suffered for his country with little in compensation. During seven years of service, he claimed to have been paid only once in real (not paper) money, and that only because the Army borrowed hard cash from French officers. Then Martin watched in wonder as the very citizens who had callously neglected the army began to take full credit for independence. Promised bounties failed to materialize, and speculators raked in the land grants supposedly destined for veterans. His 1830 autobiography expressed a deep sense of betrayal: "When the country had drained the last drop of service it could screw out of the poor soldiers, they were turned adrift like old worn-out horses" (Martin 2001, 241–245).

The reasons for these harsh conditions varied from year to year. During the first few years of the war, the supply system was a shambles. Corruption and graft ran rampant throughout the entire chain of supply. No one exercised a firm hand to coordinate the military's logistical support. The supply administration eventually improved, but other problems proved harder to overcome. Most roads in the United States were simple ruts in the ground or paths of dirt. Rain turned them into impassable mud, and snow blocked traffic in the winter. This made it nearly impossible to carry provisions any distance to the army. When wagons became stuck, teamsters simply abandoned them and returned to camp empty-handed. As mentioned, farmers had a choice of whom to sell their produce to. If they took their crops to the American camp, they would receive volatile paper currency. The British, on the other hand, offered solid pounds sterling. Leaving aside politics, a farmer concerned with keeping his farm going and his family fed until the next harvest naturally felt the pull of British money. Deep-rooted structural problems like inflation and substandard roads could not be solved without investing

Baron Friedrich Wilhelm von Steuben drills troops at Valley Forge in 1777. Steuben's introduction of discipline to the motley assortment of Continental troops of the American Revolution was a major contribution to the success of the army. (*National Archives and Records Administration*)

massive amounts of money and time, neither of which the struggling United States had in abundance during the Revolutionary War (Carp, 1984).

Because strategic information flowed almost exclusively among the officer corps, the average private in the Continental Army knew little about the war effort beyond his immediate surroundings. His world largely consisted of his tent mates, mess companions, and the fellows of his company. When pay failed to arrive or food ran out, he did not blame roads or inflated currency, because these culprits were too abstract and distant. He blamed those he could see and hear: citizens apparently indifferent toward the needs of the desperate men fighting for the country's liberty and officers who seemed not to care if their men suffered. During bad times, which seemed all too common, soldiers took out their frustrations on these two groups. Civilians became the victims of theft or plunder, while officers faced insubordination, desertion, and mutiny.

Officers and Enlisted Men

Becoming an officer in the Continental Army conferred not only military rank, but social status as well. A commission bestowed "gentleman" status on its recipient, and officers strove to live the life of a gentleman even in wartime. A defining feature of eighteenth-century gentlemen was that they did not work, and early officers took this to heart. Officers and enlisted men stood on opposite sides of a social gap that neither side wanted to cross. Officers rode instead of walked, employed personal servants to carry their belongings, bypassed camp food in favor of dining in taverns or homes, and at night looked up to see a solid roof overhead rather than tent canvas or open sky. Tasks like drilling, setting out guards, and looking after the men were delegated to sergeants. To the common soldier, commanders were cold, distant figures who inspired neither emotional attachment nor respect. Only three officers gained any real popularity among the enlisted men during the war: "The General" (George Washington), "the Marquis" (the Marquis de Lafayette), and "the Baron" (Baron Friedrich Wilhelm August Heinrich Ferdinand von Steuben). Each showed a willingness to work and a concern for the basic well-being of their men. Steuben in particular criticized his American counterparts for their unwillingness to work hard and lead by example. He could often be seen demonstrating military maneuvers personally to soldiers, regardless of whether the men in question were his responsibility (Royster, 1979, 85–91, 215–218).

Officers and men of the rank and file had vastly different concerns when it came to provisions and pay. Privates merely hoped to receive enough food to avoid starvation and prayed for the day when their officially established ration became a reality. Officers, though, were entitled to extra food based on their rank—sometimes three or more times the amount of the standard ration. During the harsh Valley Forge winter of 1777–1778, while enlisted men starved and froze, officers held a series of substantial dinner banquets, tea parties, and social events inside their warm cabins. The stark contrast did not escape the common soldiers' notice.

Facing severe food shortages in 1778, Congress reduced officers' food entitlements to a single official ration, putting them on a par with enlisted men. As compensation, lawmakers offered an extra cash stipend for officers to buy supplemental provisions befitting men of high social status. Officers thundered in protest at this terrible injustice. No one could expect them to survive on an average soldier's ration! They voiced their outrage to anyone who would listen, though they were bewildered when the men under their command refused to join in the protests. By fierce lobbying, officers not only retained their right to multiple rations, but also began drawing the additional cash stipends (Mayer, 1996, 67–68). Enlisted men looked upon all of this with a mixture of disgust, resignation, and cynicism. Most of the men after a time stopped believing in the basic decency of their superiors. Expectations dropped lower and lower, until a "good" officer was one the enlisted men disliked less than they disliked the enemy.

"Bad" officers—the incompetent, lazy, or vicious—faced insubordinate behavior or worse. A comical example of insubordination came in response to an oft-repeated order not to fire weapons in camp. A group of soldiers propped up a loaded musket in an empty tent, set a slow fuse burning, and then ran from the scene. When the weapon went off, it caused a ruckus in the camp. Angry officers rushed toward the sound ready to order immediate punishment. When they discovered the ruse, they swore to bend the perpetrators to the lash and went back to their tents. The pranksters then repeated the game over and over through the night until officers learned to ignore the gun discharges. As a result of this incident, for several days afterward the men could fire their muskets at will in camp without drawing attention (Neimeyer, 1996, 141). Other men took matters more seriously and directly threatened their officers' lives—though this occurred rarely and nearly always anonymously. One such serious incident came to light when Private James McCormick killed Private Reuben Bishop. At the murder trial, the accused soldier confessed to the deed but in his defense claimed that Bishop's death was purely accidental. McCormick explained that he was trying to kill the company commander but had missed and hit Bishop instead (Royster, 1979, 75).

Desertion was another possible response to either real or perceived mistreatment. Many men found that they could not tolerate the material conditions in the Continental Army and so just left for home. The overall desertion rate during the war averaged between 20 and 25 percent. That average masks fairly severe peaks when food shortages, pay stoppages, or battlefield defeats devastated morale. During these peaks, officers watched helplessly while men flowed out of the army. Civilians rarely cooperated in locating deserters, and some families even offered places for the men to hide. To effectively combat the problem would have required dispatching one-half of the army to chase down the other half. Frustrated, Washington reluctantly put aside his personal feelings and offered periodic blanket amnesties if men returned to the ranks of their own accord (Royster, 1979, 71–72). Other than that, absenteeism was just one more problem the army had to accept as normal.

Desertion occurred primarily among new recruits—those only days, weeks, or a few months into their terms of service. Absentee rates plummeted among troops serving past six months. Two elements account for this pattern of declining desertion. First, men who remained with the army longer than several months became part of a community of soldiers bound together by feelings of brotherhood and loyalty. Through each difficult year, the core veterans of the army became increasingly alienated and insulated from the wider American society. They learned to distrust civilians as a rule, blaming the miseries of military life on national apathy or the disloyalty of their countrymen. Enlisted men felt that they could depend only on each other. They could not even trust their officers. Common soldiers shared a unique bond of understanding based upon their mutual experiences of endurance and suffering. Deserting meant shattering that precious bond and abandoning brothers in arms. A few could not bring themselves to stay away, even when their terms of service legally ended. Joseph Plumb Martin received a discharge at the end of 1776 and vowed that nothing could drag him back into the war. The following spring he encountered a man he had grown close to while serving and who was still in the army. The friend pressed Martin to reenlist and return to his "mates." Though Martin claimed to feel no preference one way or the other, he signed up for a new term. As he later wrote, "that little insignificant monosyllable—No—was the hardest word in the language for me to pronounce" (Martin, 2001, 52).

The second reason for the decline in desertion was that soldiers had different motives for fighting. Some arrived with unrealistic dreams of glory or hoped for a steady income. They joined for adventure or cash, and within days or weeks found their expectations shattered. Such individuals probably accounted for the majority of desertions. Other men might have enlisted because of the future promise of free land, but self-interest does not explain why they remained. Prolonged exposure to the horrible conditions of Continental Army life dispelled any illusion that common soldiers would profit from the war. Therefore, veterans likely stayed because they believed they were fighting for a greater cause than themselves. The war was a struggle for liberty and for their country's future. Those goals were worth whatever treatment they had to endure or sacrifices they had to make (Royster, 1979, 373–378; Martin, 2001, 157–162).

A willingness to endure and sacrifice, however, did not mean that common soldiers surrendered the right to complain. Long-term veterans took organized action to try and improve conditions. Soldiers called them "protests," officers labeled them "mutinies." Three incidents occurred in early 1780 involving units from Massachusetts, New York, and Connecticut. The winter had been the worst in decades, and food shortages and pay interruptions ratcheted up the misery level. Of the three mutinies, only the last one appeared serious. On May 25, 1780, two Connecticut regiments formed up with weapons and prepared to march out of the army and back to their homes. A Pennsylvania division surrounded them and blocked the planned departure, but the angry New Englanders spent that night audibly pouring out their anger at Congress, army officers, uncaring citizens, and the country in general. One colonel who considered himself a "soldiers' friend" tried to talk the men into returning to their duties but received a bayonet wound in reply. The standoff ended peacefully the following day, however, when promises of more food and regular pay convinced the mutineers to resume their positions in the ranks. Some officers breathed a sigh of relief that the uprising ended so easily, but more realistic observers saw more trouble ahead (Royster 1979, 299–301).

A half-year after the Connecticut protest ended, the largest mutiny in American history almost tore apart the Continental Army. The Pennsylvania Line nursed the same widespread grievances about pay and rations, but in addition challenged the terms of their enlistments. Many of them had signed up for three years or the duration, which by customary interpretation held that their terms expired whichever deadline came first. When some of the men wanted to leave in 1780 after putting in three years, Washington and the Pennsylvania officers used trickery to convince the men that they had committed for the entire war. The men got wind of the deception, and their simmering resentment boiled over on New Year's Day, 1781. Led by their sergeants, 1,500 Pennsylvanians rose up, gathered their muskets and artillery, and marched out of winter camp toward Philadelphia. Most wanted to stay in the army, but felt cheated out of the bonus they would have received upon formally reenlisting. Officers who tried to stop them received rough treatment—two of them were wounded, one killed. Their commander, General Anthony Wayne, trailed along behind the column, unable to assert control. Ominously, soldiers from other states resisted orders to move against the Pennsylvanians, thereby lending implicit support to the mutiny.

British general Henry Clinton hurriedly sent spies to the Pennsylvanians, offering bribes and riches if they switched sides in the war. Leaders among the disaffected troops immediately handed the spies over to American authorities for execution. They were mutinous, not treasonous. Anxiety in the army as a whole finally began to subside when a delegation of sergeants opened negotiations with Wayne and other officers. With the firm support of their state government, the Pennsylvanians eventually agreed to terms. The army

George Washington informs Congress of a mutiny by the Connecticut Line in this 1780 letter. (*Library of Congress*)

agreed to make up all back pay, to pursue no prosecutions for mutiny, and to discharge some thirteen hundred men from service. Within a short time, many reenlisted and pocketed their new bounties. The soldiers in 1781 had won significant concessions from their superiors (though wages remained erratic), and that left officers concerned about the precedent it set. They swore never to allow another successful mutiny. Army officers responded quickly to mutinies later in 1781 with crackdowns and executions instead of negotiations, and this uncompromising policy continued throughout the remainder of the war. Discontent in the ranks continued but no longer led to mass action (Van Doren, 1943; Royster, 1979, 303–306).

When the British government agreed to a generous peace in 1783 and Americans celebrated their independence, many in the Continental Army officer corps felt underappreciated and hard-pressed. During the war, they had been promised a pension of half-pay for life. Now in 1783, Congress went back on that pledge and agreed only to give each officer a lump sum equal to five years' full salary.

If officers felt cheated, enlisted men felt absolutely betrayed. Officers got five years' income; the common soldier got a pat on the back and a shove out the door. As a parting package, each man received a "final settlement certificate" that promised three months' worth of pay at some unspecified future date—far less than many were owed in unpaid wages from previous years. The men could take with them their muskets and whatever clothes they wore. Finally, those soldiers who had been promised a land allotment after the war were given a land warrant, redeemable again sometime vaguely in the future. The Congress considered this settlement final and all obligations toward the soldiers fulfilled. For their long years of endurance, enlisted men returned home with only the clothes on their backs and a handful of paper promises—the exact kind that had consistently been broken during the war. The anguished cries and pleas of the common soldiers fell upon deaf ears. Even General Washington's vigorous appeals for better treatment for his departing men could not sway public opinion.

At every turn, the veterans ran into shattered promises and unfulfilled expectations. The final settlement certificates of 1783 suffered the same fate as the state promissory notes of 1780. Impoverished veterans in dire need of cash sold them for pennies on the dollar to investors who could afford to wait several years to collect at full face value. When Congress and the states finally began to redeem the notes in the 1790s, most of the money went to speculators. Since the payments came from tax revenues, many former soldiers actually ended up paying for rather than collecting their final settlements. The land allotment bounties also took too long to materialize. Peace had reigned for a decade and a half before Congress distributed the first land grants. By then, most of these too had been sold off to wealthy speculators for a tiny fraction of their value. Investors once again reaped the rewards intended for veterans.

Adding insult to injury, many Americans began playing down the importance of the Continental Army in securing independence. Victory came about through the combined effort of a patriotic citizenry, they claimed, not because a few ragamuffin soldiers marched around plundering farms and plotting mutinies. In the minds of some Americans, the Continental Army was posthumously reduced to irrelevance. The state militias—unsteady troops called up for short-term emergencies and disbanded quickly—were elevated to a new position of importance as the deciding factor in defeating the British. By the early 1800s, all the Continental veterans seemingly had to comfort themselves were their bonds of brotherhood and the shared belief that without their efforts the Revolution would have failed.

Conclusion

Not until 1818 did the country take steps to acknowledge the Continental Army's enlisted men. President James Madison successfully lobbied to provide financial relief for poverty-stricken Revolutionary soldiers. Officers in need received half-pay, common soldiers $5 per month. In 1832, Congress granted life pensions to everyone who had taken up arms from 1775 to

1783, though the measure lumped together militiamen, state troops, and Continental Army soldiers all as equally deserving of recognition. By that time, most veterans had died. The average survivor was seventy-four years old and drew his long-sought "life" pension for only a few years (Martin and Lender, 1982, 194–199).

References and Further Reading

Bodle, Wayne. *The Valley Forge Winter: Civilians and Soldiers in War.* University Park: Pennsylvania State University Press, 2002.

Bolton, Charles K. *The Private Soldier under Washington.* New York: Scribner's, 1902.

Carp, Wayne E. *To Starve the Army at Pleasure: Continental Army Administrators and American Political Culture, 1775–1783.* Chapel Hill: University of North Carolina Press, 1984.

Fast, Howard. "Did Washington's Wisecrack Tip the Balance?" *Americana* 20 (1992): 6.

Frey, Silvia. *Water from the Rock: Black Resistance in a Revolutionary Age.* Princeton, NJ: Princeton University Press, 1991.

Gross, Robert A. *The Minutemen and Their World.* New York: Hill and Wang, 1976.

Higginbotham, Don. *The War of American Independence: Military Attitudes, Policies, and Practice, 1763–1789.* New York: Macmillan, 1971.

Martin, James Kirby. "A 'Most Undisciplined, Profligate Crew': Protest and Defiance in the Continental Ranks, 1776–1783." In *Arms and Independence: The Military Character of the American Revolution*, ed. Ronald Hoffman and Peter J. Albert. Charlottesville: University Press of Virginia, 1984.

Martin, James Kirby, and Mark E. Lender. *A Respectable Army: The Military Origins of the Republic, 1763–1789.* Arlington Heights, IL: Davidson, 1982.

Martin, Joseph Plumb. *A Narrative of a Revolutionary Soldier*, ed. Thomas Fleming. New York: Signet, 2001.

Mayer, Holly A. *Belonging to the Army: Camp Followers and Community during the American Revolution.* Columbia: University of South Carolina Press, 1996.

Neimeyer, Charles Patrick. *America Goes to War: A Social History of the Continental Army.* New York: New York University Press, 1996.

Royster, Charles. *A Revolutionary People at War: The Continental Army and American Character, 1775–1783.* New York: Norton, 1979.

Wright, Robert K. *The Continental Army.* Washington, DC: Center of Military History, United States Army, 1986.

Van Doren, Carl. *Mutiny in January.* New York: Viking Press, 1943.

"Both Parties Trembled for the Ark of God": Transatlantic Methodism and the American Revolution

8

Anna M. Lawrence

The rise of American Methodism was coincident with the American Revolution. Even before the Revolution, though, the First Great Awakening
and the missionary efforts of Methodism's founder John Wesley influenced the formation of this sect in England in the 1730s and 1740s. Thus,
the history of Methodism is a profoundly transatlantic one, and this transatlantic movement was seriously affected by the rise of republican ideology
and the Revolutionary War in America. This movement was transatlantic
in the sense that there was a circulation of ideas, language, and people who
crossed the Atlantic constantly throughout the eighteenth century. Methodism did not develop solely as a British transplant on American soil; both
English and American Methodisms matured within a culture of exchange.
This flow of personnel and ideas was of course profoundly altered by the
events of the Revolution. When the Revolution began, Methodism in many
ways worked against it. Its leaders helped preserve the religious group as a
united body through the tumultuous times. Yet at the same time, paradoxically, the Revolution and its challenges to traditional authority played a role
in bringing both the American and the English branches of Methodism to a
new level of independence.

Methodism in the Revolutionary Era

The conservative, often promonarchy politics of John Wesley complicated
the establishment of Methodism in America during these revolutionary
years. Often, Methodism seems to have been a paradoxically unrevolution-
ary sect, not growing alongside Revolutionary sentiment, but rather in spite
of it. As historian Dee Andrews wrote, the Methodist preachers hindered the
republican cause "by not only attracting a devoted following among women
and blacks—often outsiders to the Revolutionary agitation—but also turning

British political cartoon shows a bishop climbing aboard a ship labeled "Hillsborough" having been chased there by angry American colonists who use long poles to push the ship away from the quay, 1768. (*Library of Congress*)

potential militia and Continental Army recruits into pacifist noncombatants" (Andrews, 2000, 3–4). The American Methodist leader and preacher Francis Asbury himself practiced and believed in a pacifist stance, refusing to speak for or against the Patriot cause, and he wished more Americans would follow his lead. He was terribly distraught at how the Revolution seemed to distract people from religious causes. During the Revolutionary period, Methodists were dissenters both religiously and politically. They were seeking to establish their religion in a time of severe political upheaval, but more than that, their position as religious dissenters was complicated by the fact that Methodist leaders were publicly advocating against the Revolutionary War. Adding to this complication was the fact that there were struggles within Methodism, echoing some of the larger issues within the war, such as hierarchy, democratic control, and representative politics.

Yet the Revolutionary period was incredibly important to the establish-ment of Methodism and the building of denominational religion in America more generally. The Revolutionary era saw Methodists form a separate de-nomination from the Anglican Church. From Methodism's birth in the 1730s and 1740s, John Wesley was always an ordained minister in the Church of England. His movement immediately diverged from the general practices of the Church of England, but many prominent Methodist preachers were ordained Anglican ministers, despite the fact that Methodists were recogniz-ably different from Anglicans. They believed in the transformative power of religious experience and in pursuing and practicing a "heart religion," and they held that salvation was attainable by all souls. While some of their practices were still wedded to the Church of England during the years of the American Revolution, the Methodist Church in America experienced its own revolution, breaking away from its mother church. This formation as a separate church in America finalized Methodism's separation from the Church of England as well as threatening to split the Methodist Church in-ternally. Americans denied aspects of English leadership, and some English Methodists were upset at the fact that the Methodist Church was now truly distinct from the Church of England.

The surprising part of the history of American and British Methodists during this period is that they did not splinter into a myriad of different groups; instead they remained unified after the Revolution. Of course, there were significant numbers of people who became alienated from the central Methodist leadership, never to return. The Inghamites and the Republican Methodists, just to name two splinter groups, were never reconciled with the central leadership (Rack, 1989, 216–217; Lawrence, 2004). The primary factors that held Methodism together were the force of its leadership and its accommodation of individual religious expression and practice. Wesley remained the leader of English and American Methodists until his death in 1791, and he made his role as their leader explicitly paternal. His leader-ship was so natural, so dominant, that he held their allegiance and affection almost as unquestionably as a father would—almost. The American sons did begin to question the rightfulness of Wesley's leadership and increas-ingly saw the power of "Dear Old Daddy," as he was called by some, as an anathema to republican politics, which had begun to infuse the American Methodist leadership by the 1780s.

One of the themes of the Revolution was of course the questioning of leadership—its shape and its methods. Many revolutionaries spoke ardently against the ideals of deference and presumed paternalism that had once reigned as natural authority in Anglo-America. Methodists on both sides of the Atlantic were keenly aware of Wesley's fatherly role and the deference he expected.

Wesley promoted many democratic features within Methodism, includ-ing lay preachers and exhorters, religious structures that depended upon close bonds within the laity, and individual attention to moral perfection. However, he was still interested in preserving the hierarchy of religious and political orthodoxy. The Loyalist/Tory vein of Wesley's political thinking was much more prominent than his Whiggish tendencies were in his response to leadership struggles, both among the Methodists and between the Americans and British. As we can see in the following discussion of American leadership, his love of traditional hierarchy led him to cling very tightly to the role of father to American and British Methodists. More particularly, in the case of American Methodists, his behavior throughout the Revolutionary period revealed his sense that "father knows best," that his decisions needed no discussion or explanation, and that he deserved a natural and absolute authority over the American branch.

Dissent in the Colonies

Methodists trace their origins to the meetings of Oxford University's Holy Club in the early 1730s, where John and Charles Wesley met with a number of fellow students to perfect their religious lives. Oxford turned a blind eye to these extra-institutional meetings, and their stance echoed a broader move toward religious tolerance (Rack, 1989, 35–37). Andrews explains that, in the eighteenth century, "English religion became 'denominationalized': nonconformists were not sectarians, schismatics from an established church, so much as 'denominated' Christians, calling themselves by a particular name for distinction from the established church" (Andrews, 1986, 2). Andrews saw this new attitude as the essential precondition of Wesley's syncretistic approach to religious traditions, combining his Anglican training with Pietist and early Christian theology (Andrews, 1986, 5–6). Linda Colley and many other scholars have argued that, whereas religious dissension had of course almost torn the country apart during the civil war period, by the eighteenth century it was met with cool disregard. This shift in attitude toward dissent was significant. In the previous century, religious dissent had been viewed as a political and social scourge, but for most of the eighteenth century, dissension seemed to be reduced to a legal stigma. The Toleration Act of 1689 had taken the sting out of dissenting status, even though adherence to the Church of England was still a requirement for public office. Colley even maintained that in practice Protestant dissenters faced no discrimination, and that the emotional and political center of religious discord was English opposition to Catholicism rather than internal Protestant divisions (Colley, 1992, 18–54).

American attitudes toward religious dissent were definitely shifting in the eighteenth century as well. In the period leading up to the Revolution, over 125 new churches had been established. The Great Awakening, which began with small revivals in New England during the late 1730s, had opened the way for the establishment of multiple churches. Additionally, new immigration, particularly to the middle colonies, had brought new religious institutions, especially in the form of Lutheran and Presbyterian churches. The Puritan hegemony of the north and the formal Anglican culture of the South were rapidly fading, to be replaced by a deeply pluralistic religious culture.

Certainly, a real change was under way, but the new attitude of tolerance was far from universal, nor did it result in immediate religious freedom.

Portrait of Methodist
leader John Wesley
(1703–1791). (*Cirker,
Hayward, and Blanche
Cirker, eds. 1967.*
Dictionary of American
Portraits. *New York:
Dover Publications, Inc.*)

In America and England, Methodists faced violence on the streets and repudiation in the press. Many preachers repeatedly experienced the wrath of
mobs on their circuits (the areas in which they preached). Wives incurred
their husbands' wrath when they joined evangelical groups, and children
felt their parents' displeasure after attending meetings. Pamphlets warned
society that Methodists were a political and social scourge equal to the dissenters of the seventeenth century. Furthermore, critics made an association
between Catholics and Methodists in the eighteenth century, a damning association indeed. The eighteenth-century Methodist experience casts doubt
on Colley's assertion that hatred of dissenters dissolved in the face of anti-
Jacobite fears, or that there was an unbridgeable division in people's minds
between Catholicism and dissenting Protestantism. Methodists were labeled
as dissenters as well as Catholics in disguise. The Methodist story points to
the fact that eighteenth-century religious culture was still an inhospitable
place for dissenting religious groups to grow. The level of response may have
been different toward seventeenth-century and eighteenth-century dissenters, but there was still a great risk in identifying with a dissenting religious
society.

The Church of England had reason to fear nonconformist sects, which threatened to woo believers away from the established church in eighteenth-century England. Methodists, even as they remained attached to the Church of England, suffered persecution on both sides of the Atlantic into the nineteenth century. Dissent was at work both within and outside the Church of England. There were many people who called themselves adherents to the Anglican Church while attending dissenting group meetings. Although the Church of England could claim 90 percent of English people as its members, their formal allegiance masked the fact that many English were no longer very centrally involved with the Anglican Church. The Church of England had already lost numbers to the dissenting splinters of radical Protestantism, such as the Quakers and Baptists. As the eighteenth century progressed, the Anglican Church seemed to be withering while nonconformist sects bloomed. By the time of Wesley's death in 1791, despite losses to splinter groups, Wesleyan Methodists claimed 72,000 souls in England and 60,000 in America (Watts, 1978, 404). Methodist societies, once planted in America, grew phenomenally during the early national period and claimed half a million members by 1830 (Hatch, 1989, 3).

Growth in the Colonies

Methodism had taken root in most areas of the colonies by the 1740s, but Wesley waited a while to include America in his missionary plan. He seemed content to allow lay Methodists to drive the American Methodist movement until the 1770s. After the Seven Years' War, many Wesleyan Methodists emigrated to America, and this seems to have led Wesley toward advancing his mission there (Andrews, 1986, 17). The most significant growth took place in the Maryland, Delaware, New York, and Philadelphia areas, where many Irish immigrants settled.

According to Methodist lore, it was an Irish Wesleyan convert, Barbara Heck, who originally helped light the Methodist fires in America. Heck and other immigrants, who had originally followed Methodist practices in Ireland, began to assimilate to the Lutheran church after settling in New York City. One night in the fall of 1766, Heck interrupted a card game in an Irish immigrant's home by seizing the cards on the table and throwing them into the fireplace. Heck was symbolically renewing her vow to keep to the Methodist rules of generally avoiding trivial diversions, and perhaps pointing out the fate of the players' souls if they kept at this: Their souls would burn in Hell, like so many cards in the fire. She also reportedly urged Philip Embury, a fellow Irish immigrant, to begin itinerating, or working as a traveling preacher in New York (Baker, 1976, 42). Barbara Heck and Philip Embury formed classes in New York City in 1766. By the late 1760s, there was a Methodist community in Philadelphia as well (Baker, 1976, 33–50; Andrews, 1986, 18–23).

Captain Thomas Webb, an early organizer of American Methodism deeply influenced by John Wesley, played an important role in the growth of Methodism in New York. Captain Webb had fought in the Seven Years' War; he converted to Methodism in England and was close to John Wesley, who encouraged his enthusiasm, religious and otherwise. After returning from military service, he began preaching in various New York meeting spaces and organized a Methodist class in Brooklyn with a mixed black and white membership. Webb, Embury, and other newly immigrated English Methodists built the first meetinghouse in New York City, and this was done largely without formal support from Wesleyan Methodists in England or leadership on Wesley's part. Captain Webb also ventured into the many centers of new Methodist converts springing up throughout the middle colonies and upper South.

Evangelizing Methodists were encouraged by the ripe field of America in the 1760s, since there were a number of denominations and a variety of new immigrants, especially in the middle colonies. Unlike Methodists in England, American Methodists did not have to contend with a dominant Church of England. There were areas of America that were altogether free of any religious authority, and Methodism's itinerant evangelical system was well suited to exploit these open areas.

Up to the beginning of the 1770s, American Methodism was largely led by the laity, but after this period, Wesleyan Methodists began to systematize the American societies in earnest. The first step in organizing was to send over licensed preachers and to send someone to oversee these official preachers as well as the lay preachers and the various societies that had already formed without Wesley's help. The first wave of Wesleyan preachers came over in 1769; Richard Boardman, who had traveled a preaching circuit for some time under Wesley, and Joseph Pilmore, a junior preacher, were the first volunteers to come to America. To lead these societies and preachers, John Wesley sent over English preacher Francis Asbury in 1771. Francis Asbury began his American itinerancy just prior to the Revolution, and his struggles for leadership reveal the difficulties between American and English preachers during this period as well as the difficulties caused by Wesley's paternal role, as discussed above.

At the August 1771 British conference in Bristol, Asbury volunteered for service in America. A scant two months later, he landed in Philadelphia with fellow itinerant Richard Wright. Since Boardman and Pilmore had been sent over in 1769, they had found their work overwhelming and petitioned Wesley for help in preaching to the American societies. Asbury threw himself into disciplining American societies, as he thought Wesley would do, superseding Boardman and Pilmore's authority. In New York, Asbury complained, the leadership was especially lax; Methodists were allowing folks outside the ranks to infiltrate the select bands and other groups. The lines were not properly drawn, and this was largely due, Asbury said, to the lack of leadership.

In 1772, John Wesley named Asbury "assistant in America" (Potts, 1958, 1:46), but he was quickly replaced as leader by Thomas Rankin, who was named general assistant by Wesley in 1773. Rankin was senior in years and service to Asbury, but perhaps more important, he was closer to Wesley and more likely to adhere to Wesley's wishes. Asbury was more resistant to being led than Rankin. Furthermore, Rankin was also superior in education to Asbury, who was the son of a gardener, young and untutored (Andrews,

2000, 43–44). Rankin convened the first conference in America in 1773, shortly after he arrived. He came to America with a directive to make the American Methodists shipshape, according to Wesley's ideals. This meant following the printed guidelines of the Methodist discipline more closely, as well as keeping closer accounts of membership numbers. He repeatedly wrote in his diary about the lack of discipline of the various societies he encountered as he toured the American colonies from the middle of 1773 through August 1777 (when he started to head back to England during the Revolution) (Tees, 1773–1778). Soon after Rankin's arrival he wrote: "From what I see and hear, and so far as I can judge, if my brethren who first came over had been more attentive to our discipline, there would have been, by this time, a more glorious work in many places of this continent. Their love-feasts, and meetings of society, were laid open to all their particular friends; so that their number did not increase, and the minds of our best friends were thereby hurt" (Rankin, "Journal" 2, ca. June 12, 1773).

Rankin outwardly blamed Asbury for what he perceived as American Methodism's failure to thrive, disciplinary weaknesses, and organizational confusions. In New York and Philadelphia, he complained of women's extravagant dress, and the lack of discipline (Rankin, "Journal" 4, June 14, 1773, and 9, December 5, 1773). But even though his criticisms were based upon the behavior of the laity, he blamed American Methodist leadership. He had taken over the supervision of American societies and not given an official role to Asbury. He opined in several places that Asbury was an effective preacher but deficient as a leader. He wrote in his journal in December 1774, "Brother Asbury preached this evening, and not without the Divine blessing. Next day we talked over different matters respecting the work and also removed some little and foolish misapprehensions, that had taken place in his mind" (Rankin, "Journal" 20, December 4, 1774).

The conflict between Rankin and Asbury went deeper than two brothers fighting over Wesley's affections. In the context of the Revolutionary struggle, they represented different modes of leadership in a rapidly changing period. Even by the time Rankin arrived, Asbury had become "American" in some ways. He was not distinguished in his education and therefore more readily associated with the lay preachers who served with him than did the well-educated British ministers who ruled Methodism in England. As Asbury got older, and even after he became a bishop of American Methodists, he increased the distance he would travel and braved rougher terrain as an itinerant preacher. Rankin, on the other hand, believed in ruling from above. He set about to correct the American discipline and organize American Methodists along Wesleyan lines. He often criticized the work of other preachers and in Asbury's opinion, "assumed too much authority over the preachers and people" (Bangs, 1860, 1:86).

A Strained Transatlantic Relationship

At the same time that American Methodists were beginning to become organized, strained relations between England and America developed. Asbury wrote that Wesley had counseled the American Methodists to stay out of the politics of war, "to have nothing to do with the affairs of this world if he could help it, and mind the business of our spiritual calling" (Francis Asbury to Joseph Benson, January 15, 1816). Rankin, Asbury argued, violated this directive by declaring that Revolutionary America was a lost cause for Methodists. As a result of this pessimism and fear for the well-being of leading Methodist preachers, Rankin and Wesley supported the recall of all English preachers. This was in response to the heightening of conflict between England and the American colonies. In March 1775, Wesley wrote to Rankin that he wanted "Brother Asbury to return to England [at] the first opportunity." In the same letter, Wesley wrote to all Americans preachers that they should act as "peace-makers" and not commit themselves to any side in the conflict. Overall, they should be united as a group and follow Rankin's lead in all things. Charles Wesley also added a more directly worded appeal in the same letter that urged Rankin to be "like-minded with me. I am of neither side, and yet of both; on the side of New England and old. Private Christians are excused, exempted, privileged, to take no part in civil troubles" (John Wesley to Thomas Rankin, March 1, 1775, in *Letters of John Wesley*, 1931, 6:142–143). Asbury interpreted this recall of preachers as reflecting a desire to stay within the fold of both the mother country and the mother church. Asbury interpreted Rankin's support of the recall of preachers as reflecting his desire to stay within the fold of both the mother country and the mother church. Asbury wrote: "It appeared to me that his [Rankin's] objective was to sweep the continent of every preacher that Mr. Wesley had sent to it and of every respectable travelling preacher from Europe who had graduated among us, whether English or Irish. He told us that if we returned to our native country, we should be esteemed as such obedient, loyal subjects that we should obtain ordination in the grand episcopal Church of England and come back to America with respectability after the war was ended."

Joseph Pilmore and Richard Boardman returned to England in 1774, as the first wave of preachers to return. In July 1775, the remaining leading English preachers, Rankin, Martin Rodda, and James Dempster, had all resolved to return as well (though they did not leave immediately). Wesley made repeated appeals to Asbury to leave the colonies, but Asbury expressed his desire to stay, and eventually Wesley resigned himself to this (John Wesley to Thomas Rankin, August 13, 1775, *Letters of John Wesley*, 1931, 6:173). Asbury said he had a calling to stay and wrote, "I can by no means agree to leave such a field for gathering souls to Christ, as we have in America. It would be an eternal dishonour to the Methodists . . . neither is it the part of a good shepherd to leave his flock in time of danger: therefore, I am determined, by the grace of God, not to leave them, let the consequence be what it may" (Clark, 1958, 1:161, August 7, 1775).

The recall of all English preachers was not just a political move within the context of the Revolution; it also reflected the internal politics of Methodism. At a preachers' conference in May 1776, Wesley again called for the return of the English preachers. Most of those who had ignored his earlier advice answered his call by leaving America within the next year as the war started to encroach upon the middle colonies (Kirby, 1996, 4). Non-Methodists may have seen this retreat as confirming the political status of Methodists as Loyalists. Others within the society may have seen this retreat as underlining how dangerous and relatively unimportant Wesley considered the project of trying to promote Methodism during the Revolution. Furthermore, his recall of preachers to England tested Wesley's power over the American branch of Methodism and the loyalty of American preachers.

Wesley himself contradicted his advice to American Methodists to remain above the political fray and focus solely on spiritual matters. His *Calm Address to Our American Colonies* was published in 1775, and certainly caused American colonists to become suspicious of Methodists' political stance. Wesley had copied, with little alteration, a pamphlet previously published by Samuel Johnson. In *Calm Address*, Wesley is staunchly anti-Republic and pro-king. The pamphlet urges Americans to acquiesce in their powerless status as subjects of the king and to accept British authority. *Calm Address* further argues that the Seven Years' War, the ostensible cause for increased taxes and the root of the conflict, was all about the mother country protecting America. Raising taxes to pay for that war was reasonable and well within Parliament's prerogative. Displaying deeply Tory philosophy, he argued that the English ideals of liberty were already well established in American society. Wesley wrote:

> What more religious liberty can you desire, than that which you enjoy already? May not every one among you worship God according to his own conscience? What civil liberty can you desire, which you are not already possessed of? Do you not sit without restraint, every man under his own vine? Do you not, every one, high or low, enjoy the fruit of your labour? This is real, rational liberty, such as is enjoyed by Englishmen alone; and not by any other people in the habitable world. (Wesley, 1775, 15)

In this passage, Wesley (following Johnson) described the nature of disestablishment of religious worship within the context of English liberal Enlightenment thought. If religion should be separate from government, then Methodists should also stay out of the Revolutionary War. Wesley thought that all Christians should be neutral in politics, a position that derived from his pietistic Moravian connections and also from his parents' stance as dissenters who were also nonjurors, that is, people who refused on principle to take any oaths of loyalty (see Rack, 1989; Andrews, 2000, 14–18). Of course, Wesley also directly contradicted his appeal for religious neutrality by publishing such a clear defense of the Loyalist position. Furthermore, he effectively converted any American Methodist neutrality into presumed loyalism. Wesley's pamphlet was well circulated, selling 40,000 copies in the first three weeks it was out in England. He also published a number of other addresses and pamphlets in the same promonarchy vein. His position, then, was well known to Americans and put a certain antipatriot stamp on American Methodists.

Wesley's *Calm Address* made life more difficult for American Methodists during the Revolution. In his journal in March 1776, Asbury wrote that he was "sorry that the venerable man [Wesley] ever dipped into the politics of America." Asbury went on to speculate that if Wesley had "been

A CALM

ADDRESS

TO

OUR AMERICAN

COLONIES.

By *JOHN WESLEY,* M. A.

Ne, pueri, ne tanta animis affuefcite bella,
Neu patriæ validas in vifcera vertite vires.
VIRGIL.

LONDON,
Printed by R. HAWES, in *Dorfet-Street,* Spitalfields,
And Sold at the Foundry, Moorfields.

Title page of treatise written by
Methodist leader John Wesley.
(*Library of Congress*)

a subject of America, no doubt he would have been as zealous an advocate of the American cause. But some inconsiderate persons have taken occasion to censure the Methodists in America, on account of Mr. Wesley's political sentiments" (Clark, 1958, 1:181). It was not, however, simply a publication from the leading Methodist that caused Methodists in general to become targets of anti-Tory sentiment after 1775. Some prominent Methodists, including Rankin's assistant, Martin Rodda, had been outspoken in their support of the Loyalist cause. Other Methodists proclaimed neutrality or, like Asbury, claimed their nonjuror status exempted them from participating in any political cause.

In 1777, Martin Rodda campaigned for the Loyalist cause and actively joined the Loyalist resistance. Rodda had hardly refrained from mixing politics and religion as Wesley had commanded; instead, he distributed Loyalist material while on his circuit. Rodda was arrested and narrowly escaped execution, returning to England with the help of a fellow Methodist (Simpson, 1984, 4). Patriots were generally very suspicious of Methodists, claiming that Methodists were acting as Loyalist spies. The accusation of duplicity was not new to Methodists, who had been seen before as hiding their true motives behind their religion (Lawrence, 2004).

Many Methodists did try to stay above the fray, turning a blind eye to the political and martial turmoil they were surrounded by. Asbury made frequent reference in his diary to the war movements in the middle colonies where he preached during the war. He seemed distressed that people's minds were distracted by the war, which prevented them from considering their religious well-being (Clark, 1958, 1:155, April 30–May 4, 1775, and 186, May 8, 1776). As he rode into Burlington, New Jersey, on April 17, 1776, he wrote that he "was filled with holy peace, and employed in heavenly contemplations: but found, to my grief, that many had so imbibed a martial spirit that they had lost the spirit of pure and undefiled religion" (Clark, 1958, 1:184, April 23, 1776). The violent feelings and actions of war were certainly in opposition to the pacific religious spirit Asbury hoped to inspire. His disappointment during this period was also that more people did not see the parallel between earthly struggles and those in the next world. After noting the commotion in Baltimore over the recent arrival of a British man-of-war in 1776, he wrote: "Alas for fallen man! He fears his fellow creatures, whose breath is in their nostrils, but fears not Him who is able to destroy body and soul in hell. If fire and sword at a small distance can so alarm us, how will poor impenitent sinners be alarmed when they find, by woeful experience, that they must drink the wine of the wrath of God, poured out without mixture?" (Clark, 1958, 1:180, March 7, 1776). The real battle, as Asbury and other revivalists struggled to remind those living through the Revolutionary War, was being fought over their souls. The message was that this earthly war was just a passing trifle, soon to end, and not worth so much energy and emotion.

Rankin, Asbury, and other Methodists did not take an active stance in the war, but maintained their pacifism. Rankin was publicly sympathetic to the American cause, but he also wrote in his journal that he opposed war for any cause (Rankin, "Journal" 68–69, July 1, 1777–July 27, 1777). Yet the worsening war did have effects on the Methodists, despite some of their best efforts to ignore it. In September 1777, Rankin described his own hasty departure from Maryland, when he believed his life was in danger. He did not leave immediately following Wesley's call, perhaps in order to retain his supervisory position over Asbury and the American Methodists. In a letter to Wesley, while aboard a ship waiting to leave the harbor, he wrote that English troops had landed on August 25, and that Methodists in eastern Maryland had been captured by the rebels. The Methodists had refused to fight with them. "Such [has been] the conduct of these patrons of liberty against the peaceable inofensive people!" Rankin suspected that his life was in danger, since he had been named as a Tory; rebels had reportedly threatened Rankin's life. Rankin wrote, "I looked upon it as a call from divine providence and so went on board the next day Having sent an account of all that has passed to Mr. Shadford and Asbury, who I apprehend unless God appear for them will be exposed to sever Sufferings." The oftentimes brutal treatment of Methodists as suspected Tories during the war seemed only to confirm the negative view Wesley held of American independence. Wesley wrote on the reverse of Rankin's letter, "The Rebels in Scotland did not even hang or Shoot those who refused to Join with them. But if they had what mercy had that been compared to the death inflicted by the Rebels in America? Can Englishmen Still open their Mouth in favor of those worse than Indian Savages?" (Thomas Rankin to John Wesley, September 17, 1777, Preachers Collection). Rankin left Maryland and went to Philadelphia, which was then under British control. He waited until March 17, 1778, to return to England with a number of other prominent English preachers—Rodda, George Shadford, and Robert Lindsay.

After the English Preachers Headed Home

After hearing of Rankin's and Rodda's departure, Asbury wrote in his journal, "So we are left alone" (Clark, 1958, 1:249, September 22, 1777). Since 1773, sixty American and English preachers had itinerate preaching circuits in the American connection. After March 1778, only one licensed itinerant preacher, Asbury, remained, and less than half of the unlicensed preachers were still on their circuits (Andrews, 2000, 55).

While Wesley's recall of preachers did not decimate American Methodism altogether, it clearly did create a power vacuum. There were still American lay preachers, and certainly American societies continued to meet, but the leadership ranks were devastated by this recall. Most of the leading itinerant preachers were English, Irish, or Scottish, and all but Asbury had returned; Rankin, Richard Boardman, John King, Joseph Pilmore, George Shadford, Thomas Webb, Abraham Whitworth, Richard Wright, and Joseph Yearby all left before or during the early years of the war (Buckley, 1912, 16). Like Rankin, though, Asbury framed his decision on whether to stay in America as a "calling," and Asbury never wrote that his decision was a direct repudiation of Wesley's wishes. Asbury, as the only English-born and -trained preacher who remained, became the only Methodist leader left in America. He was somewhat uncertain about whether he had made the right decision and wondered at times if he should go back to England. He wrote on March 13, 1778, that he was "under some heaviness of mind. But no wonder: three thousand miles from home—my friends have left me—I am considered by some as an enemy of the country—every day liable to be seized by violence, and abused. However, all this is but a trifle to suffer for Christ, and the salvation of souls. Lord, stand by me!" (Clark, 1958, 1:263–264). Asbury's rather pathetic lament in his journal underscores the difficulty and isolation that Methodists in general must have felt. Even if they were born in the colonies, and especially if like Asbury they were foreign-born, their allegiance to the Revolutionary struggle and America as homeland was suspect. By the beginning of the war in 1776, Asbury had only been in America for five years, and he clearly still considered England his home.

Asbury's isolation increased with time. After April 1778, his journeys were much more circumscribed by his refusal to take an oath of fidelity to Maryland. He was taken in by Judge Thomas White, a staunch Methodist, who was prosecuted as a Loyalist as a result of his association with Asbury and others. He was able to preach in the state of Delaware for the next two and a half years, which despite its diminutive size held a great number of Methodists; the part of the Delmarva Peninsula in Delaware alone accounted

Portrait of Francis Asbury, first bishop of the Methodist Church in America. (*Library of Congress*)

for nearly 15 percent of American Methodists during the Revolution. Still, Asbury was accustomed to covering huge swaths of land in his circuits; previously he had preached in the states of New York, Pennsylvania, New Jersey, Maryland, Virginia, and West Virginia. Thus, his sense of desolation is understandable. Nevertheless, as scholars have pointed out, Asbury, "despite persecution, seclusion, and inability to travel retained, even increased, his influence" (Kirby, 1996, 3).

Despite a deficit of leadership, Methodists managed to increase, unlike many denominations during the war, actually tripling their numbers in eight years. They went from just under 5,000 members in May 1776 to almost 9,000 in 1777, and 10,500 in 1781. At the end of the war in 1784, the numbers had increased to 15,000 members. During the war, Asbury was continually drawing up new circuits and appointing new preachers, 90 between 1774 and 1784 (Baker, 1972; Simpson, 1984, 7). How did the sect manage to thrive in the face of maltreatment and neglect from its father John Wesley? How did they attract new numbers, despite the public perception of counter-revolutionary politics?

Methodists took an ecumenical stance to embrace the followers of other Christian denominations, a stance that served them well as the religious environment shifted during the Revolutionary War (Andrews, 1986, 5). While the Anglican Church in the South was struggling to retain its already weak hold over the area, Methodists easily stepped into the gap. Their itinerant structure was well suited to areas that lacked churches, which was true of many areas of the South. While the cannons of war were sounding, leaders in America sent triumphant accounts to Wesley of their spectacular growth in areas like Virginia. By the end of the Revolutionary War, the South accounted for a stunning 89 percent of Methodist members (Simpson, 1984, 7).

As they experienced this impressive growth, Asbury and Methodist leadership in general came to rely on young, energetic preachers who were not daunted by the challenges of the Revolution—preachers like Freeborn Garrettson. He became an itinerant preacher at the very start of the war in 1776. Garrettson was American-born and free to travel, so Asbury used him to oversee the work in other parts of the Methodist southern and middle colonies. Garrettson had also refused to take arms or oath, and he openly opposed slavery. His circuit was the Delmarva Peninsula area, with its huge concentration of both Methodists and anti-Methodists. In 1779, while Asbury was in confinement, Garrettson oversaw American Methodism, traveling to Philadelphia as Asbury's agent to bolster the societies there. In New Jersey and Pennsylvania, he managed to preach twelve sermons a week. In 1780, Garrettson's conflict with Patriots and the law intensified; he was accused as a Tory, and on February 25, 1780, placed in a Maryland jail. After appeals to the governor, he was released (Simpson, 1984, 96–97).

During 1779 and 1780, the struggle between American and English authority continued in Methodist societies. In 1779 an "irregular" session of the conference of Methodists in Baltimore recognized Asbury's leadership and resolved "that brother *Asbury* ought to act as *general assistant* in America." The conference decided that this should be the case "because [he was] originally appointed by Mr. Wesley" (Lee, 1810, 67). Soon after this Baltimore conference, Garrettson was assigned to travel to Virginia and North Carolina and "help convince preachers and people of the Wesleyan viewpoint," which was that there should be no ordinations conferred or sacraments given and Asbury should be the leader for all Methodists, north and south (Simpson, 1984, 6).

Due to the difficulties of traveling during the war, the full body of preachers was not able to meet regularly. On May 18, 1779, southern preachers came together in Fluvanna, Virginia, without the northern preachers (and without Asbury), and decided to administer the sacraments, including baptism, until the next scheduled preachers' conference in 1780. Some historians have seen Robert Strawbridge, the Irish itinerant, as the key figure behind the independent move (see Baker, 1976, 39; Andrews, 2000, 63–64). It was a statement against Wesleyan authority as well as continued association with Anglicanism in both religious and political manners. It was also a statement supporting democratic decisions among Methodists and the revolutionary spirit of the times (Kirby, 1996, 4).

American Methodists understood that this was a rejection of Asbury's authority as well as a rejection of Wesley and perhaps English Methodism altogether. As Jesse Lee, who had been an active Methodist during this period, wrote in the early nineteenth century, "There was great cause to fear a division, and both parties trembled for the ark of God, and shuddered at the

Freeborn Garrettson

Freeborn Garrettson was the most significant American-born leader of Methodism during the Revolution. A young and energetic twenty-four-year-old, he was the ideal Methodist preacher. Garrettson was born August 15, 1752, into a prosperous family that had been in America for three generations. Like many Methodists at the time, he was not born into the church. His mother had been active in the Church of England in Maryland, but had also been attracted to evangelical preaching. When she died, he was only ten years old; he described the next decade of his life as superficial and decadent. As a young man, "I was as destitute of the power of religion as a hottentot. . . . I kept company with the pleasure-takers about town" (Simpson, 1984, 2).

In 1770, Garrettson heard Robert Strawbridge, a Methodist itinerant who preached frequently in the Maryland circuits. This was his first real experience with Methodism, but it took repeated exposure to preaching and religious literature for him to feel like a true Methodist. He met Francis Asbury in August 1773, and he "determined to choose God's people for my people." When his father died soon after, he inherited all of his holdings, property and slaves included. Garrettson, however, did not hold slaves for very long. In June 1775, he gathered his "family together for prayer. [and] this thought powerfully struck my mind. 'It is not right for you to keep your fellow creatures in bondage; you must let the oppressed go free'" (Simpson, 1984, 48–49).

As the War of Independence was starting in 1776, Garrettson became a Methodist preacher. These were difficult years for any religious organization, but the work of Garrettson, among

Itinerant Methodist preacher Freeborn Garrettson was instrumental in spreading Methodism throughout the newly formed United States. (*Courtesy of the Pitts Theology Library, Candler School of Theology, Emory University*)

other new preachers and many lay Methodists, contributed to the ongoing success of American Methodism. Garrettson resisted fighting in the war, but he supported the Revolutionary cause. Because his mentor Francis Asbury was a suspected Tory and spent much of the war secluded, Garrettson became Asbury's agent, overseeing the work, attending conferences, and visiting different circuits and preachers. In 1779, Garrettson effectively ran American Methodism. As an American, Garrettson was indispensable, since he was less likely to draw the Patriots' suspicions than his English Meth-

thought of dividing the Church of Christ" (Lee, 1810, 70). There was a real concern that schisms would form and American Methodists would be weakened by this division. After the war began, as English leadership became unavailable in the colonies, American Methodists looked with a jaundiced eye on any of Wesley's appointed leaders, including Asbury. The decision to

odist colleagues. Preaching in the Delmarva Peninsula during the war, Garrettson oversaw the largest single Methodist community, accounting for about one-seventh of all American Methodists. He traveled to different societies to bolster them during the war, and indefatigably preached up to a dozen sermons in one week, traveling hundreds of miles on horseback.

While he was overseeing the largest Methodist society, he was also affected by anti-Methodist and strong Patriot sentiments. Garrettson was accused of being a Tory and put into jail in Cambridge, Maryland, on February 25, 1780. After he appealed to the governor of Maryland, the governor granted his release. At the same time that political conflict brewed in secular society, religious conflicts brewed in his own Methodist society. When southern and northern Methodists were divided over the issues of sacraments and authority in 1779 and 1780, "democratic and conciliatory" Freeborn Garrettson was an ideal mediator. While Asbury saw himself as the leader and was rankled that the southern preachers would not obey his wishes, Garrettson was in a better position to negotiate a compromise.

In order to knit the Methodist societies together and preach his circuits, Garrettson continued to travel while a dangerous war was being waged. He traveled extensively in Virginia during the war, where a number of important battles were fought in the final years of the war. He preached in Cornwallis and near Yorktown, and heard cannons while preaching. In 1781, he traveled 5,000 miles in Virginia and North Carolina, preaching 500 sermons that year (Simpson, 1984, 6–7).

In the years of 1782 to 1784, his preaching circuit was in Delaware, where he attracted a large following among African Americans. He preached to large crowds, both black and white, in this area. With the overwhelming majority of Methodists located in the South throughout the Revolutionary period, Garrettson was instrumental in creating a vibrant and exciting outbreak of evangelical fever. At the close of the war, Garrettson and other Methodists were only beginning to form an independent church in America. To gather preachers together for the Christmas conference of 1784, he rode a remarkable 1,200 miles in six weeks.

After Methodists formed this new church in America, Garrettson began to think more about the American project as a whole. This led him to focus on New York as the area most in need of new organization. In 1788, he encouraged a dozen young preachers to go with him and evangelize New York State under his leadership. It was there that he met his future wife, Catherine Livingston. They had a lengthy, remarkable courtship of five years. Livingston was his match in evangelical energy, having formed her own Methodist meeting and encouraged the kindling of evangelicalism in the Rhinebeck area of upstate New York. Despite considerable opposition from her family, they were married in 1793 at a Methodist Episcopal church in Rhinebeck. She was thirty-eight years old and he was forty when they married, and both had already lived full lives. Well into the nineteenth century, both Catherine and Freeborn Garrettson continued to travel, preach, and exhort extensively in order to spread Methodism in America.

reject Asbury's authority had been made mainly by southern preachers, and it was repudiated by the northern preachers. The northern and southern preachers remained divided for almost a year. During that time, the South saw dramatic increases in membership, which only confirmed to them that their independent actions were correct.

At a meeting of northern preachers with Asbury in April 1780, a number of resolutions were passed. One of the first resolutions was against slavery, and the other major resolution was to declare that they viewed the southern preachers "as no longer Methodists in connection with Wesley and us till they come back." The northern preachers dreaded the thought of losing such a thriving society of Methodists and splitting the formerly strong fellowship of preachers. Therefore, once Asbury could travel again, his first business was to arrange a compromise between the two groups of preachers. In 1780, Asbury went with Freeborn Garrettson and William Watters to the Virginia conference and proposed that they rescind the previous measures. After much debate and a last-minute reversal by the southern preachers, the conferences reunited and in 1782 unanimously chose Asbury to act as general assistant, which they were careful to say was "according to Mr. Wesley's original appointment." Finally, in 1783, Wesley officially backed him as the general assistant in America (Kirby, 1996, 4). This was a just reward for his valiant backing of Wesley at a crossroads in the formation of American Methodism. Eventually, though, even Wesley had to concede that Americans were on their way to forming an independent church, completely separate from the Church of England, and somewhat separate from Wesley as well.

Despite some conciliatory moves on both sides of the ocean, Asbury felt that the Revolution had irrevocably sundered his relationship to Wesley and English Methodists. He wrote retrospectively that his "greatest sorrow" was "that our dear father [Wesley] from the time of the Revolution to his death grew more and more jealous of myself and the whole American connection; that it appeared that we had lost his confidence almost entirely." How did the Americans supposedly lose Wesley's confidence? Asbury, rather petulantly, saw the problem as caused by Rankin, concluding that Wesley "was told, and possibly made to believe, that no sooner had he granted the Americans what they wished than they declared themselves independent of him" (Francis Asbury to Joseph Benson, January 15, 1816, Preachers Collection).

Wesley was certainly insecure about his power over the Americans. In October 1783, Wesley wrote to Jesse Lee a letter that he wanted conveyed to all American Methodists. Wesley was concerned that some English preachers were working in America without his permission. He insisted that any English preacher going to America had to have his permission to do so, as well as accepting the local authority of Asbury and the American conference (Potts, 1958, 1:450; Neely, 1892, 211).

Despite Wesley's need for control of the American leadership, by at least as early as 1784, Wesley understood that the American church should have some sort of separate and independent status. There were logistical reasons for giving some independence to the American church; administering sacraments and the ordination of new ministers had become difficult issues, threatening to divide the church. But one of the underlying reasons was that Wesley felt the American Revolution had separated England and America, perhaps irrevocably. His other reasons included the lack of an Anglican bishop in America to ordain ministers, the expansion of American societies, which had left them disorganized, and the fact that Asbury had asked for a different form of government that would address these specific needs of American Methodists (*Minutes of Several Conversations*, 1785). American Methodism had become more than simply an arm of British Methodism—it was now a unique and particular movement. In 1784, Wesley chose Thomas Coke, who had been ordained in the Church of England, to become superintendent and oversee American ordinations and administration of sacraments. In this role, he would have the power of an Episcopal or Anglican bishop without the title. Wesley showed some political sensitivity in his decision here, since, given the antihierarchical sentiments of post-Revolutionary America, American Methodists would not have stood for a bishop overseeing the American church.

Coke sailed to America in September 1784 with two preachers whom Wesley had ordained to administer sacraments, Richard Whatcoat and Thomas Vasey. Coke feared that he would be rejected as the leader of American preachers. He told Wesley, "I may want all the influence, in America, which you can throw into my scale" (Thomas Coke to John Wesley, August 9, 1784, in Tyerman, 1872, 3:429). His comment reflected Coke's need to control Asbury and Asbury's apparent unwillingness to submit to the English Methodist leadership. The establishment of a Methodist superintendent in America further cemented the status of American Methodism as a separate, dissenting religion—separate from American Anglicans (now Episcopalians), the Church of England, and perhaps English Methodists as well. Seeing the transatlantic dynamic of this period reveals how the scales tipped back and forth between American sovereignty and British control during the last decades of the eighteenth century. What was interesting, though, was the way that this departure for American Methodists marked a departure for Methodists as a whole. Upon granting the powers they did to the Methodist superintendent in America, both the British and American Methodists felt themselves taking a further step of separation from the Church of England. Thus, through Methodism, the American Revolution had an impact in England.

An Independent Church

American Methodists increasingly proclaimed their independence from the mother church and their father Wesley. When Coke met with Asbury in Delaware in November 1784, Asbury brought a council of preachers with him to accept or deny Coke's appointment. They did not blindly fulfill Wesley's wishes; they pulled together an irregular conference of preachers to meet in Baltimore and decide whether to accept Coke as the superintendent (Kirby, 1996, 6). A contemporary observer named Jonah Tigert wrote: "Wesley never intended to originate an American General Conference . . . that gave the American Church autonomy: i.e., the independence of Mr. Wesley and the English Conference" (Tigert, 1908, 192). However, that level of independence is indeed what the 1784 Christmas conference established.

At this 1784 Christmas conference, the American Methodists underlined the republican nature of their leadership, even while affirming the structure and leadership that Wesley wanted. They formed themselves as the Methodist Episcopal Church and made "the elected superintendent amenable to the body of ministers and preachers." Their leadership had to be confirmed by the whole body of preachers. At the same time, they pledged their allegiance to Wesley, agreeing, "During the life of the Rev. Mr. Wesley, we acknowledge ourselves his sons in the gospel, ready in matters belong[ing] to church government to obey his commands" (*Minutes of Several Conversations*, 1785, 3). In this conference, they formed an Episcopal Church—under the direction of a superintendent, elders, deacons, and helpers. The conference also elected Coke and Asbury both as co-superintendents. The conference sought to make the power structure of Methodism more democratic; the superintendent had veto power on major decisions, yet the conference could depose a superintendent if it saw fit. It furthermore checked Wesley's power and made his appointments to the American connection subject to its approval. Wesley had given Coke and Asbury some fuller powers in the right to oversee the connection and ordain and appoint preachers, but he presumed that they would see him as the ultimate authority, a presumption implicitly challenged by the conference, even as the participants expressed their acceptance of it.

Wesley's presumption of power came into question again in September 1786 when Wesley wrote to Coke and directed him to appoint a General conference meeting in Baltimore on May 1 of the following year, in order to appoint Richard Whatcoat co-superintendent with Asbury (Wesley to Coke, September 6, 1786, in Telford, 1931, 7:190–191). The preachers met and agreed that this directive was objectionable, because Wesley "was not qualified to take the charge of the connection" (Lee, 1810, 126). They also feared that this appointment would weaken Asbury's position, and Asbury, among the

Lovely Lane Meeting House, location of the Christmas conference of 1784, the meeting of American Methodist leaders that determined the future direction of Methodism in America. (*Library of Congress*)

various leaders, had now firmly established himself as the *American* leader. In a statement of protest, the American preachers erased the Wesley allegiance clause and Wesley's name altogether from the Discipline, the annually updated rules of the society. At the same time, they sent a conciliatory letter to Wesley, requesting that he visit America. That he had never visited was one of the bones of contention. Their father had presumed to be a parent in absentia, much as the British government had.

Coke was also in trouble with the American preachers for being too willing to follow Wesley's commandments, for doing this as a British minister, as well as being ordained in the Church of England. While Coke was in Europe, at Wesley's request, he changed the date that the American preachers had settled on for the next conference meeting. As a response, the preachers made Coke sign an agreement that he would not make any decisions involving the governance of American Methodists when he was not in America (Lee, 1810, 125). Furthermore, the preachers decided that Coke would not be able to assign preachers' circuits; only preachers would have the right to decide where and when to station other preachers.

All of these decisions on the part of the American preachers mortified Wesley, who explicitly blamed Asbury for the decision to take his name out of the Discipline. He wrote to Whatcoat: "It was not well judged of Brother Asbury to suffer, much less indirectly encourage, that foolish step in the late Conference. Every preacher present ought, both in duty and in prudence, to have said: 'Brother Asbury Mr. Wesley is your father, consequently ours, and we will affirm this in the face of all the world'" (Wesley to Whatcoat, July 17, 1788, in *Works of John Wesley*, 2:23).

Wesley had expected Asbury as leader of American Methodists to reaffirm his paternal leadership, and to do this by example. If Asbury had treated Wesley as a father to follow and obey, the American preachers would have done so too, Wesley reasoned. The conference did acquiesce to Wesley in electing Whatcoat bishop, and they wrote Wesley's name back into the Discipline in 1789, listing him a leader (alongside Coke and Asbury). However, much to Wesley's continuing consternation, they never reinstated the expression of their allegiance to him as their father and ultimate leader.

Wesley's relationship with American leadership continued to be strained in the final years of his life. Asbury alluded to the idea that Wesley was still alienated from American leaders due to his Tory stance during the Revolution. Asbury wrote to Jasper Winscom in 1788, "There is not a man in the world so obnoxious to the American politicians as our dear old Daddy, but no matter, we must treat him with all the respect we can and that is due him" (Asbury to Jasper Winscom, August 15, 1788, in Potts, 3:62).

The mode of leadership that Wesley had presumed to exercise was part and parcel of the issues of the Revolution. In his love of king and country, Wesley had internalized the ideology of paternal power, the expectation of deference and the unquestioning right to authority. If his American sons loved and valued their father, they would submit to his decisions. At the same time that Asbury and other American preachers claimed that they loved and cherished their "dear old Daddy," they saw that he was hopelessly out of step with the American ethos of governance from below.

Thus as American Methodism developed and became more independent of its English counterpart, it still shared a common evangelical ethos, language, print culture, and personnel. Moreover, in the establishment of American Methodism as a church, with its own powers of ordination, both English and American Methodism became formalized as separate entities from the Church of England.

Politically, as American preachers emphasized the roles of brotherhood, they resisted the absolute power of the father in the role of Wesley. In the post-Revolutionary period, the American leadership's resentment of the idea of a more hierarchical arrangement extended to Wesley's appointed leaders, Coke and even Asbury (though to a lesser extent), whom they suspected were more British and, therefore, more likely to be simply following Wesley's word on American matters. Certainly, it also became clear that American leaders saw themselves as having particular concerns and challenges that the British Methodists could not understand or share. At the same time, the structure and form of Methodist practice was exactly as Wesley had wished for America. Their commonalities, in many ways, were more significant than their differences.

The ways in which this power struggle was described as a struggle between fathers and sons were reflected in many of the letters between American and English leadership. The ideas of paternalism were strongly imbedded in authority throughout the eighteenth century. The Revolutionary period and the alienation between the two sides saw some contestation over the terms of fatherhood; Wesley was the wise father at times, the doddering, presumptuous father at others. Still, the power of the term *father* survived this struggle, and American Methodists would go on to call Asbury and Wesley their spiritual fathers into the nineteenth century.

References and Further Reading

Andrews, Dee. *The Methodists and Revolutionary America, 1760–1800: The Shaping of Evangelical America*. Princeton, NJ: Princeton University Press, 2000.

Andrews, Doris. "Popular Religion and the Revolution in the Middle Atlantic Ports: The Rise of Methodists, 1770–1800." Ph.D. diss., University of Pennsylvania, 1986.

Baker, Frank. *From Wesley to Asbury: Studies in Early American Methodism*. Durham, NC: Duke University Press, 1976.

Baker, Gordon Pratt. *Those Incredible Methodists: A History of the Baltimore Conference of the United Methodist Church*. Baltimore: Baltimore Conference, 1972.

Bangs, Nathan. *The History of the Methodist Episcopal Church*. New York: Carlton and Porter, 1860.

Buckley, James M. *Constitutional and Parliamentary History of the Methodist Episcopal Church*. New York: Methodist Book Concern, 1912.

Butler, Jon. *Awash in a Sea of Faith: Christianizing the American People*. Cambridge, MA: Harvard University Press, 1990.

Clark, Elmer T., ed. *Journal and Letters of Francis Asbury.* 3 vols. London: Hazell, Watson and Viney, 1958.

Colley, Linda. *Britons: Forging the Nation, 1707–1837.* New Haven, CT: Yale University Press, 1992.

Hatch, Nathan. *The Democratization of American Christianity.* New Haven, CT: Yale University Press, 1989.

Isaac, Rhys. *The Transformation of Virginia, 1740–1790.* Chapel Hill: University of North Carolina Press, 1982.

Kirby, James E., Russell E. Richey, and Kenneth E. Rowe. *The Methodists.* Westport, CT: Greenwood, 1996.

Lawrence, Anna. "The Transatlantic Methodist Family: Gender, Revolution and Evangelicalism in America and England, c. 1730–1815." Ph.D. diss., University of Michigan, 2004.

Lee, Jesse. *A Short History of the Methodists in the United States of America.* Baltimore: Magill and Clime, 1810.

Minutes of Several Conversations between the Rev. Thomas Coke, LLD, the Rev. Francis Asbury, and Others, at a Conference begun in Baltimore in the State of Maryland on Monday, the 27th of December, in the Year 1784. Composing a Form of Discipline for the Ministers, Preachers, and Other Members of the Methodist Episcopal Church in America. Philadelphia: Charles Cist, 1785.

Neely, Thomas B. *A History of the Origin and Development of the Governing Conference in Methodism, and Especially the General Conference of the Methodist Episcopal Church.* New York: Hunt and Eaton, 1892.

Potts, J. Manning, ed. *The Journal and Letters of Francis Asbury.* 3 vols. London: Epworth, 1958.

Preachers Collection, Methodist Archives, Manchester, UK.

Rack, Henry. *Reasonable Enthusiast: John Wesley and the Rise of Methodism.* London: Epworth, 1989.

Simpson, Robert, ed. *American Methodist Pioneer: The Life and Journals of the Rev. Freeborn Garrettson, 1752–1827.* Rutland, VT: Academy, 1984.

Tees, Francis, comp. "Journal of Thomas Rankin, 1773–1778." Drew University Library, Madison, NJ.

Telford, John, ed. *Letters of John Wesley.* 8 vols. London: Epworth, 1931.

Tigert, Jonah. *A Constitutional History of American Episcopal Methodism* [1894]. Nashville, TN: Methodist Episcopal Church, 1908.

Tyerman, Luke. *The Life and Times of Rev. John Wesley, M.A., Founder of the Methodists.* New York: Harper and Brothers, 1872.

Watts, Michael R. *The Dissenters.* Oxford: Clarendon, 1978.

Wesley, John. *A Calm Address to Our American Colonies.* London: R. Hawes, 1775.

Wigger, John H. *Taking Heaven by Storm: Methodism and the Rise of Popular Christianity in America.* New York: Oxford University Press, 1998.

"This Time of Deep Affliction and Difficulty": The Society of Friends and the American Revolution

9

A. Glenn Crothers

I n March 1781 the Coffin family of New Garden, North Carolina, located just a few miles from Guilford County Courthouse, found themselves in the middle of war. Though the American Revolution had already been raging for over six years, it was not until the army of British general Lord Cornwallis made its way through the Carolinas that the Coffins, a Quaker family who espoused the sect's pacifist ideology, saw firsthand the consequences of battle. The Coffins, along with their Quaker neighbors, could not escape the maneuvers and clashes of Cornwallis's British forces and General Nathaniel Greene's American Army as they swept through local communities in the days before and after the Battle of Guilford Courthouse. In fact, a few days after the battle, Greene, himself a lapsed Quaker, issued a plea to the New Garden Friends Meeting to care for the wounded on both sides. He need not have done so. For local Quakers had not just witnessed the battles that swirled around their communities; they had from its outset offered aid to both American and British casualties. Years later, Elijah Coffin remembered one particular casualty: "During the progress of the battle," he recalled, "a soldier came in great haste to my mother at the dwelling, having two fingers shot off and bleeding which she kindly dressed for him as well as she could and he hastened back to the conflict." Though Coffin never identified this soldier, the same day Lieutenant Colonel Banastre Tarleton, the British cavalry officer known to the Americans as "Bloody Tarleton" for the bloodthirsty tactics of his legion, was hit by a musket ball that "shattered the first and middle fingers of his right hand." Unbeknownst to them, the Coffins—a peaceable Quaker family—had aided one of the American Revolution's most infamous military men (Newton, 1994, 11).

The Revolutionary Dilemma

This episode was just one small part of the Guilford Courthouse clash, and an even smaller part of the Revolutionary War in the South. But it stands

The First Maryland Regiment retaking British field artillery at the battle of Guilford Courthouse in March 1781. (*North Wind Picture Archives*)

as a good introduction to the dilemmas members of the Society of Friends—known as Friends, or Quakers—faced during the Revolution. As pacifists, Quakers believed that all war was to be avoided, and the vast majority of American Quakers refused to choose sides or offer support of any kind to the military efforts of either the Patriots who championed American independence or the Loyalists who wished to remain under British rule. For this refusal, they faced regular harassment, financial hardships, and deep suspicion. At the same time, their spiritual beliefs also led them to aid those who suffered because of the war, and they regularly took care of the wounded and offered financial aid to the suffering, regardless of political or religious orientation. For this service they were often praised. As Nathaniel Greene wrote, there is "no order of people more remarkable for the exercise of humanity and benevolence" (quoted in Kashatus, 1990, 48). But this exercise of charity was not enough to pacify the animosity of the most ardent American patriots. For such individuals, Quakers who refused to offer any support for the Revolution—despite their charitable work and generosity—could only be viewed as Loyalists. As a result, for Quakers the Revolution was a time a trial. Despite many Friends' initial support for the American cause, once the struggle threatened to turn violent, their spiritual convictions—specifically their pacifist beliefs—required of them a course of action that deeply alienated them from the broader American community.

Thus the behavior of Quakers during the Revolution was shaped by their distinctive spiritual beliefs, which Friends called their "testimonies." At the core of Quaker belief was the conviction that all human beings possessed the "Inner Light" and were thus all equally capable of receiving God's grace.

From this belief in humanity's spiritual equality arose the Quaker emphasis on the Golden Rule—"Whatsoever ye would that men should do to you, do ye even so to them" (Matthew 7:12)—and their rejection of a professional clergy. Second, Quakers believed that spiritual truth's simplicity should be reflected in their own lives. From this conviction came their distinctive plain dress, simple and direct language (using "thee" and "thou" for the upper as well as the lower classes and refusing to swear oaths), and their rejection of ostentatious displays of wealth. Their peculiar dress and language, of course, immediately set them apart from the communities in which they lived. Similarly, Quakers celebrated industry and diligence, believing that useful labor—following a "calling"—was one sign that an individual was committed to carrying out God's will in this life.

Most radically, Quakers espoused pacifism, believing that it was wrong to take a human life, because every individual potentially possessed the "light within." The Society rejected the use of force in favor of appeals to people's spiritual nature. Consequently, Friends refused to serve in the military, pay war taxes, or become complicit in war making in any way, including by taking sides. The Quaker refusal to proclaim allegiances during war stood in contrast to their attitude toward government during times of peace. Believing government to be divinely inspired, they adhered to a policy of active obedience to any secular authority that did not force them to act against their conscience. When a government's actions violated their testimonies, however, they practiced passive disobedience, refusing to cooperate with secular authorities in nonviolent fashion and suffering the consequences—which could often be severe—as a form of peaceful protest (Brinton, 1973, 5–7; Mekeel, 1979, 2–3).

Following these beliefs, the Quakers who settled in America flourished. By 1775, there were approximately 60,000 Friends in the thirteen colonies, with over a third of that number settled in Pennsylvania, the colony founded in 1681 by the Quaker leader William Penn. Significant concentrations of Friends also lived in New England (12,000), New Jersey and New York (11,000), and the southern colonies (13,000). Though scattered throughout the colonies, Friends maintained tight bonds of contact through an elaborate system of yearly, quarterly, monthly, and preparative meetings. There were six yearly meetings in the colonies, the largest and most influential located in Philadelphia. The yearly meetings ultimately decided the content of the Quaker testimonies, though decisions in such matters were arrived at slowly and only after reaching a consensus among the membership. Each yearly meeting consisted of a number of quarterly meetings that met for worship and business. Each quarterly meeting, in turn, consisted of numerous monthly meetings, and each monthly meeting of multiple preparative meetings where Quakers met for worship.

It was at the level of the monthly meetings that Friends enforced the Society's testimonies and disciplined those members who violated them. Individuals who failed to uphold the sect's practices—or discipline—could face a variety of sanctions, the most serious being "disownment," or removal from the Society. But such decisions were not taken lightly. Only after lengthy "treating" and visiting with wayward Friends—a process that could often

Quakers became known for their quiet worship, waiting to be moved by the Spirit. (*Special Collections, Davidson Library, University of California, Santa Barbara*)

take months—did monthly meetings remove unrepentant members. Meetings also established an extensive correspondence with one another, offering advice and recommendations, and querying one another about their adherence to the Society's discipline. Finally, "traveling Friends"—members divinely inspired to visit meetings far from home—helped ensure the Quaker unity and coherence (Mekeel, 1979, 2–3).

Quakers, then, were a group that stood apart from the broader communities of which they were apart—though they actively participated in the economic life of the colonies, and before the French and Indian War (1754–1763) they even played prominent roles in colonial governments. Nowhere was this public role more pronounced than in Pennsylvania, where the Society of Friends had tried to create a "peaceable kingdom" in which they could live in harmony among themselves and with the world. If not entirely successful in achieving these goals, the colony did become extremely prosperous, and in Philadelphia Quaker merchants grew wealthy from their involvement in the Atlantic trade between Great Britain and her American colonies. In the 1750s, however, the Quakers' "Holy Experiment" foundered when warfare erupted on the Pennsylvania frontier and the governor requested and frontier settlers demanded large military appropriations from the colonial assembly. Such demands posed a dilemma for Quaker legislators, who could not both meet the broad public demand for active military measures and uphold their pacifist ideology. In response, most resigned from office. Meanwhile, non-Quakers viewed the refusal of wealthy Quakers to contribute to the colony's war effort as self-serving. When the war ended in the early 1760s, many Friends returned to public office and continued their participation in the imperial trade, but the episode provided a foretaste of

New-York, May 17, 1770.

Advertisement.

THE Subscribers to the Non-Importation Agreement, are desired to meet at the Exchange To-morrow Morning, precisely at 11 o'Clock, to consider of a Letter received from Philadelphia, relative to the Non-Importation Agreement; and as it is a Matter of great Consequence, it is hoped that every Subscriber will punctually attend.

Advertisement calling for a meeting of New Yorkers to reconsider the nonimportation agreement of 1768. (*Library of Congress*)

the dilemmas they faced during the imperial crisis (Marietta, 1984, 150–186; Brock, 1968, 63–140).

But such problems were not apparent to most in 1765, when the British government passed the Stamp Act and the conflict between Britain and her American colonies began in earnest. In fact, most American Quakers supported efforts to protect American liberties against British incursion, particularly the right of English subjects to be taxed only with their own consent. The Stamp Act, under which the British Parliament taxed all printed documents in the colonies, represented a clear breach of this basic English principle, and in September 1765, Quaker members of the Pennsylvania legislature helped pass a series of resolves protesting it. Similarly, Quaker merchants played a leading role in forming a nonimportation agreement to stop the influx of British goods until the Stamp Act was repealed. However, leading Friends were also concerned that participation in these protest activities might violate the testimonies of the Society, and they worked hard to moderate Pennsylvania's response. For example, in June 1766, after the repeal of the Stamp Act, Friends in the Pennsylvania Assembly helped compose an address to the British king, George III, that stressed the loyalty of the colony and thanked him for his magnanimity (Mekeel, 1979, 12–33).

As the Revolutionary crisis deepened, however, Friends found their position increasingly difficult. In 1767, Parliament passed the Townshend Duties, which introduced taxes on a variety of manufactured goods imported into the colonies. Prepared by the Stamp Act crisis, American leaders responded with another nonimportation agreement. In Philadelphia, many Friends initially supported these efforts, and Quaker merchant John Reynell chaired the town's nonimportation committee. However, more conservative Friends, such as the influential Israel Pemberton, were deeply worried about the activities of the committee and the leading role taken by its Quaker members because one of the committee's foremost tasks was to deal with those merchants who refused to participate in the boycott. While Reynell believed that his presence helped moderate the committee's decisions, Pemberton feared that public meetings called to decide the fate of importers were an invitation to violence and intimidation. Such extralegal activities, he believed, promised to violate the Quaker peace testimony and represented an act of disloyalty against British authorities during peacetime.

The Philadelphia Yearly Meeting soon endorsed Pemberton's point of view. An epistle of advice issued to Friends in Pennsylvania and neighboring colonies in July 1769 stressed that "we cannot join" with any members who "manifest a disposition to contend for liberty by any methods . . . contrary to the peaceable spirit and temper of the Gospel." The threat of violence and the extralegal methods of the Patriot committees were, the Philadelphia meeting decided, inconsistent with the Quaker peace testimony and its loyalty to the legally constituted government. In response, many Quakers—as they had during the French and Indian War—began to step down from public positions (Mekeel, 1979, 47; also 34–52).

Though Quaker fears declined in the early 1770s, the Tea Act of 1773 and the ensuing violence in Boston once more placed Friends in a difficult position. After an October 1773 meeting of the Philadelphia Yearly Meeting, James Pemberton, brother of Israel, concluded, "Altho' we are not insensible of the incroachments of power and of the value of civil rights, yet in matters contestable we can neither join with nor approve the measures which have been . . . proposed . . . for asserting and defending them." As the imperial crisis deepened in 1774 and 1775, this conservative Quaker stand only deepened. Seeking a unified Quaker response to the crisis, a January 1775 epistle of the Philadelphia meeting addressed to Friends declared that Quakers could not participate in the resistance movement "without deviating from . . . our religious principles," and called on "every meeting" in which members who were participating in the resistance movement lived "speedily to treat with them . . . and endeavor to convince them of their error." To the broader public, the Philadelphia meeting issued a public declaration of their position. Radical Patriot tactics, they contended, "have involved the Colonies in confusion," and "appear likely to produce violence and bloodshed." Opposing such violence, and believing that "decent and respectful addresses" to the king were the best method for restoring "the just rights of the people," Friends condemned "all combinations, insurrections, conspiracies, and illegal assemblies," while stressing their "fidelity to the King and his government." In short, Quakers argued that the Patriot movement represented an illegitimate opposition to a legally constituted government, and that further resistance would only lead to violence. The only conscionable course of action for Friends was noninterference in political affairs (Brock, 1968, 143; Gilpin, 1848, 282–287).

After violence erupted in 1775 between British and American forces at Lexington and Concord and later at Bunker's Hill outside Boston, Quakers became more resolute in their adherence to a position of loyalty to the established government and a rigorous neutrality when it came to fighting. In January 1776, ten days after lapsed Quaker Thomas Paine published his inflammatory and wildly popular pro-independence pamphlet *Common Sense*, the Philadelphia Yearly Meeting issued another statement of Quaker beliefs to non-Quakers. Contrasting the "calamities and afflictions which now surround us" with the "peace and plenty" Americans had enjoyed under the "kings and government" of England, the address concluded that Quakers "firmly unite in the abhorrence of all . . . measures" designed "to break off the happy connexion we have heretofore enjoyed with the kingdom of Great Britain, and our just and necessary subordination to the king." Designed to explain the reasons for the Quaker doctrine of passive neutrality and to avert a final break between the colonies and Great Britain, in an increasingly partisan environment it was interpreted by Patriots as a sign of the Friends' Loyalist sentiments. Consequently, the response to the Friends' public address was immediate and overwhelmingly negative. Patriot newspapers published a series of blistering attacks on the Society, and warned that it should not give offense to Patriots by "endeavoring to counteract the measures of their fellow citizens for the common safety." Others wondered how a group that professed neutrality could express support for the monarchy. As Samuel Adams pronounced, "if they would not *pull down Kings*, let them not support *tyrants*" (Gilpin, 1848, 287–291; Mekeel, 1979, 138; Brock, 1968, 146–147).

The most withering response, however, came from Paine, who to subsequent editions of *Common Sense* appended an address "To the Representatives of the Religious Society of People called Quakers." Accusing Friends of "dabbling in matters which your professed . . . Principles instruct you not to meddle in," Paine argued that the Society could not claim both that "the setting up and putting down of kings and governments is God's peculiar prerogative," and make political pronouncements that condemned Patriot actions. Instead, Quakers must—if they were to be true to their principles— "wait with patience and humility for the event of all public measures, and . . . receive *that event* as the divine will towards you," rather than trying have a "share in the business." Directly addressing Friends, Paine argued that their attempts to influence public opinion revealed "that either ye do not believe what ye profess, or have not virtue enough to practise what ye believe." In short, the Society had "mistaken party for conscience," and such "mingling [of] religion with politics" should "*be disavowed and reprobated by every inhabitant of* AMERICA" (Paine, 1995, 54–59).

If being lambasted by America's foremost polemicist for their actual pronouncements was not enough, the next year the reputation of the Society sank even further as a result of a fabricated letter from the nonexistent "Spanktown Yearly Meeting." The note, found in the papers of an American officer who defected to the British and later published by Congress, provided an account of the size and location of Washington's army in Pennsylvania. Informing Congress of the letter, American general John Sullivan condemned Friends as "the most Dangerous Enemies America knows & such as have it in their power to Distress the Country more than all the Collected Force of Britain." "Covered with that Hypocritical Cloak of Religion," Sullivan continued, "they have with Impunity . . . Long Acted the part of Inveterate Enemies of their Country," and have "Prostituted" "their Religious Meetings . . . to the Base purposes of betraying their Country." Though Friends informed Congress and the public repeatedly that there was "no meeting throughout our whole Society" called Spanktown, "nor was that letter, or any one like it, ever written in any of our meetings," the widely publicized spurious letter had done its damage. Appearing at a time when British general William Howe was threatening to occupy Philadelphia, the new nation's capital, the letter caused many Americans to agree with Sullivan and see the Quakers as a threat to the Patriot cause. In Virginia, for example, Edmund Pendleton assumed that Friends—whom he labeled "the broad brims" after their distinctive dress—had great "hopes of How[e]'s success" (Gilpin, 1848, 58, 61–62, 299; Sullivan to John Hancock, August 24, 1777, quoted in Mekeel, 1979, 173–174; Pendleton to William Woodford, September 13, 1777, in Mays, 1967, 1:223).

In the face of growing hostility, the Philadelphia Yearly Meeting worked to clarify the sect's discipline and ensure that Quakers throughout the colonies responded to threats in a unified fashion. The September 1776 Philadelphia meeting issued explicit instructions to its subordinate meetings—and ultimately to all the other yearly meetings in America—on how to enforce the Quaker peace testimony and maintain uniformity within the sect. All Friends, the Philadelphia meeting decided, were required to resign from any positions within the new governments because they were founded on violence. Similarly, Friends were enjoined to refuse payment of any war tax, or any penalties or fines they might incur for refusing to pay war taxes or serve in the military. Finally, they were directed to disengage from any war-related business or trade from which they could personally profit. Most important, these strictures were not offered as advice; violating any of these testimonies, the Philadelphia meeting stress, was punishable by disownment from the Society. Soon, all the yearly meetings embraced these measures, ensuring that American Friends followed a consistent pattern of conduct throughout the war. In December, the Philadelphia meeting issued another epistle to fortify the convictions of "weak" and "wavering" Friends. Recognizing that this was a "time of deep . . . affliction and difficulty," the epistle urged Friends nonetheless to "withstand and refuse to submit to the arbitrary injunctions and ordinances of men who assume to themselves the power of compelling others." Girded by the "truth" of the inner light, Quakers could do no other than "steadily . . . bear our testimony against every attempt to deprive us of it" (Mekeel, 1979, 162–163; Brock, 1968, 147–148, 189–190; Gilpin, 1848, 291–293).

The Hardships of War

As heartening as these words must have been for beleaguered Friends throughout America, they did not change the real hardships members of the sect faced during the war years. Though circumstances were different in each province and pacifists faced particular problems when American military fortunes were most in jeopardy, all Friends faced a similar set of dilemmas. The most basic dilemma was caused by the attempts by various Patriot governments to recruit Quakers for military service (the British military never tried to recruit Friends).

Though the Continental Congress had recognized in July 1775 that religious pacifists should be excused from military duties, they did urge them to "do all other services to their oppressed country, which they can consistently with their religious principles." Moreover, in times of manpower shortages—which were often in the later years of war—Congress issued troop requests to the states without exempting conscientious objectors. Likewise, the state governments often made no effort to protect pacifists, and most required objectors to pay a fine for their refusal to serve. As a

Petition to the Convention of Virginia requesting military exemption for Quakers and Menonites, but suggesting they pay a tax in return, 1776. (*Library of Congress*)

result, many male Friends faced harsh treatment for their refusal to serve. In Philadelphia, for example, a military company forcibly paraded through the streets before a jeering mob three Quakers who would not serve. Other Philadelphia Friends faced jail sentences for upholding their pacifist beliefs. In Virginia, one young Friend suffered forty lashes "very heavily laid on by three different persons with a whip having nine cords" for refusing guard duty after he had been drafted, and in 1777 officers of the Virginia militia forcibly removed fourteen Quakers from their homes in Frederick County and marched them 200 miles to Philadelphia. When they refused to bear arms officers "with drawn swords" pushed the men into rank and threatened to "have their blood if they did not comply." When threats did not work, soldiers tied guns to three of the men. Eventually, lapsed Quaker Clement Biddle interceded on their behalf with George Washington, who ordered their immediate release (Brock, 1990, 146; Pemberton, 1844, 97–98; Mekeel, 1979, 167; Gilpin, 1848, 181).

Quakers meticulously documented these examples of "sufferings" in specially-created "Meetings for Sufferings." For Friends, such trials represented, in the words of traveling Friend John Pemberton, an opportunity to "spread the testimony of truth." Still, not all Friends were able to resist the strong and persistent social pressures and occasional physical intimidation employed by Patriots, particularly because so many Quakers found Patriot goals—if not tactics—so attractive. Sharing with the revolutionaries a belief in religious and political liberty, some Friends viewed the Society's opposition to the Revolution and the new American governments as a mistake. Such principled opponents of the Society's interpretation of the peace testimony included a number of prominent Friends, and most left the sect in the early years of the war. In addition, young men lured by the adventure of military life often succumbed to the broader social pressures. As Philadelphia Quaker James Pemberton noted in 1775, "A military spirit prevails . . . and many younger members of the Society are daily joining" the Patriots. Whether backsliders were principled opponents or wayward youth, the Society acted decisively with individuals who joined the military. Monthly meetings treated at length with such individuals, but if they refused to express regret for and renounce their behavior, the meeting disowned them. As a result, over the course of the war over 1,000 Friends—less than 2 percent of all members—were disowned for serving in the military. Thus, despite the hardships faced by Friends, it is clear that the vast majority remained faithful to the peace testimony and refused to serve in a military function (Pemberton, 1844, 97–98; James Pemberton, quoted in Hirst, 1923, 400; Mekeel, 1979, 200–201, 336).

A more widespread problem among Quakers was created by the fines imposed by the states for nonservice or for refusing to hire substitutes, fines mandated in laws that eventually existed in every state. Moreover, most states progressively raised such fines to keep pace with inflation. In Pennsylvania, for example, the state initially set fines for nonservice at £2.10s.; by the early 1780s, such penalties reached £1,000. Some states, in an effort to accommodate religious pacifists, allowed individuals to hire substitutes to serve in their place, but for Friends such laws offered no relief. Seeking to avoid complicity in war making in any way, they refused to hire substitutes, nor would they pay fines for nonservice. In response, state governments responded by distraining—or seizing—Friends' property, and jailing those who did not own anything of value. Ultimately, the loss of property—most of it through distraint—was the biggest problem Quakers faced during the war. In Rhode Island, for example, Friends suffered from distraint of goods on 496 separate occasions, losing livestock, food and crops, household goods, clothing, and in the case of Thomas Lapham, a dictionary. These exactions were sometimes severe enough to bankrupt Friends. In 1778 the Providence Meeting for Sufferings reported "one Friend with a large family" who had been "turn'd out of his house and stript of most of his property." As Friends regularly noted, the value of the property seized by state officials regularly exceeded the amount of fines assessed on Friends. In 1781 Chester County, Pennsylvania, Quakers complained about the "rapacious and unreasonable men, who have sported with [our] property." The following year, Quakers in Wrightstown, Georgia, charged that American officials who seized their property acted in an "Arbitrary manner . . . taking what they pleased." In all, Friends lost over £100,000 worth of property during the course of the war. Upholding the peace testimony, then, required significant material sacrifice (Foster et al., 1977, 16, 43; Brock, 1968, 157, 205–209; Davis, 1982, 9; Mekeel, 1979, 328).

Unfortunately, it was a sacrifice that some Quakers could not make. For example, some Friends tried to find ways to circumvent the society's rules. In North Carolina, William Townsend of Perquimans Monthly Meeting was disowned after it was discovered he was "a partner in hiring a man to serve in a military capacity to save himself from the penalty of the law." Another North Carolina Quaker, John Charles, was dealt with for arranging to have another man pay his militia fine. In New Jersey, a member of the Haddonfield Monthly Meeting was disowned after he directed his apprentices to fulfill his militia service. In all, over 450 members of the Society were dealt with during the war for paying militia fines or hiring someone to fight in their stead. Of these, about 250 were eventually disowned by the local meetings. Still, given the extent of the property losses suffered by Friends, what is striking is how few members violated this aspect of the peace testimony. Pacifism lay at the heart of the Quakers' spiritual beliefs; suffering on its behalf was testimony to the world of their seriousness. As the New England Meeting for Sufferings put it in July 1776, "We have enlisted ourselves as soldiers under the Prince of Peace, [we] must wear his uniform and march according to his step" (Thorne, 1961, 325–326; Brock, 1968, 158–159; Mekeel, 1979, 336–337; Brock, 1990, 145).

A third issue that plagued Friends throughout the war was the taking of loyalty oaths. After the Declaration of Independence, each state required that inhabitants take a test oath or affirmation in which they declared their allegiance to the new government and renounced their loyalty to the crown. Those who refused to take such oaths—known as nonjurors—could face serious consequences, including fines, the loss of civil rights, the distraint of property, and imprisonment. Quakers would not take oaths or affirmations because, they believed, to do so was to participate—however tangentially—in

Oath of allegiance, required by Virginia's assembly, signed by Samuel Duncan, 1777. (*Reuben T. Durrett Collection on Kentucky and the Ohio River Valley, Special Collections Research Center, University of Chicago Library*)

pulling down the legally constituted government. Moreover, Friends asserted that if they pledged their loyalty to the new regimes they were in effect sanctioning the violence that helped create these governments. The consequence of this Quaker "scruple" soon became apparent. In Pennsylvania a 1778 law stipulated that those who refused to take the state's loyalty oath would no longer be able to sue in the courts, and had to pay double (and later treble) taxes. More damaging still, nonjurors could not work as doctors, druggists, lawyers, or schoolteachers. This last provision was particularly onerous because it effectively shut down the extensive Quaker school system and, as the North Carolina Friends put it, led to "the Ruin of many Honest Families." Nowhere were such hardships more pronounced than in Perquimans County, North Carolina, where in 1779 the county court ordered the seizure of nonjurors' estates and their banishment from the state. Though the state government later overturned the county court's decision, the impact on the local Quaker population was dramatic. Still, the Society of Friends remained united in its opposition to oaths. Despite widespread suffering and extensive public pressure, only 187 Friends were disowned for taking oaths of allegiance (Brock, 1968, 162–164; Mekeel, 1979, 189–190, 193, 271–272, 336; Thorne, 1961, 330–333).

Friends were also united in their refusal to provide direct aid to either army or to accept payment for any coerced aid, and they made doing so grounds for removal from the Society. Ultimately, monthly meetings disowned 115 Friends for this offense, including one individual who willingly manufactured munitions, another who made "wheels for gun carriages," and a few who worked as teamsters for the army. Usually, the American and British forces coerced Friends into providing assistance or supplies. Members of the Society could not stop military forces from taking their property, of course, but their scruples required them to refuse payment for any confiscated goods. For example, when "two armed men" burst into the home of Pennsylvania Quaker James Bennett in 1779 "& demanded a Blanket of me," he complied, as he did some days later when American officers ordered him to "draw fifty Bushels of wheat to the mill." More problematic, he accepted "and made use of" the money they offered in exchange. Brought before his monthly meeting to "reflect on" his actions, he acknowledged with "shame" his "misconduct" and was accepted back into the meeting.

A year earlier in Maryland, American forces "forcibly" requisitioned the wagon and horses of Quaker Jeremiah Brown to carry military stores, for which Brown "receive[d] wages"; he was also paid for a horse that "was lost in the journey." With a troubled conscience, Brown acknowledged before his local meeting that "weakness" had led him to accept payment, and "hop[ed] and desir[ed] for the future to give closer attention to the inward principles which preserve [us] out of error." The problem of forcible requisition was a particular problem for Quakers who lived in contested areas such Queens County, New York. Both the Patriot forces that originally controlled the county in 1774–1775 and the British forces that occupied it thereafter discovered to their chagrin that Quakers offered assistance to neither side. The strict neutrality of the sect required no less (Mekeel, 1979, 336; Brock, 1968, 180–185; Cope, 1902–1903, 21; Tiedemann, 1983, 224–225).

In contrast, the Society was far less unified in its response to the payment of taxes. Nearly all Friends agreed that paying war taxes—money collected to support the military directly—constituted a violation of the peace testimony, and the Yearly Meetings throughout America made payment of them a disownable offence. Likewise, the vast majority of Friends agreed that taxes earmarked for nonmilitary purposes should be paid. Quakers vehemently disagreed, however, on whether members should pay general taxes in which a portion of the money was used to support the military effort. Opposition to the payment of such levies was most pronounced within the Philadelphia and Virginia Yearly Meetings, though neither meeting made doing so a disownable offence. In 1778, for example, the Philadelphia Yearly Meeting recommended that Friends should take "care to avoid complying with the injunctions and requisitions made for the purpose of carrying on War," adding that members who could not pay general taxes without "uneasiness to themselves" should be supported by the Society. But they recommended no disciplinary action for those who did pay such levies (Brock, 1968, 167–169, 171–172; Mekeel, 1979, 192, 266).

This ambiguous response reflected the real divisions that existed within the Society. A minority of Quakers, driven by their support for the revolutionary cause, believed that members should pay all the demands of the new American governments, and pointed to the sect's history to make their point. In 1776, New England Friend Timothy Davis published *A Letter . . . on the Subject of Paying Taxes* in which he noted that Quakers had in the past paid war taxes to the colonial governments; thus, refusal to make such payments in the present conflict would be, in effect, taking sides. Two years later, Pennsylvania Quaker Isaac Grey repeated Davis's arguments in his own pamphlet, *A Serious Address to . . . the People called Quakers*. Like Davis, Grey emphasized that historically Quakers had paid war taxes, both in England and the colonies. Moreover, he argued, refusing to pay taxes to the revolutionary governments belied Quaker neutrality. If, Grey concluded, Quakers "choose not to have any hand in the formation of governments," they must, "take governments as they find them, and comply with their laws, so far as they are clear of infringing rights and matters of faith towards God." For their troubles, both Davis and Grey were disowned. In 1781, some of the Philadelphia dissenters established their own meeting and labeled themselves "Free Quakers." However, the group failed to attract a significant number of followers and collapsed in the early nineteenth century. Still, their voices reveal the extent of the disagreement among Quakers on the issues of taxation and support for the Patriot cause (Davis, 1776; Grey, 1778).

Job Scott, a traveling Friend from Rhode Island, represented the opposite, more radical view. In a "Truly Conscientious Scruple," written in 1780, he argued that Quakers should resist all taxes in times of war. Friends, he believed, could not financially support the revolutionary regimes because the actions of these governments—most notably, "the promiscuous shedding of human Blood in War"—violated the most basic principles of the Society. A slightly less radical position on the tax issue was enunciated the same year by Samuel Allison, a respected New Jersey Friend. His "Reasons against War, and Paying Taxes for Its Support" argued that Friends should not pay general taxes if the government used the money to make citizens perform tasks that Quakers could not themselves undertake in good conscience. All nonmilitary taxes, however, were acceptable. As Allison put it, "We pay our proportion to the support of the poor, the maintenance of roads and the support of civil order in government. . . . These include every benefit we ask or receive. We desire not war or any of its consequences." Both Allison and Scott submitted their tracts to the Philadelphia meeting, but it declined to publish them because the Society had not reached a consensus on the issue of general taxes. Still, if calls for broader tax resistance failed to generate widespread support, the American Revolution was the first time Friends as a body refused to pay levies specifically earmarked for military purposes. As Virginia Quaker Robert Pleasants noted in 1779, "Friends can no more pay [war taxes] than take the test [oath], for they are both calculated to promote the same ends and make us parties to the destruction, violence and confusion consequent to such intestine commotion" (Foster, 1977, 60–62; Mekeel, 1979, 204, 233–234; Brock, 1968, 173–176; Brock, 1990, 192–193; Pleasants, quoted in Archer, 1921, 179).

For this stance, as for their position on oaths, Friends suffered. The standard penalty for refusing to pay taxes was distraint of personal property, and Meetings for Sufferings throughout the states reported extensive property losses among members. Ironically, Friends generally paid far higher sums to the military when their property was seized than if they had voluntarily paid the assessed war taxes. But members wanted to avoid the charge of hypocrisy that would arise if they paid taxes that sent others into battle when they refused to fight. These losses were greatest in Pennsylvania, where Friends reported that the state government seized £38,000 worth of property, over half of which was for refusal to pay taxes. In New England, where the Quaker population was much smaller, property losses for nonpayment of taxes amounted to just over £3,000, though at least one Friend was jailed for tax evasion. In contrast, North Carolina Friends suffered the loss of over £10,000, about half of which was for unpaid taxes. Despite the economic losses and the internal discord over acceptable taxes, few Friends violated this testimony. In all, fewer than 200 Friends were disowned for paying war taxes (Brock, 1968, 180; Mekeel, 1979, 202, 236–237, 273, 336).

Quakers also divided on whether their peace testimony allowed them to use Continental currency in good conscience. The most radical Friends argued that Congress created the currency to help finance the American war effort, and thus its use was akin to paying war taxes. Equally important, these Friends argued that using the currency granted legitimacy to an illegally constituted government. However, this remained a minority opinion, and outside of Virginia, no yearly meeting made the rejection of paper money mandatory. Instead, the yearly meetings left the matter up to the conscience of individual members, even when—as in the case of the Philadelphia meeting—the use of paper money was condemned. Still, a significant number of Friends became currency objectors and faced widespread public condemnation as a result. In Delaware, for example, Quaker John Cowgill was twice hauled before the local Committee of Safety in 1778 for his refusal to accept paper money. The committee proclaimed him "an enemy of his country" in local newspapers, requisitioned his livestock and foodstuffs, and established an economic boycott against him. When he still refused to handle American currency, Cowgill was carted through the town of Dover with a placard on his back inscribed with the message, "On the Circulation of the Continental Currency Depends the Fate of America." "For several years," Cowgill's daughter wrote later, "when we went to bed at night we did not know what would be the issue before day." But public humiliation and intimidation could not cow the most steadfast Friends. Virginia Quaker Warner Mifflin, for example, wondered if he could "make the stand" against paper money, but ultimately his conscience demanded that he reject its use (Mekeel, 1979, 133, 144–145, 149, 232; Brock, 1968, 164–167).

Similar acts of bravery on behalf of their testimony recur frequently in the records of the Quaker meetings. But the most public persecution of Friends took place in September 1777, when, on the orders of Congress, Pennsylvania's Supreme Executive Council arrested over forty suspected Loyalists, including many of Philadelphia's leading Quakers. The arrests came at a critical time for the American cause. In late August, the spurious Spanktown meeting letters came to light, casting grave suspicion on the motives of Friends throughout the country. At the same time, Congress, meeting in the Quaker city of Philadelphia, expected a British attack at any moment. In this dire atmosphere, Friends' obstinate neutrality appeared deeply suspect, and an anxious Congress concluded "that those persons are, with much rancour and bitterness, disaffected to the American cause." In the eyes of many Patriots, Quakers and Loyalists had become synonymous. The behavior of the arrested Friends did little to lessen Patriots' suspicions. All of those arrested were offered their freedom in exchange for pledging loyalty to the state, and most of those arrested were eventually released after doing so. Eighteen Friends, however, could not in good conscience take the oath, and they remained incarcerated. Held without charge, the suspected Loyalists were transported to Winchester, Virginia, where they were kept in custody over seven months (Gilpin, 1848, 261; Mekeel, 1979, 173–184; Oaks, 1972, 298–325).

For Friends, the arrests and incarceration of the "Virginia exiles" were a bitter experience. The physical conditions of their confinement in Virginia were tolerable if spartan, and as the months passed the prisoners enjoyed more freedoms. Most important, they were allowed to worship with and draw support from the local Quaker population. Nonetheless, two of the exiles, John Hunt and Thomas Gilpin, died during their incarceration, and

Warner Mifflin, the "Good Quaker"

During the eighteenth century, European travelers flocked to the New World to study the social and cultural life of the American people. Among the groups travelers found of interest were the Society of Friends or Quakers. French writers in particular were intrigued by the Quakers, regarding members of the sect as the epitome of honesty, simplicity, and fair dealing. When Jacques-Pierre Brissot de Warville visited the United States in the 1780s, for example, he praised the virtue of the Quakers, singling out Warner Mifflin (1745–1798) of Virginia for particular commemoration. "What humanity! and what charity!" exclaimed Brissot. "It seems, that to love mankind, and to search to do them good constitutes his only pleasure" (De Warville, 1797, 104). In short order, Mifflin came to personify the "good Quaker" for much of educated Europe. It

was a reputation well earned, for Mifflin exhibited both the mild disposition and the strong convictions of the most earnest eighteenth-century Friends. He was among the first Virginia Quakers to free their slaves in 1774–1775, and in subsequent years visited Quaker meetings throughout America to convince fellow Friends of the inequity and brutality of slavery. He even resigned his position as a Virginia justice of the peace because he no longer wished to participate in a legal system that supported slavery. In the 1780s and 1790s, he continued his antislavery efforts, helping to write and present numerous petitions to Congress calling for an end to the slave trade and domestic slavery.

When the American Revolution erupted, he adhered strictly to Quaker peace principles, refusing military service and taxes, and reject-

all of them experienced great economic and emotional trauma because of the enforced separation from their families, who were trapped in British-held Philadelphia. Communications between the exiles and their families were as a result always unreliable and constantly subject to Patriot scrutiny. Nonetheless, the exiles did their best to maintain a regular correspondence with family and friends. The letters of Henry Drinker and his wife Elizabeth, for example, reveal the emotional hardships faced by the exiles and their families. For her part, Elizabeth had trouble explaining to their children "the long absence of their Father," and worried constantly about Henry's health. She could only condemn "those wicked men who have been the cause of our separation," and the "injustice and cruelty of taking Exemplary and innocent men from their growing Families." For his part, Henry brooded about his family's safety in British-held Philadelphia, particularly after Elizabeth was forced to board an English officer. "Who is it," he fumed, "that could urge to be received in my House, after a proper representation of the situation the Master is in?" But fume was all he could do. (This correspondence survives in the Haverford College Library Quaker Collection, from which all these letters are taken. See also Oaks, 1972.)

Most galling to the exiles was that they were held without charge and without trial. This denial of habeas corpus seemed to belie the very cause that the Americans were fighting for. In repeated petitions to American authorities, they protested their "illegal" arrest and demanded a fair trial. But these petitions had little immediate impact. Henry Drinker, for one, could

ing the use of Continental currency because it was used to finance the American military effort. As a result, Mifflin, like many Friends, faced public ridicule, accusations of Toryism, and the loss of property. Still, he remained undeterred, noting to his wife after the war ended, "If every farthing we were possessed of, was seized for the purpose of supporting war, and I was informed it should all go, except I gave voluntarily one shilling . . . I was satisfied I should not so redeem it." Moreover, as Brissot noted, Mifflin generously extended aid to any who suffered as a result of the war, an "angel of mercy" who was "equally a friend to the French, the English, and the Americans." Most dramatic, Mifflin and five leading Friends traveled without passes between the American and British lines during the battle of Germantown in October 1777. The group hoped that explaining the peace testimony to American general George Washington would help to exonerate the Virginia Exiles, the Philadelphia Quakers suspected of treason but held without charge by American forces in the Shenandoah Valley. After visiting Washington, Mifflin and his fellows crossed British lines into Philadelphia in order to deliver the same peace testimony to British general William Howe. Traveling without passes, the group risked the charge of spying, but their efforts helped undermine the commonly held belief among Patriots that Quaker pacifism amounted to disloyalty. Indeed, by war's end Washington conceded the value of Quaker principles, noting to Mifflin after he became president, "Mr. Mifflin, I honor your sentiments; there is more in that than mankind have generally considered" (De Warville, 1797, 104).

not contain his anger, when in February 1778, after some four months of confinement, Congress repeated their initial offer to release the exiles if they would take an oath of allegiance. His words thick with sarcasm, he wondered how the "Guardians of Liberty" in Congress thought "a Test of allegiance," which Quakers could not in good conscience take, could end "the injustice they have heretofore exercized in the most lawless & unprecedented manner." The exiles' incarceration continued, largely because neither Congress nor the state of Pennsylvania would take responsibility for the matter. But as the affair dragged on, many Patriots began questioning the Friends' arrest and the violation of their rights. Indeed, even the Pennsylvania Council worried about "the dangerous example which their longer continuance in banishment may afford," and the "uneasiness" their arrest had caused "to some good friends to the independency of these states." Nevertheless, it was mid-April before both Congress and Pennsylvania concurred and ordered that the exiles be returned to Pennsylvania and released (Oaks, 1972; Mekeel, 1979, 173–184; Gilpin, 1848).

If this episode represented the most notorious example of the repression faced by the Quakers, it was certainly not the last. Throughout the Revolutionary War, Friends suffered for following their peace testimony, though the severity of their ordeal waxed and waned with the fortunes of the American cause. At the same time, Quaker spiritual beliefs dictated another response to the conflict: Aid those who suffered because of the war. Thus, despite their own economic problems, Friends generously provided aid to Quakers and non-Quakers alike who faced hardship as a result of the fighting. For Friends, service to the broader community became a central way to put into action their spiritual principles of nonviolence and respect for all humanity, while at the same time enabling them to make a positive contribution to the new civil society taking form in America. They also realized, of course, that such generosity could help restore the good image of the Society, but ultimately their behavior was motivated by their spiritual beliefs.

These efforts began almost as soon as violence erupted. In November 1775, after the British occupied Boston, the Philadelphia Yearly Meeting sent almost £2,000 to New England, to be distributed to all who suffered because of the conflict—excluding those who took an active role in the fighting. Ultimately, Friends sent over £4,400 to New England, and over 5,220 people received some kind of relief, either in cash or supplies. Similarly, when the British fleet commanded by Lord Dunmore bombarded Norfolk in November 1776, Virginia Quakers sent aid to the beleaguered town. The British occupations of New York, in 1776, and Philadelphia, in 1777–1778, elicited an equally generous response from American Friends. When the war turned south in 1778, Quakers again raised funds to aid the suffering in Georgia, the Carolinas, and Virginia. Moreover, Friends frequently tended to the wounded soldiers and buried the dead of both armies when the fighting took place in their vicinity. Thus, it was that the Quakers of North Carolina offered aid to the wounded soldiers at Guildford Courthouse, including the notorious British officer Banastre Tarleton. As they wrote to American general Nathaniel Greene after the battle, "We are determined . . . while we have anything among us, that the distressed of both [armies] at the [Guilford] Courthouse . . . shall have part of it with us." "We hold it the duty of true Christians," they concluded, "at all times to assist the distressed" (James, 1962, 369–377; Mekeel, 1979, 294–313; Thorne, 1961, 336–339).

Conclusion

When the war ended in 1783 and the passions of the Revolution subsided, many Americans came to recognize the significant relief Quakers had provided to those who suffered because of the war. Speaking to Congress in 1790, Elias Boudinot, commissary general of prisoners during the war, praised the Society of Friends for the aid it dispensed to "the miserable prisoners," who "felt the happy effects of their exertions in his favor, but participated in their money, their food, and clothing." Their behavior, he concluded, "did honor to human virtue." After the ordeal of the war, this was high praise indeed. Few noncombatants faced such regular vilification during the American Revolution, and few faced such great economic deprivation for putting their spiritual beliefs into action. Still, the War of Independence—paradoxically—had positive consequences for the group, as well as for the new nation. Having survived the gauntlet of war, the Quakers achieved a new unity and strengthened their internal discipline. Forced by outsiders to define the meaning of their testimonies—particularly the peace testimony—more clearly, they did so with vigor, disciplining and disowning those who failed to measure up. More important, however, Friends forged for themselves a novel role in the new United States of America. When the Revolution ended, Quakers accepted the new government—just as they had accepted British rule before 1776. But building on the precedent of their relief efforts during the war, they set it as their task to become "a holy army" that would fight for the good of the entire nation by spreading virtue. In practice, this meant establishing schools that accepted the poor and free African Americans, it meant providing social services for and defending the interests of the new nation's Indian population, and it meant working to end slavery and aid enslaved African Americans throughout the nation. Out of the distress of the Revolution, then, was born a new role for Quakers: the conscience of the nation (quoted in Mekeel, 1979, 294; James, 1962, 377–382).

References and Further Reading

Archer, Adair P. "The Quaker's Attitude towards the Revolution." *William and Mary Quarterly*, 2d ser., 1 (1921): 167–182.

Brinton, Howard H. *The Religious Philosophy of Quakerism: The Beliefs of Fox, Barclay, and Penn as Based on the Gospel of John*. Wallingford, PA: Pendle Hill Publications, 1973.

Brock, Peter. *Pioneers of the Peaceable Kingdom*. Princeton, NJ: Princeton University Press, 1968.

Brock, Peter. *The Quaker Peace Testimony, 1660–1914*. York, UK: Sessions Book Trust, 1990.

Cope, Gilbert. "Chester County Quakers during the Revolution." *Bulletin of the Chester County Historical Society* (1902–1903): 15–26.

Davis, Robert Scott, Jr., ed. "The Wrightsborough Quakers and the American Revolution." *Southern Friend* 4 (1982): 3–16.

Davis, Timothy. *A Letter from a Friend to some of his Intimate Friends, on the Subject of Paying Taxes, &c*. Watertown, MA: Edes, 1776.

De Warville, J. P. Brissot. *New Travels in the United States of America, Performed in 1788*. Boston: Joseph Bumstead, 1797.

Foster, Thyra Jane, et al. *Rhode Island Quakers in the American Revolution, 1775–1790*. Providence, RI: Published for Providence Monthly Meeting of Friends, 1977.

Gilpin, Thomas, ed. *Exiles in Virginia: With Observations on the Conduct of the Society of Friends during the Revolutionary War*. Philadelphia: Sherman, 1848.

Grey, Isaac. *A Serious Address to Such of the People called Quakers, on the Continent of North America, as Profess Scruples Relative to the Present Government*. Philadelphia: Styner and Cist, 1778.

Hirst, Margaret E. *The Quakers in Peace and War: An Account of Their Peace Principles and Practice*. New York: Doran, 1923.

James, Sydney V. "The Impact of the American Revolution on Quakers' Ideas about Their Sect." *William and Mary Quarterly*, 3rd ser., 19 (1962): 360–382.

Kashatus, William C. *Conflict of Conviction: A Reappraisal of Quaker Involvement in the American Revolution.* Lanham, MD: University Press of America, 1990.

Marietta, Jack D. *The Reformation of American Quakerism, 1748–1783.* Philadelphia: University of Pennsylvania Press, 1984.

Mays, David John, ed. *The Letters and Papers of Edmund Pendleton.* 2 vols. Charlottesville: University Press of Virginia, 1967.

Mekeel, Arthur J. *The Relation of the Quakers to the American Revolution.* Washington, DC: University Press of America, 1979.

Newton, Algie I. "The Battle of New Garden." *Southern Friend* 16 (1994): 11.

Oaks, Robert F. "Philadelphians in Exile: The Problem of Loyalty during the American Revolution." *Pennsylvania Magazine of History and Biography* 96 (1972): 298–325.

Paine, Thomas. *Common Sense.* In *Thomas Paine: Collected Writings,* ed. Eric Foner. New York: Library of America, 1995.

Pemberton, James. *The Life and Travels of John Pemberton, A Minister of the Gospel of Christ.* London: Gilpin, 1844.

Thorne, Dorothy Gilbert. "North Carolina Friends and the Revolution." *North Carolina Historical Review* 38 (1961): 323–340.

Tiedemann, Joseph S. "Queens County, New York Quakers in the American Revolution: Loyalists or Neutrals?" *Historical Magazine of the Protestant Episcopal Church* 52 (1983): 215–227.

A Sea of Rebellion: Maritime Workers in the Age of the American Revolution

10

Matthew Raffety

Seafarers, whether those in naval service or those who worked on merchant vessels, played an active role in American life before, during, and after the Revolution. Sailors not only participated in the Revolution itself, but were on the front lines of the conflict long before independence had been declared. Despite the importance of seamen to the Revolution, however, their contribution has often been undercounted or overlooked in the history of the American Revolution. Even during the Revolution, the importance of seamen, not only to the Revolution itself, but to American economy and society, remained invisible to both British and colonial leaders. Seafarers were critical to the economic, cultural, and political life of the Atlantic world. Nevertheless, most accounts pay little attention to the role that seafarers played in the major political events of the day.

Sailors became important figures in the American struggle for independence. Sailors and other maritime workers served in many capacities; they joined in the protests that preceded the Revolution, and they lent organizational (and physical) strength to the growing public discontent that lead to the push for independence. The plight and mistreatment of sailors by the British Navy offered revolutionaries a powerful illustration of the excesses of empire. Once the war began, sailors fought in a number of capacities, and their contribution was critical to securing independence.

The Dangers of Maritime Life

Nothing came easily for America's seafarers in the Revolutionary era. Their workplace was dangerous and dirty. Going to sea meant living in cramped conditions and performing strenuous and hazardous labor, under the often harsh command of the ship's officers. Sailors worked (when work could be found at all) for small wages, which were often withheld on the whims of the ships' officers, who held sweeping powers over them. Although a wide range

The USS *Alfred*, a 30-gun former merchantman commissioned in Philadelphia in December 1775, took part in the raid on Nassau and captured numerous prizes in European waters before being captured by the British ships *Adriane* and *Ceres* in March 1778. (*National Archives and Records Administration*)

of men went to sea in the Revolutionary era for varied reasons, they tended to be young men of limited means, who had a career of only a few years on the water. At the same time, sailors took great pride in their craft and had a long-standing tradition of defending their rights—by violence when necessary—long before the American Revolution.

Sailors were identifiable by the distinctive clothing of their profession, including a short jacket and striped and brightly colored trousers. They traditionally wore their hair pulled back into a tight queue, and topped their kit with a broad-brimmed straw hat decorated with trailing ribbons and liberally treated with tar as waterproofing. "Jack Tar," as the sailor was universally known, was a regular presence in the port cities of the British Empire. Although in many ways they were much like other workers of the late eighteenth century, sailors had a singularly bad reputation. Often poor and in unfamiliar surroundings, seamen became associated with the most dangerous parts of a city and were frequent customers of the more dubious forms of recreation. In areas like Philadelphia's evocatively named "Hell Town," sailors mingled with others on the bottom rungs of colonial society. Dockside haunts and taverns provided an important site for the politicization of seafarers, slaves, and other "undesirables" (Gilje, 2003).

Despite the dubious reputation of their profession, sailors were not, as many on both sides of the conflict believed, merely a part of the excitable rabble that could be whipped into a dangerous frenzy in any political direction. Rather, American seafarers had an often sophisticated understanding of the issues that precipitated the Revolution, and knowingly and intelligently participated in the politics of the era. They understood that their reputation as a dangerous and unruly class of society made their presence in the public protests of the era all the more powerful. They used this power to defend the rights of their own craft and melded that tradition into the developing larger revolutionary movement.

Indeed, it can be argued that seafarers were in rebellion against Britain long before 1776. What is certain, however, is that the Revolution owed a considerable debt to seamen of all stripes. Sailors fought for independence, both at sea and in American ports throughout the war. They also helped precipitate that conflict by providing tactics, communication, organization, and enthusiastic participation to the fledgling movement for independence. Seafarers made ready revolutionaries because they were all too familiar with the excesses and abuses of the empire. Whether from serving on a merchant slaver traveling the middle passage, or experiencing the brutal and often arbitrary discipline of the British Navy, seamen saw firsthand the violent power of the British Empire. It is little wonder, then, that many seafarers were radicalized long before the American Revolution, nor that, once the war began, they were prepared to fight and sacrifice for the American cause in large numbers.

A Rebellious Lot

The unwilling impressment of sailors into the Royal Navy had soured many seafarers on both sides of the Atlantic on the British Empire long before other colonists began to clamor for independence during the 1760s. The voracious demand of the Royal Navy for sailors meant resorting to forced labor. Gangs of naval officials, often little more than a brute squad, would sweep through the dockside neighborhoods "impressing" by force any able-bodied men they could capture. These "press gangs" swept through British ports on both sides of the Atlantic with increasing frequency throughout the eighteenth century.

In response to the press gangs, Jack Tar was in rebellion long before his landlubber countrymen. Protests over impressments ranging from the symbolic to the violent became commonplace in the 1740s throughout the British Empire. Increasingly, sailors banded together to halt the press gangs in their actions. Often they threatened and mobbed naval officers, trading the officers' safe return to their vessels in exchange for the release of the press gangs' victims. In other cases, they attacked the boats used by the press gangs to shuttle the new "recruits" back to the ships, often burning or scuttling them. New York alone saw five major anti-impressment riots between 1758 and 1807. As the Revolution approached, seamen became more daring in their attacks on impressment. Newport, Rhode Island, in 1765, saw an anti-impressment mob grow more than 500 strong. Two years later, a multiracial mob attacked a British captain in Norfolk, Virginia (Linebaugh and Rediker, 2000, 228).

Sailors were an active and vocal presence in the protests and public actions leading up to open conflict. They had long been an important presence in the rough political theater of colonial urban centers. Jack Tar was a familiar face and a lusty participant in mob actions throughout the colonial period, but particularly during the period leading up to the Declaration of Independence. In port cities throughout the colonies, seafarers joined in (and often led) the growing tide of mob action in response to Parliamentary actions (Linebaugh and Rediker, 2000, 234). Not only did they lend their voices and fists to this rugged political theater of the early opposition to the British, sailors also provided a model of organization for the radical groups beginning to form. The sailors' waterside haunts had developed a network of loose clubs and secret societies that helped warn of press gangs and rally the mob to the defense of those captured.

The Sons of Liberty, an organization that helped to organize American resistance in the 1770s, may have taken as its model the older Sons of Neptune, a secret fraternity present along the waterfront earlier that precipitated actions to free sailors from the naval press gangs (Linebaugh and Rediker, 2000, 237; see also Morris, 1946, 138). Revolutionary leaders in the Sons of Liberty and other groups appropriated the tactics developed by waterfront mobs for public actions. The growing revolutionary movement made great use of the public demonstrations pioneered by groups like the Sons of Neptune. Even the forms that public action took owed much to the sailors among the participants. The practice of tarring and feathering those whose actions had offended the mob, which began to appear in the Northeast in the protests of the late 1760s, owed its origins to traditional punishments and hazing rituals at sea (Gilje, 1987, 65). More broadly, the use of mass demonstrations, in which sailors had long participated, became a key tool of colonial leaders during the crisis following the passage of the Stamp Act in 1765.

Sailors represented a critical site for the transfer of information and ideas throughout the Atlantic world. They were among the best-traveled people in the world in the eighteenth century, and they had contact with other regions, cultures, and nations that few could match at any social level. They acted as an important underground and unofficial source of news throughout the empire. Workers throughout the empire relied on the news sailors brought with them from distant ports to keep tabs on the wider world. Seamen quickly spread word of the growing protests and assaults on British authority that spread through colonial American in the 1760s. Additionally, the sea was the most diverse working environment of the era. Seafarers from throughout Europe, Africa, the Caribbean, and North America often shipped out in the same forecastle. Some scholars argue that this diversity helped make sailors a radical force, acting to halt the expansion of state power in the Atlantic world long before the American Revolution. Sailors, argue these historians, were radicalized long before the specific issues that precipitated the explicit severing of America from Britain in 1776 (Linebaugh and Rediker, 2000, 211–247; Gilje, 1987, 5–35; Gilje, 2003; Lemisch, 1968, 371–407; Lemisch, 1997, xviii; Rediker, 1987, 205–253).

But sailors were not just a passive conduit for revolutionary news and spirit. Seamen continued to participate in the protests that had become part of a broader movement. Sailors played important roles in the burning of the customs ship HMS *Gaspee* off Newport, Rhode Island, in 1772. Although the mob that rowed out in three longboats boasted members from many occupations, seafarers took the lead in burning the ship to the waterline.

Sailors were also among the first to pay the most drastic price in the struggle for independence. After more than a year of occupation by British troops, the situation in Boston had become extremely tense. On March 5, 1770, anxious British troops opened fire on a boisterous crowd of around fifty to sixty. What had begun as one of many tense incidents throughout the colonies ended by giving the American cause some of its first martyrs. When the smoke cleared, five lay dead, and another eight wounded in the event that the press soon labeled the Boston Massacre. Two sailors lay among the dead, and at least two of the wounded survivors also worked at sea.

One of those first casualties was Crispus Attucks, a sailor of African and Native American ancestry. According to a newspaper report, he was, "killed instantly, two balls entering his breast, one of them in special goring of the

Paul Revere's sensational illustration of the Boston Massacre, a skirmish on March 5, 1770, in which British soldiers fired on and killed five townspeople. Revere's historic print, released within a month, publicized the event and was hugely influential in stoking anti-British sentiment in the years before the American Revolution. An interesting example of Revere's emphasis on impact over accuracy is the depiction of one of the victims, Crispus Attucks, a man of both Native and African American roots, as a white man. (*National Archives and Records Administration*)

right lobe of the lungs and a great part of the liver most horribly." What little is known about Attucks's life before that fatal day at Faneuil Hall suggests he was in many ways a typical seafarer of the late eighteenth century. Attucks, like many black seamen, had escaped slavery in his youth to enjoy the relative freedom of the sea. He had worked on a Nantucket whaler earlier and by 1770 was in Boston working as a dockworker until he could find another appealing berth to go to sea. As a man in his late forties, Attucks was a bit of an "old salt," toward the end of his seafaring career. Nevertheless, his story was typical in many ways. The sea was the most diverse workplace of the age, bringing together men of many backgrounds, including those of mixed heritage like Attucks, to forge the society of the forecastle. Additionally, both in his escape from slavery and in his participation in anti-British protests like the one that took his life, Attucks reflected the importance of "freedom" and "liberty" to seamen throughout the colonies and the world (*Boston Gazette and Country Journal*, March 12, 1770; Belton, 1972, 149–152).

If Crispus Attucks reflected the actions and ideology of many less famous seamen who had been protesting British power and striving for freedom long before March 1770, his death made him an icon both within and outside the seafaring community. Paul Revere's famous engraving of the event was created to rally converts to the cause, even if those who have fallen to the redcoats' musket balls in his depiction are decidedly white. Although the revolutionary leaders began to try to pull the movement back from the more radical aspects of the pre-Revolutionary fervor, the power of sailor-led mobs like that of the Boston Massacre were clearly a force to be reckoned with. Although few of the ideological leaders of the Revolution had spent time at sea, many looked to the waters for both inspiration and examples of British tyranny.

The Importance of the Atlantic

In more abstract ways, the sea played an enormous role in Revolutionary America's culture. Indeed, from its beginnings as tiny settlements clinging to the Atlantic coast, the Anglo-American colonial world saw the ocean (if not always those who made their living upon it) as the critical lifeline to the "civilization" of the mother country. Early Americans wrested their very survival from the waters. It is no surprise, then, that the 1639 *Almanack Calculated for New England, by Mr. Pierce, Mariner*, reputedly the first English-language book printed in the Americas, focused primarily on the waterways and fishing grounds of New England (Tebbel, 1987, 6).

The waters also represented a site of manly adventure in late colonial America. Most young men at least toyed with the idea of going to sea, even if most, including Benjamin Franklin and George Washington, managed to recover from their "sea fever" without shipping out (Lemisch, 1968, 373–374). Even if they never sailed themselves, however, the powerful economic and cultural presence of the maritime world influenced the revolutionary generation in many ways.

Beyond the wanderlust and desire for adventure that drew many young American men to the sea, sailor's lives, works, and political actions directly influenced many of those who sought to bring order and coherence to the revolutionary movement. Samuel Adams, James Otis, Thomas Jefferson, Benjamin Franklin, and Thomas Paine all acknowledged an intellectual debt to the actions of the "multiracial seaport crowds" that asserted in deed the resistance to oppression that the newly forming committees of correspondence argued for in their writings. Benjamin Franklin noted that naval impressment injured not only seafarers themselves, but the colonial economy as a whole. During the Seven Years' war, he commented in frustration that the drain on labor caused by the navy's voracious appetite for manpower often hurt trade "more than the Enemy hurts it." Not all of Franklin's objections were economic, however. He also saw the injustice of impressment as a black mark on British society, noting that "it doth not secure liberty but destroys it" (quoted in Lemisch, 1997, 18, 35). Thomas Paine, author of the 1776 pamphlet *Common Sense*, saw sailors as critical not only to the Revolution itself, but to the new nation's survival. According to Paine, "No country on the globe is so happily situated, so internally capable of raising a fleet as America." He went on to suggest that the maritime economy was the "natural manufactory" of the new nation and would guarantee both its security and its prosperity (Paine, *Common Sense*, 1995).

Perhaps Paine understood the importance of sailors to the nation because he himself had sailed as a crew member on the privateer *Terrible* as a nineteen-year-old during the Seven Years' War. Although Paine's time at sea was short, its impact reverberated throughout the Revolution. Although Paine was somewhat unique among the key revolutionaries in having gone to sea himself, he was not the only one to see the rhetorical value of sailors to the American cause (Linebaugh and Rediker, 2000, 237–239).

The struggles of seafarers against impressment served as a compelling example of British tyranny—an example that could be exploited powerfully by those seeking to rally colonials to the revolutionary standard. The practice of impressment seemed antithetical to the notion of inalienable rights that the revolutionaries began to claim as justification to form a new nation. Radicals were quick to point out the ways that the harsh realities of seafaring life failed to live up to claims of the vaunted rights of Englishmen. As early as 1754, the London *Post-Boy* editorialized, "That the hardy Sailor, who has just survived the Fury of the Seas, and the Rage of Elements, should be immediately torn from the Bosom of his friends and Family, and, without the least Prospect of Honour or Advantage, compelled to revisit barbarous Shores, is inconsistent with Civil Liberty, and the natural Rights of Man" (cited in Lemisch, 1997, 36).

Benjamin Franklin commented that naval impressment marked a singular example of British tyranny: "The very means which the Navy used to fill out its ranks—reminiscent as they are of the means of catching Africans for slavery—suggest that to be in the Navy was to be unfree" (Lemisch, 1997, 16). More succinctly, he argued, there is "no slavery worse than that sailors are subject to" (cited in Lemisch, 1997, 35).

The impressment crisis gave revolutionaries a concrete and evocative example of Britons' trampling of American rights. So important was the issue to the Americans that Thomas Jefferson included it among the justifications in

Alexander White

It would be impossible to find a truly typical seafarer of the Revolutionary era. Young men went to sea for a constellation of reasons, and came together from all corners of the Atlantic world and beyond to work at sea. Nevertheless, the short life of Alexander White has themes many late eighteenth-century seamen would recognize, even if his career came to a somewhat grimmer end than most.

White was born in County Tyrone in Ireland in 1762, just as the first rumblings of the Revolutionary era were beginning across the Atlantic. As a boy from a family of limited means, he "got what education my parents thought necessary," before the lure of the sea proved too strong for him to remain at home. Like many young men going to sea, White found the prospect of travel and adventure irresistible, and, his "mind being inclined to see strange countries against . . . parents' wishes," he fled home for England to seek a berth on a merchant ship (Russell, 1784, 27).

Significantly, White left little information about his life as a seafarer in his brief and misnamed "dying confession," even though he began his career in the midst of the American Revolution. In no surviving account did he describe either his view of or his participation in the world events swirling around him as a young man. We cannot even reconstruct what, if anything, the Irish-born seaman who sailed from both British and American ports during this bloody and contentious era thought of the Revolution, or how, if at all, he served directly for either side.

White's failure to describe the politics and protests he must have witnessed in his travels frustrates modern historians. But his reticence suggests that he was, like many seafarers of the day, merely a young man trying to make his way in a complicated world and in a difficult and dangerous profession. White saw himself as typical for a seaman of his era, noting that he was so typical a tar that "it is needless of me to give an account how I spent my life" (Russell, 1784, 28). Although he was proud of the skill he developed, noting that by the end of his career his studious attention to his craft made him a valuable crew member of any ship as either a before-the-mast hand or an officer, he nevertheless referred to his chosen life somewhat grimly, noting that he "gave himself up to" the sea as a young man and had known no other life since. He also noted that he shared the culture of the forecastle with his bunkmates, explaining that in both his virtues and his vices

the Declaration of Independence, commenting that among the outrages perpetrated by the British Crown was that the king had "constrained our fellow Citizens taken captive on the high seas to bear arms against their Country, to become executioners of their friends and Brethren, or to fall themselves by their Hands." To men like Franklin and Jefferson, impressment marked not only an unusually onerous injustice of British rule. It also served as an opportunity to dramatize the plight of "fellow citizens" for emotional effect.

Not all the revolutionary leadership saw the influence of sailors in the revolutionary movement as a good thing, however. More conservative revolutionaries saw danger in the mob actions that seamen participated in and often led. Even those who relied on seamen for inspiration and pointed to them as an example of the cost of British tyranny had no intention of sharing the new republic with them on equal footing. Fear of "the mob," even as it became an important tool of the revolutionary effort, meant that many saw the participation of seamen as dangerous. James Madison felt that sail-

he was a typical Jack Tar, and "had never been guilty of any vices but such as are common to sailors" (White, 1784, 2).

As with most seafarers, his profession may have brought him the travel and adventure he had desired as a boy; it did not, however, bring him riches. Seafaring life was economically difficult even for skilled men with good reputations like White.

Desperately poor, White found himself in Philadelphia in 1784, awaiting a promised berth as a mate on a journey to the West Indies. Ashamed of his poverty (particularly because of a budding romance with a woman of more comfortable means) White was pushed by his need for money to sign on to a sloop bound for Nova Scotia rather than waiting for a more lucrative promised berth.

It was during this voyage to Nova Scotia that White's career took a dramatic turn. Off Long Island, New York, he and a fellow seaman named Johnson sought to seize the ship by killing the captain (also named White) and another passenger (Russell, 1784, 28). White's mutiny and murders were motivated by the riches the sloop was carrying, and he admitted in his confession that, blinded by love, he

sought a quick and sanguine solution to his financial situation.

White's "solution" to his financial problems may have been unusually drastic, but the desperation of his situation was certainly not unusual. Although murderous incidents like White's case were rare even in the confusion of the Revolutionary era, violence always remained a ready response at sea. Seamen faced difficult economic pressures and exerted little if any control over their employment and working conditions. Although White's response to his economic desperation may have been unusual, his frustration at the vagaries of fortune and the economic displacements of war was not. Indeed, the frustrations faced by White were precisely what drew so many seafarers to revolutionary causes during this period.

White's career (and life) ended at the gallows in Portsmouth, Massachusetts, after his conviction for murder and piracy in 1784. His outcome was grimmer than most, but understood in the context of the difficult, violent, and dangerous world of the sea, a world White himself was so accustomed to that he scarcely commented upon it, his story seems perhaps more typical than it might at first glance.

ors were important to the revolutionary fight, but less important to the new nation that was to follow. Rather harshly, he mocked the contribution sailors could make to the new republic, asking, "At home in his vessel, what new ideas and occurrences can shoot from the unvaried use of the ropes and the rudder, or from the society of comrades as ignorant as himself?" (cited in Linebaugh and Rediker, 2000, 239). Ironically, to Madison and other leaders, seamen were important agents in bringing about the new nation, but of limited utility to it once independence was obtained. Samuel Adams even served as legal counsel for the British soldiers charged with Attucks's death, earning an acquittal by claiming that any reasonable person would have been terrified by someone who looked like Attucks coming at him (Linebaugh and Rediker, 2000, 237).

For their part, seafarers did not need lofty theoretical appeals to natural law or the acceptance of the revolutionary elite to make the Revolution their own. Rather, sailors had been waging a concerted campaign against the practice of impressment throughout the British Atlantic for decades by the time it came to the notice of men like Franklin, Paine, and Jefferson. Sailors dealt with the theoretical issues of the Revolution in practical, pragmatic, and everyday ways. After all, "liberty," one of the central themes of the revolutionary movement, had a concrete meaning for sailors—it was the time they were permitted to be off the ship. Although debate continues about whether sailors' participation in the violence and spectacle of mass demonstrations before 1776 was out of an understanding of and connection to revolutionary ideology, or was prompted by more immediate aims, such as avoiding impressments or simply being a part of the action, sailors did have a profound effect on those who sought a broader and more theoretical revolutionary movement.

In part, sailors participated so actively in the mobs of the Revolutionary era because they more than almost any other class of workers felt the sting of these "intolerable" acts of Parliament directly. The Parliamentary maneuverings that raised so much colonial ire in the 1760s had real and direct effects on seamen. The regulation and taxation of the goods traveling throughout the far-flung British Empire meant changes in the patterns of shipping. In turn, this meant real differences for individual sailors regarding when, how often, and at what wage they could follow their trade. The increased billeting of British soldiers in American ports after 1766 meant even stiffer competition and lower wages for already scarce waterfront jobs. Moonlighting redcoats put downward pressure on wages in port cities, a pressure that was felt throughout the maritime economy. Most dramatically, the punitive closing of Boston Harbor after the Boston Tea Party in 1775 meant wholesale unemployment for those plying maritime trades. Not that the coming of the war solved all problems; in fact war made things at once better and more difficult for seafarers. The outbreak of hostilities effectively closed many of the traditional opportunities open to seafarers and waterfront workers. As the

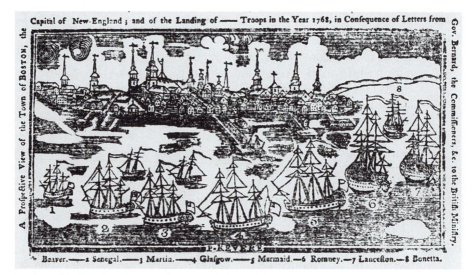

Landing of the British troops in Boston, 1768. (*Library of Congress*)

war halted merchant commerce, seafarers in many ports found themselves out of work. Over 200 sailors in Philadelphia struck to protest low wages and the scarcity of work in 1779 (Foner, 1976, 165).

On the other hand, the coming of war sometimes proved an economic boon to those who followed the maritime trades. Those who escaped the press gangs and did not rally immediately to the revolutionary cause had their pick of merchant berths in ports held by the British. Nevertheless, most American seamen who had been involved in their own revolt against impressment and the Royal Navy sought ways to aid the American cause.

Before the focus of this chapter shifts completely to the war itself, it is worth reiterating that, from ship owners to the men who served before the mast, maritime workers were among the Americans most frustrated with British revenue policies of the 1760s and 1770s. Wealthy merchants like John Hancock grew outraged when his provocatively named sloop *Liberty* was seized by British officials in 1768, but it was regular tars who rioted in defense of both their liberty and Hancock's *Liberty* on the streets of Boston, forcing the newly appointed Board of Customs Commissioners to flee in fear of their safety. It was not only the affluent merchants like Hancock who suffered under the tightening restrictions of imperial commercial regulation, and sailors understood that these policies affected their livelihood. Impressment was only the most drastic injustice that the empire cast upon seamen. As has been discussed above, the shifting regulatory landscape meant displacement and unemployment, and maritime Americans of all walks of life became increasingly frustrated with the engines of empire (Maier, 1970, 3–35).

Sailors and the War

Due to their long frustration with the Royal Navy and the ways that Parliamentary whims wrought sometimes dire consequences on their livelihood, most American seamen found themselves firmly on the revolutionary side when the fighting began. Nevertheless, the call to revolution was not universally accepted along the American waterfront. Many affluent captains, merchants, and ships' officers, although frustrated by imperial actions, feared the even more disruptive consequences of independence. Even some regular tars remained loyal to Britain, such as New York's Alpheus Avery and Richard Jenkins. The sailors who rejected the American cause tended to be unusually well-off financially as compared to their bunkmates, which was the case with both Avery and Jenkins. Loyalists mariners found themselves decidedly unpopular once the war began, and the waterfront became a dangerous place to be identified as a Tory. Neither Avery nor Jenkins felt safe remaining even in British-controlled New York. Avery fled with his father to England and rose to be captain of a merchant vessel, while Jenkins fled to New Jersey to join the British Army (Lemisch, 1997, 151–152).

Sailors' role in the birth of the nation was obviously not limited to the protests and rallies that lead up to the actual fighting. Seamen fought, bled, and died on both sides of the conflict throughout the war. Some scholars would even go so far as to say that the American victory owed more to what happened on the seas than to all of the battles that took place ashore. Despite the overwhelming power of the massive Royal Navy, sailors provided great strength to the American cause. British officials were stunned by the speed with which the Americans were able to build a small but viable navy at the beginning of the war. What was to become the United States Navy began in late 1775, when the Continental Congress authorized the creation of a naval force for an independent America. In order to create a navy for the American cause, the Continental Congress turned to a small group of captains ready to forge a new force for the revolutionary cause. In particular, the task fell to a Scottish-born seaman named John Paul Jones. Despite having only left Britain in 1774 to flee legal troubles, Jones was willing to bring to America's nascent naval force his organizational genius as well as considerable skill as a captain on the water (Mahan, 2001).

Jones, a seafarer who had risen up the ranks since going to sea at age sixteen, sought to build a force that could match in some small measure the might of the Royal Navy on the water. Unlike Washington, who could rely on existing colonial militias to form the core of the new Continental Army, Jones and other officers of the new naval force had to create the new navy without any existing colonial structure upon which to build. To make matters

John Paul Jones was the first great American naval officer. He fought brilliantly against great odds, and his victory over HMS *Serapis* during the American Revolution remains one of the most celebrated ship-to-ship encounters in history. (*Library of Congress*)

worse, although skilled seafarers abounded in American ports, many of whom had had experience in the Royal Navy, the American forces could boast almost no captains with military experience. Exceptions included Jones and Philadelphian Nicholas Biddle, who had served as a young man with the future British naval hero Horatio Nelson (Beach, 1986, 14–18).

Despite American shortcomings in equipment, experience, and organizational structure, the Continental Navy came to number sixty-four ships, and it was able to harass British forces even within sight of British shores. Although much of the American Navy might be described as a disaster, some captains like Jones and Biddle scored several decisive and, for the Royal Navy, embarrassing victories on the water (Howarth, 1991, 17–43).

Despite the limitations that the Americans faced in countering British sea power, the skill of American sailors and shipbuilders meant that, though small, the American presence on the water was occasionally effective. New England had long been a site of shipbuilding, using the plentiful old-growth timber of the Maine woods for material, and American-built ships soon won a reputation for both hardiness and speed. Additionally, skilled American tars and officers often had an advantage in the familiar waters of the American coast. Perhaps the greatest advantage the Americans had on the water was one of morale. Whether serving in Jones's navy or on the scores of privateers fighting in the American cause, American sailors fought because they chose to do so.

In contrast, the largely impressed seamen of the Royal Navy were often at best ambivalent about the British cause. Even worse, many were American Patriots serving Britain only at the point of an officers' cutlass. That a single privateer, commanded by Captain Jonathan Haraden of Salem, Massachusetts, could seize three ships of the Royal Navy in the same battle illustrates the importance of morale in marine combat. The Royal Navy, subject to mutinies and desertions in the best of times, found itself awash with disciplinary problems after 1776. Captain Jones himself counted superior morale as among the chief advantages of the American side. Many sailors serving on British ships of the line were only too willing to desert or be "captured" by Americans. Estimates suggest that over 40,000 sailors deserted between 1776 and the end of the war in 1783. Indeed, many of the sailors serving on the American side of the conflict by the end of the war had begun it in the employ of the Royal Navy (Linebaugh and Rediker, 2000, 241; Howarth, 1991, 21).

The new Continental Navy, while effective for its size, represented only a small fraction of the American presence on the seas during the war. A far larger and more important force was constituted by the large number of independent vessels and sailors who joined the American cause as privateers. Privateers, privately owned vessels engaged in capturing ships of other nations as "prizes," became the heart of the official American presence on the water during the Revolution. Privateers were distinguished from pirates by a "letter of marque," a license issued by the government to engage in maritime combat. During the Revolution, however, the British did not recognize the new American nation issuing the letters of marque, which meant that those captured aboard privateers could be treated as simple pirates. Even though the new naval service offered the possible protection of a recognizable flag that privateers could not fly, patriotic American seamen strongly preferred serving on privateers to joining Jones's new navy. Jones was frustrated by the limited success of his efforts in trying to lure men into the service of the new nation. When he began his recruitment drive in New York before its reconquest by British forces in 1776, he discovered that most available Patriots had already either joined Washington's army or elected to sign on a privateer rather than join the new naval service.

Moreover, the American Navy as well as the British Navy suffered large desertions to American privateers (Lemisch, 1997, 151–153). Sailors preferred to serve on privateers for good reason. Ever the pragmatist, Jack Tar sought to benefit not only his nation, but his own finances at the same time. While the navy paid wages little above those of a merchant seaman and used harsh discipline in the bargain, a successful privateering cruise could yield hundreds of dollars to regular crewmen. Such a payday represented a rare opportunity in a field that paid less than ten dollars a month in normal times. Additionally, service on a privateer meant unusual opportunities for advancement in the dangerous and chaotic maritime terrain of the war. Adventurous and talented seamen moved up through the ranks, and both the financial rewards of success and the dire need for talented officers meant young men who would have waited years for a command in the navy, if indeed it had ever become available to them, found themselves moving up from the below-decks home of regular seamen in the forecastle to the captain's plush cabin on the quarterdeck before war's end. The combination of patriotic appeals and the potential financial rewards drew over 55,000 to sign articles and serve on privateers. American forces issued over 1,600 letters of marque over the course of the war, and as many as 450 American privateers were preying on British shipping at one time.

Privateering was critical to American success. This massive force harassed and disrupted Great Britain's ability to move information and material. American ships took over 16,000 prisoners, more than the total taken by Washington's army. Additionally, American privateers captured more than 2,200 prizes, providing the American cause with ships and weapons. More than 2 million pounds of gunpowder seized by privateers kept Washington's army prepared for battle. Even Washington himself acknowledged the importance of the American presence on the water, noting that "without a decisive presence on the water, we can do nothing definitive" (Howarth, 1991, 5).

Not all privateers were successful, however, and although substantial rewards awaited the brave and fortunate who signed onto successful privateers, the less lucky paid heavily for the risks they had taken. The overwhelming size and power of the Royal Navy meant that capture was likely for even the most skilled American tar. In total, over 1,300 American privateering vessels were either sunk or captured by British forces. Although relatively few died from combat at sea during the war (at least as compared to the mortality of those who fought on land), crew members of privateers captured by the Royal Navy often met a grim end. Many found themselves simply impressed into the British Navy, the very fate that had prompted so many to join the rebel cause. Even though impressment was often seen as a death sentence, those impressed might easily be better off than their bunkmates who either refused or were unable to serve in the British Navy. More than 10,000 sailors met their end aboard overcrowded, filthy prison ships in British-controlled ports. These ships, usually little more than aged hulls transformed into floating jails, housed the flood of captured Americans pulled off of privateers and other ships that dared show American colors. The conditions ranged from the grim to the unspeakable. Inmates had to struggle for limited food and water, and even fresh air came at a premium, as inattention and overcrowding meant that prisoners often shared their billet with the decaying corpses of those who had expired from the conditions.

One such prisoner was James Forten, a black seaman from Philadelphia who had served in the Continental Army before signing on to the *Royal Louis* for a privateering cruise. After a first successful cruise that saw the capture of a royal brig, the *Royal Louis* sailed again, but with less success. Once captured, Forten was lucky not to be sold into slavery, which was the fate of many black sailors captured fighting in the American cause. Instead, Forten was placed on board the prison ship *Jersey* moored in New York harbor. He suffered imprisonment on the *Jersey* for seven months until he was finally released in a prisoner exchange. Forten was one of the luckier inhabitants of the *Jersey*. Not only did he survive his time caged below the decks of the rotting hulk, but after the war Forten returned to his native Philadelphia and

Interior of the *Jersey* prison ship during the Revolutionary War. Thousands of American captives died of disease and malnutrition aboard such vessels, usually hulks moored in ports like New York. (*Library of Congress*)

used the money he had made on board the *Royal Louis* to set himself up in business and become a leader of the free black community and an outspoken advocate for the abolition of slavery.

Another survivor of the *Jersey*, Captain Thomas Dring, described his 1779 arrival on the ship. He received a chilling hello from a fellow inmate upon his transfer to the infamous *Jersey*, moored in the East River, who cried out that it was "a lamentable thing to see so many young men in full strength, with the flush of health upon their countenance, about to enter that infernal place of abode. . . . Death had no relish for such skeleton carcasses as we are, but he will now have a feast upon you fresh comers." Fearful he would not survive the *Jersey*, Dring eventually made his escape by swimming to the New Jersey shore (quoted in Gilje and Rock, 1992, 175).

Sailors served in many capacities during the era of the American Revolution. Whether as provocateurs, as inspiration to Revolutionary theoreticians, as participants in mass demonstrations or as combatants under British or American colors, or on a privateer, seamen were central to the era. However, with independence won, the leaders of the new nation turned their back on the more revolutionary implications of their own actions. Sailors, workers, and slaves, all vital participants in the powerful revolutionary coalition that began the push for independence in the waterfront protests of the 1760s, discovered after 1783 that they had been written out of the victory.

As the fighting ended for most Americans, seafarers continued to feel the unfinished aspects of the Revolution, both on land and at sea. As the new nation began the long turn away from the more radical implication of the Revolution that had been embodied in the work of Paine, seamen found themselves written out of the political life of the new nation. Few met the property qualifications offset by individual states for participating directly in the new nation. Significantly, it was not until noncoastal states like Ohio were added to the Union that property qualifications began to fall away. Even more dramatically, seafarers felt few of the new benefits of the American victory on the water. The British Navy continued to impress Americans, pulling them off ships flying the American flag into the nineteenth century. As a result, seafarers continued, often to the dismay of the new leadership of the United States, to press for change and participation as they had before and during the struggle for independence. Dockside protests and riots continued to serve as means by which "the mob's" voices could still be heard, and the old tactics of revolution remained important and powerful tools in the hands of those silenced by the new regime.

Conclusion

Neither sailors' most specific goal—to be free of the specter of impressment—nor their larger claims for equal participation in the newly formed society were realized by the coming of independence. Even though true equality remained in the distance, however, seamen had proven themselves as an undeniably important part of the struggle for American independence and a loud voice for liberty in the new nation.

References and Further Reading

Beach, Edward L. *The United States Navy: 200 Years.* New York: Holt, 1986.

Belton, Bill. "The Indian Heritage of Crispus Attucks." *Negro History Bulletin* 35 (1972): 149–152.

Boston Gazette and Country Journal.

Creighton, Margaret S., and Lisa Norling, eds. *Iron Men, Wooden Women: Gender and Seafaring in the Atlantic World, 1700–1920.* Baltimore: Johns Hopkins University Press, 1996.

Foner, Eric. *Tom Paine and Revolutionary America.* New York: Oxford University Press, 1976.

Gilje, Paul A. *The Road to Mobocracy: Popular Disorder in New York City, 1763–1834.* Chapel Hill: University of North Carolina Press, 1987.

Gilje, Paul A. *Liberty on the Waterfront: American Maritime Culture in the Age of Revolution.* Philadelphia: University of Pennsylvania Press, 2003.

Gilje, Paul A., and Howard B. Rock. *Keepers of the Revolution: New Yorkers at Work in the Early Republic.* Ithaca, NY: Cornell University Press, 1992.

Howarth, Stephen. *To Shining Sea: A History of the United States Navy, 1775–1991.* New York: Random House, 1991.

Lemisch, Jesse. "Jack Tar in the Streets: Merchant Seamen in the Politics of Revolutionary America." *William and Mary Quarterly*, 3rd ser., 25 (1968): 371–407.

Lemisch, Jesse. *Jack Tar vs. John Bull: The Role of New York's Seamen in Precipitating the Revolution.* New York: Garland, 1997.

Linebaugh, Peter, and Marcus Rediker. *The Many-Headed Hydra: Sailors, Slaves, Commoners, and the Hidden History of the Revolutionary Atlantic.* Boston: Beacon, 2000.

Mahan, Alfred Thayer. *The Influence of Sea Power upon History, 1660–1783* [1890]. New York: Barnes and Noble, 2001.

Maier, Pauline. "Popular Uprisings and Civil Authority in Eighteenth-Century America." *William and Mary Quarterly*, 3rd ser., 27 (1970): 3–35.

Morris, Richard B. *Government and Labor in Early America.* New York: Harper and Row, 1946.

Paine, Thomas. *Common Sense.* In *Thomas Paine: Collected Writings*, ed. Eric Foner. New York: Library of America, 1995.

Rediker, Marcus. *Between the Devil and the Deep Blue Sea: Merchant Seamen, Pirates, and the Anglo-American Maritime World, 1700–1750.* New York: Cambridge University Press, 1987.

Russell, E. *The American Bloody Register.* Boston: Russell, 1784.

Tebbel, John. *Between Covers: The Rise and Transformation of American Book Publishing.* New York: Oxford University Press, 1987.

White, Alexander. *A Narrative of the Life and Conversion of Alexander White.* Boston: Powars and Willis, 1784.

Ladies of Liberty: The Lives of Women during the American Revolution | 11

Lisa Ennis

The experiences of women during the American Revolution were as varied and dynamic as the women themselves. While the individual experiences of women differed, depending on numerous factors such as level of education, socioeconomic status, and physical location, the Revolution affected women from all walks of life. Further, since women made up approximately half the population of colonial America, their active participation made the War for Independence a woman's war as well as a man's war (Engle, 1976, xvii; De Pauw, 1976, 11).

Sadly, the historical record only contains bits and pieces of the story of most women's contributions to the struggle for independence. Most of the information available concentrates on the elite women of the time, such as Abigail Adams and Mercy Otis Warren, who left volumes of letters and other writings, or women in the public eye, such as Martha Washington. Middle- and lower-class women are generally mentioned only in passing by people recording "larger" stories. Piecing together the wartime roles and experiences of women during the American Revolution remains a challenge for historians.

The Constraints of the Common Woman

During the colonial period, the patriarchal system was in full effect. Women had few, if any, legal rights. Colonial America's male-dominated society dictated that women dedicate themselves to the home, bearing and raising children, and being good wives. Committed to home and hearth, women were generally prohibited from making legal contracts, owning property, and voting, although exceptions did exist. As a result, women were excluded from the public sphere, including education; many could neither read nor sign their own names. From an early age, girls were taught to believe that they were inferior to men. Further, an overall societal ideology served to strengthen the colonial ideal of a subordinate, submissive, passive, silent, and weak woman. Once married, a woman legally surrendered everything she owned to her husband, which included all property, profits, and land (Evans, 1975, 2). For example, if a widow held land from her first marriage, complete control of that land would go to her new husband if she married again. Despite the subordinate legal status of married women, marriage was preferable to remaining single. One of the worst social stigmas was that of spinster. These unmarried women, often ostracized and the subject of pity, depended largely on the help of male relatives to ensure their livelihoods (De Pauw, 1976, 5).

For women of color, the social and legal constraints were even stricter, whether they were slave or free. Laws restricted women of color in the same manner as white women but added many more rules. For instance, laws directed people of color as to where they could and could not go; they were not afforded trial by jury, nor could they marry outside their race, bear arms, or even fire a gun or buy liquor (Newman, 1976, 280). Black women, whether slave or free, were relegated to the domestic sphere. Free women of color had very few options. The majority worked as seamstresses, laundresses, cooks, servants, ragpickers, and the like. Many free women of color offered themselves as indentured servants. Those who could not find work usually found themselves in the poorhouse or jail. Free black women in northern states also lived under the constant fear of being kidnapped and transported south into slavery (Newman, 1976, 282–284). While there are exceptions, this was the nature of life for women of color during the Revolutionary era, and it remained unchanged until the American Civil War.

One exception was Phillis Wheatley. Born in Gambia and taken from her parents at age seven, Phillis was bought by John and Susannah Wheatley of Boston and became their personal servant. The intelligent young girl learned English quickly and began writing poetry. Her first book of poetry, *Poems of Various Subjects Religious and Moral* (1773), published in England since no American publisher would print her works, brought her some renown. Her poetry was so good that she had to subject herself to examination to prove that she was actually black and that she could also write poetry. In deference to her talent, she was freed by the Wheatleys. She married John Peters in 1778. Despite her talent and freedom Phillis, who suffered from poor health, died in poverty; most of her poems were not even published until after her death. She is known as the first major black poet in American history (Sidwell, 1999, 38–39).

Practically every religious group reinforced the societal role of women as subordinate and demure. Most Americans followed some form of Christianity, which relied on the New Testament writings of Paul and Peter to teach women how a good Christian wife should behave. Both Peter and Paul repeatedly instructed women that they should obey men without question. Only three religious groups allowed women any sort of active role: the Society of Friends, also known as the Quakers, the society founded by Ann Lee,

Phillis Wheatley was kidnapped as a child in Africa in the 1750s and sold at a slave auction to a prosperous Boston family. The family raised her as their own and gave her freedom. As a young adult she became an accomplished poet, traveling to London to publish her collection of poetry. (*Library of Congress*)

called the Shakers, and the society founded by Jemima Wilkinson. Quakerism, founded in the mid-seventeenth century, allowed women to ask questions and express their opinions as well as to preach. Quakers also believed in the equality of men and women and accordingly in providing girls and boys an equal education (Evans, 1975, 7–8).

Neither Ann Lee nor Jemima Wilkinson had the advantage of an already established religion. Lee and nine of her followers immigrated to New York in August 1774. They were called Shakers because they shook and trembled during services. Lee preached that celibacy and confession were the only way to achieve salvation. She so threatened the traditional view of the family and male dominance that she was often the victim of attacks and was arrested numerous times. Her group eventually settled in Albany, New York.

Wilkinson started her religious journey after a long illness. Wilkinson was convinced that her first soul had gone on to heaven and that God had filled her with a new spirit. She called herself the Public Universal Friend and preached throughout Connecticut and Rhode Island. She eventually gained enough of a following to establish a settlement in Genesee County, New York, called New Jerusalem. Her community disbanded after her death in 1819 (Evans, 1975, 9–10).

Another female religious leader was a free woman of color from New Jersey. Jarena Lee became a maid at age seven and was converted at twenty. Discouraged from preaching by her preacher, Richard Allen, Lee decided to marry a preacher, Joseph Lee. Unfulfilled, Lee returned to her childhood church when her husband died; this time Allen supported her in becoming an exhorter. Lee embarked on an itinerant tour all over the Northeast and as far west as Ohio (Sidwell, 1999, 39–40).

Most women played no such leadership roles. They were not, however, the passive and weak creatures the prevalent ideology seemed to prescribe. In fact, the harsh reality of American life equipped most of them to play a far more important role in the Revolution than any British woman would have been able to play. Few colonial women had the luxury of leading a genteel lady's life. The colonies were overwhelmingly rural. Thus, women usually worked alongside the men to farm and clear the land in addition to their more traditional tasks of making household goods, cooking and storing food, cleaning, weaving cloth, and raising large broods of children. Women usually did not dress in their best clothes unless visiting a large city like New York. Opting for comfort instead of fashion, women often wore skirts that stopped at midcalf with bright stockings and went barefoot in warmer weather (De Pauw, 1976, 5–6). While working around the house, women had no need to don elaborate clothing. Such finery would get in the way of their labor, and the dirty hard work would ruin their best clothing. It simply was not practical for women to concern themselves with fashion while working in primitive conditions and harsh weather. Necessity made colonial women strong and independent. Visitors were often astonished at what a colonial woman could and would do as a matter of course. For instance, women bridled and rode horses, traveled long distances without male companions, wielded axes, endured harsh cold and heat, and handled boats. Many women also learned how to handle guns and rifles. Some women even successfully defended their homes and families during the French and Indian Wars from 1689 to 1763 (Engle, 1976, xvii; De Pauw, 1976, 6).

The severe daily existence of colonial life also led women into a variety of business ventures, both large and small, to help supplement their families' income. For instance, some women, usually widows or those who obtained permission from the male head of the household, ran a business of some sort. Advertisements appeared in numerous colonial newspapers describing different wares, produce, and seeds, all of which were sold by women. Though blacksmithing was not a typical occupation for females, in Massachusetts at least two women advertised that they shoed horses. Widows frequently took over their late husbands' businesses, often doing very well and even turning a profit. Anne Katharine Green of Maryland and Anna Zenger of New York are just two examples of widows who managed newspapers after the death of their husbands. Moreover, both Green and Zenger used their papers and positions to criticize England and support the Independence movement (Engle, 1976, xii–xiii). Most of these female-run businesses were offshoots from small farms, but some women ran taverns, small shops, or owned small factories such as mills or forges. The most common household industry was the making of linen or wool cloth, a physically demanding and repetitive task. Women usually wove all that their family needed and sold the excess (De Pauw, 1976, 7). The tasks involved with everyday living for American women proved invaluable to the Revolutionary effort and gave the colonies a definite advantage over the British.

Domestic Politics

As the Revolution geared up, one of the most important weapons the colonists employed was the boycott. England attempted to exercise its influence over the colonies by imposing taxes on goods, so the colonists decided to rebel by refusing to import English commodities. The key to any boycott's success, however, was the women. For example, without the support and participation of women, the boycott created by the Nonimportation Act would have failed miserably. Not only did women have to refuse to purchase English goods and wares, but they also had to increase their own production of goods to meet colonial demand. Women organized themselves into groups, such as the Daughters of Liberty, which held all-day sewing events in order to fill the need for cloth and other goods created by women's participation in the boycott (Engle, 1976, xiii). Even a wealthy woman like Deborah Franklin made her family's clothing in support of the colonies (Gundersen, 1996, 150). For the first time, women found themselves and their actions playing a role in a larger struggle. For example, the decision to purchase clothing made and imported from England rather than weaving homespun became a political choice and an issue of loyalty as well (Hoffman and Albert, 1989, 18–19).

The Daughters of Liberty actively participated in the conflict against the British by organizing women to spin cloth so that the colonists could become independent of foreign-made goods. (*North Wind Picture Archives*)

Women often came together and signed public agreements to support the Patriot cause. For example, in Edenton, North Carolina, women wrote a manifesto and signed it, agreeing that they would not purchase imported tea. Other women made public promises to be only courted by Patriot soldiers. This politicization of women could also turn less than friendly. Women began to operate in social circles dictated by political affiliation. Neighbors who had once been friends now shunned each other over differing political beliefs. Further, women who refused to sign manifestos or agreements often found their names in the local paper, announcing their political leanings to the whole community. In the worst cases, women and their families could be victims of mob protests (Gundersen, 1996, 148–150).

As mistresses of the home and hearth, women held a special form of influence over their men: shame. Since the social norm was for men to be brave and courageous and above all to do their duty, women were in a position to shame them into going off to war. Admonishments for men to fight bravely even appeared in newspapers. For example, the *Pennsylvania Evening Post* carried a letter from a grandmother begging soldiers not to be wounded in the back, since this would indicate that they were running from battle and were thus cowards (Hoffman, 1989, 21). With the mere suggestion that a man would be considered a coward if he did not fight bravely, women could shame men into doing their very best. As they sent their husbands and sons off to fight, the women always reminded them to bring honor to themselves and their families and expressed contempt for soldiers who were a source of embarrassment. Elizabeth Marshall Martin of South Carolina, whose daughter and daughter-in-law, Rachel and Grace, were also active Patriots, told her eight sons to "fight till death, if you must, but never let your country be dishonored! Were I a man, I would go with you" (Diamant, 1998, 174). A woman might even tell her husband she would prefer him to come home a corpse rather than a coward.

Doing what they did best, women found a number of ways to support the war effort from their homes. In Connecticut, Ruth Draper organized her neighbors and spent two days and nights baking bread for Patriot troops. As troops passed by her farm, she gave away the bread along with cheese and cider. Later, when Washington called for pewter and lead to make munitions, Mrs. Draper unselfishly collected all her pewter plates and dishes for the cause, some of which were family heirlooms brought from England. Other women sewed clothes and bandages for soldiers. For example, in Charleston, South Carolina, Sabina Elliot knitted socks with 1776 sewn into the pattern. Women also organized themselves into various associations to collect money for the Patriots. One group, headed by Ester Reed and Deborah Franklin Bache of Philadelphia, included women from all levels of society, including free women of color and a countess (Engle, 1976, xiv). Another group in Trenton, New Jersey, in a joint effort with similar New Jersey associations, collected over $15,000 in just a few weeks (De Pauw, 1976, 23). The Revolution, moreover, was not fought in a distant land; it was fought in the cities, towns, and neighborhoods, and on the farms of the colonists. Thus, for many women the war came right into their neighborhoods and homes and affected them every bit as much as the men.

The Disruptions and Opportunities of War

Women left behind at home by their husbands, brothers, and sons going off to fight faced a multitude of challenges. Not only did the women continue to manage all aspects of the household, but they were now also confronted with the daunting task of completing the physically demanding work usually done by men. Chores such as making house repairs, chopping wood, hunting, and bringing in the harvest became the sole responsibility of the women. Further, if the now absent men were involved in businesses ventures, the women had to step in and take care of those issues as well. In addition to taking care of their own families, women faced the very real prospect of being forced to quarter British or American troops, as well as the possibility that actual fighting and bombardments might occur on their property. The quartering of soldiers from either side meant housing them, taking care of their basic needs such as food and supplies, and the quartering and tending of any of their horses or other animals. There was, however, a significant difference between the Patriot soldiers and the British. From all accounts, the Patriot troops seemed to understand the importance of maintaining a decent relationship with the civilian population. The Patriot soldiers knew that victory depended on the civilians supplying them with money, food, clothing, and a multitude of other necessities. It is true that American soldiers, dirty and hungry, usually brought lice and disease into homes and sometimes resorted to theft if they were refused a meal. One soldier wrote that after catching a hen, he simply walked into the first kitchen he came to, cooked the hen, and left. Neither the occupants nor the soldier spoke (De Pauw, 1976, 21). Thus, they were not always welcome visitors, but on the whole, American soldiers avoided antagonizing the Patriot civilian population.

British troops posed much more of a threat to all civilians, whether neutral, Loyalist, or Patriot. Redcoat troops plundered private and public property as they marched through the colonies. They destroyed any food stores, crops, trees, and animals they could not take for themselves. Of all the horrendous acts of British troops, none stirred more public outrage than the act of rape. While Patriot soldiers no doubt committed some attacks on women, British soldiers perpetrated the vast majority of rapes. In one day in the New Jersey county of Hunterdon, six different women delivered depositions charging rape by British soldiers; the youngest girl was only thirteen years old (De Pauw, 1976, 16, 19; Evans, 1976, 25).

Given their strength, it is not surprising that many women refused to submit tamely to British pillage. Catherine Schuyler, wife of Major General Philip Schuyler, burned her own wheat fields rather than have the British take what they could of her crop before destroying the rest. In South Carolina, Rebecca Mott helped the Patriots set fire to her own house while it was occupied by British troops, forcing a British surrender (Engle, 1976, xiv–xv). Another defiant woman was Tempe Wick from New Jersey. When American soldiers demanded that Wick surrender her horse, she refused and raced home. She cleverly hid the horse in a first-floor guest bedroom in the family home until the soldiers gave up looking for the animal (De Pauw, 1976, 23).

Nancy Morgan Hart of Georgia, called "War-woman" by local Creeks, was another formidable woman. Over six feet tall and cross-eyed, Hart was an ardent Patriot, frontierswoman, and sharpshooter. She is credited with taking a number of British prisoners and even capturing an enemy spy by throwing boiling lye in his face. However, Hart's most famous encounter with British troops occurred at her dinner table. A group of five British soldiers out searching for Patriot supporters raided Hart's farm, shot a turkey, and then demanded that she cook it for them. Realizing she was too outnumbered to defy the soldiers, the usually fiery Hart sent her daughter to sound an alarm under the guise of retrieving water from a nearby spring. Meanwhile, the soldiers made themselves at home, helping themselves to the Harts' food and whiskey. As Hart served the soldiers food and drink, she purposely walked between the soldiers and the corner where they had stacked their rifles. As the soldiers became more and more comfortable and relaxed, having been satisfied with food and drink, Nancy quietly began sliding rifles between the logs of her house and onto the ground outside. The soldiers caught her attempting to slide the third rifle outside, but Nancy was too fast for them. Turning the rifle on the soldiers, she threatened to shoot if they made a move. Before help arrived, Hart had killed one soldier and fatally wounded another. The remaining three soldiers were hanged in her front yard (Booth, 1973, 203–205).

Nancy Hart was also a known spy. She once gathered important enemy plans from the British stronghold in Augusta, Georgia. Dressed like a man and faking insanity, she was able to move freely through Augusta (Booth, 1973, 204). Hart, moreover, was just one of the many women who risked

An illustration of Nancy Hart's famous capture of Loyalist soldiers at her cabin during the American Revolution. (*North Wind Picture Archives*)

their lives spying and delivering vital intelligence for the Americans. Unless they were known to be spies, women often moved freely in and out of British lines and camps usually under the pretense of selling wares and goods (De Pauw, 1976, 24). Women also attempted daring acts of bravery to strip British couriers of their papers. In South Carolina, sisters-in-law Rachel and Grace Martin, armed with pistols and dressed like men, ambushed a courier and his escorts. The Martin women successfully stole the courier's papers and forced the group to retreat. In Massachusetts, a whole group of women in men's clothing ambushed Captain Leonard Whiting, stole the vital documents he was carrying in his boots, and marched him off to jail (Evans, 1975, 14).

A number of women also served as couriers for the American cause. One of the more colorful Patriot couriers was Anne Bailey from Virginia. Dressed in buckskin and an expert with a rifle, Bailey made numerous trips through the harshest frontier conditions from the eastern colonies to the remotest western frontier forts. She was so efficient at escaping capture that the local Natives were convinced she was possessed and called her Mad Anne (Cole, 1980, 323–324). In South Carolina, a young girl named Emily Geiger volunteered to deliver a message for General Nathanial Greene to General Thomas Sumter, over a hundred miles away. On the second day of her trip, British scouts stopped Emily. While waiting for a British woman to come search her, Emily tore the letter into pieces and ate them. When the woman found nothing Emily was allowed to leave, but she had memorized the message and was able to successfully deliver Greene's orders to Sumter, thus helping Greene defeat Lord Rawdon (Diamant, 1998, 165). Similar stories from every colony tell of women risking their lives and traveling hundreds of miles to deliver vital military information.

Women also played a role in army camps on both sides of the struggle. Most women and children became camp followers out of economic necessity. Women who were unable to make ends meet at home alone went with their male family member into army camps. Some women, however, followed soldiers because they could not bear the separation, while other women were refugees. Army life for middle- and lower-class women was one of toil and drudgery. Women generally took in laundry, cooked, foraged, carried supplies, nursed the sick and wounded, and worked at whatever other domestic chores remained. These women were also hired by officers and officers' wives to complete their household chores as well. Unfortunately, most of the Patriots, both enlisted men and officers, remained unpaid for long periods of time, and since they received no wages, they could only offer these women army rations in return for their labor (De Pauw, 1976, 29).

Women and children camp followers presented an interesting challenge for General Washington. Women and children drained the army of rations needed for the soldiers. Women drew half rations and children drew a quarter each. Even though women helped gather, produce, and cook food, what they contributed never reached the amount that they consumed. Camp followers also hindered the army's movement by either taking up space on wagons or tailing behind the men. Further, women and children were often disorderly and an obstacle to the discipline that Washington liked and needed (Hoffman, 1989, 14). He most definitely felt that women should be at home growing crops for the war effort or serving as nurses. Washington

Lydia Barrington Darragh

Born in Dublin, Ireland, in 1728, Lydia Barrington married William Darragh on November 2, 1753. William was a clergyman's son and a tutor in the Barrington house. In 1753, Lydia and William migrated to Philadelphia, where they settled into a relatively comfortable life. While William was most likely a teacher and did not earn much income, Lydia became the breadwinner, supporting their family by working as a midwife and nurse, and even opening a mortuary and making funeral clothes. The Darraghs had nine children, but only five of them lived to adulthood: Charles, Ann, John, William, and Susannah. Lydia was well respected, and her career flourished; and the Darragh family lived comfortably in one of Philadelphia's best neighborhoods. During General Howe's occupation of Philadelphia from September 1777 to June 1778, circumstance placed Lydia and her family in the right place at the right time to help the Patriot cause.

Described as a delicate, soft-spoken, and small woman, Lydia was a member of the Society of Friends, also called Quakers, a faith that demanded strict pacifism. Lydia and her family were among a minority known as Fighting Quakers and ardently supported the Patriot cause. General Howe set up his headquarters right across the street from the Darraghs' home in a house known as Loxley House, at 177 South Second Street. Lydia was in a unique position to gather information. She and her husband carefully watched and recorded what they saw on small pieces of paper. Lydia sewed the messages behind the buttons of her fourteen-year-

Lydia Darragh giving warning to a Continental Army officer. (*Library of Congress*)

old son's coat. The youngster, John, then faked errands to deliver the messages to his older brother, Charles, who was a Continental officer (Bohrer, 2003, 134).

On the evening of December 2, 1777, Lydia's espionage activities reached a new level of urgency and danger. Since Lydia's house was right across the street from Howe's headquarters, close to the wharves and the Golden Fleece Tavern, rooms were often commandeered by the British for meetings. On the night of the second, however, Howe's adjunct instructed Lydia that they would be using her back room

only tolerated the women because he knew that a good many men would either desert or refuse to reenlist if he sent the women home (Evans, 1975, 12). Washington also knew that women usually only joined the army camp out of desperation (De Pauw, 1976, 29).

Officers' wives usually only remained in camp during the winter, since the cold weather meant much less fighting and the soldiers settled into a

for a meeting at 7 p.m., and to ensure the privacy of the officers, she was to have her family in bed before the meeting. The officer's urgency and careful attention to secrecy made Lydia suspicious, but she did as she was told. While her family slept, Lydia welcomed the officers, asked if they needed anything, and then went off to bed, but she did not go to sleep. Instead, risking her life and the safety of her family, she snuck back downstairs and eavesdropped on the meeting.

With an ear to the keyhole, she heard plans for a surprise attack on the Continental troops at Whitemarsh, just north of Philadelphia, scheduled for two days later. She carefully recorded what she heard; Howe planned to leave for Whitemarsh on December 3 with 5,000 men, 13 cannons, and 11 boats. As the meeting ended, Lydia hurried back upstairs. Just moments later, the adjunct knocked at Lydia's bedroom door to let her know they were leaving. Cleverly, Lydia made him knock three times before she answered, making him think she had been sound asleep (Engle, 1976, 12).

Knowing she had to get this information to General Washington, Lydia devised a dangerous plan. Believing the information was too important for young John to carry, she obtained a pass from the British to travel past their lines to a nearby flourmill at Frankford. Once she got to Frankford, however, she dropped off her empty flour sack and headed toward Washington's camp. On her way, she met Washington's director of intelligence, Elias Boudinot. Lydia gave Boudinot the notes she had taken and continued toward Whitemarsh. Boudinot raced ahead to deliver the message to Washington. He later described the encounter in his journal. Lydia then met an American patrol led by Colonel Thomas Craig, a friend of the Darraghs. She carefully recited what she had heard to Craig, who then took Lydia to a safe place where she could rest and eat before retrieving her flour and heading home (Bohrer, 2003, 142–143). Lydia returned home with her flour and then sat up all night watching the British preparing to leave.

On December 8, 1777, the British returned from Whitemarsh dejected and defeated. Knowing that the Americans had been told of the attack, Howe's adjunct questioned Lydia about her family's possible involvement. Lydia remained outwardly calm and could honestly say that her family had been in bed that night. The adjunct never asked if Lydia herself had been in bed, instead telling her that he knew she had been asleep because he had to knock three times to get her attention (Engle, 1976, 15). Despite her close call, Lydia continued to support the Revolution. She often served as a nurse for refugees and wounded soldiers. Her husband William died in 1783, leaving her with just enough to money to purchase their house on Second Street, where she opened a small store. Lydia was suspended from the Quakers for her involvement in the American Revolution but was later readmitted. She received a Quaker burial when she died in December 1789 at the age of sixty.

more permanent campsite to wait out the colder months. While army life was far from what these aristocratic women were accustomed to, they were still much better off than women from the lower and middle classes. For instance, while Washington was encamped in Middleton, the officers and their wives enjoyed dances, dinner parties, and sleigh rides. Women also formed "circles," making social events of knitting, sewing, canning, and the like.

They enjoyed the best food and shelter available and usually hired one of the lower-class women camp followers to do the more menial tasks. Overall, women made up approximately 5 to 10 percent of the Patriot camps' population (De Pauw, 1976, 31; Diamant, 1998, 3).

However, far more women were attached to the British Army. As the war progressed and the Patriots enjoyed more victories, many Loyalist women found the British Army to be their only source of protection. There were few women who traveled from England to be with their husbands, and the vast majority of the women in British Army camps were Loyalist refugees. In fact, the number of women and children increased steadily, and by the end of the war, the number of women in British camps had doubled. The number of camp followers was so great that the British were unable to feed and care for all of them. As a result, many women and children turned to theft and even outright plundering, along with the British soldiers. As in Patriot camps, Loyalist women often hired themselves out as domestics in an effort to earn money. However, unlike women in American camps, women in the British camps also engaged in prostitution. British men held a very different idea of what was acceptable behavior. Far away from home, men quite commonly had mistresses. Also, unlike the American soldiers, the British had the money to pay women for whatever services were rendered (De Pauw, 1976, 26–27).

As with the women who had stayed home, those who were with the soldiers often performed services for the American Army and the struggle for independence far outside the normal sphere of traditional female activities. For instance, whereas carrying water to men on battlefields under fire was a common task, at least two women took over the actual firing of artillery when their husbands were wounded. On November 16, 1776, at the Battle of Fort Washington in New York, Margaret Corbin sponged out the bore between firings and helped reload the cannon. When her husband John, a private in the Pennsylvania Regiment of Artillery, was killed, she took over firing the cannon until she was hit with grapeshot, which injured her shoulder, jaw, and chest, and cost her the use of one arm. The army sent her to the Invalid Regiment at West Point, where she remained on muster lists. In 1779, Corbin was awarded 50 percent of a soldier's monthly salary, one new outfit per year, and a monthly ration of liquor. In 1926, her remains were moved to West Point, where she was buried with military honors (Evans, 1975, 10).

Mary Hays, traditionally known as Molly Pitcher, was another battlefield wife who engaged in actual fighting. She stayed with her husband William, a gunner in the same regiment as John Corbin, during his seven years of service. Hays also played an active role in battle, carrying water, tending the wounded, and helping with the cannons. During the Battle of Monmouth in New Jersey on June 28, 1778, Hays was assisting her husband with the cannons. As she was stretching for a cartridge, an enemy cannon ball passed between her legs, tearing off the bottom of her petticoat; she kept on loading the cannon despite the close call. Then later, when her husband William was injured, she stepped into his place and continued to fire the cannon. She eventually received an army pension of forty dollars a year in 1822 (Evans, 1975, 10).

Mary Ludwig Hays, known as "Molly Pitcher," at the Battle of Monmouth. Hays was a washerwoman in the Continental Army, and at the Battle of Monmouth she brought water to the soldiers. After her husband was injured, she replaced him at an artillery piece. The troops affectionately nicknamed her "Molly Pitcher," and her fame quickly spread throughout the colonies, making her a heroine of the American Revolution. (*National Archives and Records Administration*)

A more usual activity for women was that of tending to the wounded and dead. Women not only worked in hospitals nursing wounded and sick soldiers back to health, but they also scoured battlefields searching for wounded soldiers in need of help. Another grim task that women took charge of was burying all the dead, both friend and foe. In addition to the informal nursing that so many women did, Washington also assigned a number of the American camp followers to be official nurses, although no training was ever provided. The army was authorized to hire one nurse for every ten sick or wounded soldiers. These women earned two dollars a month and a single ration per day. Other women helped the sick and wounded in less direct ways. For instance, Catherine Greene of Rhode Island, wife of General Greene, allowed the army to use her house as a hospital for smallpox inoculations. Martha Washington organized groups of women and made home remedies for the ill (Engle, 1976, xiv–xv; De Pauw, 1976, 31). Women also cared for Patriot prisoners by bringing them various supplies and baked goods. Since British prisons were abysmal, prisoners depended on women to bring them the basics as well as an occasional treat like a fresh pie. There were even examples of women organizing prisons breaks. In 1779, for instance, Elizabeth Burgin helped 200 Patriot prisoners escape (Blumenthal, 1974, 57–58; Gundersen, 1996, 154).

Despite the rigid and predefined roles that society expected women to play, some females completely shattered societal mores and participated in the Revolution as full-time soldiers. Since these women soldiers had to keep their gender a secret, few records of their service exist, although there are a few exceptions. One of the most successful woman soldiers was Deborah Sampson of Plympton, Massachusetts. Sampson enlisted in the Fourth Massachusetts Regiment as Robert Shurtleff in April 1781 (some accounts say 1782). She was able to keep her secret for approximately two years even though she was wounded twice. In 1783, the ruse was discovered during a medical exam after Sampson was admitted to the hospital with a high fever. Washington granted Sampson an honorable discharge and the U.S. government granted her a pension of eight dollars a month (Engle, 1976, xv).

A number of other women also tried to enlist with varying degrees of success. For instance, Sally St. Clair enlisted to be with her boyfriend but was killed at the Battle of Savannah in 1779. Another woman, whose name remains unknown, enlisted under the name Samuel Gay and was supposedly promoted to a sergeant before she was discovered and discharged. A third woman, Anna Marie Lane, remained with her husband throughout the war, first as a camp follower and then as a soldier, when Washington threatened to send the women home. Lane's service is well documented in pension records.

Conclusion

The Revolutionary ideals of freedom and equality combined with the often courageous and selfless acts of women during the War for Independence should have brought about a shift in the expectations of women and in the value society placed on women, but few saw any connection. Women and men in the eighteenth century simply accepted the superior position of men as a sign of civilization (De Pauw, 1976, 10). Even though women contributed in every aspect of the struggle for independence and often operated outside of their defined and normal gender roles, once the Revolution was over, they went back into their normal spheres, with only a few exceptions. The place and status of women did not change legally or within society. The wartime experience of women demonstrated that women could be as brave, courageous, independent, and self-sufficient as men, but it took years for these women and their acts of bravery and valor to be acknowledged and recognized.

References and Further Reading

Blumenthal, Walter Hart. *Women Camp Followers of the American Revolution.* New York: Arno, 1974.

Bohrer, Melissa Lukeman. *Glory, Passion, and Principle: The Story of Eight Remarkable Women at the Core of the American Revolution.* New York: Atria, 2003.

Booth, Sally Smith. *The Women of '76*. New York: Hastings House, 1973.

Cole, Adelaide. "Anne Bailey: Woman of Courage." *DAR Magazine* 114 (1980): 322–325.

De Pauw, Linda Grant. *Fortunes of War: New Jersey Women and the American Revolution*. Trenton: New Jersey Historical Commission, 1976.

Diamant, Lincoln, ed. *Revolutionary Women in the War for American Independence: A One-Volume Revised Edition of Elizabeth Ellet's 1848 Landmark Series*. Westport, CT: Praeger, 1998.

Engle, Paul. *Women in the American Revolution*. Chicago: Follett, 1976.

Evans, Elizabeth. *Weathering the Storm: Women of the American Revolution*. New York: Scribner's, 1975.

Gundersen, Joan R. *To Be Useful to the World: Women in Revolutionary America, 1740–1790*. New York: Twayne, 1996.

Hoffman, Ronald, and Peter J. Albert, eds. *Women in the Age of the Revolution*. Charlottesville: University Press of Virginia, 1989.

Juster, Susan. *Disorderly Women: Sexual Politics and Evangelicalism in Revolutionary New England*. Ithaca, NY: Cornell University Press, 1994.

Kerber, Linda. *Women of the Republic: Intellect and Ideology in Revolutionary America*. Chapel Hill: University of North Carolina Press, 1980.

Newman, Debra L. "Black Women in the Era of the American Revolution in Pennsylvania." *Journal of Negro History* 61 (1976): 211–225.

Norton, Mary Beth. *Liberty's Daughters: The Revolutionary Experience of American Women, 1750–1800*. Ithaca, NY: Cornell University Press, 1996.

Sidwell, Mark. "The Fruit of Freedom." *Christian History* 18 (1999): 38–41.

"Allegiance to a Fall'n Lord": The Loyalist Experience in the American Revolution

12

Margaret Sankey

Writing to his friend Thomas McKean in 1814, John Adams guessed that a third of Americans during the Revolution were for the rebellion, a third neutral, and a third Tories, or supporters of the continuation of British rule. For a population of 2.5 million colonists in 1776, more modern estimates of 500,000 men and women who gave some sign of loyalty to George III and as many as 80,000 who went into exile for that choice may be more accurate. In comparison to the French Revolution, whose well-known exodus of *ci-devant* aristocrats may have been 5 per 1,000 citizens, R. R. Palmer suggested the American Loyalists were a far greater proportion, at 24 per 1,000. Whatever their numbers, the existence of counter-Revolutionaries and their experience provides a crucial lens through which to view the American Revolution, which was far from universally popular. Vilified and painted as enemies by both their contemporaries and later Whig histories of the period, Tories clung fast to their principles of loyalty and empire, deeply shocked at being labeled "disaffected" or "a party." For these British subjects, it was the rebels who had strayed from the path into a faction, imperiling their Anglo-American world (Adams, 1856, 10:87; Evans, 1969, 3; Palmer, 1959, 1:187–189; Norton, 1972, 9; Ritcheson, 1973, 5; Ousterhout, 1987, 4).

Tories and Critics

Ironically, in the years before 1776, the men who were later identified as Tories were some of the most insistent critics of British imperial policy, believing that in their capacity as good subjects, they had not just the right, but the duty to supply the ministry with good information and corrections to their reading of the American situation. The 1765 Stamp Act met with almost universal disapproval, even among officers appointed by the king.

Loyalist refugees fled the colonies during and after the Revolutionary War by choice and by compulsion. The greatest number of exiles chose to settle in Canada. (*North Wind Picture Archives*)

John Wentworth, the governor of New Hampshire, protested that the stamps would pull more desperately needed hard currency out of the economy. William Samuel Johnson, although his law partner was a stamp distributor, sat as a member of the Stamp Act Congress. Thomas Hutchinson, soon to be the hated governor of Massachusetts, pointed out that the tax had been levied without representation. All these men, however, stopped short of advocating violent protest, believed strongly that Great Britain did possess the power to tax the colonies, and counted on the ministry to realize its mistake and repeal the act; after the repeal they breathed an enormous sight of relief at the easing of the situation. Governor James Wright of Georgia did not stop there, but addressed the ministry with an exasperated memo demanding time to prepare his colony for measures like the Stamp Act, rather than having them sprung on the colonial administration (Nelson, 1961, 5; McCaughey, 1980, 58; Calhoon, 1973, 11; Welderson, 1994, 64; Berkin, 1974, 42).

Wright was not alone in his willingness to stand up to British policies when they were found to be unjust or unsuited to American conditions, or, most important, contrary to individual principles. William Franklin, governor of New Jersey, evaded the Currency Act by declaring bills of credit to be legal tender in his colony, and petitioned the Privy Council to accept his decision. Jonathan Sewall, acting as attorney general of Massachusetts, refused to rubber-stamp British customs orders, ruling in favor of colonists in key decisions about loading procedures and illegal searches of vessels like John Hancock's *Lydia*. Thomas Hutchinson and William Franklin both pleaded for troops to be removed from their colonies, pointing out the expense and the social problems caused by their presence. In the interests of tolerance and a personal sense of fairness, William Smith, himself an Anglican, wrote against both the Vice-Admiralty Court in Halifax and an American episcopate (Calhoon, 1973, 125; Berkin, 1974, 52; Nelson, 1961, 31; Benton, 1969, 114).

Nor were Tories reticent about suggesting alterations to the imperial structure. As early as the Stamp Act crisis, Joseph Galloway was writing as "Americanus," suggesting that American colonies receive representation in the House of Commons or in an American legislature. In 1770, lawyer William Smith of New York suggested that the ministry appoint a lord lieutenant for America, while Thomas Hutchinson countered with a proposal for dividing the colonies into three regions, each with a governor-general. The most elaborate plan, offered by Galloway in September 1774 as a last-ditch effort

An influential politician in colonial Pennsylvania, Joseph Galloway served in the First Continental Congress in 1774 and, in an effort to diffuse the growing political crisis, proposed a plan of imperial unification with England in which Parliament and a colonial congress would both have to approve colonial legislation. As the American position grew more radical, pushing closer to independence, Galloway remained loyal to the Crown, eventually leaving his native Pennsylvania and seeking refuge in England. (*Cirker, Hayward, and Blanche Cirker, eds. 1967.* Dictionary of American Portraits. *New York: Dover Publications, Inc.*)

William Franklin

Born sometime between September 1730 and March 1731, William Franklin was the illegitimate son of Benjamin Franklin and an unknown woman. As an infant, William was taken into the household of his father's new wife, Deborah Read Franklin, and raised with his half-sister Sally. At his father's insistence, William received the education of a gentleman, attending Alexander Annand's Classical Academy, a measure of Benjamin Franklin's ambition for his son, since this background made him unsuited for the trades expected of a bastard child in colonial society. William toyed with a military career, but when the 1746 campaign planned for Canada failed to come together, he realized the precarious career prospects of an American with a British commission. Instead, he studied law with his father's ally Joseph Galloway, and in 1705 he entered his name in the Inns of Court, an association that all English barristers must join. As Benjamin Franklin ascended the ladder of colonial posts, he used his influence to have William appointed as clerk of the Pennsylvania Assembly, postmaster of Philadelphia, and eventually controller of the North American Postal System. In 1757, William accompanied his father to London, where he studied law and acted as his father's deputy before the Board of Trade as a colonial agent. Impressed with Britain, he was honored to receive an honorary Oxford M.A. when his father was given a doctorate. At some point, William fathered an illegitimate son, William Temple Franklin, who was born shortly before his London marriage to Elizabeth Downes, the daughter of a Barbadian planter, in August 1762.

When Josiah Hardy, governor of New Jersey, was abruptly removed from office, Franklin, with the aid of Lord Bute, maneuvered William into position to be appointed to the office. Leaving William Temple behind to be raised by his grandfather, William sailed for his new post as a sworn representative of George III, an oath that shaped the rest of his life. William proved an able governor, navigating the bipolar world of New Jersey's two capital cities and factional politics, winning over William Alexander (Lord Stirling), convincing the legislature to fund internal improvements and to send troops to help suppress Pontiac's Rebellion. Benjamin Franklin, in his argument for a royal governor for Pennsylvania, used his son's administration as a positive model.

However, William increasingly found himself caught between the aggressive moves of his legislature to resist British taxation and his own duty to carry out royal orders. As an American-born governor, William thought himself an ideal messenger to explain to the ministry colonial complaints and negotiate a peaceful and advantageous settlement to the Stamp Act crisis. Instead, the legislature gave him no credit for his own lobbying for paper currency and a removal of royal troops from New Jersey, focusing instead on his place as an unelected official. William remained optimistic, especially when Lord Hillsborough withdrew troops from New Jersey in 1771 and praised his actions in keeping the peace over the Townshend Acts, even though the legislature did approve the nonimportation agreement.

William, who saw the British Empire as an organic whole, became nervous, as his father seemed to be on a collision course with the ministry and was coming closer to attacking the king's authority. William refused Benjamin

to head off a break with Britain, outlined a colonial government headed by a "President General" acting in consultation with a grand council appointed by colonial legislatures every three years and responsible for placing laws before Parliament for assent, except in emergencies in America. As they urged these fundamental alterations to the status quo, these Tories felt patriotic and

William Franklin, last royal governor of New Jersey and illegitimate son of Benjamin Franklin. A firm Loyalist, he was arrested in June 1776, but exchanged two years later and allowed to settle in British-controlled New York. (*Library of Congress*)

Franklin's request to resign his governorship after Ben's humiliating confrontation with the council in January 1774; William believed that Joseph Galloway's moderate plans for the Continental Congress would prevail in negotiating the Coercive Acts and trusted that when his father returned to America, he too would be appalled by the vulgar nature of the Patriot Party. William even suggested an upper house to Galloway's plan of union in order to provide a greater balance of powers. Believing in the power of Britain to crush resistance, William en-

couraged humble petitions and patience to his agitated legislature. Ultimately, William thought he owed his position and loyalty to George III and the British Parliament, rather than the colony or its legislature, and he acted to preserve royal authority in the face of defiance.

New Jersey formed a provisional assembly separate from William's authority in 1775, leaving him a powerless head of state until January 1776, when William Alexander arrested him for passing intelligence to the British ministry and held him under house arrest in the governor's mansion. From June 1776 until September 1778, he was removed to a series of local jails and house arrests in Connecticut until traded for Delaware governor John McKinley and given safe passage to New York. William was heartbroken to learn that, during his imprisonment, his wife Elizabeth had died and his son William Temple had sided with grandfather Ben.

In New York, William established himself as the head of the Board of Associated Loyalists, feeding intelligence to the British, collecting money, and organizing military guerillas for raids and vicious retaliation against New York rebels. A fierce critic of restraint and Cornwallis's surrender at Yorktown, Franklin's embarrassingly outspoken calls for revenge endangered treaty negotiations and eventually led to his "promotion" to London, where he advocated for exiled Loyalists. William never reconciled with his father, although he did reestablish a relationship with his son, whose own illegitimate child, Ellen Franklin, he raised. Paid a paltry £1,800 pounds in compensation for his losses, Franklin married wealthy Anglo-Irishwoman Mary d'Evelyn in 1788 and lived comfortably, if bitterly, in London, where he died in 1814.

dutiful toward George III as their sovereign (Ousterhout, 1987, 17; Nelson, 1961, 27; Ferling, 1977, 26).

Instead of violent protest, Tories advocated working with the British imperial system. Most governors and many wealthy Tories had been to London, where they had seen in person the chaotic inner workings of the House of

Commons. They completely discounted Whig theories of a British conspiracy to oppress, pointing out that Parliament itself labored under constitutional limitations and thus could not work quickly or without fractious debates and party politics. As evidence, they pointed to Parliament's willingness to correct a law that inadvertently cut the colonies out of Irish trade. Wentworth, a personal friend of the Marquis of Rockingham, understood that the colonies need only wait out the unstable ministries then in power to seek redress through very sympathetic men in high places, including John Pownell, the undersecretary of the Board of Trade, Henry Cruger of New York, who sat as an MP for Bristol, Stephen Saye, an American who had been selected as sheriff of London, and William Lee, made a London alderman in 1774. Americans were far more represented in British bureaucracy and politics than many Britons, and should strive for patience. Even more important, these men had seen the effect of colonial defiance in Britain, where angry politicians had picked up Stamp Act and Townshend Acts protests as leverage against the ministry (Berkin, 1974, 34; Van Tyne, 1929, 10; Ousterhout, 1987, 43; Welderson, 1994, 9; McCaughey, 1980, 107; Einstein, 1969, 246).

For these political Tories, waiting out poorly judged policy was worth it in exchange for the benefits of a place in the British Empire. They agreed that even if the authorities were faltering, the government had been ultimately beneficial to the colonies. Hutchinson and Jonathan Boucher both stressed the disunity of the colonies and their vulnerable position vis-à-vis the Spanish and hostile frontier coalitions like that led by Pontiac. Galloway went so far as to compare the colonies to Poland, ready to be torn apart by internal flaws and external invasion. All pointed to the vital importance of the Royal Navy, an asset the colonies could not hope to create for themselves, in preventing French hegemony during the French and Indian War. Instead, for the prosperity, security, and personal advantage of colonists, the British could be "trained" through demonstrations of gratitude to be more responsive to America's important place in the empire. Wentworth steered New Hampshire's economic development into things like potash, the manufacture of which was desirable, and sweetened his contacts with British politicians by naming things after important men like Lord Dartmouth (Zimmer, 1978, 153; Benton, 1969, 160; Calhoon, 1973, 15; Potter, 1983, 113; Welderson, 1994, 107).

Until July 1776, then, the best course of action, many Tories felt, was to work within the system, participating in the Continental Congress, staying on protest committees, and remaining in local positions as judges, clergy, and militiamen. By doing so, they had been able to keep town meetings moderate during the 1765 Stamp Act furor, and they were pressing for reconciliation and negotiation with Britain until the last debates about independence. Individual Tories drew different lines in their commitments—some balked at serving in any extralegal body, while Galloway, Johnson, Daniel Leonard, and John Joachim Zubley were willing to sit in Congress, even serve on Samuel Adams's Committee of Nine or work with the Sons of Liberty. Of these men, however, Johnson was unwilling to take up arms against Great Britain, seeing his right to protest as ending with using a pen and his voice.

Independence was the final and most trying decision they faced about their participation in rebel organizations, an acid test that irrevocably separated Tories from their colleagues (Benton, 1969, 71; Blakely and Grant, 1982, 66; Brown, 1969, 33; McCaughey, 1980, 168).

Just as some Tories had feared, the extralegal protest bodies were taking on a life of their own, and men outside the traditional power structure of the colonies increasingly dictated policy that was startlingly radical and violent, and excluded expressions of dissent. Some New England "associations" established to police nonimportation were taking it upon themselves to restrict dancing, gambling, and stylish dress according to strict moral standards not shared by the community, even examining a young woman charged with fornication. Loyalist leaders had already confronted violent and radical mobs in 1765, and had become convinced that they represented less any real ideological stance than a desire to tyrannize over their neighbors and terrorize personal enemies. Lewis Penard had personal experience with the effects of such motives, having shamed a mob ostensibly protesting the Stamp Act through attacking his New York house by pointing out that its leaders had only come to loot his wine cellar. It had become difficult to believe that Sons of Liberty were protecting individual freedoms while smashing printing presses, shouting down dissidents, and convening extralegal bodies to exclude moderates. The point was particularly driven home when Tories in Queens took part in 1775 elections for congressional delegates and overwhelmingly won the vote, only to have 1,200 rebel troops arrive to void the ballots and arrest more than twenty Anglican clergymen. Within months, pro-British and moderate men had been surgically removed from power, or new offices installed to get around their authority and exclude disagreement. As Rev. Matthew Byles, a Congregationalist, had pointed out in 1770, it was better "to be ruled by one tyrant 3,000 miles away than 3,000 tyrants one mile away" (Potter, 1983, 30; Tyler, 1977, 14; Van Buskirk, 2002, 71; Ranlet, 1986, 23, 70; Brown, 1965, 37).

An Unorganized and Diverse Group

Despite including some of the most eloquent, educated, and wealthy men in the colonies, the Tories never organized themselves well in comparison to the Whig rebels. Although possessed of some organizations like the Society for the Propagation of the Gospel that might have been altered to provide contact across colonial borders, the Loyalists put such stock in British strength and were so influenced by the fact that the crisis after 1763 ebbed and flowed, leading them to believe it would not in the end come to a head, that they avoided coming out publicly to protest rebel actions until it was too late and Tories had been disarmed or identified. The British, for their part, putting little stock in the Loyalists' influence during the crisis, did nothing to encourage the formation of correspondence circles, militia companies, or any structure to rival that of the revolutionaries (Nelson, 1961, 72; Fingerhut, 1983, 51; Bradley, 1971, 57; Einstein, 1969, 190).

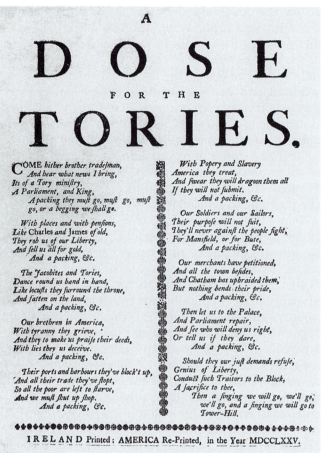

Broadside of the Revolutionary War period titled, *A Dose for the Tories.* (*Library of Congress*)

Tories were also poor propagandists, unwilling to court public opinion in the cause of counterrevolution, and hampered by the control of the mail and many presses by the rebels. Loyalists preferred to show allegiance through traditional rituals, such as celebrating the king's birthday, or as New York Tories did in February 1775, by raising a 75-foot "mast" in honor of George III, and using oral methods of communication like sermons, almost always "preached to the choir" in Anglican services. Only occasionally did the Tories come down to the level of their scathing Whig critics, using viciously pointed farce to display the bigoted Cromwellian face of "Rev. Ebenezer Snuffle" in a New York play, or loudly trumpeting disbelief at the alliance of "patriots" with absolutist, Catholic, arch-enemy France (Van Tyne, 1973, 48, 156; Nelson, 1961, 19; Potter, 1983, 150; Fingerhut, 1983, 43; Crary, 1973, 300).

Beyond political ideology, other Tories remained British subjects because they trusted the British, as an impartial and overseeing power, to preserve their rights as minorities far better than the colonial majorities with whom they lived. These minorities included religious groups such as the Sandemanians in Massachusetts, "Old Light" Congregationalists in Connecticut who had been alienated by the Great Awakening, Dutch Reformed congregations who wished to keep the center of the faith in Amsterdam, French Catholics in Quebec and in pockets in upstate New York, and Anglicans in Congregationalist-dominated New England, particularly those Church of England communicants who were campaigning for an American episcopate. Quakers, whose privileges of avoiding military service and enjoying religious toleration were prized concessions from Great Britain, saw their Philadelphia General Meeting issue a letter charging all Friends to "fear god, honor the king" in 1775 (Blakely and Grant, 1982, 31; Tyler, 1977, 6; Brown, 1965, 122; Ranlet, 1986, 121; Brown, 1969, 75; Nelson, 1961, 90, 106).

Ethnic and economic minorities also counted on the British to insulate them from the aggression, expansion, or bigotry of their American neighbors. Recently arrived or unassimilated groups of Palatine Germans in South Carolina, French Huguenots in New York, and Dutch-speaking communities in New Jersey and New York looked to the British to preserve their languages and land grants. Established British settlers feared encroachments by rowdy and increasingly influential frontiersmen such as the Pennsylvania "Paxton Boys," Crackers in Georgia, and the land speculators of the Susquehanna Company. Justus Sherwood, a former Green Mountain Boy, realized that the survival of his land grant in Vermont was more likely under the British than if exposed to the gaze of predatory New York speculators. At the western edge of the colonies, British military retirees with substantial land grants expected the imperial government to restrict creeping encroachment by squatters, while the Scottish clans of the backcountry owed personal loyalty to the Hanoverian monarchs who had spared their lives and transported them after the failed Jacobite rebellions of 1715 and 1745; also, they understood from experience the power of the victorious British empire (Brown, 1965, 226; Nelson, 1961, 8, 89; Hall, 2001, 11; Tyler, 1977, 12; Wright, 1975, 19; Brown, 1969, 47).

Other Loyalist men had personal reasons for remaining tied to Great Britain. Those who believed that keeping their oaths to the king, taken as royal officials or clergymen, was a matter of honor were reluctant to blaspheme or to commit what they believed to be treason. Jonathan Sewall was reluctant to turn his back on the beliefs of the distinguished men like Chambers Russell and Edmund Towbridge who had sponsored his career. Placemen holding royal offices and drawing salary from the Treasury, as well as those merchants dependent on sales of naval stores or bounty crops, were unwilling to gamble their prosperity on revolution. For William Franklin, royal recognition as governor of New Jersey canceled the social stigma of his illegitimacy in a way no colonial-bestowed status could replace (Berkin, 1974, 27; Fingerhut, 1983, 65; Allen, 1972, 290; Brown, 1965, 209; Welderson, 1994, 3).

Native Americans, including members of the Mohawk, Shawnee, Creek, Cherokee, Oneida, Tuscarora, Seneca, and Cayuga nations, joined with the British and should be considered Loyalists. Even when not happy with British authority in comparison with previous French contact, leaders among the Iroquois were deeply concerned about settlers violating of the Proclamation of 1763 and moving west across the Appalachian Mountains. Additionally,

Anglican ministers running schools and providing competition for the New England rantings of Presbyterian missionaries like Samuel Kirkland and Ebenezer Wheelock proved far more attractive to indigenous people. The British were aided in forming connections with the tribes by the excellent work of their agents, Sir William Johnson, John Stuart, and Alexander McKee, whose respect for and knowledge of native culture won the allegiance of many men, whose willingness to fight for the British added valuable knowledge of the region and guerilla abilities to the counter-Revolution (Graymont, 1972, 40; Ousterhout, 1987, 256).

Joseph Brant, the younger brother of Sir William Johnson's Mohawk consort, Molly Brant, proved to be a formidable combat commander as well as a respected diplomat and negotiator. Alongside the Johnson sons and nephews, Brant and the Loyalist Mohawks led devastating raids into the Wyoming Valley and defended St. Johns against American invasion in 1775. Molly, meanwhile, won over the Mohawk mistress of rebel Philip Schuyler and provided not only crucial intelligence to aid Tories fleeing the colonies to Canada, but vital warning at the Battle of Oriskany. For their actions, the Brants and Johnsons were driven out of the Mohawk Valley and into Niagara, where the British used their prestige to keep order among Native American and British refugees and rewarded the Brants and their dependents with pensions and land grants. A similar plan to arm the tribes in the South failed badly when John Stuart, the British Indian agent for the South, encouraged the Cherokee to attack on the Carolina borders, but carried out raids indiscriminately, killing as many Tories as rebels and terrifying some Loyalists into joining with the rebel government of South Carolina (Crary, 1973, 253; Graymont, 1972, 136, 239; Nelson, 1961, 114).

African Americans, both free and enslaved, formed a special category of Tories, whose commitment to the British cause stemmed from the immediate potential for freedom rather than political ideology. As early as April 1775, slaves were approaching Virginia governor Lord Dunmore with offers to enlist in exchange for manumission, far in advance of his November 7 declaration that would later sanction their use as soldiers and provide freedom to slave men willing and able to fight on behalf of the British. Quickly, with the British policy spreading through the network of slave communication, more than 800 men found their way to Dunmore (17 from Mount Vernon), with an additional hundred offered by Tory masters, whom the governor outfitted as "Lord Dunmore's Ethiopian Regiment." By the end of the war, perhaps 80,000 slaves had fled to British lines, while 5,000 men were in active British service as a squadron of dragoons and as Hessian General von Reidesel's drum corps, as well as serving as foragers, spies, coastal pilots, and laborers on the siege fortifications at Charleston and Savannah (Quarles, 1961, 29, 149; Kaplan, 1973, 67; Wilson, 1976, 21).

The presence of manumitted men in occupied cities, where the British allowed Tories to keep their slaves, added to the tension, as did incidents in which officers treated slaves as booty, including Benedict Arnold's Chesapeake raid, in which the newly Loyalist general returned runaway volunteers to their owners. British reality, however, still trumped halfhearted rebel policies allowing only free blacks into the militia or the Continental Army, and the use of confiscated Loyalist-owned slaves as enlistment bounties or labor in lead mines. In 1780, two particularly daring free black men, John and Paul Cuffee, sued the rebel Massachusetts government for "taxation without representation," a serious embarrassment to prominent people like Abigail Adams and Lafayette. Large numbers of African Americans chose to leave with the British, at least 4,000 from New York, 4,000 from Savannah, and 5,300 from Charleston. At embarkation, British officials such as Brigadier General Samuel Birch offered "free papers" without asking questions about free status. One group of these ex-slaves, led by Thomas Peters, a member of the British Black Pioneers regiment, found Nova Scotia a poor relocation and with the aid of abolitionists William Wilberforce and Oltobah Cugano in London organized a move to Sierra Leone in 1791 (Van Buskirk, 2002, 139; Quarles, 1961, 131; Wilson, 1976, 5; Kaplan, 1973, 69).

Tory women, who with rare exceptions had little say in their family's political allegiances, deserve particular mention. Unlike Patriot women, who were celebrated after the Revolution as "Founding Mothers," Loyalist women received little attention and few rewards for their services to the British cause. Molly Brant was granted a substantial claim against the loss of her property and a generous pension as the consort of a British imperial agent, but most relied on the bounties or pensions paid to male relatives for Tory military service. When daring enough to follow the Loyalist troops into Canada, women served as vital support, nursing, cooking, and organizing the camps of the regiments. Left behind, they attempted to preserve family property and could become priceless conduits for intelligence and saboteurs of the rebel economy through the passage of large amounts of counterfeit money. Women of status within ethnic societies could also take leadership positions and act on their own convictions. Flora MacDonald of North Carolina, already famous for her rescue of Bonnie Prince Charlie in 1745, railed the MacDonald clansmen into action with Gaelic curses after Whigs abused her family. Widow Sarah McGinnis, respected by the Mohawks, worked tirelessly to keep them connected to British orders and loyal to George III. Officially, however, the most valued Loyalist women were the most traditional, holding tea clubs and raising money for donations, such as the spectacular 1780 New Year's gift of a privateer, *Fair American*, to the Royal Navy in occupied New York City (Potter-MacKinnon, 1993, 106; Crary, 1973, 51; Graymont, 1972, 158; Brown, 1969, 90; Bradley, 1971, 92).

The rebel governments were hardly blind to the actions of Tory women and increasingly targeted them with demands for loyalty oaths after it was discovered that they were ideally positioned to pass messages and take part in aiding the British. In the beginning of the conflict, rebel officials classified women as *femmes covert*, the legal extension of their husbands or other male authority, and thus not in need of separate bonds or oaths for good behavior. However, they could not ignore the women who accepted paroles to visit family and instead fled to husbands under arms in Canada or were apprehended spreading counterfeit money, such as Mrs. Charles Slocombe, who was branded on both cheeks and had her ears cut off as punishment in Rhode Island. Local mobs could also take out their frustrations on Tory spouses who remained behind, as four men did, attacking Mrs. Philip Empy as she walked home from the local jail. They had learned that her husband and sons had escaped from jail, and angry at recent rebel military reverses, they beat her so badly that although found by neighbors, she died several days later (Potter-Mackinnon, 1993, 58; Brown, 1969, 88).

Wartime Insecurity

As the pressure to declare sides increased, Tories realized that the coming conflict was likely to tear their families apart. Leading Loyalists had relatives high in revolutionary circles, and were deeply hurt when political ideals trumped bonds of blood and friendship. John Jay never reconciled with his Tory brother, Sir James, and Colonel Ephraim Leonard disowned his son Daniel, while Henry Knox cut ties with his father-in-law, Thomas Flucker, John Hancock with brother-in-law Jonathan Sewall, and Henry Laurens with son-in-law Sir Egerton Leigh, all of whom left Boston in 1775. As one-quarter of Harvard graduates alive in 1776 were Tories, men found themselves at odds with lifelong colleagues, friends, and classmates. Margaret Draper brokered with her business partner to run a Tory newspaper, while Jonathan Boucher resigned as tutor to Jacky Custis, George Washington's stepson. We can only guess at the deep wounds created by the demands faced by Mary Cruger Meyers, whose rebel in-laws demanded custody of her infant before allowing her to join her Tory husband in Canada, or the tension in the house of Captain William Howard of New Jersey, who posted the sign "No Tory Talk Here" on his mantle to silence his Loyalist wife (Evans, 1969, 26; Benton, 1969, 156; Einstein, 1969, 197–198; Brown, 1965, 26; Zimmer, 1978, 80; Potter, 1983, 87).

The nature of the conflict and the close ties among participants made the treatment of Loyalists that much more painful because it came at the hands of former friends and neighbors. Nearly every Tory had at least one festering, bitter charge against the Revolution. Jonathan Boucher gave his last sermons armed with pistols against violent harassment from his Virginia congregants; John Wentworth found himself arguing politics with Dr. Hall Jackson during Mrs. Wentworth's life-threatening labor; John Champneys of South Carolina was held in jail without parole while his two-year-old son was dying; Peter Oliver was deliberately prevented from attending his brother's funeral; and Peter Van Schaack's dying wife was refused permission to visit a captured British specialist in New York City (Zimmer, 1978, 175; Welderson, 1994, 255; Einstein, 1969, 193; Lambert, 1987, 60).

The persecutions could be even more violent, with regular elements of ritual humiliation as mobs tarred and feathered, stripped, beat, and ransacked. Peter Guires was branded on the forehead with "G.R" (George Rex); Daniel Leonard's pregnant wife was in labor when a mob attacked their house, and she gave birth to a premature and retarded child; Filer Diblee's family home was looted four times by rebels who eventually stripped his children of their clothing when there were no more possessions to steal; William Davies was beaten so severely in the head with musket butts that he suffered permanent memory loss; and Elizabeth Cary Wiltees saw her log

In this 1775 British political cartoon titled "The Alternative of Williamsburg," a Virginia loyalist is being forced to sign a document while another man is being led toward the gallows from which a sack of feathers and a barrel of tar hangs. (*Library of Congress*)

cabin destroyed in midwinter by vengeful neighbors who left her standing in the snow. Even without violence, the pressure of being put on published lists of men to be ostracized and thus losing the ability to protect their families drove Filer Diblee and William Byrd III of Westover, West Virginia, to suicide, and Reverend Ebenezer Kneeland, son-in-law of Samuel William Johnson, to a collapse that ended in his death while suffering house arrest (Brown, 1965, 64–65; Potter, 1983, 56; Calhoon, 1973, 282; Wright, 1975, 12; Benton, 1969, 158; McCaughey, 1980, 186).

With rebels in control of local Committees of Safety and the governments of the new states, Whigs were in a position to demand that Tories declare themselves through oaths and other gestures of renouncing allegiance to Great Britain. Early in the Revolution, sympathetic men like John Jay and Patrick Henry allowed Tory neighbors and friends to give incredibly vague answers, avoid oaths, and live quietly at home, but increasingly radical revolutionaries put laws in place after the Declaration of Independence that closed loopholes and forced a Test Act on any Tory owning property or holding a professional license, or anyone who came to the attention of Committees of Observation. In New York, the Whig legislature passed an "Act More Effectively to Prevent the Mischief Arising from the Influence and

Example of Persons of Equivocal and Suspected Character" to identify and root out Tories, while in other colonies, individuals like Thomas McKean formed People's Courts, extralegal grand juries of local residents to charge known Tories for activities such as naming their children after the royal family or singing "God Save the King."

While a minority of Tories held oaths to rebels to be so worthless that they took them and then immediately broke their word by fleeing to the British, others, such as Colonel Richard Saltonstall and Isaac Wilkinson, could not reconcile personal honor and an oath to local Whig rebels and left for London. Quakers and other religious minorities who could not take oaths became particular targets for the rebels. Although the Christian Brethren established a fund to pay the fines of their members who could not take oaths, local officials gleefully exhausted it by repeatedly visiting to demand an oath or a fine. In Pennsylvania, some Quaker families were bankrupted when committees began seizing household goods in lieu of fines for repeated refusals to take oaths of allegiance. Until those challenged took the oath, they had no legal rights, were allowed no lawyers, and had no status in the eyes of the new state governments (Potter, 1983, 36; Ousterhout, 1987, 123; Calhoon, 1973, 385; Nelson, 1961, 146; Bradley, 1971, 93).

When Tories refused loyalty oaths, they became vulnerable to a new wave of legislation issuing from the rebel state governments that seized their property. The well-known estates went first, with New York taking the DeLancey property (worth £140,000) and the huge grants owned by the Johnsons in the Mohawk Valley. Smaller fry were turned in by informers who received rewards for revealing hidden property and telling authorities about legal dodges, such as Tories transferring estates to underage heirs or wives. The states also moved on the property of Tories who had fled, evicting Grace Galloway from her home in 1779 and seizing two-thirds of the personal estate (including half of his slaves) of Robert Alexander, whose wife and children paid tripled taxes on the remainder. Most states only began sales of confiscated land after 1780, and they stepped up auctions in 1782 in order to get around any treaty provision requiring restitution of Tory real estate. In the meantime, administrators plundered the forfeitures, stripping them of trees, draining the fishponds, and looting the houses. While some Tories managed to have their homes purchased through friends, most went to covetous neighbors, some of whom had been the informers in the first place (Bradley, 1971, 113; Tyler, 1977, 18; Ferling, 1977, 44; Benton, 1969, 196; Van Tyne, 1973, 276).

Committees of Safety also preemptively disarmed Tories and imprisoned those likely to emerge in threatening leadership roles. Without trials, they were placed in local jails, sentenced to removal from the state, or collected in locations such as the horrendous Simsbury copper mine in Connecticut, where Tories were locked underground in abandoned tunnels. Tories caught in service to the British were often flogged, and sometimes, as with Connecticut native Moses Dunbar in 1777, executed for accepting a British military commission. Other states found it more convenient to charge Tories with criminal rather than political crimes, jailing them for larceny, trespassing, perjury, or banditry instead of treason. To be fair, some residents did use the circumstances of the war to turn to lawlessness, like the Doanes family of Plumstead, Pennsylvania, which, outside of any political loyalty, became dangerous banditti (Evans, 1969, 14; Crary, 1973, 216; Blakely and Grant, 1982, 248; Calhoon, 1973, 401).

Loyalists and the Army

One option taken by as many as 10,000 Loyalists was to take up arms for the British. The siege of Boston saw many Tories participating in a defense effort, but it took almost a year before the British realized the necessity of enlisting and commissioning Tories for military use. In the meantime, royal governors such as William Tryon of New York and Dunmore created units of Tories, allowing James DeLancey to form a "cowboy" cavalry in Westchester or arming runaway slaves. In East Florida, General Patrick Toyn commissioned refugee men to form the East Florida Rangers, which turned back an invasion by Georgians in 1775. Part of the delay came from the regular British Army, which jealously guarded its commissions and privileges, creating situations in which Tory officers automatically had junior rank to British regulars and were not entitled to medical care, wound bonuses, or half pay until 1779. Tories were also rarely included in prisoner exchanges or the demands for the proper treatment of prisoners of war that the British routinely made for Hessians and their own officers. To make enlistment attractive to Tories, the British often had to do things that restricted the effectiveness of a unit, naming the most prominent (not necessarily the most talented) local man as commander, keeping the regiments close to home, and treating them with a mixture of condescension and mistrust that either damaged morale or inspired independent and often disastrous uncoordinated actions on the part of the Tory troops. The delay in organizing Tory regiments meant that often the most willing men had been preemptively picked up by the rebels, and the remaining units, without a strong British vision for using them, took on rebel forces at low strength and at inopportune times, losing badly at Moore's Creek Bridge in March 1776 and Ramsaver's Mill in June 1780 for this reason (Fingerhut, 1983, 113; Lambert, 1987, 150; Ranlet, 1986, 149; Bradley, 1971, 59; Cuneo, 1958, 72; Smith, 1964, 25, 142).

The British Army eventually formed fifty provincial corps of 312 companies. Loyalist regiments formed an important part of the Burgoyne campaign leading to Saratoga, although Burgoyne ungratefully found them a convenient scapegoat for his defeat. Abandoned after the surrender, the Johnson- and Mohawk-led companies of Tories took to guerilla actions out of Canada. The Queen's Rangers, led by British adventurer Robert Rogers, served at Brandywine, Germantown, and Monmouth Courthouse before being taken at Yorktown. The Rangers, however, refused to surrender their colors and smuggled them to Great Britain. In the South, the premier Tory regiments were organized by Major Patrick Ferguson, who led them to destruction at King's Mountain, Georgia, July 12–15, 1780. Remaining Loyalists in the South often meant being involved in fighting that shocked both British and rebel commanders, brutal vendettas across the backcountry. Personal feuds and revenge killing stemming from the war probably killed more than actual battles fought between recognized military units. Frustration with the rules of war and the slow progress of the British in New York similarly inspired William Franklin, Governor Tryon, and Robert Alexander to form the Associated Loyalists board in 1780 to launch raids across the Connecticut coast and engage in the revenge execution of Joshua Huddy after rebels killed Loyalist soldier Philip White. Although British officers like Banastre Tarleton occasionally participated in the harsh reprisal actions, senior commanders on both sides attempted to restrain atrocities and remain professionals, much to the anger of many Tories (Graymont, 1972, 156; Blakeley and Grant, 1982, 292; Smith, 1964, 143; Ranlet, 1986, 80; Brown, 1969, 107).

Wherever the British occupied a major city and stationed troops, Loyalists flocked for protection and opportunities to take part in the war. Beginning with Tory refugees in Boston, the dislocated also experienced a pattern that persisted in New York, Philadelphia, Charleston, and Savannah. The British, although sometimes generous with the newly arrived, insisted on martial law and treated the Tories as Americans, continuing to keep them out of British trade and leaving much city administration and fund-raising to the Tories themselves. Despite crowded conditions and financial difficulties, the occupied cities offered Tories their best chance for mutual support and news through royalist newspapers and relief subscriptions (Norton, 1972, 35; Nelson, 1961, 144; Van Tyne, 1973, 261).

The situation in New York, held by the British from September 1776 to 1783, was particularly difficult. After it was abandoned by the rebels, it was quickly reoccupied by a flood of Tories. The crowded situation was made far worse by the looting that British soldiers conducted as the original inhabitants fled and as result of a devastating fire that erupted on September 21, and razed nearly a quarter of the city. As the population rose to more than 180,000, Tories complained about the lack of garbage collection, dangerous street crime, and corruption among petty British government officials who controlled food and housing offices. The presence of soldiers and a military bureaucracy guaranteed that the Tories suffered hundreds of small indignities as they went about their daily routines. British frivolity shocked the more conservative New Yorkers as they watched the British celebrate royal holidays and hold theatrical entertainments, often on a stage erected in the grounds of the burned-out Trinity Church (Bradley, 1971, 66; Ranlet, 1986, 74; Van Buskirk, 2002, 34).

Similar situations occurred in Philadelphia and Charleston, although having learned from New York, the commanders installed competent Tory authorities—Joseph Galloway in Philadelphia and a board of local merchants in Charleston—to form volunteer police forces, monitor price gouging, and handle disagreements among refugees. The British also paid generously for the use of private property as military quarters and were openhanded when possible with food and supplies. Charleston in particular had to deal with a large population of women and children whose male relatives had been killed in the fighting and who used their time under British protection to reconstitute their families. Many women remarried, some, like Mary Mail, with British soldiers, while Jane Downs met a Tory officer, Colonel Zacharias

Gibb. Charleston Tory officials even hired a schoolteacher to handle the many children stranded because of the conflict (Brown, 1969, 85; Lambert, 1987, 193, 233).

Beginning with the evacuation of Boston that took place in the aftermath of the Battle of Lexington and Concord in 1776, many Tories, perhaps 8,000 of them, went directly to London for assistance, confident that once they were heard, not only would the ministry win the war using better information provided by Tories, but it would return them to their antebellum status. Even for Loyalists who had been to Great Britain previously, the shock of exile and relocation was extremely unsettling. Nelly, the wife of Jonathan Boucher, was overwhelmed by the noise and filth of the metropolis, while the much more conservative Americans, even the relatively well-traveled and sophisticated ones, were shocked by the riotous atmosphere. Americans had little status among elite Britons who still denigrated fortunes made in "trade," and they found the city hideously expensive for their limited budgets. After the first wave, Tories found that they were no longer "news" and had lost the transient sympathy of Londoners; as Thomas Hutchinson explained wearily, "We Americans are plenty here, and very cheap." To their amazement, they also encountered British Whigs such as Isaac Barre and Adam Smith celebrating American success and realized that they might not, after all, be going home in triumph (Norton, 1972, 36; Callahan, 1967, 91; Ferling, 1977, 47; Ritcheson, 1973, 7).

The Tory expatriate community in Britain organized itself to provide support for newcomers, raising money to tide them over between the

British board ships to leave Boston. Cannon barrels are being dumped off a wharf to prevent capture. (*Grafton, John, ed. 1975.* The American Revolution, a Picture Sourcebook. *New York: Dover Publications, Inc.*)

twice-a-year Treasury meetings at which pensions were given, and offering social support in the form of meeting places such as the New England Coffee House. Loyalist lawyers offered others advice on their petitions, while experienced travelers to Britain aided the least wealthy to move to cheaper areas like Bristol. This kind of self-help became increasingly necessary, as Tories discovered that the Church of England jealously guarded its jobs and that the professionals of Britain refused to accept American legal or medical training as adequate preparation to practice in their fields. The pressure of poverty and social snubbing led to petty quarrels blowing up into duels, such as the one in Hyde Park between Lloyd Dulaney and the Reverend Bennett Allen over accusations of disloyalty to the Crown in order to save a family estate. Some Tories, such as Alexander Harvey of Charleston, went mad from the strain; Harvey ended his life in a London asylum. A few Tories took some satisfaction in pointing out the presence of Americans of anti-British leanings in London, pressing for their arrests. John Trumbull, in the capital to study art, was picked up and tried for treason on the affidavits of vengeful Loyalists, but to the Tories' deep disappointment, was rescued by Edmund Burke (Norton, 1972, 59; Einstein, 1969, 207; Benton, 1969, 210; Berkin, 1974, 120; Brown, 1969, 132).

Tories were extremely concerned after Yorktown, and exerted whatever influence they had mustered in Britain to influence the treaty negotiations in their own favor. At the suggestion of Lord North, who wished to harass the Shelburne ministry using Loyalist demands, they organized themselves under Sir William Pepperell, Joseph Galloway, and William Bull as the Loyalist Association. Their anecdotes and testimony allowed North to decry the "base treatment" of British subjects and topple Shelburne. Sadly, once it had used them, the new ministry moved on, approving a treaty in which Articles 5 and 6 recommended leniency to Tories and restoration of property, but accepted that the Articles of Confederation government had no authority to require states to cooperate. Some cynical Tories even observed that the ministry had less interest in their plight than in collecting examples of treaty violations (states mistreating Loyalists) in order to have leverage on things the British were more interested in, such as merchant debts and western forts. After 1783, the few Loyalists remaining in London attempted to affect policy, William Knox and Brook Watson pushing for the Orders in Council barring American ships from British ports in the Caribbean, and others lobbying for a bill that would protect Loyalists from being sued by American firms for debts (while Americans hid behind Byzantine state-national conflicts to avoid paying). The debt bill failed, reinforcing for many Tories their belief that Britain had little place for them and more interest in their American betrayers (Wright, 1975, 48; Callahan, 1967, 120; Ritcheson, 1973, 2).

Many Tories, who had sacrificed so much for their loyalty, had experienced this attitude from the British throughout the war. From the beginning, the British regarded Tories with a mix of distrust and contempt, an attitude that had shown through dramatically in their treatment of Loyalist soldiers and civilians within occupied cities. Loyalist committees gave what, in retrospect, would have been valuable advice, attempting to tell the British that the Americans would not be pushovers on the battlefield, advocating a strategy centered on pursuing and destroying the Continental Army rather than taking cities, and working for the creation of a two-tier "army in being" similar to Washington's arrangement of the rebels. Because overoptimistic Tory appraisals of manpower and morale rarely panned out, the British fell into the habit of discounting their good information as well. Some British decisions directly damaged Tories, as when Hessians were allowed to get away with indiscriminately terrorizing New Jersey early in the war, including Loyalists, or when J. Hector St. John Crèvecoeur, Tory author of *Letters from an American Farmer*, escaped in 1780 to occupied New York, only to be jailed as a spy. Tories rejoiced when liberated by Commodore George Collier's raid on Portsmouth and Norfolk in 1779, but they were then abandoned when the military withdrew without making provision for them. Worst of all, from a Tory point of view, the British commanders, secure in the loyalty of the Tories, offered rebels generous forgiveness and paroles rather than punishment (Van Tyne, 1973, 160; Fingerhut, 1983, 112; Brown, 1965, 112; Van Buskirk, 2002, 38; Smith, 1964, 110; Nelson, 1961, 134).

Resettlement

Unable to return the Tories to America, the British now approached resettlement and restitution. Since 1775, the Treasury had been paying out the salaries of officials and pensions for Loyalists, a substantial amount that was becoming unpopular in the House of Commons. Parliament needed to come to a permanent settlement with the Tories and move them on into new lives, preferably in another colony. From 1783 to 1790, a five-man commission examined 2,291 Tory claims for loss of income and property in the American colonies. After consultation with the Loyalist Association, which attempted to police claims before they were submitted, in the interests of efficiency and preventing outlandish claims, the commission granted £3,033,091 worth of damages out of £8,216,126 requested. The commission made its decision based on the degree of zeal shown by the claimant and on provable loss, both subjective and difficult-to-prove criteria that frustrated the Tories immensely. The commission established polices ruling out claims on loss pertaining to potential income, damage by British troops, devalued paper money, sales of property at a loss, loss of slaves, or impossible-to-quantify issues such as loss of limb. To make things easier for refugees already in Canada, boards of inquiry were set up in Quebec and Nova Scotia to take claims back to the commission. By 1790, the British government had spent £10.5 million pounds, and it was anxious for the Tories to stand on their own feet (Norton, 1972, 192, 216; Brown, 1969, 181; Van Buskirk, 2002, 302; Ritcheson, 1973, 10).

Solutions to the problem were to relocate Tories to thinly populated regions of Canada to form new British communities or integrate Loyalists into established areas like Jamaica and Barbados. The relocation to Canada had begun even before the Declaration of Independence. Tories began arriving in Canada in 1775 after the surrender of Boston and came in waves after every evacuation. Sir Guy Carleton arranged for generous land grants in New Brunswick and Nova Scotia, while refugees from the fighting in the Mohawk Valley crossed over into southern Ontario and took up residence around the British forts at Kingston and Niagara. Many of the Tories had been extremely proud of being the descendants of the founders of the American colonies, but now were overwhelmed by the reality of being pioneers themselves and carving out new towns from the Canadian wilderness. The hard conditions gave rise to the nickname "Nova Scarcity" for their new lands, and some even felt bitter that one of the new settlements had been named Shelburne, after the politician they felt had been too easy in treaty negotiations. The Tories adapted, however, demanding reform of political policies that worked for a wilderness fort, but not for a community of highly educated and politically charged émigrés; they founded universities, built up infrastructure, and proudly placed the rescued royal arms from the Massachusetts Council Chamber over the door of the new Trinity Church at St. Johns, Nova Scotia. Amazingly, in 1812 American war hawks convinced themselves that Canadians in Ontario, many of whom had been protesting for reform exactly the same way they had in America before 1776, were ripe for Americanization. Instead, the Tories flocked to defend their new homes, successfully turning back invaders with the help of British troops and pro-British Native Americans (Bradley, 1971, 145, 200; Callahan, 1967, 7; Van Tyne, 1973, 276; Blakely and Grant, 1982, 15).

Southern Tories tended to head to the Caribbean or East Florida, where the situation was more congenial to slaveholding and reestablishment of plantation farming. The 10,000 who arrived in East Florida were horribly disappointed when the British turned the area over to the Spanish, and they found themselves once more at the mercy of American raiders and harassment from Georgia. Their migration had to include a second stage to the British islands or Nova Scotia. In Jamaica, refugees were given aid to acquire land and exempted from taxes on slaves for seven years. In Barbados, each head of household received 40 acres and 20 for each dependent. Like their Canadian counterparts, the governors of these islands were surprised at the political savvy of the newcomers, who immediately demanded more representation in the conservative and governor-centered administration of the British Caribbean (Callahan, 1967, 142, 150; Lambert, 1987, 266).

The British attempted to honor the ranks of former colonial officials and made genuine efforts to place them in jobs commensurate with what they had lost. Samuel Quincy, the former solicitor general of Massachusetts, became attorney to the Crown on Antigua; William Brown and Daniel Leonard became governor and chief justice of Bermuda, respectively; New York Supreme Court justice George Duncan Ludlow became chief justice of New Brunswick; and Governor John Wentworth of New Hampshire accepted the jobs of His Majesty's Surveyor of Nova Scotia and governor in 1792, and a baronetcy in 1795. The 1791 separation of Upper Canada from Quebec and the establishment of New Brunswick and Nova Scotia as separate provinces were partially motivated by a need to create as many administrative jobs as possible for the Tory refugees (Norton, 1972, 103; Callahan, 1967, 56; Welderson, 1994, 269; Bradley, 1971, 147).

Only a handful of Tories ever returned to America, motivated by homesickness, family ties, and the changing course of the American Revolution.

The cooling-off period between Yorktown and the final evacuation of New York allowed the state governments and Congress to rethink harsh laws against Tories and to consider the effects of allowing extremely powerful local officials to use arbitrary power as they had against Loyalists during the war. Quietly, the New York attorney general dropped indictments against Tories in 1782 and encouraged pending charges to be dropped to misdemeanors like disturbing the peace. Pennsylvania also restored the estate of John Roberts, who had been hung as a scapegoat by angry Whigs after the British evacuation of Philadelphia, to his widow and paid her a pension. Other states followed suit, with South Carolina and Georgia arranging "amercement" programs that allowed returning Tories to pay a fine proportionate to their estates, keep their property, and be restored to voting rights and citizenship after three years. Tories who took the states up on these generous reintegration plans, however, discovered that local enmity still existed, and that their former neighbors often waited to tar and feather, despite embarrassing condemnation by the British government and crackdowns by the state governments (Ousterhout, 1987, 294; Van Buskirk, 2002, 188; Hall, 2001, 168; Crary, 1973, 309; Ritcheson, 1973, 16).

In elite circles, some Americans were anxious to reestablish ties, and they reached out to Tory colleagues. John Jay, who had compared the loss of the Loyalists to the loss of the Huguenots to Louis XIV's France, and Alexander Hamilton, who was building his legal career on his performance in the suit of a Loyalist in *Waddington vs. Rutgers*, arranged for the return of Peter Van Schaack, who wanted his son to attend Yale. Culturally, the United States benefited from the return of Count Rumsford; Dr. William Paine, founder of the American Antiquarian Society; and Francis Greene, a pioneer in the study of the deaf. Anglicans actually found the Episcopal Church (no longer the Church of England but still in communion with it) welcoming, as Washington arranged the return of former congressional chaplain Jacob Duche in 1790, and Samuel Seabury came back to New York as a missionary (Chernow, 2004, 195; Brown, 1969, 76; Nelson, 1961, 167; McCaughey, 1980, 194; Benton, 1969, 209).

Some Tories even joined the new government, finding in the Federalist Party and the new constitution the reformed government that they had pushed for in the crisis of the 1760s. William Samuel Johnson attended the Constitutional Convention and advocated a strong central government with the power to tax the states and manage foreign affairs. James Sheafe was elected to the Senate in 1801, as was Philip Barton Key of Maryland, a senator elected in 1806, who gave up his British half-pay commission to become an American citizen. Van Schaack refused Federalist overtures to become a candidate, but opened a private law school that groomed a generation of New York politicians.

A proud tradition of Empire Loyalism continued in parts of British Canada, but the Tories were forgotten in Britain and absorbed into the island societies of Bermuda, Barbados, and Jamaica. In America, former Tories and returned expatriates had to continue to conceal or downplay their histories in the face of the new nation's celebrations of the Revolution, memorials, and increasingly Whig version of events, which painted a frustratingly simple dichotomy

William Samuel Johnson represented Connecticut at the Constitutional Convention in 1787. (*Pixel That*)

of Whig-Tory, Patriot-Loyalist, Good-Evil. Pennsylvania published *A Blacklist: A List of Those Tories Who Took Part With Great Britain in the Revolutionary War and Were Attainted of High Treason* in 1802, while the War of 1812 brought out scathing attacks on Tories, many remembered and repeated verbatim from the Revolution (Purcell, 2002, 70; Ousterhout, 1987, 221).

References and Further Reading

Adams, John. *The Works of John Adams*. Edited by Charles Francis Adams. 10 vols. New York: Little, Brown, 1856.

Allen, Anne Alden. "Patriots and Loyalists: The Choice of Political Allegiance by the Members of Maryland's Proprietary Elite." *Journal of Southern History* 38 (1972): 283–292.

Benton, William Allen. *Whig Loyalism: An Aspect of the Political Ideology in the American Revolutionary Era*. Rutherford, NJ: Fairleigh Dickinson University Press, 1969.

Berkin, Carol. *Jonathan Sewall: Odyssey of an American Loyalist*. New York: Columbia University Press, 1974.

Blakely, Phyllis, and John Grant, eds. *Eleven Exiles: Accounts of Loyalists of the American Revolution.* Toronto: Dundurn, 1982.

Bradley, Arthur. *The United Empire Loyalists.* London: Thornton Butterworth, 1971.

Brown, Wallace. *The King's Friends: The Composition and Motives of the American Loyalist Claimants.* Providence, RI: Brown University Press, 1965.

Brown, Wallace. *The Good Americans: The Loyalists in the American Revolution.* New York: Morrow, 1969.

Calhoon, Robert McCluer. *The Loyalists in the American Revolution, 1760–1781.* New York: Harcourt Brace, 1973.

Callahan, North. *Flight from the Republic: The Tories of the American Revolution.* Indianapolis, IN: Bobbs-Merrill, 1967.

Chernow, Ron. *Alexander Hamilton.* New York: Penguin, 2004.

Crary, Catherine. *The Price of Loyalty: Tory Writings from the Revolutionary Era.* New York: McGraw-Hill, 1973.

Cuneo, John R. "The Early Days of the Queen's Rangers, August 1776–February 1777." *Military Affairs* 22 (1958): 65–74.

Einstein, Lewis. *Divided Loyalties: Americans in England during the War of Independence.* Freeport, NY: Books for Libraries, 1969.

Evans, G. N. D., ed. *Allegiance in America: The Case of the Loyalists.* Reading, MA: Addison-Wesley 1969.

Ferling, John. *The Loyalist Mind: Joseph Galloway and the American Revolution.* University Park: Pennsylvania State University Press, 1977.

Fingerhut, Eugene. *Survivor: Cadwallader Colden II in Revolutionary America.* Washington, DC: University Press of America, 1983.

Graymont, Barbara. *The Iroquois in the American Revolution.* Syracuse, NY: Syracuse University Press, 1972.

Hall, Leslie. *Land and Allegiance in Revolutionary Georgia.* Athens: University of Georgia Press, 2001.

Kaplan, Sidney. *The Black Presence in the Era of the American Revolution, 1770–1800.* Washington, DC: National Portrait Gallery, 1973.

Lambert, Robert Stansbury. *South Carolina Loyalists in the American Revolution.* Columbia: University of South Carolina Press, 1987.

McCaughey, Elizabeth. *From Loyalist to Founding Father: The Political Odyssey of William Samuel Johnson.* New York: Columbia University Press, 1980.

Nelson, William. *The American Tory.* Oxford: Clarendon Press, 1961.

Norton, Mary Beth. *The British-Americans: The Loyalist Exiles in England, 1774–1789.* Boston: Little, Brown, 1972.

Ousterhout, Anne M. *A State Divided: Opposition in Pennsylvania to the American Revolution.* Westport, CT: Greenwood, 1987.

Palmer, R. R. *The Age of Democratic Revolutions.* Princeton, NJ: Princeton University Press, 1959.

Potter, Janice. *The Liberty We Seek: Loyalist Ideology in Colonial New York and Massachusetts.* Cambridge, MA: Harvard University Press, 1983.

Potter-MacKinnon, Janice. *While the Women Only Wept: Loyalist Refugee Women.* Montreal: McGill-Queens University Press, 1993.

Purcell, Sarah. *Sealed with Blood: Sacrifice and Memory in Revolutionary America.* Philadelphia: University of Pennsylvania Press, 2002.

Quarles, Benjamin. *The Negro in the American Revolution.* Chapel Hill: University of North Carolina Press, 1961.

Ranlet, Philip. *The New York Loyalists.* Knoxville: University of Tennessee Press, 1986.

Ritcheson, Charles R. "Loyalist Influence on British Policy towards the United States after the American Revolution." *Eighteenth Century Studies* 7 (1973): 1–17.

Skemp, Sheila. *Benjamin and William Franklin: Father and Son, Patriot and Loyalist.* Boston: Bedford, 1994.

Smith, Paul H. *Loyalists and Redcoats: A Study in British Revolutionary Policy.* Chapel Hill: University of North Carolina Press, 1964.

Tyler, John. *Connecticut Loyalists.* New Orleans: Polyanthus, 1977.

Van Buskirk, Judith. *Generous Enemies: Patriots and Loyalists in Revolutionary New York.* Philadelphia: University of Pennsylvania Press, 2002.

Van Tyne, Claude Halstead. *Loyalists in the American Revolution.* New York: Smith, 1929.

Welderson, Paul. *Governor John Wentworth and the American Revolution: The English Connection.* Hanover, NH: University Press of New England, 1994.

Wilson, Ellen Gibson. *The Loyal Blacks.* New York: Putnam's, 1976.

Wright, Esmond, ed. *A Tug of Loyalties: Anglo-American Relations, 1765–1785.* London: Athlone, 1975.

Zimmer, Anne Y. *Jonathan Boucher: Loyalist in Exile.* Detroit: Wayne State University Press, 1978.

"Young Ladies in Town"

The Townshend Acts of 1767 enacted a tax on paper, lead, glass, and tea. The money raised was to be used to pay the salaries of British colonial officials. In addition to the general outrage about the nature of the new taxes, many colonists resented that the tax was imposed by Parliament without any participation of the colonial assemblies. In response, colonists initiated a boycott of imported British goods. The nonimportation agreements lasted more than two years. During this time many women spun their own textiles, and their families proudly wore clothing made of homespun rather than the finer weaves from Britain. They found substitutes for tea, allowed their homes to go unpainted, and used paper that they began to make themselves, rather sparingly. The burden of these measures fell to a great extent on women. This popular song from 1769 called on American women to support the boycott of British textiles. The Townshend Acts were repealed in 1770.

Young ladies in town, and those that live 'round
Wear none but your own country linen;
Of economy boast, let your pride be the most
To show clothes of your own make and spinnin'.
What if homespun, they say, be not quite as gay
As brocades. Be not in a passion
For once it is known 'tis much worn in town
One and all will cry out 'tis the fashion!
And as one all agree, that you'll not married be,
To such as will wear London factory;
But at first sight refuse, tell 'em you will choose,
As encourage our own manufactory.
No more ribbons wear, nor in rich silks appear,
Love your country much better than fine things,
Begin without passion, 'twill soon be the fashion,
To grace your smooth locks with a twine string.
Throw away your bohea, and your green hyson tea,
And all things of a new fashioned duty;

Get in a good store of the choice Labrador,
There'll soon be enough here to suit ye.
These do without fear and to all you'll appear,
Fair charming, true, lovely and clever,
Though the times remain darkish,
Young men will be sparkish,
And love you much stronger than ever.

Source: Boston Newsletter, *1769.*

Petition of Regulators (1769)

In the 1760s, frustrations in the Carolina backcountry resulted in two Regulator Movements. In North Carolina, Scottish, German, and Scots-Irish farmers vented their frustrations against predominantly English officeholders in the eastern part of the colony. When petitions failed to address their concerns and the colonial assembly passed a poll tax in order to build a mansion for the colony's royal governor, they turned to violence. The fighting continued into 1771, when Governor Tyron's militia soundly defeated the Regulators at the Battle of Alamance Creek. Although the Regulator resistance dissipated, especially with the execution of seven of its leaders, the tensions remained in the backcountry. The following petition expressed the grievances of the western farmers and offered several means of redress. The concerns of the petition went largely unaddressed until the Revolution.

Petition dated 9 October 1769.

Mr. Speaker and Gen't of the Assembly.

Humbly Showeth:

That the Province in General labour under general grievances, and the western part thereof under particular ones; which we not only see, but very sensibly feel, being crouch'd beneath our sufferings and not withstanding our sacred privileges, have too long yielded ourselves slaves to remorseless oppression. — Permit us to conceive it to be our inviolable right to make known our grievances, and to petition for redress as appears in the Bill of Rights pass'd in the reign of King Charles the first, as well as the Act of Settlement of the Crown of the Revolution. We therefore beg leave at the Act of the Settlement of the Crown of the Revolution. We therefore beg leave to lay before you a specimen thereof that your compassionate endeavors may tend to the relief of your injured Constituents, whose distressed condition call aloud for aid. The alarming cries of the oppressed possibly may reach your ears; but without your zeal how they shall ascend the throne — how relentless is the breast without sympathy, the heart that cannot bleed on a view of our calamity; to see tenderness removed, cruelty stepping in; and all our liberties and privileges invaded and abridg'd (by as it were) domestickes; who are conscious of their guilt and void of remorse. — O how darling! how relentless whilst impending Judgements loudly threaten and gaze upon them, with every emblem of merited destruction. A few of the many grievances are as follows, (viz't)

1. That the poor inhabitants in general are much oppress'd by reason of the disproportionate Taxes, and those of the western Counties in particular; as they are generally in mean circumstances.

2. That no method is prescribed by law for the payment of the taxes of the Western Counties in produce (in lieu of a currency) as in other Counties within this Province to the Peoples great oppression.

3. That Lawyers, Clerks, and other petitioners; in place of being obsequious Servants for the Country's use, are become a nuisance, as the business of the people is often transacted without the least degree of fairness, the intention of the law evaded, exorbitant fees extorted, and the sufferers left to mourn under their oppressions.

4. That an Attorney should have it in his power, either for the sake of ease or interest, or to gratify their malevolence and spite, or commence suits to what courts he pleases, however inconvenient it may be to the Defendants; is a very great oppression.

5. That all unlawful fees taken in Indictment, where the Defendant is acquited by his Country (however customary it may be) is an oppression.

6. That Lawyers, Clerks, and others, extorting more fees than is intended by law; is also an oppression.

7. That the violation of the King's Instructions to his Delegates, their artfulness in concealing the same from him; and the great injury the People thereby sustains: is a manifest oppression.

And for remedy whereof, we take the freedom to recommend the following mode of redress, not doubting audience and acceptance which will not only tend to our relief, but command prayers at a duty from your humble Petitioners.

1. That at all elections each suffrage be given by Ticket & Ballot.

2. That the mode of Taxation be altered, and each person pay in proportion to the proffits arising from his Estate.

3. That no future tax be laid in Money, until a currency is made.

4. That there may be established a Western as well as a Northern and Southern District, and a Treasurer for the same.

5. That when a currency is made it may be let out by a loan office (on land security) and a Treasurer for the same.

6. That all debts above 60s (shillings) and under 10 pounds be tried and determined without lawyers, by a jury of six freeholders, impaneled by a Justice, and that their verdict be enter'd by the said Justice, and be a final judgement.

7. That the Chief Justice have no perquisites, but a Salary only.

8. That Clerks be restricted in respect to fees, costs, and other things within the course of their office.

9. That Lawyers be effectively Barr'd from exacting and extorting fees.

10. That all doubts may be removed in respect to the payment of fees and costs on Indictments whereas the Defendant is not found guilty by the jury, and therefore acquited.

11. That the Assembly make known the Remonstrance to the King, the conduct of the cruel and oppressive Receiver of the Quit Rents, for omitting the customary easie and effectual method of collecting by distress, and pursuing the expensive mode of commencing suits in the most distant Courts.

12. That the Assembly in like manner make known that the Governor and Council so frequently grant lands to as many as they think proper without regard to Head Rights, notwithstanding the contrariety of his Majesties instructions, by which means immence sums has been collected, and numerous Patents granted, for much of the most fertile lands in this Province, that is yet uninhabited and cultivated, environed by great numbers of poor people who are necessitated to toil in the cultivation of bad Lands whereon they hardly can subsist, who are thereby deprived of His Majesties liberality and Bounty nor is there the least regard paid to the cultivation clause in said Patent mentioned, as many of the said Council as well as their friends and favorites enjoy large quanitities of Lands under the above-mentioned circumstances.

13. That the Assembly communicates in like manner the Violation of His Majesties Instructions respecting the Land Office by the Governor and Council, and of their own rules, customs and orders. If it be sufficiently proved, that after they had granted Warrants for some Tracts of Land, and that the same was in due time suvey'd and returned and the Patent fees timely paid into the said office; and that if a private Council was called to avoid spectators, and peremptory orders made that Patents should not be granted; and Warrants by their orders arbitrarily to have been issued in the names of other Persons for the same Lands, and if when intreated by a solicitor they refus'd to render so much as a reason for their so doing, or to refund any part of the money paid by them extorted.

14. That some method may be pointed out that every Improvement on Lands in any of the Proprietors part be proved when begun, by whom, and every sale made, that the eldest may have the preference of at least 300 acres.

15. That all taxes in the following Counties be paid as in other Counties in the Province (i.e.) in the produce of the County and that warehouses be erected as follows (viz), In Anson County at Isom Haleys Ferry Landing on PeeDee River, Rowan and Orange at Cambleton in Cumberland County, Mecklenburg at __?__ on the Catawba River, and in Tryon County at __?__ on __?__ River.

16. That every denomination of People may marry according to their respective mode Ceremony and customs after due publication or License.

17. That Doc't Benjamin Franklin or some other known patriot be appointed agent, to represent the unhappy state of this Province to his Majesty, and to solicit the several Boards in England.

[signed by 254 men]

Source: William L. Saunders, ed., The Colonial Records of North Carolina, 10 vols. (Raleigh: Hale, 1886–1907), 8:81–82, 241–244.

Description of the Boston Massacre (1770)

On March 5, 1770, a crowd of angry Bostonians congregated at the customhouse in the port city. While they heckled and threw chunks of ice, oyster shells, and other items at the lone guard, several British soldiers arrived at the scene. The soldiers fired on the crowd, killing four Bostonians immediately. A fifth person died several days later, and six others were injured. Among the dead was Crispus Attucks, a man of mixed Indian and African heritage. Within weeks, word of the events spread to all of the thirteen colonies, and many newspaper editors used the "Boston massacre" to anger colonists about British tyranny. The following is the description of the events from a local Boston newspaper.

On the evening of Monday, being the fifth current, several soldiers of the 29th Regiment were seen parading the streets with their drawn cutlasses and bayonets, abusing and wounding numbers of the inhabitants.

A few minutes after nine o'clock four youths, named Edward Archbald, William Merchant, Francis Archbald, and John Leech, jun., came down Cornhill together, and separating at Doctor Loring's corner, the two former were passing the narrow alley leading to Murray's barrack in which was a soldier brandishing a broad sword of an uncommon size against the walls, out of which he struck fire plentifully. A person of mean countenance armed with a large cudgel bore him company. Edward Archbald admonished Mr. Merchant to take care of the sword, on which the soldier turned round and struck Archbald on the arm, then pushed at Merchant and pierced through his clothes inside the arm close to the armpit and grazed the skin. Merchant then struck the soldier with a short stick he had; and the other person ran to the barrack and brought with him two soldiers, one armed with a pair of tongs, the other with a shovel. He with the tongs pursued Archbald back through the alley, collared and laid him over the head with the tongs. The noise brought people together; and John Hicks, a young lad, coming up, knocked the soldier down but let him get up again; and more lads gathering, drove them back to the barrack where the boys stood some time as it were to keep them in. In less than a minute ten or twelve of them came out with drawn cutlasses, clubs, and bayonets and set upon the unarmed boys and young folk who stood them a little while but, finding the inequality of their equipment, dispersed. On hearing the noise, one Samuel Atwood came up to see what was the matter; and entering the alley from dock square, heard the latter part of the combat; and when the boys had dispersed he met the ten or twelve soldiers aforesaid rushing down the alley towards the square and asked them if they intended to murder people? They answered Yes, by G-d, root and branch! With that one of them struck Mr. Atwood with a club which was repeated by another; and being unarmed, he turned to go off and received a wound on the left shoulder which reached the bone and gave him much pain. Retreating a few steps, Mr. Atwood met two officers and said, gentlemen, what is the matter? They answered, you'll see by and by. Immediately after, those heroes appeared in the square, asking where were the boogers? where were the cowards? But notwithstanding their fierceness to naked men, one of them advanced towards a youth who had a split of a raw stave in his hand and said, damn them, here is one of them. But the young man seeing a person near him with a drawn sword and good cane ready to support him, held up his stave in defiance; and they quietly passed by him up the little alley by Mr. Silsby's to King Street where they attacked single and unarmed persons till they raised much clamour, and then turned down Cornhill Street, insulting all they met in like manner and pursuing some to their very doors. Thirty or forty persons, mostly lads, being by this means gathered in King Street, Capt. Preston with a party of men with charged bayonets, came from the main guard to the commissioner's house, the soldiers pushing their bayonets, crying, make way! They took place by the custom house and, continuing to push to drive the people off, pricked some in several places, on which they were clamorous and, it is said, threw snow balls. On this, the Captain commanded them to fire; and more snow balls coming, he again said, damn you, fire, be the consequence what it will! One soldier then fired, and a townsman with a cudgel struck him over the hands with such force that he dropped his firelock; and, rushing forward, aimed a blow at the Captain's head which grazed his hat and fell pretty heavy upon his arm. However, the soldiers continued the fire successively till seven or eight or, as some say, eleven guns were discharged.

Source: Boston Gazette and Country Journal, *March 12, 1770.*

Broadside Warning Pilot of the Ship Polly *Not to Dock in Philadelphia (1773)*

When the British Parliament passed the Tea Act in 1773, many colonists were angry about what appeared to be an illegal monopoly on tea imports. In response, many colonists began to drink replacement brews made of local roots and herbs. Others sought to eliminate the ability to drink tea by preventing East Indian Company boats from docking in the colonial ports. In the following broadside, the local "Committee on Tar and Feathering" warned the Delaware pilots not to allow the ship *Polly* to dock in Philadelphia with its cargo. This broadside was one of several warnings posted in Philadelphia and elsewhere.

TO CAPT. AYRES Of the Ship *Polly*, on a Voyage
from London to Philadelphia

Sir,

We are informed that you have imprudently, taken charge of a quantity of tea which has been sent out by the India Company, under the auspices of the ministry as a trial of American virtue and resolution.

Now, as your cargo, on your arrival here, will most assuredly bring you into hot water; and as you are perhaps a stranger to these parts, we have concluded to advise you of the present situation of affairs in Philadelphia that, taking time by the forelock, you may stop short in your dangerous errand—secure your ship against the rafts of combustible matter which may be set on fire and turned loose against her; and more than all this, that you may preserve your own person from the pitch and feathers that are prepared for you.

In the first place, we must tell you that the Pennsylvanians are, to a man, passionately fond of freedom, the birthright of Americans, and at all events are determined to enjoy it.

That they sincerely believe no power on the face of the earth has a right to tax them without their consent.

That in their opinion the tea in your custody is designed by the ministry to enforce such a tax which they will undoubtedly oppose, and in so doing, give you every possible obstruction.

We are nominated to a very disagreeable, but necessary service—to our care are committed all offenders against the rights of America; and hapless is he, whose evil destiny has doomed him to suffer at our hands.

You are sent out on a diabolical service; and if you are so foolish and obstinate as to complete your voyage by bringing your ship to anchor in this port, you may run such a gauntlet as will induce you in your last moments most heartily to curse those who have made you the dupe of their avarice and ambition.

What think you Captain, of a halter around your neck—ten gallons of liquid tar decanted on your pate—with the feathers of a dozen wild geese laid over that to enliven your appearance?

Only think seriously of this and fly to the place from whence you came—fly without hesitation—without the formality of a protest—and above all, Captain Ayres, let us advise you to fly without the wild geese feathers.

Your friends to serve

THE COMMITTEE, as before subscribed Philadelphia, Nov. 27, 1773.

Source: The Pennsylvania Magazine of History and Biography *15 (1891): 390–391.*

George Robert Twelve Hewes Remembers the Boston Tea Party (1834)

On December 16, 1773, in response to the Tea Act of 1773, about sixty frustrated colonists dressed up as Mohawk Indians, boarded three ships of the East Indian Company which recently docked in Boston Harbor, and threw 342 containers of tea overboard. The Boston Tea Party, as it became known, resulted in the closing of Boston Harbor and increased animosity between colonists and the British officials. In 1834, several decades after the Boston Tea Party, George Robert Twelve Hewes, a Boston shoemaker, recounted from memory his experiences. Hewes's account reminds us that the Tea Party was not the result of a chaotic mob, but rather a measured response to what the colonists understood as a conspiracy against their liberties.

The tea destroyed was contained in three ships, lying near each other at what was called at that time Griffin's wharf, and were surrounded by armed ships of war, the commanders of which had publicly declared that if the rebels, as they were pleased to style the Bostonians, should not withdraw their opposition to the landing of the tea before a certain day, the 17th day of December,

1773, they should on that day force it on shore, under the cover of their cannon's mouth.

On the day preceding the seventeenth, there was a meeting of the citizens of the county of Suffolk, convened at one of the churches in Boston, for the purpose of consulting on what measures might be considered expedient to prevent the landing of the tea, or secure the people from the collection of the duty. At that meeting a committee was appointed to wait on Governor Hutchinson, and request him to inform them whether he would take any measures to satisfy the people on the object of the meeting.

To the first application of this committee, the Governor told them he would give them a definite answer by five o'clock in the afternoon. At the hour appointed, the committee again repaired to the Governor's house, and on inquiry found he had gone to his country seat at Milton, a distance of about six miles. When the committee returned and informed the meeting of the absence of the Governor, there was a confused murmur among the members, and the meeting was immediately dissolved, many of them crying out, "Let every man do his duty, and be true to his country"; and there was a general huzza for Griffin's wharf.

It was now evening, and I immediately dressed myself in the costume of an Indian, equipped with a small hatchet, which I and my associates denominated the tomahawk, with which, and a club, after having painted my face and hands with coal dust in the shop of a blacksmith, I repaired to Griffin's wharf, where the ships lay that contained the tea. When I first appeared in the street after being thus disguised, I fell in with many who were dressed, equipped and painted as I was, and who fell in with me and marched in order to the place of our destination.

When we arrived at the wharf, there were three of our number who assumed an authority to direct our operations, to which we readily submitted. They divided us into three parties, for the purpose of boarding the three ships which contained the tea at the same time. The name of him who commanded the division to which I was assigned was Leonard Pitt. The names of the other commanders I never knew.

We were immediately ordered by the respective commanders to board all the ships at the same time, which we promptly obeyed. The commander of the division to which I belonged, as soon as we were on board the ship appointed me boatswain, and ordered me to go to the captain and demand of him the keys to the hatches and a dozen candles. I made the demand accordingly, and the captain promptly replied, and delivered the articles; but requested me at the same time to do no damage to the ship or rigging.

We then were ordered by our commander to open the hatches and take out all the chests of tea and throw them overboard, and we immediately proceeded to execute his orders, first cutting and splitting the chests with our tomahawks, so as thoroughly to expose them to the effects of the water.

In about three hours from the time we went on board, we had thus broken and thrown overboard every tea chest to be found in the ship, while those in the other ships were disposing of the tea in the same way, at the same time. We were surrounded by British armed ships, but no attempt was made to resist us.

We then quietly retired to our several places of residence, without having any conversation with each other, or taking any measures to discover who were our associates; nor do I recollect of our having had the knowledge of the name of a single individual concerned in that affair, except that of Leonard Pitt, the commander of my division, whom I have mentioned. There appeared to be an understanding that each individual should volunteer his services, keep his own secret, and risk the consequence for himself. No disorder took place during that transaction, and it was observed at that time that the stillest night ensued that Boston had enjoyed for many months.

During the time we were throwing the tea overboard, there were several attempts made by some of the citizens of Boston and its vicinity to carry off small quantities of it for their family use. To effect that object, they would watch their opportunity to snatch up a handful from the deck, where it became plentifully scattered, and put it into their pockets.

One Captain O'Connor, whom I well knew, came on board for that purpose, and when he supposed he was not noticed, filled his pockets, and also the lining of his coat. But I had detected him and gave information to the captain of what he was doing. We were ordered to take him into custody, and just as he was stepping from the vessel, I seized him by the skirt of his coat, and in attempting to pull him back, I tore it off; but, springing forward, by a rapid effort he made his escape. He had, however, to run a gauntlet through the crowd upon the wharf nine each one, as he passed, giving him a kick or a stroke.

Another attempt was made to save a little tea from the ruins of the cargo by a tall, aged man who wore a large cocked hat and white wig, which was fashionable at that time. He had sleightly slipped a little into his pocket, but being detected, they seized him and, taking his hat and wig from his head, threw them, together with the tea, of which they had emptied his pockets, into the water. In consideration of his advanced age, he was permitted to escape, with now and then a slight kick.

The next morning, after we had cleared the ships of the tea, it was discovered that very considerable quantities of it were floating upon the surface of the water; and to prevent the possibility of any of its being saved for use, a number of small boats were manned by sailors and citizens, who rowed them into those parts of the harbor wherever the tea was visible, and by beating it with oars and paddles so thoroughly drenched it as to render its entire destruction inevitable.

Source: James Hawkes, A Retrospect of the Boston Tea Party *(New York: Bliss, 1834), 28–32.*

Letter of Phillis Wheatley to Reverend Samson Occum, February 11, 1774

Phillis Wheatley was a Senegal-born woman and published poet who lived in Boston, Massachusetts, during the Revolution. Wheatley lived as the slave of a Quaker family until her emancipation in 1778. Her owners, unlike most slave owners, encouraged Wheatley's education even as they kept her in bondage. Wheatley's poem lamenting the death of preacher George Whitfield made her famous in the 1760s. As tensions grew between Great Britain and her colonies, Wheatley became an outspoken supporter of independence and revolution. In this letter to a Native American reverend, she declares her belief that slavery is incompatible with the notion of the inalienable right of equality.

Rev'd and honor'd Sir,

I have this Day received your obliging kind Epistle, and am greatly satisfied with your Reasons respecting the Negroes, and think highly reasonable what you offer in Vindication of their natural Rights: Those that invade them cannot be insensible that the divine Light is chasing away the thick Darkness which broods over the Land of Africa; and the Chaos which has reign'd so long, is converting into beautiful Order, and [r]eveals more and more clearly, the glorious Dispensation of civil and religious Liberty, which are so inseparably Limited, that there is little or no Enjoyment of one Without the other: Otherwise, perhaps, the Israelites had been less solicitous for their Freedom from Egyptian slavery; I do not say they would have been contented without it, by no means, for in every human Breast, God has implanted a Principle, which we call Love of Freedom; it is impatient of Oppression, and pants for Deliverance; and by the Leave of our modern Egyptians I will assert, that the same Principle lives in us. God grant Deliverance in his own Way and Time, and get him honour upon all those whose Avarice impels them to countenance and help forward the Calamities of their fellow Creatures. This I desire not for their Hurt, but to convince them of the strange Absurdity of their Conduct whose Words and Actions are so diametrically, opposite. How well the Cry for Liberty, and the reverse Disposition for the exercise of oppressive Power over others agree,—

I humbly think it does not require the Penetration of a Philosopher to determine.—

Source: The Connecticut Gazette, *March 11, 1774.*

Petition of Slaves to Thomas Gage, Royal Governor of Massachusetts, May 25, 1774

By 1774, a succession of events had led many colonists to complain that their natural rights had been violated by British Parliament. Some African Americans logically concluded that they too had natural rights and should enjoy the same liberties as whites. They sent petitions to colonial assemblies and British officials. In this document, slaves in Massachusetts borrowed from the revolutionary logic in their appeal to Governor Thomas Gage. They asked for gradual emancipation so that they could "obtain our Natural right our freedoms." Although their appeal was rejected, some colonists in Massachusetts recognized the incongruity of asserting inalienable human rights and universal equality while sanctioning slavery. As a result, Massachusetts banned slavery in 1783.

The Petition of a Grate Number of Blacks of this Province who by divine permission are held in a state of Slavery within the bowels of a free and Christian Country

Humbly Shewing

That your Petitioners apprehind we have in common with all other men a naturel right to our freedoms without Being depriv'd of them by our fellow men as we are a freeborn Pepel and have never forfeited this Blessing by aney compact or agreement whatever. But we were unjustly dragged by the cruel hand of power from our dearest frinds and sum of us stolen from the bosoms of our tender Parents and from a Populous Pleasant and plentiful country and Brought hither to be made slaves for Life in a Christian land. Thus we are deprived of every thing that hath a tendency to make life even tolerable, the endearing ties of husband and wife we are strangers to for we are no longer man and wife than our masters or mistresses thinkes proper marred or on-marred. Our children are also taken from us by force and sent maney miles from us wear we seldom or ever see them again there to be made slaves of for Life which sumtimes; is vere short by Reson of Being dragged from their mothers Breest Thus our Lives are imbittered to us on these accounts By our deplorable situation we are rendered incapable of shewing our obedience to Almighty God how can a slave perform the duties of a husband to a wife or parent to his child How can a husband leave master to work and cleave to his wife How can the wife submit themselves to there husbands in all things How can the child obey thear parents in all things. There is a great number of us sencear . . . members of the Church of Christ how can the master and the slave be said to fulfil that command Live in love let Brotherly Love con-tuner and abound Beare yea onenothers Bordenes How can the master be said to Beare my Borden when he Beares me down whith the Have chanes of slavery and operson against my will and how can we fulfill our parte of duty to him whilst in this condition and as we cannot searve our God as we ought whilst in this situation. Nither can we reap an equal benefet from the laws of the Land which doth not justifi but condemns Slavery or if there had bin aney Law to hold us in Bondage we are Humbely of the opinion ther never was aney to inslave our children for life when Born in a free Countrey. We therfor Bage your Excellency and Honours will give this its deer weight and consideration and that you will accordingly cause an act of the legisla-tive to be pessed that we may obtain our Natural right our freedoms and our children be set at lebety at the yeare of twenty one for whoues sekes more petequeley your Petitioners is in Duty ever to pray.

Source: Collections of the Massachusetts Historical Society, *5th Series, III (Boston: Massachusetts Historical Society, 1877), 432–437.*

Letter Responding to Lord Dunmore's Declaration Regarding the Emancipation of Slaves (1775)

On November 15, 1775, Lord Dunmore, governor of Virginia, issued a proclama-tion that terrified slaveholders in the region. Slaves who were willing to fight against their Patriot masters would obtain their freedom. Throughout the region, hundreds of black slaves ran away, and several hundred men were armed by Dunmore so that they could fight their masters. They formed the all-black Ethiopian Regiment, and they wore sashes that stated "Liberty to Slaves." Nevertheless, Dunmore's attempt to convince Patriot slaveholders to back down from their revolutionary threats backfired. Preventing the further emancipation of slaves and the arming of blacks became a rallying cry of the Patriots. Only independence could prevent future outrages by the British government.

The second class of people, for whose sake a few remarks upon this proclamation seem necessary, is the Negroes. They have been flattered with their freedom, if they be able to bear arms, and will spedily join Lord Dunmore's troops. To none then is freedom promised but to such as are able to do Lord Dunmore service: The aged, the infirm, the women and children, are still to remain the property of their masters, masters who will be provoked to severity, should part of their slaves desert them. Lord Dunmore's declaration, therefore, is a cruel declaration to the Negroes. He does not even pretend to make it out of any tenderness to them, but solely on his own account; and should it meet with success, it leaves by far the greater number at the mercy of an enraged and injured people. But should there be any amongst the Negroes weak enough to believe that Dunmore intends to do them a kindness, and wicked enough to provoke the fury of the Americans against their defenceless fathers and mothers, their wives, their women and children, let them only consider the difficulty of effecting their escape, and what they must expect to suffer if they fall into the hands of the Americans. Let them farther consider what must be their fate, should the English prove conquerors in this dispute. If we can judge of the future from the past, it will not be much mended. Long have the Americans, moved by compassion, and actuated by sound policy, endeavoured to stop the progress of slavery. Our Assemblies have repeatedly passed acts laying heavy duties upon imported Negroes, by which they meant altogether to prevent the horrid traffick; but their humane intentions have been as often frustrated by the cruelty and covetousness of a set of English merchants, who prevailed upon the King to repeal our kind and merciful acts, little indeed to the credit of his humanity. Can it then be supposed that the Negroes will be better used by the English, who have always encouraged and upheld this slavery, than by their present masters, who pity their condition, who wish, in general, to make it as easy and comfortable as possible, and who would willingly, were it in their power, or were they permitted, not only prevent any more Negroes from losing their freedom, but restore it to such as have already unhappily lost it. No, the ends of Lord Dunmore and his party being answered, they will either give up the offending Negroes to the rigour of the laws they have broken, or sell them in the West Indies, where every year they sell many thousands of their miserable brethren, to perish either by the inclemency of the weather, or the cruelty of barbarous masters. Be not then, ye Negroes, tempted by this proclamation to ruin yourselves. I have given you a faithful view of what you are to expect; and I declare, before GOD, in doing it, I have considered your welfare, as well as that of the country. Whether you will profit by my advice I cannot tell; but this I know, that whether we suffer or not, if you desert us, you most certainly will.

Source: Virginia Gazette, *November 5, 1775.*

A Sermon Preached on the Day of the Continental Fast (1775)

As tensions between Britain and the colonies turned to violence, religious leaders guided their communities through the ethical and political issues they faced. While many preachers advocated a continued search for amicable relations, others spoke out for revolution. In the following sermon, which was delivered in front of troops in Chester County, Pennsylvania, on July 20, 1775, Reverend David Jones argued for the ethical common sense of revolution. A month later, on August 16, the *Pennsylvania Gazette* announced the publication of this sermon from which the excerpts below are taken under the title of "Defensive War in a Just Cause Sinless." Reverend Jones later served as a chaplain in the Continental Army.

The reason why a defensive war seems so awful to good people is, they esteem it to be some kind of murder: but this is a very great mistake; for it is no more murder than a legal process against a criminal. . . .

Suppose, a villain was to rob you of a valuable sum of money, and thereby expose you and your family to distress and poverty, would you not think it your duty to prosecute such a public offender? yes, without doubt, or else you could not be a friend to the innocent part of mankind.

But suppose, he not only robs you, but in a daring manner, in your presence, murders your only son, will you not think that blood calls aloud for punishment? Surely both reason and revelation will justify you in seeking for justice in that mode by which it can be obtained.

The present case is only too similar:—by an arbitrary act all the families that depended on the Newfoundland fishery are abandoned to distress and poverty, and the blood of numbers spilt already without a cause. Surely it is consistent with the purest religion to seek for justice.

Consider the case in this point of view, and he that is not clear in conscience to gird his sword, if he would act consistently, must never sit on a jury to condemn a criminal.

This brings me . . . to present a few particulars to your consideration, which will demonstrate the alarming call . . . to take up arms, and fight in our own defence.—

We have no choice left to us, but to submit to absolute slavery and despotism, or as free-men to stand in our own defence, and endeavor a noble resistance. Matters are at last brought to this deplorable extremity;—every reasonable method of reconciliation has been tried in vain;—our addresses to our king have been treated with neglect or contempt.

It is true that a plan of accommodation has been proposed by the administration; but they are men of more sense than to think it could be accepted. It could be proposed for no other purpose than to deceive England into an opinion, that we did not desire reconciliation. What was the substance of this pretended plan? In short, this, that we should give them as much money as they were pleased to ask, and we might raise it in our own mode. Slaves therefore we must be, only we shall be indulged to put on our fetters, to suit ourselves.

This plan is no better than that clause, which says, "That the parliament have a right to make laws to bind us in all cases whatsoever." For if they may fix the sum, and we must raise it, the case is the same, we have nothing left, but what they have no use for: all is at their disposal, and we shall have no voice in the application of our own money. They may apply it to raise forces in Canada, to cut our throats. The call therefore is alarming—we cannot submit to be slaves—we were born free, and we can die free. . . .

Even our religion is not excepted—they assume a right to bind us in all cases. Agreeable to this proposition, they may oblige us to support popish priests, on pain of death: they have already given us a specimen of the good effects of their assumed power, in establishing popery in near one half of North America. Is not this the loudest call to arms?

All is at stake—we can appeal to GOD, that we believe our cause is just and good. . . . [Our] brethren in the Massachusetts are already declared rebels; they are treated as such, and we abettors are involved in the same circumstances; nothing can be more unjust than such a proclamation. Rebels are men disaffected with their sovereign in favour of some other person. This is not the case of America. . . .

We very well know what follows this proclamation, all our estates are confiscated, and were we even to submit, we should be hanged as dogs. Now therefore let us join, and fight for our brethren.

Remember our Congress is in eminent danger. It is composed of men of equal characters and fortunes of most, if not superior to any in North-America. These worthy gentlemen have ventured all in the cause of liberty for our sakes; if we were to forsake them, they must be abandoned to the rage of a relentless ministry. Some of them are already proscribed, and no doubt his would be the fate of the rest:

How could we bear to see these worthy patriots hanged as criminals of the deepest dye? their families plundered of all they possess, and abandoned to distress and poverty? This, my countrymen, must be the case, if you will not now as men fight for your brethren: Therefore if we do not stand by them, even unto death, we should be guilty of the basest ingratitude, and entail on ourselves everlasting infamy.

But if the case of our brethren is not so near as suitably to effect us, let us consider the condition of our sons and daughters. Your sons are engaged in the present dispute, and therefor subject to all the consequences:

Oh! remember if you submit to arbitrary measures, you will entail on your sons despotic power. Your sons and daughters must be strangers to the comforts of liberty; they will be considered like beasts of burden, only made for their masters use. If the groans and cries of posterity in oppression can be any argument, come now, my noble countrymen, fight for your sons and daughters.

But if this will not alarm you, consider what will be the case of your wives, if a noble resistance is not made: all your estates confiscated, and distributed to the favourites of arbitrary power, your wives must be left to distress and poverty. This might be the better endured, only the most worthy and flower of all the land shall be hanged, and widowhood and poverty both come in one day.

The call to arms is therefore alarming, especially when we consider the tender mercies of the wicked are cruel, we can expect no favour from the administration. They seem to be callous, so as to have no feeling of human distress. What can be a greater demonstration than to excite the barbarous savages against us? These, instead of coming against our armed men, will beset our defenceless frontiers, and barbarously murder with savage cruelty poor helpless women and children. Oh, did ever mortal hear of such inhuman barbarity!

Come then, my countrymen, we have no other remedy, but, under GOD, to fight for our brethren, our sons, and daughters, our wives and our houses.

Source: David Jones, A Sermon Preached on the Day of the Continental Fast (Philadelphia, 1775), 16–26.

Letter of Abigail Adams Urging Her Husband John to Remember the Ladies (March 31, 1776)

As representatives in the Continental Congress drafted the Declaration of Independence, women across the colonies understand that any revolution would reshape their lives as well as those of their families. Although excluded from the assemblies and various committees that shaped the revolution, many women were carefully following what happened in the public domain. In the following letter, Abigail Adams tried to sway her husband and thus wield her influence in the political sphere. Although Adams did not call for female suffrage, she boldly demanded that any statement of grievances would acknowledge the gender inequalities faced under the British system. Despite her eloquence, the Declaration was silent on issues of gender relations.

I wish you would ever write me a Letter half as long as I write you; and tell me if you may where your Fleet are gone? What sort of Defence Virginia can make against our common Enemy? Whether it is so situated as to make an able Defence? Are not the Gentery Lords and the common people vassals, are they not like the uncivilized Natives Brittain represents us to be? I hope their Riffel Men who have shewen themselves very savage and even Blood thirsty; are not a specimen of the Generality of the people.

I am willing to allow the Colony great merit for having produced a Washington but they have been shamefully duped by a Dunmore.

I have sometimes been ready to think that the passion for Liberty cannot be Eaquelly Strong in the Breasts of those who have been accustomed to deprive their fellow Creatures of theirs. Of this I am certain that it is not founded upon that generous and christian principal of doing to others as we would that others should do unto us.

Do not you want to see Boston; I am fearfull of the small pox, or I should have been in before this time. I got Mr. Crane to go to our House and see what state it was in. I find it has been occupied by one of the Doctors of a Regiment, very dirty, but no other damage has been done to it. The few things which were left in it are all gone. Cranch has the key which he never deliverd up. I have wrote to him for it and am determined to get it cleand as soon as possible and shut it up. I look upon it a new acquisition of property, a property which one month ago I did not value at a single Shilling, and could with pleasure have seen it in flames.

The Town in General is left in a better state than we expected, more oweing to a percipitate flight than any Regard to the inhabitants, tho some individuals discoverd a sense of honour and justice and have left the rent of the Houses in which they were, for the owners and the furniture unhurt, or if damaged sufficient to make it good.

Others have committed abominable Ravages. The Mansion House of your President [John Hancock] is safe and the furniture unhurt whilst both the House and Furniture of the Solisiter General [Samuel Quincy] have fallen a prey to their own merciless party. Surely the very Fiends feel a Reverential awe for Virtue and patriotism, whilst they Detest the paricide and traitor.

I feel very differently at the approach of spring to what I did a month ago. We knew not then whether we could plant or sow with safety, whether when we had toild we could reap the fruits of our own industery, whether we could rest in our own Cottages, or whether we should not be driven from the sea coasts to seek shelter in the wilderness, but now we feel as if we might sit under our own vine and eat the good of the land.

I feel a gaieti de Coar to which before I was a stranger. I think the Sun looks brighter, the Birds sing more melodiously, and Nature puts on a more chearfull countanance. We feel a temporary peace, and the poor fugitives are returning to their deserted habitations.

Tho we felicitate ourselves, we sympathize with those who are trembling least the Lot of Boston should be theirs. But they cannot be in similar circumstances unless pusilanimity and cowardise should take possession of them. They have time and warning given them to see the Evil and shun it.—I long to hear that you have declared an independancy—and by the way in the new Code of Laws which I suppose it will be necessary for you to make I desire you would Remember the Ladies, and be more generous and favourable to them than your ancestors. Do not put such unlimited power into the hands of the Husbands. Remember all Men would be tyrants if they could. If perticuliar care and attention is not paid to the Laidies we are determined to foment a Rebelion, and will not hold ourselves bound by any Laws in which we have no voice, or Representation.

That your Sex are Naturally Tyrannical is a Truth so thoroughly established as to admit of no dispute, but such of you as wish to be happy willingly give up the harsh title of Master for the more tender and endearing one of Friend. Why then, not put it out of the power of the vicious and the Lawless to use us with cruelty and indignity with impunity. Men of Sense in all Ages abhor those customs which treat us only as the vassals of your Sex. Regard us then as Beings placed by providence under your protection and in immitation of the Supreem Being make use of that power only for our happiness.

April 5

Not having an opportunity of sending this I shall add a few lines more; tho not with a heart so gay. I have been attending the sick chamber of our Neighbour Trot whose affliction I most sensibly feel but cannot discribe, striped of two lovely children in one week. Gorge the Eldest died on wednesday and Billy the youngest on fryday, with the Canker fever, a terible disorder so much like the thr[o]at distemper, that it differs but little from it. Betsy Cranch has been very bad, but upon the recovery. Becky Peck they do not expect will live out the day. Many grown person[s] are now sick with it, in this [street?]. It rages much in other Towns. The Mumps too are very frequent. Isaac is now confined with it. Our own little flock are yet well. My Heart trembles with anxiety for them. God preserve them.

I want to hear much oftener from you than I do. March 8 was the last date of any that I have yet had.—You inquire of whether I am making Salt peter. I have not yet attempted it, but after Soap making believe I shall make the experiment. I find as much as I can do to manufacture cloathing for my family which would else be Naked. I know of but one person in this part of the Town who has made any, that is Mr. Tertias Bass as he is calld who has got very near an hundred weight which has been found to be very good. I have heard of some others in the other parishes. Mr. Reed of Weymouth has been applied to, to go to Andover to the mills which are now at work, and has gone. I have lately seen a small Manuscrip de[s]cribing the proportions for the various sorts of powder, fit for cannon, small arms and pistols. If it would be of any Service your way I will get it transcribed and send it to you.—Every one of your Friend[s] send their Regards, and all the little ones. Your Brothers youngest child lies bad with convulsion fitts. Adieu. I need not say how much I am Your ever faithfull Friend.

Source: Charles Francis Adams, ed., Letters of Mrs. Adams, the Wife of John Adams, *4th ed. (Boston: Wilkins, Carter, 1848).*

Virginia Bill of Rights (June 12, 1776)

On June 12, 1776, the Virginia House of Burgesses issued a declaration that was echoed less than a month later in the Declaration of Independence. In this Bill of Rights, Virginians declared the equality of citizens and called upon Parliament to recognize their inalienable rights. Written by George Mason and later edited by a committee, Virginia's Bill of Rights asserted the idea that governments obtained their power from the people, declared the importance of the separation of powers, and safeguarded the personal freedoms of individuals to pray, speak, and print.

A DECLARATION OF RIGHTS *made by the representatives of the good people of Virginia, assembled in full and free Convention; which rights do pertain to them, and their posterity, as the basis and foundation of government.*

1. That all men are by nature equally free and independent, and have certain inherent rights, of which, when they enter into a state of society, they cannot, by any compact, deprive or divest their posterity; namely, the enjoyment of life and liberty, with the means of acquiring and possessing property, and pursuing and obtaining happiness and safety.

2. That all power is vested in, and consequently derived from, the people; that magistrates are their trustees and servants, and at all times amenable to them.

3. That government is, or ought to be, instituted for the common benefit, protection, and security, of the people, nation, or community; of all the various modes and forms of government that is best, which is capable of producing the greatest degree of happiness and safety, and is most effectually secured against the danger of maladministration; and that whenever any government shall be found inadequate or contrary to these purposes, a majority of the community hath an indubitable, unalienable, and indefeasible right, to reform, alter, or abolish it, in such manner as shall be judged most conducive to the publick weal.

4. That no man, or set of men, are entitled to exclusive or separate emoluments or privileges from the community, but in consideration of publick services; which, not being descendible, neither ought the offices of magistrate, legislator, or judge, to be hereditary.

5. That the legislative and executive powers of the state should be separate and distinct from the judicative; and that the members of the two first may be restrained from oppression, by feeling and participating the burthens of the people, they should, at fixed periods, be reduced to a private station, return into that body from which they were originally taken, and the vacancies be supplied by frequent, certain, and regular elections, in which all, or any part of the former members, to be again eligible, or ineligible, as the laws shall direct.

6. That elections of members to serve as representatives of the people, in assembly, ought to be free; and that all men, having sufficient evidence of permanent common interest with, and attachment to, the community, have the right of suffrage, and cannot be taxed or deprived of their property for publick uses without their own consent, or that of their representatives so elected, nor bound by any law to which they have not, in like manner, assented, for the publick good.

7. That all power of suspending laws, or the execution of laws, by any authority without consent of the representatives of the people, is injurious to their rights, and ought not to be exercised.

8. That in all capital or criminal prosecutions a man hath a right to demand the cause and nature of his accusation, to be confronted with the accusers and witnesses, to call for evidence in his favour, and to a speedy trial by an impartial jury of his vicinage, without whose unanimous consent he cannot be found guilty, nor can he be compelled to give evidence against himself; that no man be deprived of his liberty except by the law of the land, or the judgment of his peers.

9. That excessive bail ought not to be required, nor excessive fines imposed, nor cruel and unusual punishments inflicted.

10. That general warrants, whereby any officer or messenger may be commanded to search suspected places without evidence of a fact committed, or to seize any person or persons not named, or whose offence is not particularly described and supported by evidence, are grievous and oppressive, and ought not to be granted.

11. That in controversies respecting property, and in suits between man and man, the ancient trial by jury is preferable to any other, and ought to be held sacred.

12. That the freedom of the press is one of the great bulwarks of liberty, and can never be restrained but by despotick governments.

13. That a well regulated militia, composed of the body of the people, trained to arms, is the proper, natural, and safe defence of a free state; that standing armies, in time of peace, should be avoided, as dangerous to liberty; and that, in all cases, the military should be under strict subordination to, and governed by, the civil power.

14. That the people have a right to uniform government; and therefore, that no government separate from, or independent of, the government of *Virginia*, ought to be erected or established within the limits thereof.

15. That no free government, or the blessing of liberty, can be preserved to any people but by a firm adherence to justice, moderation, temperance, frugality, and virtue, and by frequent recurrence to fundamental principles.

16. That religion, or the duty which we owe to our CREATOR, and the manner of discharging it, can be directed only by reason and conviction, not by force or violence; and therefore all men are equally entitled to the free exercise of religion, according to the dictates of conscience; and that it is the mutual duty of all to practice Christian forbearance, love, and charity, towards each other.

Source: Francis Newton Thorpe, ed., The Federal and State Constitutions, Colonial Charters, and Other Organic Laws of the States, Territories, and Colonies Now or Heretofore Forming the United States of America *(Washington, DC: Government Printing Office, 1909).*

Memoirs of a Patriot Recruiter (1776)

American colonists understood that declaring rights was quite different from securing them. After the colonists declared independence in July 1776, they turned their attention to fighting for their newly declared freedoms. Alexander Graydon was one of many colonists who were charged with recruiting soldiers for a new army. In 1775, Congress appointed Graydon a captain, explicitly so that he could raise troops. When the war began, Graydon continued as a recruiter but also served as a soldier. He fought at the Battle of Long Island and was captured during the fight on Harlem Heights. He obtained his freedom through a prisoner exchange in 1778. In the following excerpt from his memoir, Graydon recalled his experiences as a recruiter.

1776

The object now was to raise my company, and as the streets of the city had been pretty well swept by the preceding and contemporary levies, it was necessary to have recourse to the country. My recruiting party was there-fore sent out in various directions; and each of my officers as well as myself, exerted himself in the business. Among the many unpleasant peculiarities of the American service, it was not the least that the drudgery, which in old military establishments belongs to serjeants and corporals, here devolved on the commissioned officers; and that the whole business of recruiting, drilling, &c. required their unremitted personal attention. This was more emphati-cally the case in recruiting; since the common opinion was, that the men and the officers were never to be separated, and hence, to see the persons who were to command them, and above all, the captain, was deemed of vast importance by those inclining to enlist: for this reason I found it necessary, in common with my brother officers, to put my feelings most cruelly to the rack; and in an excursion I once made to Frankford, they were tried to the utmost. A number of fellows at the tavern, at which my party rendezvoused, indicated a desire to enlist, but although they drank freely of our liquor, they still held off. I soon perceived that the object was to amuse themselves at our expense, and that if there might be one or two among them really disposed to engage, the others would prevent them. One fellow in particular, who had made the greatest shew of taking the bounty, presuming on the weakness of our party, consisting only of a drummer, corporal, my second lieutenant and myself, began to grow insolent, and manifested an intention to begin a quarrel, in the issue of which, he no doubt calculated on giving us a drub-bing. The disgrace of such a circumsts[a]nce, presented itself to my mind in colors the most dismal, and I resolved, that if a scuffle should be unavoid-able, it should, at least, be as serious as the hangers which my lieutenant and myself carried by our sides, could make it. . . . At length the arrogance of the principal ruffian, rose to such a height, that he squared himself for battle and advanced towards me in an attitude of defiance. I put him by, with an admonition to be quiet, though with a secret determination, that, if he re-peated the insult, to begin the war, whatever might be the consequence. The occasion was soon presented; when taking excellent aim, I struck him with the utmost force between the eyes and sent him staggering to the other end of the room. Then instantly drawing our hangers, and receiving the manful cooperation of the corporal and drummer, we were fortunate enough to put a stop to any further hostilities. It was some time before the fellow I had struck, recovered from the blow, but when he did, he was quite an altered man. He was as submissive as could be wished, begging my pardon for what he had done, and although he would not enlist, he hired himself to me for a few weeks as a fifer, in which capacity he had acted in the militia; and during the time he was in this employ, he bore about the effects of his insolence, in a pair of black eyes. This incident would be little worthy of relating, did it not serve in some degree to correct the error of those who seem to conceive the year 1776 to have been a season of almost universal patriotic enthusiasm. It was far from prevalent in my opinion, among the lower ranks of the people, at least in Pennsylvania. At all times, indeed, licentious, levelling principles are much to the general taste, and were of course popular with us; but the true merits of the contest, were little understood or regarded. The opposition to the claims of Britain originated with the better sort: it was truly aristocratic in its commencement; and as the oppression to be apprehended, had not been felt, no grounds existed for general enthusiasm. . . .

Recruiting went on but heavily. Some officers had been more successful than others, but none of the companies were complete: mine perhaps contained about half its complement of men, and these had been obtained by dint of great exertion. In this situation, captain Lenox of Shee's regiment also, suggested the trying our luck on the Eastern shore of Maryland, particularly at Chester, situated on the river of that name. It having been a place of some trade, it was supposed there might be seamen or longshoremen there, out of employ. . . . Mr. Heath . . . helped us . . . to a recruit, a fellow, he said, who would do to stop a bullet as well as a better man, and as he was a truly worthless dog, he held, that the neighborhood would be much indebted to us for taking him away. . . .

With such unfavorable prospects in Maryland, it would have been folly to have proceeded further: we therefore, set off on our way home the next morning. . . . Returning by Warwick, we sent forward our solitary recruit, for whom we tossed up; and in winning, I was, in fact, but a very small gainer, since his merits had been set at their full value by Mr. Heath; and he was never fit for any thing better than the inglorious post of camp colour man.

After this unsuccessful jaunt I bent my course to the Four-lane ends, Newtown, and Corryell's ferry; thence passing into Jersey, I proceeded to the Hickory tavern, to Pittstown, Baptisttown, Flemmingtown, and other towns, whose names I do not remember. . . . In the whole of my tour, therefore, I picked up but three or four men. . . .

Source: Alexander Graydon, Memoirs of a Life, Chiefly Passed in Pennsylvania *(Edinburgh: Blackwood, 1822).*

"Tradesmen's Song" (1777)

Music and poetry were important morale boosters for both Patriots and Loyalists during the American Revolution. They spoofed the opposition, praised specific causes, and made clear the righteousness of the cause. Written for the king's birthday, this Loyalist song was written soon after the British occupied Philadelphia. The British remained in the city for nine months, and during this time, this and other Loyalist songs were sung across the city. Like most Revolutionary-era songs, residents learned of "The Tradesmen's Song" when it was published as a broadside, printed in a newspaper, and otherwise spread by word of mouth. This song was sung to the widely known tune of "When Britain First at Heaven's Command."

Again, my social Friends, we meet
To celebrate our annual display
This great, this glorious Natal Day:
'Tis George's Natal Day we sing,
Our firm, our steady Friend and King.
For Britain's Parliament and Laws
He waves his own Imperial Power,

For this (Old England's glorious Cause)
May Heaven on him its blessings shower,
And Colonies, made happy, sing,
Great George their real friend and King.
Since Britain first at Heaven's command
Arose from out the Azure Main,
Did ever o'er this jarring Land
A Monarch with more firmness reign?
Then to the Natal Day we'll sing,
Of George our sacred Friend and King.
To Charlotte fair, our matchless Queen,
To all his blooming heavenly Line,
To all their Family and Friends,
Let us in hearty chorus join,
And George's Natal Day let's sing,
Our gracious Father, Friend, and King.
And may the heavenly Powers combine,
While we with loyal hearts implore
That one of his most sacred Line
May rule these Realms till time's no more.
And we with chearful voices sing
Great George our steady, natal King.

Source: Pennsylvania Ledger, *October 22, 1777.*

Loyalist Editorial (1779)

Loyalists comprised roughly a third of all the colonists. With another third uncertain of their loyalties and desirous of peace, the American Revolution was often a battle for the hearts and minds of the undecided. Writers frequently turned to newspapers, broadsides, and pamphlets to sway the public. This newspaper article, taken from the *New York Gazette*, recounted the recent military events in New York while telling readers about the "wanton cruelties" committed by Patriots toward Loyalists. In addition, the author declares that the war was chosen and perpetuated by selfish colonists who spread rumors of misdeeds in order to obtain supporters. The article was likely written by Loyalist James "Candidus" Chalmers.

July 20.—We have just seen a rebel newspaper which contains a very curious article relative to the late attack on Stony Point. The article is written in that turgid style, and in that little spirit of triumph, which distinguish almost all the rebel publications, on the acquisition of any trifling advantage; and is at once a just sample of the eloquence and temper of the rebels. . . .

Our writer goes on to extol the "humanity of the rebels" and contrasts it with the "savage barbarity of burning unguarded towns, deflowering defenceless women," &c. As far as truth will permit, I am willing to believe, for the honour of America, that the rebels on this occasion relaxed in their usual barbarity. As it is the first instance, it should be recorded, though it would have lost nothing had it been expressed in less exaggerated terms.

The rebels have hitherto been infamous for their wanton cruelties. Their brutal treatment of Governor Franklin, and many other persons of distinction whom I could mention,—their barbarity to loyalists in general, and at this present hour—hanging men for acting according to the dictates of conscience—whipping men almost to death because they will not take up arms—publicly whipping even women, whose husbands would not join the militia—their confiscations, fines, and imprisonments; these things which they daily and indubitably practice, very ill agree with the character of humanity so lavishly bestowed on them by this writer. Nothing but a long, very long series of conduct the reverse of this can wipe off the infamy which they hereby incurred.

The charge of "deflowering defenceless women" is one of those deliberate, malicious falsehoods which are circulated by the rebels, purely to incense the inhabitants against the British troops. As to burning "unguarded towns," this writer should know that the King's troops burn no houses except public magazines, and those from which they are fired at, or otherwise annoyed. This was lately the case at Fairfield and Norwalk, the towns to which, I suppose, the author alludes; and when houses are thus converted into citadels, it is justifiable to burn them by the rules of war among all civilized nations.

New Haven was in the possession of the King's troops, yet they did not burn it. The reason was, they were not fired at from the houses during their approach to, or retreat from, the town. Some of the inhabitants, however, did what would have justified the British troops in consigning it to the flames. Sentries placed to guard particular houses have been fired at from those very same houses, and killed. An officer of distinction took a prisoner who was on horseback, and had a gun; the prisoner apparently submitted, but watching for an opportunity, he discharged his gun at the officer, and wounded him. The wounded officer was carried into an adjoining house to have his wound dressed; the owner of the house seemed to be kind and attentive to the officer; the latter, in gratitude for his attention, ordered the soldiery, on his departure, to be particularly careful of the house, that no injuries should be offered to it. Yet, no sooner was the officer gone, and at the distance of fifty yards, than this very man discharged a loaded musket at him. These are samples of rebel humanity, which sweetly harmonize with our writer's sentiments.

This writer, and all others of his stamp, should remember that the colonies are now in a state of revolt and rebellion against their rightful sovereign. The British legislature is unalterably determined to bring them back to their allegiance. The most generous overtures have been made to them—a redress of grievances, an exemption from taxes, and a free trade, have been offered. These liberal terms would indubitably make America the happiest, freest, and most flourishing country in the world. But the American Congress have madly and insolently rejected these terms. The Congress, therefore, and their partisans, are justly chargeable, before God and the world, with all the calamities which America now suffers, and with all those other and greater calamities which it will probably hereafter suffer in the course of this unnatural contest.

Source: New York Gazette, *August 16, 1779.*

Treaty between the United States and the Delaware Indians (1778)

The ending of British rule necessitated that the newly formed United States forge new agreements with its Native American neighbors. As the war began poorly for the American military, securing Indian allies proved rather important. The following treaty with the Delaware Indians took place in the shadows of the demoralizing winter at Valley Forge. As a result, the United States offered the Indians access to necessary trade goods and weapons, as well as the potential to form a state of their own in the new nation. The Treaty with the Delaware was the United States' first successful negotiation with a Native American nation.

ARTICLE I.

That all offences or acts of hostilities by one, or either of the contracting parties against the other, be mutually forgiven, and buried in the depth of oblivion, never more to be had in remembrance.

ARTICLE II.

That a perpetual peace and friendship shall from henceforth take place, and subsist between the contracting: parties aforesaid, through all succeeding generations: and if either of the parties are engaged in a just and necessary war with any other nation or nations, that then each shall assist the other in due proportion to their abilities, till their enemies are brought to reasonable terms of accommodation: and that if either of them shall discover any hostile designs forming against the other, they shall give the earliest notice thereof that timeous measures may be taken to prevent their ill effect.

ARTICLE III.

And whereas the United States are engaged in a just and necessary war, in defence and support of life, liberty and independence, against the King of England and his adherents, and as said King is yet possessed of several posts and forts on the lakes and other places, the reduction of which is of great importance to the peace and security of the contracting parties, and as the most practicable way for the troops of the United States to some of the posts and forts is by passing through the country of the Delaware nation, the aforesaid deputies, on behalf of themselves and their nation, do hereby stipulate and agree to give a free passage through their country to the troops aforesaid, and the same to conduct by the nearest and best ways to the posts, forts or towns of the enemies of the United States, affording to said troops such supplies of corn, meat, horses, or whatever may be in their power for the accommodation of such troops, on the commanding officer's, &c. paying, or engageing to pay, the full value of whatever they can supply them with. And the said deputies, on the behalf of their nation, engage to join the troops of the United States aforesaid, with such a number of their best and most expert warriors as they can spare, consistent with their own safety, and act in concert with them; and for the better security of the old men, women and children of the aforesaid nation, whilst their warriors are engaged against the common enemy, it is agreed on the part of the United States, that a fort of sufficient strength and capacity be built at the expense of the said States, with such assistance as it may be in the power of the said Delaware Nation to give, in the most convenient place, and advantageous situation, as shall be agreed on by the commanding officer of the troops aforesaid, with the advice and concurrence of the deputies of the aforesaid Delaware Nation, which fort shall be garrisoned by such a number of the troops of the United States, as the commanding officer can spare for the present, and hereafter by such numbers, as the wise men of the United States in council, shall think most conducive to the common good.

ARTICLE IV.
For the better security of the peace and friendship now entered into by the contracting parties, against all infractions of the same by the citizens of either party, to the prejudice of the other, neither party shall proceed to the infliction of punishments on the citizens of the other, otherwise than by securing the offender or offenders by imprisonment, or any other competent means, till a fair and impartial trial can be had by judges or juries of both parties, as near as can be to the laws, customs and usages of the contracting parties and natural justice. The mode of such trials to be hereafter fixed by the wise men of the United States in Congress assembled, with the assistance of such deputies of the Delaware nation, as may be appointed to act in concert with them in adjusting this matter to their mutual liking. And it is further agreed between the parties aforesaid, that neither shall entertain or give countenance to the enemies of the other, or protect in their respective states, criminal fugitives, servants or slaves, but the same to apprehend, and secure and deliver to the State or States, to which such enemies, criminals, servants or slaves respectively belong.

ARTICLE V.
Whereas the confederation entered into by the Delaware nation and the United States, renders the first dependent on the latter for all the articles of clothing, utensils and implements of war, and it is judged not only reasonable, but indispensably necessary, that the aforesaid Nation be supplied with such articles from time to time, as far as the United States may have it in their power, by a well-regulated trade, under the conduct of an intelligent, candid agent, with an adequate salary, one more influenced by the love of his country, and a constant attention to the duties of his department by promoting the common interest, than the sinister purposes of converting and binding all the duties of his office to his private emolument: Convinced of the necessity of such measures, the Commissioners of the United States, at the earnest solicitation of the deputies aforesaid, have engaged in behalf of the United States, that such a trade shall be afforded said nation conducted on such principles of mutual interest as the wisdom of the United States in Congress assembled shall think most conducive to adopt for their mutual convenience.

ARTICLE VI.
Whereas the enemies of the United States have endeavored, by every artifice in their power, to possess the Indians in general with an opinion, that it is the design of the States aforesaid, to extirpate the Indians and take possession

of their country to obviate such false suggestion, the United States do engage to guarantee to the aforesaid nation of Delawares, and their heirs, all
their territorial rights in the fullest and most ample manner, as it hath been
bounded by former treaties, as long as they the said Delaware nation shall
abide by, and hold fast the chain of friendship now entered into. And it is
further agreed on between the contracting parties should it for the future be
found conducive for the mutual interest of both parties to invite any other
tribes who have been friends to the interest of the United States, to join the
present confederation, and to form a state whereof the Delaware nation
shall be the head, and have a representation in Congress: Provided, nothing
contained in this article to be considered as conclusive until it meets with
the approbation of Congress. And it is also the intent and meaning of this
article, that no protection or countenance shall be afforded to any who are
at present our enemies, by which they might escape the punishment they
deserve.

In witness whereof, the parties have hereunto interchangeably set their
hands and seals, at Fort Pitt, September seventeenth, anno Domini one
thousand seven hundred and seventy-eight.

Andrew Lewis, [L. S.]
Thomas Lewis, [L. S.]
White Eyes, his x mark, [L. S.]
The Pipe, his x mark, [L. S.]
John Kill Buck, his x mark, [L. S.]

In presence of—

Lach'n McIntosh, brigadier-general, commander the Western Department,
Daniel Brodhead, colonel Eighth Pennsylvania Regiment,
W. Crawford, collonel,
John Campbell,
John Stephenson,
John Gibson, colonel Thirteenth Virginia Regiment,
A. Graham, brigade major,
Lach. McIntosh, jr., major brigade,
Benjamin Mills,
Joseph L. Finley, captain Eighth Pennsylvania Regiment,
John Finley, captain Eighth Pennsylvania Regiment.

Source: Charles J. Kappler, ed., Indian Affairs: Laws and Treaties, *vol. 2 (Treaties) (Washington, DC: Government Printing Office, 1904).*

Baron Von Steuben Describes His Experiences in the Continental Army (1779)

Baron Friedrich Wilhelm Augustus Steuben was a German officer who was invited
to teach American officers how to drill their soldiers. He worked with small groups
of carefully chosen men, who then went off to train the rest of the Continental
Army. Steuben initially served the United States as a volunteer, but soon after he

took a salary. By the end of the war, he had been well compensated and he decided to remain in the United States. In the following excerpt, Steuben describes his experiences and his growing love for the United States.

[July 4, 1779]

I am at present on a tour of inspection for the purpose not only of reviewing all the regiments, but of introducing the system laid down in my tactics. Indeed, my friend, I have been fortunate in everything I have here undertaken. I am now fifth in rank as general; and if my career be not ended by a fever or by half an ounce of lead, the possibilities are vast enough to satisfy the most ambitious. Two or three years of toil, and then, my friend, you must promise to visit me in Paris; and there we will discuss the question whether we are to dine together in Europe or in America. Oh! my dearest F, why have I wasted my years in such a manner! Two years of work—if one is not afraid of toil and danger—can make a man successful. Experience has convinced me of this; nor can I forgive myself for my past indolence.

What a beautiful, what a happy country this is! Without kings, without prelates, without blood-sucking farmer-generals, and without idle barons! Here everybody is prosperous. Poverty is an unknown evil. Indeed, I should become too prolix were I to give you an account of the prosperity and happiness of these people. The account of them by Abbe Reynal is not entirely accurate, but it is the best. Read it and judge for yourself. . . .

I must candidly admit to you that six foreign officers cause more trouble to me here than two hundred American ones; and indeed most of the foreigners have so utterly lost their credit, that it is daily becoming more difficult to employ foreign officers. A large number of German barons and French marquises have already sailed away; and I am always nervous and apprehensive when a baron or a marquis announces himself. While here we are in a republic; and Mr. Baron does not count a farthing more than Mister Jacob or Mister Peter. Indeed, German and French noses can hardly accustom themselves to such a state of things! Our general of artillery [Knox], for instance, was a bookbinder in Boston. He is a worthy man, thoroughly understands his trade, and fills his present position with much credit.

Baron von Kalbe and myself are now the only foreign generals in the United States service; and Kalbe, who has an income of over 30,000 livres in France, will resign at the end of this campaign.

Finally, my friend, I will only state to you my prospects and then close my letter. I will finish the war here, or it will finish me. Without doubt England, at the utmost, can continue the game but two years longer. It will then be my care to put the army and the militia in the thirteen provinces on a uniform and solid footing; and this having been accomplished, I shall render an account to Congress as to what we owe each other. My ability to keep up my appointments on 16,400 livres is assured to me for life. Congress has promised me, not gifts, but a landed estate either in New Jersey or Pennsylvania, two of the best provinces. A considerable pension from France, after the (successful) termination of the war, was pledged to me by the French Court before my departure for America; besides which, I can depend upon receiving a substantial gratuity especially from the thirteen provinces. To acquire all this requires on my part only three years, at the farthest, of life, health, steadfastness of purpose and courage. The first two conditions do not depend upon me: the last two are within my power and control. And then, my friend, when these have been fulfilled! Then shall I see you in Europe; and then we can talk the matter over, and decide whether you shall in future dine with me in Paris or Philadelphia!

Believe me, my friend, this globe of ours is not so large as we imagine it! An ant does not deserve its food if it is too lazy to seek it at the other side of its hill; and I have already wasted fourteen years of my life. Now, is Canada my hunting-lodge; Georgia my country-seat; and this strip of land the eighth of the world. At each of these extreme ends an order signed by me will be executed. This is somewhat flattering to an ambitious man; and you can, therefore, recognize your friend!

Source: Albert Bushnell Hart, ed., American History Told by Contemporaries, *vol. 2: Building of the Republic (New York: Macmillan, 1899), 582–585.*

An English Account of the War (1781)

As the War of Independence progressed, the United States had difficulty paying its soldiers. This caused great frustrations within the ranks of the American troops, who often took matters into their own hands. A series of riots and near mutinies bolstered the confidence of many Britons, especially as their fortunes on the battlefields declined and the British home front tired of the mounting costs. In the following account, a British observer hints that defeat is inevitable. Soon after this document was written, the United States and Great Britain ended their major combat operations against each other, and they began to negotiate the terms of peace.

The impatience of all the rebel troops, and being long deprived of their pay in real money, and wholesome provisions, had determined many of the soldiers to a peremptory demand, that their arrears should be produced to them in solid money, and the whole army put on a respectable and well appointed establishment; many perceiving the bankrupt condition of the Congress's finances, and that no magazines, &c. &c. were formed for the future subsistence of the army, took occasion on Monday last (when the times of the enlistment of several hundred expired) boldly to require their pay in present cash and hard money: finding no revenue but the long expired paper currency produced to supply their demands, the malcontents frankly offered to give up their pay with all arrears, and return home, provided each got a formal discharge, as they were determined to a man no longer to remain in the Continental service. These overtures being rejected, a cessation immediately ensued, consisting of the whole Pennsylvania line, commanded by General St. Clair, formerly a Lieutenant in his Majesty's Royal American regiment, having under him the Brigadier Generals W. Wayne, Hand, and a successor to the deceased Brigadier General Poor.

After having spiked up all the cannon, and destroyed all the carriages, they left their Head Quarters at Morris Town, bringing with them four field pieces, all the powder and provisions, and were pursued by some militia, of whom they killed a Colonel, two Majors, two Lieutenants, and some privates; they proceeded to Veal's Town, about twenty-two miles from Elizabeth Town, where on Wednesday last they threw up works of defence; at this place they erected a standard, chose a Commander in Chief, Commissaries, Quartermasters, and other Officers, essential to the accomodation and movement of troops on service.

They presently secured four hundred head of live cattle; all the horses of the neighbouring country as they passed were surrendered to them; upwards of one hundred rifle-men had been detached to hang on and annoy their rear, but on exploring their situation, rather than molest them, they left their Officers, and preferred to join their quondam fellow soldiers, in pursuit of the same object.

Thus reinforced, the total number of the revolters now amounts to two thousand two hundred men, and are daily encreasing. Gen. Wayne overtook, harangued, and on his knees supplicated their return, but all in vain; he was informed if he ever again approached them, they should detain him as a prisoner. Yesterday morning about three o'clock, a firing of field-pieces and musquetry was heard, supposed to be near Veal's Town.

The whole body (at the time of this paper's going to press) was in motion, conjectured to be for Amboy. It is said they are commanded by Mr. Box, formerly of his Majesty's forty-third regiment. All the measures they have hitherto concerted, seem to have been dictated by skill, firmness, and animation. The only Continental troops now in Jersey, in the Congress's service, are that solitary brigade of Gen. Dayton, lately commanded by Brigadier Maxwell, who some time since bootless quitted their service; this corps consists of only three slender regiments, total number seven hundred.

On Thursday last accounts of an action were received from the rebel country, which afford us hopes of important advantages newly obtained by the royal arms in the Carolina's; but no official relation having yet been obtained, we chuse not to risk a detail of them, until it can be done from an indubitable quarter. . . .

North America, says a correspondent, continues to be the grave of Englishmen, the repository of English money, the source of Great Britain's troubles, and, it is to be feared, a monument of her indelible disgrace and infamy. Thro' her means three powerful nations have risen up against us, and more are daily expected to show their hostile intentions, without any friend or ally to assist us.

The revolt, or mutiny, of a part of Washington's army, which has just reached our ears, has this disagreeable circumstance attending it, that whatever discontents, quarrels, and animosities prevail among the people of America, whatever hardships, distresses, and even misery they undergo, they show no hearty inclination to a reconciliation with the mother country! Else why do we not hear of the revolters immediately joining the royal standard? Nay, why do we not hear of the royal army embracing that opportunity of joining them, and attacking Washington's remaining weakened

army? An invincible obstinacy in the minds of the people overcomes all —
Independence is still the cry.

Source: Norfolk Chronicle *(England), February 17, 1781.*

Freneau's Poetry in Honor of Fallen Soldiers

Philip Morin Freneau was known as the poet of the American Revolution. Prior to
the Revolution, Freneau published satires about British rule and then moved to
the West Indies in 1776. He returned to the United States as a ship captain in 1778
and soon after was captured. After he was freed from six weeks' imprisonment,
he turned to poetry to vent his bitterness toward the Crown and to give voice to
an emerging American nationalism. In the following poem, Freneau memorialized
the American soldiers who died at the Battle of Eutaw Springs near Charleston.
This was the last battle between the British and the Americans in South Carolina.

TO THE MEMORY OF THE BRAVE AMERICANS, under General Greene,
who fell in the action of September 8, 1781.

At Eutaw springs the valiant died:
Their limbs with dust are cover'd o'er;
Weep on, ye spring, your tearful tide;
How many heroes are no more!
If in this wreck of ruin, they
Can yet be thought to claim a tear,
O smite thy gentle breast, and say
The friends of freedom slumber here!
Thou, who shalt trace this bloody plain,
If goodness rules thy generous breast,
Sigh for the wasted rural reign;
Sigh for the shepherds sunk to rest!
Stranger, their humble groves adorn;
You too may fall, and ask a tear:
'Tis not the beauty of the morn
That proves the evening shall be clear.
They saw their injur'd country's woe
The flaming town, the wasted field;
Then rush'd to meet the insulting foe;
They took the spear—but left the shield.
Led by thy conquering standards, GREENE,
The Britons they compell'd to fly:
None distant view'd the fatal plain,
None griev'd in such a cause to die—
But, like the Parthians, fam'd of old,
Who, flying, still their arrows threw;
These routed Britons, full as bold,
Retreated, and retreating slew.
Now rest in peace, our patriot band;

Though far from nature's limits thrown,
We trust they find a happier land,
A brighter Phoebus of their own.

Source: Philip Morin, The Poems of Philip Freneau, Written Chiefly during the Late War *(Philadelphia: Printed by Francis Bailey, 1786), 229–230.*

Memoirs of the Life of Boston King

Boston King was one of many Loyalist African Americans during the American Revolution. Born a slave in South Carolina, King found freedom behind English lines early in the war. He served the British military in several capacities before he was captured by the Americans and taken to New Jersey, where he was enslaved. King escaped to New York, where he married, and he and his wife remained there until the Loyalist evacuation. In his memoirs, King recalls the precarious nature of being an African American during the American Revolution.

While my mind was thus exercised, I went into the jail to see a lad whom I was acquainted with at New York. He had been taken prisoner, and attempted to make his escape, but was caught 12 miles off: They tied him to the tail of a horse, and in this manner brought him back to Brunswick. When I saw him, his feet were fastened in the stocks, and at night both his hands. This was a terrifying sight to me, as I expected to meet with the same kind of treatment, if taken in the act of attempting to regain my liberty. I was thankful that I was not confined in a jail, and my master used me as well as I could expect; and indeed the slaves about Baltimore, Philadelphia, and New York, have as good victuals as many of the English; for they have meat once a day, and milk for breakfast and supper; and what is better than all, many of the masters send their slaves to school at night, that they may learn to read the Scriptures. This is a privilege indeed. But alas, all these enjoyments could not satisfy me without liberty! Sometimes I thought, if it was the will of God that I should be a slave, I was ready to resign myself to his will; but at other times I could not find the least desire to content myself in slavery.

Being permitted to walk about when my work was done, I used to go to the ferry, and observed, that when it was low water the people waded across the river; tho' at the same time I saw there were guards posted at the place to prevent the escape of prisoners and slaves. As I was at prayer on Sunday evening, I thought the Lord heard me, and would mercifully deliver me. Therefore putting my confidence in him, about one o'clock in the morning I went down to the river side, and found the guards were either asleep or in the tavern. I instantly entered into the river, but when I was a little distance from the opposite shore, I heard the sentinels disputing among themselves: One said "I am sure I saw a man cross the river." Another replied, "There is no such thing." It seems they were afraid to fire at me, or make an alarm, left they should be punished for their negligence. When I had got a little distance from the shore, I fell down upon my knees, and thanked God for the deliverance. I traveled till about five in the morning, and then concealed myself till seven o'clock at night, when I proceeded forward, thro' bushes and marshes, near the road, for fear of being discovered. When I came to the river, opposite Staten-Island, I found a boat; and altho' it was very near a whaleboat, yet I ventured into it, and cutting the rope, got safe over. The commanding officer, when informed of my case, gave me a passport, and I proceeded to New York.

When I arrived at New York, my friends rejoiced to see me once more restored to liberty, and joined me in praising the Lord for his mercy and goodness. But notwithstanding this great deliverance, and the promises I had made to serve God, yet my good resolutions soon vanished away like the morning dew: The love of this world extinguished my good desires, and stole away my heart from God, so that I rested in a mere form of religion for near three years. About which time, (in 1783) the horrors and devastation of war happily terminated and peace was restored between America and Great Britain, which diffused universal joy among all parties; except us, who had escaped from slavery and taken refuge in the English army; for a report prevailed at New York, that all the slaves, in number 2000, were to be delivered up to their masters altho' some of them had been three or four years among the English. This dreadful rumour filled us all with inexpressible anguish and terror, especially when we saw our old masters coming from Virginia, North Carolina, and other parts, and seizing upon their slaves in the streets of New York, or even dragging them out of their beds. Many of the slaves had very cruel masters, so that the thoughts of returning home with them embittered life to us. For some days we lost our appetite for food, and sleep departed from our eyes. The English had compassion upon us in the day of distress, and issued out a Proclamation, importing, That all slaves should be free, who had taken refuge in the British lines, and claimed the sanction and privileges of the Proclamations respecting the security and protection of Negroes. In consequence of this, each of us received a certificate from the commanding officer at New York, which dispelled all our fears, and filled us with joy and gratitude. Soon after, ships were fitted out, and furnished with every necessary for conveying us to Nova Scotia. We arrived at Birch Town in the month of August, where we all safely landed. Every family had a lot of land, and we exerted all our strength in order to build comfortable huts before the cold weather set in.

Source: Boston King, Memoirs of the Life of Boston King, A Black Preacher Written by Himself, during His Residence at Kingswood School. *Reprinted in* The Methodist Magazine *(March 1798).*

Reference

Adams, John (1735–1826) Represented Massachusetts in the Continental Congress and signed the Declaration of Independence. He negotiated the Treaty of Paris that ended the war in 1783, and he later became first vice president and second president of the United States.

Adams, Samuel (1722–1803) John's second cousin and one of the earliest agitators for American Independence. He formed the Sons of Liberty and organized the Boston Tea Party.

Allen, Ethan (1738–1789) Commanded the Vermont Militia (the Green Mountain Boys) and captured Fort Ticonderoga.

America The only American ship of the line built during the war. Due to construction delays, it was not launched until a year after the British surrendered at Yorktown.

American rifle Also called the long rifle, or Kentucky rifle, this gun was a hunting weapon that proved remarkably effective in battle. The inside of the barrel was carved with special grooves that greatly increased the range and accuracy of the weapon.

André, John (1751–1780) A British major who was caught while arranging General Benedict Arnold's defection. He was hung as a spy on Washington's personal orders on October 2, 1780.

Arnold, Benedict (1741–1801) An American soldier who fought with distinction at Fort Ticonderoga and at Saratoga, but then became disgruntled with George Washington and secretly negotiated to surrender West Point to the British. His name remains synonymous with treachery.

Articles of Confederation The first constitution of the United States, this agreement created a government that held the thirteen colonies together during the war from 1777 until the U.S. Constitution went into effect in 1789.

Attucks, Crispus (c. 1723–1770) An individual of mixed African American and Native American heritage. He was a leader of the American mob that provoked the Boston Massacre. He and two others were killed at the scene and became the first Americans to die for independence.

Baltimore   The temporary home of the Continental Congress after it fled from Philadelphia and the oncoming British forces in 1776.

Battalion   The standard division for both British and American armies during the war (battalions were also called regiments). American battalions fluctuated between 500 and 780 men, with numbers dwindling to around 200 by the time of Yorktown.

Bayonets   Long blades attached to the ends of rifles. British and Continental soldiers had them, but the American militia did not, because their rifles were not made for regular warfare.

Bennington, Battle of   An important victory for the Americans, where much-needed supplies were captured from the British in August 1777. This action set the stage for Burgoyne's surrender at Saratoga.

Bonhomme Richard   An American warship commanded by John Paul Jones and named after Benjamin Franklin's character Poor Richard. Jones sailed into British waters in September 1779 and engaged the Royal Navy's *Serapis*. When the British commander shouted to Jones, asking if he was ready to surrender, he uttered his famous line, "I have not yet begun to fight." The *Serapis* surrendered after a long tough fight.

Boston Massacre   Took place on March 5, 1770. An unruly mob taunted British soldiers stationed there who fired a volley into the crowd, killing five colonists.

Boston Port Bill   Closed the port of Boston on June 1, 1774, in retaliation for the Boston Tea Party.

Boston Tea Party   Took place on December 16, 1773. Patriots organized by Sam Adams and disguised as Mohawk Indians boarded three British ships anchored in the harbor and destroyed 342 chests of tea to protest passage of the Tea Act.

Brant, Joseph (1742–1807)   Brant, whose Indian name was Thayendanegea, was the Mohawk chief during the war. He allied himself with the British and took part in several raids and battles.

British Legion   A Loyalist unit commanded by Banastre Tarleton. It was defeated by the Americans at the Battle of Cowpens in 1781.

Brown, Thomas (1750–1825)   A leading Loyalist who fled to British Florida and formed the King's Rangers, who conducted harassing raids on Patriots in Georgia and South Carolina during the war.

Bunker Hill, Battle of   Also known as the Battle of Breed's Hill, it was fought on June 17, 1775, one of the earliest battles of the war. This battle was also the bloodiest of the war, with both sides suffering 40 percent casualties. The Americans were forced to retreat but were heartened that they had successfully stood up to the mighty British Army.

Burgoyne, John (1722–1792) A British general, nicknamed "Gentleman Johnny" for his friendly demeanor. Burgoyne marched his army down the Hudson River valley from Canada and was defeated and forced to surrender at Saratoga on September 17, 1777. This English defeat helped persuade France to join the American cause.

Camden, Battle of Took place in August 1780; a major defeat for the Americans. General Horatio Gates was humiliated by the British and ended up fleeing the battlefield. Of his 4,000 men, only 700 managed to escape. This ended American attempts to recapture the South

Camp followers Civilians, usually wives and children, who accompanied a marching army to attend to the needs of the soldiers. They generally performed cooking and cleaning duties.

Castillo de San Marcos The old Spanish fort in Saint Augustine, Florida. The British used it to house American prisoners of war.

Charleston, South Carolina The largest southern port in the colonies during the Revolution. British general Henry Clinton attacked and captured the city on May 12, 1780. American general Benjamin Lincoln and 5,500 Continentals surrendered to Clinton in what was the costliest defeat of the entire war.

Clinton, Henry (1738–1795) The British commander in chief from 1778 until 1782.

Continental Army The force raised and supported by the Continental Congress, and not loyal to the individual states as were the militias.

Continental Congress, First Met in September 1774, and representatives from twelve colonies issued the Statement of Rights and Grievances.

Continental Congress, Second Met in Philadelphia in May 1775. It established the Continental Army, headed by General Washington. The Second Continental Congress effectively ran the U.S. government throughout the war.

Cornwallis, Charles (1738–1805) A British general during the Revolution who commanded the South after 1780 and surrendered at Yorktown in 1781.

Cowpens, Battle of One of the colonies' greatest victories in the war. General Daniel Morgan defeated British forces on January 17, 1781, at the battle in the South Carolina backcountry, and captured hundreds of British soldiers and much-needed supplies.

Dorchester Heights A hill located just south of Boston; General Washington placed heavy artillery captured from Fort Ticonderoga here in March 1776 and forced British general William Howe to evacuate the city.

Dragoons Soldiers who rode on horses, but generally dismounted to fight.

Eutaw Springs, Battle of Fought to a draw by General Nathanael Greene and British colonel Alexander Stuart in South Carolina in September 1781, just before the British surrender at Yorktown.

Fort Johnson   Guarded the entrance to Charleston's harbor. Patriots seized the fort from the British in 1775; the British retook the fort (along with all of Charleston) in 1780 and abandoned it in 1782.

Fort Lee   An American fortification in New Jersey, across the Hudson River from New York City. Washington was forced to abandon the fort in November 1776.

Fort Mercer   An American structure on the Delaware River that guarded the approach to Philadelphia. The British captured Philadelphia in September 1777, but had to repeatedly attack Patriots at Fort Mercer and suffer many casualties before the Americans abandoned the fort in November.

Fort Ticonderoga   Located in upstate New York, south of Lake Champlain. Ethan Allen and his Green Mountain Boys, along with Benedict Arnold, captured the British-held fort in 1775 and procured badly needed artillery, which Washington was able to move and install on Dorchester Heights, forcing the British to abandon Boston.

Franklin, Benjamin (1706–1790)   Helped persuade the English Parliament to repeal the Stamp Act, represented Pennsylvania in the Continental Congress, and signed the Declaration of Independence. As minister to France, he was crucial in getting France to join the war effort, and he helped negotiate the Treaty of Paris in 1783.

French and Indian War (1756–1763)   That part of the Seven Years' War that took place in North America, it laid the groundwork for the Revolution. Britain defeated France and gained Canada and Florida. Parliament stationed troops in the colonies and raised taxes to pay for the war, resulting in the Stamp Act and the beginning of American resistance.

Gage, Thomas (1721–1787)   The British commander at Lexington-Concord and Bunker Hill. He was relieved of command and replaced by William Howe in 1775.

Gates, Horatio (1728–1806)   The American major general whose army defeated Burgoyne at Saratoga. Some wanted him to replace Washington as overall commander. Gates instead led the American Southern Army, but met disaster at the Battle of Camden in 1780; he was charged with abandoning his army and forced into retirement.

George III (1738–1820)   King of Great Britain and Ireland from 1760 to 1811.

Georgetown, Battle of   American commanders Henry Lee and Francis Marion attacked the British sixty miles north of Charleston, South Carolina, in January 1781. Though the battle technically ended in a draw, the Americans captured valuable supplies and several British officers.

German mercenaries   The British hired some 30,000 German soldiers to fight in America. Most came from the German state of Hesse-Cassel (hence the nickname Hessian). These soldiers took part in all major campaigns of the war.

Germantown, Battle of   British general William Howe captured Philadelphia in September 1777 and camped just outside the city at Germantown. Washington, having just lost at Brandywine, attacked the British on October 4, 1777, but the plan fell apart under heavy fog, and America was again defeated.

Grapeshot   Iron balls held together in a bag. When fired from cannon, the shot spread out and proved devastating to massed troops.

Great Bridge, Battle of   The first battle after Bunker Hill, and the first fought in Virginia. Virginia royal governor Lord Dunmore gathered British regulars, Loyalist militia, and freed slaves, and attacked American militia in December 1775. The Americans held, and Dunmore evacuated to a waiting British ship.

Greene, Nathanael (1742–1786)   An American major general who participated in most important northern battles and wintered at Valley Forge with Washington. Greene replaced Gates as southern commander after Gates was humiliated at Camden. Greene led local Patriot guerillas and won control of all of South Carolina except Charleston.

Green Mountain Boys   Name given to armed bands led by Ethan Allen; they captured Fort Ticonderoga and defended the territory that later became Vermont.

Guilford Courthouse, Battle of   Took place near modern Greensboro, North Carolina. American generals Nathanael Greene and Daniel Morgan engaged General Charles Cornwallis on March 15, 1781. Cornwallis evacuated north, only to become trapped at Yorktown in October.

Hale, Nathan (1755–1776)   An American officer who volunteered to spy on the British Army in New York but was captured by General William Howe and hanged for spying. His final words were reported to be, "I only regret that I have but one life to give for my country."

Hamilton, Henry (c. 1734–1796)   The commander of the British garrison at Detroit. He was known as "the hair buyer" because of rumors that he purchased American scalps from local Indians.

Hancock, John (1737–1793)   The richest merchant in Boston, he represented Massachusetts in the Continental Congress and served as president of the congress from 1775 to 1777. In his capacity as president, he was the first to sign the Declaration of Independence.

Hanging Rock, Battle of   Took place on August 6, 1780, just north of Camden, South Carolina. Patriot guerrilla leader Thomas Sumter attacked several companies of British soldiers. The fighting raged for almost four hours. The British held the field, but sustained heavy casualties. Sumter's men managed to loot the British camp and escape with valuable plunder.

Harlem Heights, Battle of   Took place on September 16, 1776, on Manhattan Island. British general William Howe attacked American troops under Washington and Nathanael Green who had constructed defensive positions on the heights. The battle ended in a draw.

Hart, Nancy Morgan (c. 1736–1830) A Georgia Patriot woman whose bravery became legendary. She single-handedly took on five Loyalists who had entered her home. After relaxing them with food and drink, she got possession of their rifles. In the end, she killed one, fatally wounded another, and held the remaining three until neighbors arrived and hanged them.

Hays, Mary Ludwig (1754–1832) The most famous of the women known as "Molly Pitcher," she is remembered for her bravery and perseverance for the cause. Hays accompanied her husband to the battle of Monmouth Courthouse and took over his gunnery duties when he passed out from the extreme heat of the June day.

Henry, Patrick (1736–1799) A Patriot orator and early Revolutionary leader. As a member of Virginia's House of Burgesses, he spoke passionately for independence, uttering the famous words, "Give me liberty or give me death."

Hessians (see **German mercenaries**)

Howe, Richard (1726–1799) The commander in chief of the British Navy in America from 1776 to 1778.

Howe, William (1729–1814) A British general and brother of Richard. William succeeded Thomas Gage as commander in chief of the British Army, serving from 1775 to 1778.

Intolerable Acts (or Coercive Acts) Five acts passed by Parliament in 1774 to punish the Americans for the Boston Tea Party. The Boston Port Bill closed that port until restitution was made for the destroyed tea, and the Quartering Act established that colonists must open their homes to British soldiers. These acts were primarily aimed against Massachusetts, but had the effect of uniting all thirteen colonies in moving toward independence.

Jaegers Hessians who were hunters in Germany. They were expert marksmen and proved especially useful to the British. They were called greencoats by the Americans because of their green uniforms.

Jay, John (1745–1829) A member of the Continental Congress from New York and the wartime ambassador to Spain. He wrote many of the Federalist Papers and later became the first chief justice of the Supreme Court.

Jefferson, Thomas (1743–1826) Represented Virginia in the Continental Congress and was chosen to author the Declaration of Independence. He served as minister to France, governor of Virginia, first secretary of state, second vice president, and third president of the United States (1801–1809). He died on July 4, 1826: exactly fifty years after the adoption of the Declaration of Independence and on the very same day John Adams died.

Jones, John Paul (1747–1792) The most famous American naval hero of the war. (See *Bonhomme Richard.*)

Kalb, Johann (1721–1780) Also known as Baron de Kalb. He came from a German peasant background but was an effective soldier and became an

American major general. Kalb accompanied General Horatio Gates to the Battle of Camden, where Gates refused to listen to Kalb's sound advice and ended up suffering a humiliating defeat. Kalb fought with bravery, was wounded eleven times in the battle, and died three days later.

Kentucky rifle   (see **American rifle**)

Kettle Creek, Battle of   Took place in Georgia on February 14, 1779. South Carolina and Georgia militia skirmished with Loyalist units; the battle slowed the British takeover of the Georgia backcountry.

King's Mountain, Battle of   Took place on October 7, 1780, in South Carolina and was an important victory for American militia. The battle boosted Patriot morale after the disastrous loss at Camden.

Knox, Henry (1750–1806)   A self-taught soldier who volunteered to fight in the Battle of Bunker Hill. He impressed General Washington, who appointed him commander of American artillery. Knox rose to major general and built the artillery into a valuable Patriot asset. Knox succeeded Washington as American commander in chief after the war in 1783.

Lafayette, Marquis de (1757–1834)   A French aristocrat who became enamored with the American Patriot movement. When he came to America with Johann Kalb and volunteered to fight without pay, Congress commissioned the nineteen-year-old as a major general. He proved invaluable in coordinating French and American movements in the final battle at Yorktown.

Lee, Henry (1756–1818)   An American cavalry leader nicknamed "Light-Horse Harry." Lee worked with Nathanael Greene and Francis Marion and fought at Yorktown.

Letters of Marque and Reprisal   Papers officially authorizing a ship to act as a privateer. The possession of these papers separated privateers working for governments from mere pirates and thus offered some protection to the captains and crews from execution for piracy.

Lexington-Concord, Battle of   The first shooting engagement of the Revolution; it took place on April 19, 1775. Massachusetts Patriots had stockpiled powder stores outside British-held Boston. British general Thomas Gage commanded 3,000 troops in the city and ordered a surreptitious action to capture some of these supplies. At night on April 18, Gage ordered some 600–800 of his men to quietly cross the bay by boat and march on Concord. Around 10 p.m., Paul Revere and William Dawes rode out toward Lexington and Concord to warn the militia.

Around 5 a.m. some 70 minutemen met the larger British advance. Outnumbered, the militia was dispersing when someone fired the first shot (the famed "shot heard 'round the world"). The British responded with two volleys and a bayonet charge that killed or wounded 18 Americans before continuing onward to Concord, where the British met a larger group of militia. After an exchange of fire, the British troops returned to Boston. Along the way, Patriot militia used guerrilla tactics to harass the British troops.

Liberty trees or **poles**   Symbols of the Revolution in American cities. The original liberty tree was an old elm in Boston where effigies were hung. Other cities erected liberty poles to protest or rally supporters to the cause of independence.

Lincoln, Benjamin (1733–1810)   An American major general who fought with distinction in the North and was named commander in chief of the Southern Army by Congress in 1778. There, he met defeat at Charleston, where he surrendered himself and his 5,000 Continentals to British general Henry Clinton. Lincoln was exchanged for two British generals and participated in the final victory at Yorktown.

Locke, John (1632–1704)   A popular British philosopher. Locke spoke of common sense and believed that humans possessed God-given natural rights that governments could not take away if they were to remain legitimate.

Long Island, Battle of   The first large-scale battle of the war; it took place on August 27, 1776. British general William Howe had based his 31,000 troops on Staten Island the previous month, and his brother Admiral Richard Howe commanded over 150 ships. George Washington's 10,000 troops were badly outnumbered, but charged with defending New York City from this massive enemy force. Washington's ablest officer, Nathanael Greene, knew the terrain around Brooklyn better than anyone else, but he fell ill and could not participate in the battle. He was replaced first by General John Sullivan, then General Israel Putnam, which caused much confusion in the American ranks. Ultimately, Washington was defeated; as a result, he was severely criticized afterward.

Loyalists (also called Tories)   Americans who sided with King George during the war. Loyalists raised troops for the British Army and also formed their own militia throughout the conflict. Loyalists have been estimated at a full one-third of the population of the colonies.

Marion, Francis (1732?–1795)   A South Carolina guerrilla leader known as the Swamp Fox. Marion and fellow guerrilla Thomas Sumter successfully harassed the British in South Carolina following British general Henry Clinton's victory at Charleston in 1780. Marion was made a brigadier general in the state militia for his efforts.

Massachusetts Government Act of 1774   One of the so-called Intolerable Acts passed by Parliament to punish the rebellious colony. The act effectively placed all governmental privileges in the hands of the royal governor.

McCrea, Jane   An American woman who was captured and murdered by Indians attached to British general John Burgoyne. The Americans used her story to recruit additional volunteers, helping to make possible Burgoyne's defeat at Saratoga.

Mercantilism   The theory and political economy in Europe during the sixteenth, seventeenth, and eighteenth centuries. The aspect of this theory that shaped Britain's treatment of the colonies was the belief that, in order to prosper, a nation needed to establish colonies whose major economic function was to provide raw materials which the mother country would then turn into finished goods that could be sold back to the colonies.

Militia   Organized bodies of part-time soldiers who reported to the individual states, whereas the Continental Army reported to Congress. Most militiamen did not have bayonets or their long rifles would not accommodate them. The British Army looked down on the American militia as little better than rabble.

Minisink, Battle of   Took place on July 19, 1779, in New York. Indian leader Joseph Brant led a group of his warriors with Loyalist allies to raid Minisink, New York. Local militia responded and pursued Brandt; however, the Indians trapped and massacred the militiamen.

Minutemen   The name given to the Massachusetts militia, who were supposed to be ready to muster at a minute's notice.

Molly Pitcher   A name given originally to Mary Hays and probably to several other Patriot women who provided soldiers with pitchers of water during battle.

Monmouth Courthouse, Battle of   The last major battle in the northern theater; it took place on June 28, 1778, in New Jersey. The British decided to abandon Philadelphia and head back to New York. General Washington attacked the British while they were marching across New Jersey. Washington had around 13,000 men to General Henry Clinton's 10,000. The battle ended in a confusing draw, with both sides suffering almost exactly the same number of deaths. Monmouth did, however, show that the newly trained Continental soldiers could face the British and stand their ground in an open field.

Moore's Creek Bridge, Battle of   Took place on February 27, 1776, in North Carolina. Even though North Carolina had ousted its royal governor, many Loyalists lived in the colony; they formed a 1,500-man militia and began a march toward Wilmington. Around 1,000 Patriot militiamen met them at Moore's Creek. The Patriots routed the Loyalists, killing or capturing most of them, along with 15,000 British pounds and much military equipment.

Morgan, Daniel (1736–1802)   A brigadier general in the Continental Army. He joined in the battles of Quebec and Saratoga and wintered with Washington at Valley Forge. Later, he moved to the southern command and defeated Tarleton at the Battle of Cowpens in 1781.

Morris, Robert (1734–1806)   Called the financier of the Revolution. He served in the Continental Congress from Pennsylvania and in 1781 became the superintendent of finances and worked desperately to shore up the worthless Continental currency.

Murphy, Timothy (1751–1818)   An illiterate Pennsylvanian who happened to be an expert marksman. He served with distinction from the Battle of Long Island to Yorktown. He was able to climb trees and pick off British officers at 300 yards.

Netherlands, The Remained neutral for most of the American Revolution, though they secretly aided America chiefly by shipping military supplies via the Dutch Caribbean. The Netherlands officially recognized the United States of America in April 1782.

Ninety-Six A backcountry town in South Carolina. Several roads converged here, so it was a natural meeting place, and two battles were fought here (in 1775 and 1781).

Ogeechee River, Battle of Took place in February 1778 in Georgia. Patriot leader Andrew Pickens ambushed some 800 Creek Indians fighting for the British. The Indians were on their way to reinforce British-held Augusta; this defeat complicated British plans to subdue Georgia.

Olive Branch Petition A document drawn up by the Continental Congress in July 1775 (after Lexington-Concord) in which the Americans listed their grievances and attempted to reconcile with Britain. King George III refused to even read the document and declared that the colonies were in open rebellion, thus pushing many colonists to support independence.

Oriskany, Battle of Took place on August 6, 1777, in New York. British lieutenant colonel Barry St. Leger commanded several hundred Mohawk warriors who attacked New York militia. The fighting quickly became brutal hand-to-hand combat, and both sides suffered heavy losses. The American leader, General Nicholas Herkimer, died from his wounds. The heavy losses of the Mohawks convinced the Mohawk leader Joseph Brant to abandon the British and return home.

Outliers Patriots in the southern colonies who would hide in the woods to avoid taking the loyalty oath to King George when Loyalist or British troops came through their towns.

Paine, Thomas (1737–1809) The English-born Patriot who authored the pamphlet *Common Sense* in 1776 that urged colonists to support the independence movement.

Paris, Treaty of (February 10, 1763) The treaty that ended the French and Indian War.

Paris, Treaty of (September 3, 1783) The treaty that officially ended the American Revolution. The treaty provided for official English recognition of an independent United States, set the borders of the new country, and dealt with navigation and fishing rights.

Parole The system of releasing prisoners of war who took an oath not to again take up arms in the struggle. Britain did this largely to spare the cost of supporting a large body of prisoners.

Paulus Hook, Battle of Took place on August 19, 1779, in coastal New Jersey. The raid was a victory for Major Henry Lee, and a badly needed boost to Patriot morale.

Penobscot Expedition Took place July–August 1779; was a naval disaster for the Patriots. Massachusetts dispatched ships and troops to dislodge

British fortifications in present-day Maine. The Americans wavered, became trapped, and were forced to destroy their ships and flee into the woods.

Pensacola, Battle of   Took place on May 9, 1781, in British-held West Florida. A combined Spanish and French force destroyed the British fort and caused the entire British garrison to surrender. This victory removed the British military from West Florida.

Philadelphia   The largest city in the colonies and the home of the Continental Congress, whose members were forced to flee the city twice to avoid British capture.

Pickens's Cherokee Expedition   Took place in 1782 in Georgia. South Carolina militia general Andrew Pickens brutally put down a Cherokee Indian uprising and forced the Native Americans to give up claims to East Georgia.

Pontiac's War   Took place following the French and Indian War in 1763–1764. The recently defeated French encouraged Indians to make war on their new British masters. Indian alliances attacked and captured many outpost forts before the British Army managed to defeat the Indians. Britain then proclaimed that the outpost lands were Indian Territory, which caused tensions with their expansion-minded colonies.

Princeton, Battle of   Took place on January 3, 1777, in New Jersey. General Washington pulled out victories here and at Trenton when American spirits were at their lowest, and doubtlessly saved the Revolution.

Privateers   Private ships authorized by Congress to raid and capture enemy ships. Since America lacked an effective navy, privateers played an important role during the Revolution.

Pulaski, Casimir (1748?–1779)   A Polish nobleman who came to fight for America. He became a brigadier general, but died from wounds received at the Battle of Savannah, in Georgia, on October 9, 1779.

Quartering Act   (see **Intolerable Acts**)

Quebec   The site of an unsuccessful American assault (1775–1776) led by General Benedict Arnold. Colonists hoped Canada would join their cause and become the fourteenth colony, but Loyalist sentiment was too strong there.

Regiment   (see **Battalion**)

Regulators   Backcountry protestors in North and South Carolina. In 1768, settlers in western South Carolina created vigilante committees to control the backcountry and resist the government in Charleston. In North Carolina, a similar movement occurred from 1768 to 1772. Their grievances against the colony's royal governor resulted in a local war. Governor William Tyron put the rebellion down with 1,100 troops in 1772.

Revere, Paul (1735–1818)   Assisted in planning the Boston Tea Party; famous for his ride in April 1775 to warn the Lexington-Concord militia that the British soldiers were approaching. He was captured and failed to complete his famous ride. He later took part in the disastrous Penobscot Expedition.

Rochambeau, Comte De (1750–1813)   Commander of all French forces in America after 1780. He worked well with Washington, and the two managed to trap British general Charles Cornwallis at Yorktown, effectively ending the war.

Samson, Deborah (1760–1827)   A woman who disguised herself as a man and fought with distinction in the Continental Army. After she was wounded, her identity was discovered. General Washington honorably discharged her from service. She became famous later in life for her patriotism, and Congress awarded her a pension in 1805.

Saratoga, Battle of   A moving series of engagements in the fall of 1777 in upstate New York that culminated in a major British defeat. General John Burgoyne was marching his army southward along the Hudson River. He was harassed and ultimately surrounded by a combined force under generals Horatio Gates, Daniel Morgan, and Benedict Arnold, and was forced to surrender himself and his force of some 5,000 British and German soldiers. This stunning victory raised American spirits and helped convince France to enter the fight against Britain.

Savannah, capture of   Took place on December 29, 1778, in Georgia. Following the deadlock at Monmouth Courthouse, the British decided to concentrate on securing the southern colonies, hoping to find many Loyalist allies to smash the Patriots. General William Howe sent some 3,500 troops to take Savannah, the colonial capital of Georgia. The Patriot defenders broke and fled before their superior enemy, allowing the British to seize the city with minimal losses. From Savannah, the British marched northward and seized Augusta, leaving only the backcountry for the Patriots.

Seven Years' War   (see **French and Indian War**)

Sons of Liberty   A clandestine Patriot organization organized by Samuel Adams in 1765 to protest the Stamp Act. The members often used violence and threats of violence to intimidate royal officials from carrying out their duties.

Southern Strategy   Employed by Great Britain in the latter part of the war, as it designed campaigns meant to take advantage of the large numbers of Loyalists, slaves, and allied Native Americans in the southern colonies.

Spain   Officially declared war on Britain in June 1779. Motivated more by the prospect of gaining British territory (especially Florida, which Spain had lost sixteen years earlier) than by a desire to support American independence, Spain confined its military action to attacking British fortifications along the Mississippi River and the Gulf Coast.

Stamp Act   Passed by Parliament in 1765; it directly taxed the colonies to help raise money that Britain had spent defeating the French in North America during the Seven Years' War. Colonists despised the Stamp Act and began violent protests upon its implementation.

Stamp Act Congress   The initial American response to the Stamp Act. Massachusetts took the lead and organized a meeting attended by nine of the thirteen colonies. The Congress lasted from October 7 to October 25, 1765, and issued the Declaration of Rights and Grievances, which described the Stamp Act as unfair taxation without representation.

Steuben, Friedrich Wilhelm Augustin von (1730–1794)   A Prussian war veteran who came to America in late 1777 and offered his services. Congress named him inspector general of the Continental Army. Though he spoke no English and only a little French, Steuben managed to drill and train the Continental Army and turn them into a more disciplined fighting force.

Sullivan's Island, Battle of   An early fight for South Carolina, in June 1776. British generals Henry Clinton and Charles Cornwallis converged on Charleston and attempted to seize the city. Fort Sullivan was hastily constructed with palmetto logs and manned by a force of Continental soldiers and local militia. British admiral Peter Parker sailed his ships close to the fort and bombarded it with cannonballs. The British cannonballs bounced off the spongy palmetto wood, allowing the Americans to return fire and force the British to withdraw.

Sumter, Thomas (1734–1832)   A successful South Carolina guerrilla leader, nicknamed "The Carolina Gamecock" for his daring fighting style. He was the last surviving Revolutionary War general when he died at ninety-seven years of age.

Tarleton, Banastre (1754–1833)   A British lieutenant colonel who commanded the British Legion in the southern theater in 1780 and 1781. He was feared and hated by southern Patriots for his brutality, and was called "The Butcher Tarleton." (see **Cowpens, Battle of**)

Tea Act   Passed by Parliament in May 1773. It propped up the economically foundering British East India Tea Company by forcing the American colonies to buy English tea only. Opposition in Massachusetts led to the Boston Tea Party.

Tories   (see **Loyalists**)

Trenton, Battle of   A crucial victory for Washington, which literally kept the Revolution alive. Washington commanded over 6,000 men in late December 1776, but the terms of enlistment for 4,000 of them were set to expire on December 31, so Washington decided to attack the German soldiers encamped across the Delaware River at Trenton, New Jersey. On Christmas night, Washington led his troops across the near-frozen river and surprised the sleeping Hessians. Washington's men routed the mercenaries, killing or capturing all of them without losing a single Continental soldier.

Valley Forge   Located outside Philadelphia; the place where the Continental Army spent a brutally cold winter in 1777–1778.

Washington, George (1732–1799)   A congressional representative from Virginia until named commander in chief of the Continental Army in June 1775. He lost more battles than he won, but Washington's greatest military achievement was keeping the ragtag Continental Army together and thereby keeping the dream of independence alive throughout the colonies. Following the surrender of the British at Yorktown, Washington resigned his commission in late December 1783. He later served as president of the Constitutional Convention in 1787 and first president of the United States from 1789 to 1797.

Wayne, Anthony (1745–1796) An American major general who participated in many crucial battles. He was called Mad Anthony for his courageous disregard for his personal safety.

West Point A fort strategically located on the Hudson River north of New York City. This fort stopped the British from sailing up and down the river and helped the Patriots maintain control of New York.

Yorktown, siege of Took place in September–October 1781 in Virginia. George Washington and French commander the Comte de Rochambeau managed to trap General Charles Cornwallis on the Yorktown peninsula, where the British commander surrendered, effectively ending the American Revolution.

Bibliography

Adams, Charles Francis, ed. *Letters of Mrs. Adams, the Wife of John Adams*. 4th ed. Boston: Wilkins, Carter, 1848.

Adams, John. *The Works of John Adams*. Edited by Charles Francis Adams. 10 vols. New York: Little, Brown, 1856.

Alexander, John K. "The Fort Wilson Incident of 1779: A Case Study of the Revolutionary Crowd." *William and Mary Quarterly,* 3rd ser., 31 (1974): 589–612.

Allen, Anne Alden. "Patriots and Loyalists: The Choice of Political Allegiance by the Members of Maryland's Proprietary Elite." *Journal of Southern History* 38 (1972): 283–292.

Allen, Robert S., ed. *The Loyal Americans: The Military Role of the Loyalist Provincial Corps and Their Settlement in British North America, 1775–1784*. Ottawa: National Museums of Canada, 1983.

Ammerman, David. *In the Common Cause: American Response to the Coercive Acts of 1774*. Charlottesville: University Press of Virginia, 1974.

Anderson, Fred. *The Crucible of War: The Seven Years' War and the Fate of Empire in British North America, 1754–1766*. New York: Knopf, 2000.

Andrews, Dee. *The Methodists and Revolutionary America, 1760–1800: The Shaping of Evangelical America*. Princeton, NJ: Princeton University Press, 2000.

Andrews, Doris. "Popular Religion and the Revolution in the Middle Atlantic Ports: The Rise of Methodists, 1770–1800." Ph.D. diss., University of Pennsylvania, 1986.

Anthony, Katharine Susan. *First Lady of the Revolution: The Life of Mercy Otis Warren*. Port Washington, NY: Kennikat, 1972.

Applewhite, Harriet B., and Darlene G. Levy, eds. *Women and Politics in the Age of Democratic Revolution*. Ann Arbor: University of Michigan Press, 1990.

Archer, Adair P. "The Quaker's Attitude Towards the Revolution." *William and Mary Quarterly,* 2d ser., 1 (1921): 167–182.

"A Speech of the Chiefs and Warriors of the Oneida Tribe of Indians, to the four New-England Provinces; directed immediately to Governor Trumbull, and by him to be communicated." *Pennsylvania Magazine; or, American Monthly Museum (1775–1776)* 1 (1775): 601–602.

Bailyn, Bernard. *Faces of Revolution: Personalities and Themes in the Struggle for American Independence.* New York: Vintage, 1992.

Bailyn, Bernard. *The Peopling of British North America: An Introduction.* New York: Knopf, 1986.

Bailyn, Bernard, and Barbara DeWolfe. *Voyagers to the West: A Passage in the Peopling of America on the Eve of the Revolution.* New York: Knopf, 1986.

Bailyn, Bernard, and Philip D. Morgan, eds. *Strangers within the Realm: Cultural Margins of the First British Empire.* Chapel Hill: University of North Carolina Press, 1991.

Baker, Frank. *From Wesley to Asbury: Studies in Early American Methodism.* Durham, NC: Duke University Press, 1976.

Baker, Gordon Pratt. *Those Incredible Methodists: A History of the Baltimore Conference of the United Methodist Church.* Baltimore: Baltimore Conference, 1972.

Bangs, Nathan. *The History of the Methodist Episcopal Church.* New York: Carlton and Porter, 1860.

Baseler, Marilyn C. *"Asylum for Mankind": America 1607–1800.* Ithaca, NY: Cornell University Press, 1998.

Beach, Edward L. *The United States Navy: 200 Years.* New York: Holt, 1986.

Becker, Carl L. *The History of Political Parties in the Province of New York, 1760–1776.* Madison: University of Wisconsin Press, 1909.

Beeman, Richard R. *The Evolution of the Southern Backcountry: A Case Study of Lunenburg County, Virginia, 1746–1832.* Philadelphia: University of Pennsylvania Press, 1984.

Belton, Bill. "The Indian Heritage of Crispus Attucks." *Negro History Bulletin* 35 (1972): 149–152.

Benton, William Allen. *Whig Loyalism: An Aspect of the Political Ideology in the American Revolutionary Era.* Rutherford, NJ: Fairleigh Dickinson University Press, 1969.

Berkin, Carol. *Jonathan Sewall: Odyssey of an American Loyalist.* New York: Columbia University Press, 1974.

Berkin, Carol. *Revolutionary Mothers: Women in the Struggle for America's Independence.* New York: Knopf, 2005.

Berlin, Ira. *Many Thousands Gone: The First Two Centuries of Slavery in North America.* Cambridge, MA: Harvard University Press, 1998.

Berlin, Ira, and Ronald Hoffman, eds. *Slavery and Freedom in the Age of the American Revolution.* Charlottesville: University Press of Virginia, 1983.

Blakely, Phyllis, and John Grant, eds. *Eleven Exiles: Accounts of Loyalists of the American Revolution.* Toronto: Dundurn, 1982.

Blumenthal, Walter Hart. *Women Camp Followers of the American Revolution.* New York: Arno, 1974.

Bohrer, Melissa Lukeman. *Glory, Passion, and Principle: The Story of Eight Remarkable Women at the Core of the American Revolution.* New York: Atria, 2003.

Bolster, Jeffrey. *Black Jacks: African American Seamen in the Age of Sail.* Cambridge, MA: Harvard University Press, 1997.

Bonomi, Patricia U. *A Factious People: Politics and Society in Colonial New York.* New York: Columbia University Press, 1971.

Bonomi, Patricia U. *Under the Cope of Heaven: Religion, Society, and Politics in Colonial America.* Oxford: Oxford University Press, 1986.

Booth, Sally Smith. *The Women of '76.* New York: Hastings House, 1973.

Bradley, Arthur. *The United Empire Loyalists.* London: Thornton Butterworth, 1971.

Branson, Susan. *Those Fiery, Frenchified Dames: Women and Political Culture in Early National Philadelphia.* Philadelphia: University of Pennsylvania Press, 2001.

Breen, T. H. *The Marketplace of Revolution: How Consumer Politics Shaped American Independence.* New York: Oxford University Press, 2004.

Breen, T. H. "Narrative of Commercial Life: Consumption, Ideology, and Community on the Eve of the American Revolution." *William and Mary Quarterly,* 3rd ser., 50 (1993): 471–501.

Breen, T. H. *Puritans and Adventurers: Change and Persistence in Early America.* New York: Oxford University Press, 1980.

Breen, T. H. *Tobacco Culture: The Mentality of the Great Tidewater Planters on the Eve of Revolution.* Princeton, NJ: Princeton University Press, 1985.

Brewer, Holly. "Entailing Aristocracy in Colonial Virginia: 'Ancient Feudal Restraints' and Revolutionary Reform." *William and Mary Quarterly,* 3rd ser., 54 (1997): 307–346.

Brinton, Howard H. *The Religious Philosophy of Quakerism: The Beliefs of Fox, Barclay, and Penn as Based on the Gospel of John.* Wallingford, PA: Pendle Hill Publications, 1973.

Brock, Peter. *Pioneers of the Peaceable Kingdom.* Princeton, NJ: Princeton University Press, 1968.

Brock, Peter. *The Quaker Peace Testimony, 1660–1914.* York, UK: Sessions Book Trust, 1990.

Brooke, John L. "To the Quiet of the People: Revolutionary Settlements and Civil Unrest in Western Massachusetts, 1774–1789." *William and Mary Quarterly,* 3rd ser., 46 (1989): 425–462.

Brooks, Joanna, and John Saillant, eds. *"Face Zion Forward": First Writers of the Black Atlantic.* Boston: Northeastern University Press, 2002.

Brown, Richard Maxwell, and Don E. Fehrenbacher, eds. *Tradition, Conflict and Modernization: Perspectives on the American Revolution.* New York: Academic, 1977.

Brown, Wallace. *The Good Americans: The Loyalists in the American Revolution.* New York: Morrow, 1969.

Brown, Wallace. *The King's Friends: The Composition and Motives of the American Loyalist Claimants.* Providence, RI: Brown University Press. 1965.

Brown, Wallace, and Hereward Senior. *Victorious in Defeat: The Loyalists in Canada.* Toronto: Methuen, 1984.

Buckley, James M. *Constitutional and Parliamentary History of the Methodist Episcopal Church.* New York: Methodist Book Concern, 1912.

Buel, Joy Day, and Richard Buel. *The Way of Duty: A Woman and Her Family in Revolutionary America.* New York: Norton, 1984.

Buel, Richard. *Dear Liberty: Connecticut's Mobilization for the Revolutionary War.* Middletown, CT: Wesleyan University Press, 1980.

Bullock, Steven C. *Revolutionary Brotherhood: Freemasonry and the Transformation of the American Social Order, 1730–1840.* Chapel Hill: University of North Carolina Press, 1998.

Bullock, Steven C. "The Revolutionary Transformation of American Freemasonry, 1752–1792." *William and Mary Quarterly,* 3rd ser., 47 (1990): 347–369.

Bushman, Richard L. "Farmers in Court: Orange County, North Carolina, 1750–1776." In *The Many Legalities of Early America,* ed. Christopher L. Tomlins and Bruce H. Mann, 388–413. Chapel Hill: University of North Carolina Press, 2001.

Butler, Jon. *Awash in a Sea of Faith: Christianizing the American People.* Cambridge, MA: Harvard University Press, 1990.

Butler, Jon. *The Huguenots in America: A Refugee People in New World Society.* Cambridge, MA: Harvard University Press, 1983.

Calhoon, Robert McCluer. *The Loyalists in the American Revolution, 1760–1781.* New York: Harcourt Brace Jovanovich, 1973.

Calhoon, Robert McCluer, Timothy M. Barnes, and George A. Rawlyk, eds. *Loyalists and Community in North America.* Westport, CT: Greenwood, 1994.

Callahan, North. *Flight from the Republic: The Tories of the American Revolution.* Indianapolis: Bobbs-Merrill, 1967.

Calloway, Colin G. *New Worlds for All: Indians, Europeans, and the Remaking of Early America.* Baltimore: Johns Hopkins University Press, 1997.

Calloway, Colin G. "'We Have Always Been the Frontier': The American Revolution in Shawnee Country." *American Indian Quarterly* 16 (1992): 39–52.

Calloway, Colin G. *The Western Abenakis of Vermont, 1600–1800: War, Migration, and the Survival of an Indian People.* Norman: University of Oklahoma Press, 1990.

Calvert, Karin. *Children in the House: The Material Culture of Early Childhood, 1600–1900.* Boston: Northeastern University Press, 1992.

Carson, James Taylor. *Searching for the Bright Path: The Mississippi Choctaws from Prehistory to Removal.* Lincoln: University of Nebraska Press, 1999.

Cashin, Edward J. *The King's Ranger: Thomas Brown and the American Revolution on the Southern Frontier.* Athens: University of Georgia Press, 1989.

Cayton, Andrew R. L., and Fredrika J. Teute, eds. *Contact Points: American Frontiers from the Mohawk Valley to the Mississippi, 1750–1830.* Chapel Hill: University of North Carolina Press, 1998.

Chernow, Ron. *Alexander Hamilton.* New York: Penguin, 2004.

Clark, Elmer T., ed. *Journal and Letters of Francis Asbury.* 3 vols. London: Hazell, Watson and Viney, 1958.

Cleary, Patricia. *Elizabeth Murray: A Woman's Pursuit of Independence in Eighteenth-Century America.* Amherst: University of Massachusetts Press, 2000.

Cole, Adelaide. "Anne Bailey: Woman of Courage." *DAR Magazine* 114 (1980): 322–325.

Collections of the Massachusetts Historical Society. 5th series, III. Boston: Massachusetts Historical Society, 1877.

Colley, Linda. *Britons: Forging the Nation, 1707–1837.* New Haven, CT: Yale University Press, 1992.

Conway, Stephen. "'The Great Mischief Complain'd of': Reflections on the Misconduct of British Soldiers in the Revolutionary War." *William and Mary Quarterly,* 3rd ser., 47 (1990): 370–390.

Cope, Gilbert. "Chester County Quakers during the Revolution." *Bulletin of the Chester County Historical Society* (1902–1903): 15–26.

Coulter, E. Merton. "Nancy Hart, Georgia Heroine of the Revolution." *Georgia Historical Quarterly* 39 (1965): 118–131.

Countryman, Edward. *The American Revolution.* 1985. Rev. ed. New York: Hill and Wang, 2003.

Countryman, Edward. "Indians, the Colonial Order, and the Social Significance of the American Revolution." *William and Mary Quarterly,* 3rd ser., 53 (1996): 342–366.

Countryman, Edward. "The Use of Capital in Revolutionary America: The Case of the New York Loyalist Merchants." *William and Mary Quarterly* 3rd ser., 49 (1992): 3–28.

Crane, Elaine Forman. *A Dependent People: Newport, Rhode Island, in the Revolutionary Era.* Bronx, NY: Fordham University Press, 1985.

Crary, Catherine. *The Price of Loyalty: Tory Writings from the Revolutionary Era.* New York: McGraw-Hill, 1973.

Creighton, Margaret S., and Lisa Norling, eds. *Iron Men, Wooden Women: Gender and Seafaring in the Atlantic World, 1700–1920.* Baltimore: Johns Hopkins University Press, 1996.

Crow, Jeffrey J. "Slave Rebelliousness and Social Conflict in North Carolina, 1775–1802." *William and Mary Quarterly,* 3rd ser., 37 (1980): 79–102.

Cuneo, John R. "The Early Days of the Queen's Rangers, August 1776–February 1777." *Military Affairs* 22 (1958): 65–74.

Daniels, Roger. *Coming to America: A History of Immigration and Ethnicity in American Life.* New York: Harper Collins, 1990.

Davis, David Brion. *The Problem of Slavery in the Age of Revolution, 1770–1823.* Ithaca, NY: Cornell University Press, 1975.

Davis, Robert Scott, Jr., ed. "The Wrightsborough Quakers and the American Revolution." *Southern Friend* 4 (1982): 3–16.

Davis, Timothy. *A Letter from a Friend to some of his Intimate Friends, on the Subject of Paying Taxes, &c.* Watertown, MA: Edes, 1776.

Degler, Carl N. *At Odds: Women and the Family in America from the Revolution to the Present.* New York: Oxford University Press, 1980.

De Pauw, Linda Grant. *Fortunes of War: New Jersey Women and the American Revolution.* Trenton: New Jersey Historical Commission, 1976.

De Warville, J. P. Brissot. *New Travels in the United States of America, Performed in 1788.* Boston: Joseph Bumstead, 1797.

Diamant, Lincoln, ed. *Revolutionary Women in the War for American Independence: A One-Volume Revised Edition of Elizabeth Ellet's 1848 Landmark Series.* Westport, CT: Praeger, 1998.

Dickson, R. J. *Ulster Emigration to Colonial America, 1718–1775.* London: Routledge, 1966.

Dinnerstein, Leonard, and David Reimers. *Ethnic Americans: A History of Immigration and Assimilation.* 4th ed. New York: Columbia University Press, 1999.

Dowd, Gregory Evans. *A Spirited Resistance: The North American Indian Struggle for Unity, 1745–1815.* Baltimore: Johns Hopkins University Press, 1992.

Dowd, Gregory Evans. *War under Heaven: Pontiac, the Indian Nations, and the British Empire.* Baltimore: Johns Hopkins University Press, 2004.

Draper, Theodore. *A Struggle for Power: The American Revolution.* New York: Times Books, 1996.

Egerton, Douglas R. *Gabriel's Rebellion: The Virginia Slave Conspiracies of 1800 and 1802.* Chapel Hill: University of North Carolina Press, 1993.

Egnal, Marc. *A Mighty Empire: The Origins of the American Revolution.* Ithaca, NY: Cornell University Press, 1988.

Egnal, Marc. "The Origins of the Revolution in Virginia: A Reinterpretation." *William and Mary Quarterly,* 3rd ser., 37 (1980): 401–428.

Einstein, Lewis. *Divided Loyalties: Americans in England during the War of Independence.* Freeport, NY: Books for Libraries, 1969.

Ekirch, A. Roger. *"Poor Carolina": Politics and Society in Colonial North Carolina, 1729–1776.* Chapel Hill: University of North Carolina Press, 1981.

Ellis, Joseph J. *Founding Brothers: The Revolutionary Generation.* New York: Knopf, 2001.

Ellis, Joseph J. *George Washington.* New York: Knopf, 2004.

Engle, Paul. *Women in the American Revolution.* Chicago: Follett, 1976.

Evans, Elizabeth. *Weathering the Storm: Women of the American Revolution.* New York: Scribner's, 1975.

Evans, G. N. D., ed. *Allegiance in America: The Case of the Loyalists.* Reading, MA: Addison-Wesley, 1969.

Fenn, Elizabeth. *Pox Americana: The Great Smallpox Epidemic of 1775–1782.* New York: Hill and Wang, 2001.

Ferling, John. *The Loyalist Mind: Joseph Galloway and the American Revolution.* University Park: Pennsylvania State University Press, 1977.

Fingerhut, Eugene. *Survivor: Cadwallader Colden II in Revolutionary America.* Washington, DC: University Press of America, 1983.

Finkelman, Paul. "Slavery and the Constitutional Convention: Making a Covenant with Death." In *Origins of the Constitution and American National Identity,* ed. Richard Beeman, Stephen Botein, and Edward C. Carter II, 188–225. Chapel Hill: University of North Carolina Press, 1987.

Fischer, David Hackett. *Albion's Seed: Four British Folkways in America.* New York: Oxford University Press, 1991.

Fischer, David Hackett. *Paul Revere's Ride.* New York: Oxford University Press, 1994.

Fischer, David Hackett. *Washington's Crossing.* New York: Oxford University Press, 2004.

Fogelman, Aaron Spencer. "From Slaves, Convicts, and Servants to Free Passengers: The Transformation of Immigration in the Era of the American Revolution." *Journal of American History* 85 (1998): 43–76.

Fogelman, Aaron Spencer. *Hopeful Journeys: German Immigration, Settlement, and Political Culture in Colonial America, 1717–1775.* Philadelphia: University of Pennsylvania Press, 1996.

Fogelman, Aaron Spencer. "Migrations to the Thirteen British North American Colonies, 1700–1775: New Estimates." *Journal of Interdisciplinary History* 22 (1991): 691–709.

Foner, Eric. *Tom Paine and Revolutionary America.* New York: Oxford University Press, 1976.

Foner, Philip S. *Blacks in the American Revolution.* Westport, CT: Greenwood, 1976.

Foner, Philip S. *Labor and the American Revolution.* Westport, CT: Greenwood, 1977.

Foster, Thyra Jane, et al. *Rhode Island Quakers in the American Revolution, 1775–1790.* Providence, RI: Published for Providence Monthly Meeting of Friends, 1977.

Fowler, William M., Jr. *Empires at War: The French and Indian War and the Struggle for North America, 1754–1763.* New York: Walker, 2005.

Frank, Andrew K. *Creeks and Southerners: Biculturalism on the Early American Frontier.* Lincoln: University of Nebraska Press, 2005.

Franklin, John Hope. "The North, the South and the American Revolution." *Journal of American History* 62 (1975–1976): 5–23.

Frey, Sylvia R. *The British Soldier in America: A Social History of Military Life in the Revolutionary Period.* Austin: University of Texas Press, 1981.

Frey, Sylvia R. *Water from the Rock: Black Resistance in a Revolutionary Age.* Princeton, NJ: Princeton University Press, 1991.

Frey, Sylvia R., and Betty Wood. *Come Shouting to Zion: African American Christianity in the American South and British Caribbean to 1830.* Chapel Hill: University of North Carolina Press, 1998.

Geggus, David P. *The Impact of the Haitian Revolution in the Atlantic World.* Columbia: University of South Carolina Press, 2001.

Geggus, David P., and Barry Gaspar, eds. *A Turbulent Time: The French Revolution and the Greater Caribbean.* Bloomington: Indiana University Press, 1997.

Gemery, Henry A. "The White Population of the Colonial United States, 1607–1790." In *A Population History of North America,* ed. Michael R. Haines and Richard H. Steckel, 143–190. New York: Cambridge University Press 2000.

Gilje, Paul A. *Liberty on the Waterfront: American Maritime Culture in the Age of Revolution.* Philadelphia: University of Pennsylvania Press, 2003.

Gilje, Paul A. *The Road to Mobocracy: Popular Disorder in New York City, 1763–1834.* Chapel Hill: University of North Carolina Press, 1987.

Gilje, Paul A., and Howard B. Rock. *Keepers of the Revolution: New Yorkers at Work in the Early Republic.* Ithaca, NY: Cornell University Press, 1992.

Gilpin, Thomas, ed. *Exiles in Virginia: With Observations on the Conduct of the Society of Friends during the Revolutionary War.* Philadelphia: Sherman, 1848.

Goddard, Nathaniel. *Nathaniel Goddard: A Boston Merchant, 1767–1853.* Cambridge, MA: Printed at the Riverside Press for private distribution, 1906.

Gordon, Colin. "Crafting a Usable Past: Consensus, Ideology, and Historians of the American Revolution." *William and Mary Quarterly,* 3rd ser., 46 (1989): 671–695.

Graham, I. C. C. *Colonists from Scotland: Emigration to North America, 1707–1763.* Ithaca, NY: Cornell University Press, 1956.

Graymont, Barbara. *The Iroquois in the American Revolution.* Syracuse, NY: Syracuse University Press, 1972.

Greene, Evarts B., and Virginia D. Harrington. *American Population before the Federal Census of 1790.* New York: Columbia University Press, 1932.

Greene, Jack P. "The Social Origins of the American Revolution: An Evaluation and an Interpretation." *Political Science Quarterly* 88 (1973): 1–22.

Greven, Philip J., Jr. *The Protestant Temperament: Patterns of Child-Rearing, Religious Experience and the Self in Early America.* New York: Knopf, 1977.

Grey, Isaac. *A Serious Address to Such of the People Called Quakers, on the Continent of North America, as Profess Scruples Relative to the Present Government.* Philadelphia: Styner and Cist, 1778.

Grimsley, Mark. *The Hard Hand of War: Union Military Policy toward Southern Civilians, 1861–1865.* New York: Cambridge University Press, 1995.

Gross, Robert A. *The Minutemen and Their World.* New York: Hill and Wang, 1976.

Gross, Robert A., ed. *In Debt to Shays: The Bicentennial of an Agrarian Rebellion.* Charlottesville: University Press of Virginia, 1993.

Grubb, Farley. "German Immigration to Pennsylvania, 1709–1820." *Journal of Interdisciplinary History 20* (1990): 417–436.

Gundersen, Joan R. *To Be Useful to the World: Women in Revolutionary America, 1740–1790.* New York: Twayne, 1996.

Hall, Leslie. *Land and Allegiance in Revolutionary Georgia.* Athens: University of Georgia Press, 2001.

Handlin, Oscar. *The Uprooted.* 2nd ed. Boston: Little, Brown, 1973.

Hansen, Marcus Lee. *The Atlantic Migration, 1607–1860: A History of the Continuing Settlement of the United States.* Cambridge, MA: Harvard University Press, 1940.

Harkness, David James. *Southern Heroines of the American Revolution: A Bicentennial Publication.* Knoxville: University of Tennessee Press, 1973.

Hatch, Nathan. *The Democratization of American Christianity.* New Haven, CT: Yale University Press, 1989.

Hatley, Tom. *The Dividing Paths: Cherokees and South Carolinians through the Revolutionary Era.* New York: Oxford University Press, 1995.

Heimert, Alan. *Religion and the American Mind from the Great Awakening to the Revolution.* New York: Cambridge University Press, 1966.

Heitzenrater, Richard P. *Wesley and the People Called Methodists.* Nashville, TN: Abingdon, 1995.

Hempton, David. *The Religion of the People: Methodism and Popular Culture, c. 1750–1900.* London: Routledge, 1996.

Heyrman, Christine. *Southern Cross: The Beginnings of the Bible Belt.* New York: Knopf, 1997.

Higginbotham, Don. *The War of American Independence: Military Attitudes, Policies, and Practice, 1763–1789.* New York: Macmillan, 1971.

Higginbotham, Don. *War and Society in Revolutionary America: The Wider Dimensions of Conflict.* Columbia: University of South Carolina Press, 1988.

Hinderaker, Eric, and Peter C. Mancall. *At the Edge of Empire: The Backcountry in British North America.* Baltimore: Johns Hopkins University Press, 2003.

Hirst, Margaret E. *The Quakers in Peace and War: An Account of Their Peace Principles and Practice.* New York: Doran, 1923.

Hoerder, Dirk. *Crowd Action in Revolutionary Massachusetts, 1765–1780.* New York: Academic, 1977.

Hoffer, Peter Charles. *Revolution and Regeneration: Life Cycle and the Historical Vision of the Generation of 1776.* Athens: University of Georgia Press, 1982.

Hoffman, Ronald. *A Spirit of Dissension: Economics, Politics and the Revolution in Maryland.* Baltimore: Johns Hopkins University Press, 1974.

Hoffman, Ronald, and Peter J. Albert, eds. *Slavery and Freedom in the Age of the American Revolution.* Charlottesville: University Press of Virginia, 1983.

Hoffman, Ronald, and Peter J. Albert, eds. *The Transforming Hand of Revolution: Reconsidering the American Revolution as a Social Movement.* Charlottesville: University Press of Virginia, 1995.

Hoffman, Ronald, and Peter J. Albert, eds. *Women in the Age of the Revolution.* Charlottesville: University Press of Virginia, 1989.

Hoffman, Ronald, Thad W. Tate, and Peter J. Albert, eds. *An Uncivil War: The Southern Backcountry during the American Revolution.* Charlottesville: University Press of Virginia, 1985.

Holton, Woody. *Forced Founders: Indians, Debtors, Slaves, and the Making of the American Revolution in Virginia.* Chapel Hill: University of North Carolina Press, 1999.

Holton, Woody. "The Ohio Indians and the Coming of the American Revolution in Virginia." *Journal of Southern History* 60 (1994): 453–478.

Holton, Woody. "'Rebel against Rebel': Enslaved Virginians and the Coming of the American Revolution." *Virginia Magazine of History and Biography* 105 (1997): 157–192.

Horton, James Oliver, and Lois E. Horton. *In Hope of Liberty: Culture, Community and Protest among Northern Free Blacks, 1700–1860.* New York: Oxford University Press, 1997.

Howarth, Stephen. *To Shining Sea: A History of the United States Navy, 1775–1991.* New York: Random House, 1991.

"How Revolutionary Was the Revolution: A Discussion of Gordon Wood's *The Radicalism of the American Revolution*." *William and Mary Quarterly,* 3rd ser., 51 (1994): 677–716.

Illick, Joseph E. *American Childhoods.* Philadelphia: University of Pennsylvania Press, 2002.

Isaac, Rhys. "Dramatizing the Ideology of Revolution: Popular Mobilization in Virginia, 1774 to 1776." *William and Mary Quarterly,* 3rd ser., 33 (1976): 357–385.

Isaac, Rhys. *The Transformation of Virginia, 1740–1790.* Chapel Hill: University of North Carolina Press, 1982.

James, Sydney V. "The Impact of the American Revolution on Quakers' Ideas about Their Sect." *William and Mary Quarterly,* 3rd ser., 19 (1962): 360–382.

Jameson, J. Franklin. *The American Revolution Considered as a Social Movement.* Princeton, NJ: Princeton University Press, 1926.

Jellison, Richard M., ed. *Society, Freedom, and Conscience: The American Revolution in Virginia, Massachusetts, and New York.* New York: Norton, 1976.

Jennings, Francis. *The Creation of America: Through Revolution to Empire.* New York: Cambridge University Press, 2000.

Jennings, Francis. "Indians' Revolution." In *The American Revolution: Explorations in the History of American Radicalism*, ed. Alfred Young, 319–382. De Kalb: University of Northern Illinois Press, 1978.

Jensen, Merrill. *The American Revolution within America.* New York: New York University Press, 1974.

Jensen, Merrill. *The Founding of a Nation: A History of the American Revolution, 1763–1776.* New York: Oxford University Press, 1968.

Jones, Maldwyn Allen. *American Immigration.* 2nd ed. Chicago: University of Chicago Press, 1992.

Juster, Susan. *Disorderly Women: Sexual Politics and Evangelicalism in Revolutionary New England.* Ithaca, NY: Cornell University Press, 1994.

Kaplan, Sidney. *The Black Presence in the Era of the American Revolution, 1770–1800.* Washington, DC: National Portrait Gallery, 1973.

Kaplan, Sidney. "The 'Domestic Insurrections' of the Declaration of Independence." *Journal of Negro History* 61 (1976): 243–255.

Kars, Marjoleine. *Breaking Loose Together: The Regulator Rebellion in Pre-Revolutionary North Carolina.* Chapel Hill: University of North Carolina Press, 2002.

Kashatus, William C., III. *Conflict of Conviction: A Reappraisal of Quaker Involvement in the American Revolution.* Lanham, MD: University Press of America, 1990.

Katz, Stanley N., John M. Murrin, and Douglas Greenburg, eds. *Colonial America: Essays in Politics and Social Development.* 5th ed. New York: McGraw-Hill, 2001.

Keller, Rosemary. *Patriotism and the Female Sex: Abigail Adams and the American Revolution.* Brooklyn, NY: Carlson, 1994.

Kerber, Linda K. *Women of the Republic: Intellect and Ideology in Revolutionary America.* Chapel Hill: University of North Carolina Press, 1980.

Kierner, Cynthia A. *Southern Women in Revolution, 1776–1800: Personal and Political Narratives.* Columbia: University of South Carolina Press, 1998.

Kim, Sung Bok. "Impact of Class Relations and Warfare in the American Revolution: The New York Experience." *Journal of American History* 69 (1982): 326–346.

Kim, Sung Bok. *Landlord and Tenant in Colonial New York: Manorial Society, 1664–1775.* Chapel Hill: University of North Carolina Press, 1978.

Kirby, James E., Russell E. Richey, and Kenneth E. Rowe. *The Methodists.* Westport, CT: Greenwood, 1996.

Klein, Rachel N. *Unification of a Slave State: The Rise of the Planter Class in the South Carolina Backcountry, 1760–1808.* Chapel Hill: University of North Carolina Press, 1889.

Kulikoff, Allan. "The Politics of Inequality in Revolutionary Boston." *William and Mary Quarterly,* 3rd ser., 28 (1971): 375–412.

Kurtz, Stephen G., and James H. Hutson, eds. *Essays on the American Revolution.* Chapel Hill: University of North Carolina Press, 1973.

Lambert, Frank. *Inventing the "Great Awakening."* Princeton, NJ: Princeton University Press, 1999.

Lambert, Robert Stanebury. *South Carolina Loyalists in the American Revolution.* Columbia: University of South Carolina Press, 1987.

Landsman, Ned C. "Nation, Migration, and the Province in the First British Empire: Scotland and the Americas, 1600–1800." *American Historical Review* 104 (1999): 463–475.

Landsman, Ned C. *Scotland and Its First American Colony, 1683–1765.* Princeton, NJ: Princeton University Press, 1985.

Laska, Vera O. *"Remember the Ladies": Outstanding Women of the American Revolution.* Boston: Commonwealth of Massachusetts Bicentennial Commission, 1976.

Lawrence, Anna. "The Transatlantic Methodist Family: Gender, Revolution and Evangelicalism in America and England, c. 1730–1815." Ph.D. dissertation, University of Michigan, 2004.

Lee, Jean B. *The Price of Nationhood: The American Revolution in Charles County.* New York: Norton, 1994.

Lee, Jesse. *A Short History of the Methodists in the United States of America.* Baltimore: Magill and Clime, 1810.

Lemisch, Jesse. "The American Revolution Seen from the Bottom Up." In *Toward a New Past: Dissenting Essays in American History,* ed. Barton J. Bernstein, 3–45. New York: Random House, 1968.

Lemisch, Jesse. "Jack Tar in the Streets: Merchant Seamen in the Politics of Revolutionary America." *William and Mary Quarterly,* 3rd ser., 25 (1968): 371–407.

Lemisch, Jesse. *Jack Tar vs. John Bull: The Role of New York's Seamen in Precipitating the Revolution.* New York: Garland Publishing, 1997.

Lemisch, Jesse. "Listening to the 'Inarticulate': William Eidger's Dream and the Loyalties of American Revolutionary Seamen in British Prisons." *Journal of Social History* 3 (1969–1970): 1–29.

Lewis, Jan. *The Pursuit of Happiness: Family and Values in Jefferson's Virginia.* New York: Cambridge University Press, 1983.

Leyburn, James G. *The Scotch-Irish: A Social History.* Chapel Hill: University of North Carolina Press, 1962.

Linebaugh, Peter, and Marcus Rediker. *The Many-Headed Hydra: Sailors, Slaves, Commoners, and the Hidden History of the Revolutionary Atlantic.* Boston: Beacon, 2000.

Lockridge, Kenneth A. "Land, Population and the Evolution of New England Society, 1630–1790." *Past and Present* 39 (1968): 62–81.

Lockridge, Kenneth A. "Social Change and the Meaning of the American Revolution." *Journal of Social History* 6 (1972–1973): 397–439.

Lyerly, Cynthia. *Methodism and the Southern Mind, 1770–1810.* Oxford: Oxford University Press, 1999.

Lynd, Staughton, and Alfred F. Young. "After Carl Becker: The Mechanics and New York City Politics, 1774–1801." *Labor History* 5 (1964): 215–276.

MacKinnon, Neil. *This Unfriendly Soil: The Loyalist Experience in Nova Scotia, 1783–1791.* Kingston, Ontario: McGill-Queen's University Press, 1986.

Mahan, Alfred Thayer. *The Influence of Sea Power upon History, 1660–1783* [1890]. New York: Barnes and Noble, 2001.

Maier, Pauline. *From Resistance to Revolution: Colonial Radicals and the Development of American Opposition to Britain, 1765–1776.* New York: Knopf, 1972.

Maier, Pauline. "Popular Uprisings and Civil Authority in Eighteenth-Century America." *William and Mary Quarterly,* 3rd ser., 27 (1970): 3–35.

Maier, Pauline. "The Revolutionary Origins of the American Corporation." *William and Mary Quarterly,* 3rd ser., 50 (1993): 51–84.

Maier, Pauline. "Why Revolution? Why Democracy?" *Journal of Interdisciplinary History* 6 (1975–1976): 711–732.

Maier, Pauline. *The Upper House in Revolutionary America, 1763–1788.* Madison: University of Wisconsin Press, 1967.

Main, Jackson Turner. *The Social Structure of Revolutionary America.* Princeton, NJ: Princeton University Press, 1965.

Mancall, Peter C. "The Revolutionary War and the Indians of the Upper Susquehanna Valley." *American Indian Culture and Resource Journal* 12 (1988): 39–58.

Mandell, Daniel R. *Behind the Frontier: Indians in Eighteenth-Century Eastern Massachusetts.* Lincoln: University of Nebraska Press, 1996.

Marietta, Jack D. *The Reformation of American Quakerism, 1748–1783.* Philadelphia: University of Pennsylvania Press, 1984.

Marsh, Ben. "Women and the American Revolution in Georgia." *Georgia Historical Quarterly* 88 (2004): 157–178.

Mays, David John, ed. *The Letters and Papers of Edmund Pendleton.* 2 vols. Charlottesville: University Press of Virginia, 1967.

McCaughey, Elizabeth. *From Loyalist to Founding Father: The Political Odyssey of William Samuel Johnson.* New York: Columbia University Press, 1980.

McConville, Brendan. *These Daring Disturbers of the Public Peace: The Struggle for Property in Early New Jersey.* Ithaca, NY: Cornell University Press, 1999.

Mekeel, Arthur J. *The Relation of the Quakers to the American Revolution.* Washington, DC: University Press of America, 1979.

Melish, Joanne Pope. *Disowning Slavery: Gradual Emancipation and "Race" in New England, 1780–1860.* Ithaca, NY: Cornell University Press, 1998.

Merrell, James H. *The Indians' New World: Catawbas and Their Neighbors from European Contact through the Era of Removal.* Chapel Hill: University of North Carolina Press, 1989.

Merritt, Jane T. *At the Crossroads: Indians and Empires on a Mid-Atlantic Frontier, 1700–1763.* Chapel Hill: University of North Carolina Press, 2003.

Meyer, Edith Patterson. *Petticoat Patriots of the American Revolution.* New York: Vanguard, 1976.

Morgan, Philip D. *Slave Counterpoint: Black Culture in the Eighteenth-Century Chesapeake and Lowcountry.* Chapel Hill: University of North Carolina Press, 1998.

Morris, Richard B. *Government and Labor in Early America.* New York: Harper and Row, 1946.

Morris, Richard B. "'We the People of the United States': The Bicentennial of a People's Revolution." *American Historical Review* 82 (1977): 1–19.

Mullin, Gerald W. *Flight and Rebellion: Slave Resistance in Eighteenth-Century Virginia.* New York: Oxford University Press, 1972.

Murray, Gail Schmunk. *American Children's Literature and the Construction of Childhood.* New York: Twayne, 1998.

Nadelhaft, Jerome J. *The Disorders of War: The Revolution in South Carolina.* Orono: University of Maine Press, 1981.

Nash, Gary B. *Forging Freedom: The Formation of Philadelphia's Black Community, 1720–1840.* Cambridge, MA: Harvard University Press, 1988.

Nash, Gary B. *Race and Revolution.* Madison, WI: Madison House, 1990.

Nash, Gary B. *The Unknown American Revolution: The Unruly Birth of Democracy and the Struggle to Create America.* New York: Viking, 2005.

Nash, Gary B. *The Urban Crucible: Social Change, Political Consciousness, and the Origins of the American Revolution.* Cambridge, MA: Harvard University Press, 1979.

Neely, Thomas B. *A History of the Origin and Development of the Governing Conference in Methodism, and Especially the General Conference of the Methodist Episcopal Church.* New York: Hunt and Eaton, 1892.

Nelson, William. *The American Tory.* Oxford: Clarendon Press, 1961.

Newman, Debra L. "Black Women in the Era of the American Revolution in Pennsylvania." *Journal of Negro History* 61 (1976): 276–289.

Newton, Algie I. "The Battle of New Garden." *Southern Friend* 16 (1994): 11.

Nobles, Gregory H. "Breaking into the Backcountry: New Approaches to the Early American Frontier." *William and Mary Quarterly,* 3rd ser., 46 (1989): 641–670.

Nobles, Gregory H. *Divisions throughout the Whole: Politics and Society in Hampshire County, Massachusetts, 1740–1775.* New York: Cambridge University Press, 1983.

Norton, Mary Beth. *The British-Americans: The Loyalist Exiles in England, 1774–1789.* Boston: Little, Brown, 1972.

Norton, Mary Beth. "Eighteenth-Century American Women in Peace and War: The Case of the Loyalists." *William and Mary Quarterly,* 3rd ser., 33 (1976): 386–409.

Norton, Mary Beth. "The Fate of Some Black Loyalists of the American Revolution." *Journal of Negro History* 58 (1973): 402–426.

Norton, Mary Beth. *Liberty's Daughters: The Revolutionary Experience of American Women, 1750–1800.* 2nd ed. Ithaca, NY: Cornell University Press, 1996.

Oaks, Robert F. "Philadelphians in Exile: The Problem of Loyalty during the American Revolution." *Pennsylvania Magazine of History and Biography* 96 (1972): 298–325.

O'Brien, Greg. *The Choctaws in a Revolutionary Age.* Lincoln: University of Nebraska Press, 2002.

O'Donnell, James H., III. *The Southern Indians in the American Revolution.* Knoxville: University of Tennessee Press, 1973.

Okoye, F. Nwabueze. "Chattel Slavery as the Nightmare of the American Revolutionaries." *William and Mary Quarterly,* 3rd ser., 37 (1980): 3–28.

Olwell, Robert A. "'Domestick Enemies': Slavery and Political Independence in South Carolina, May 1775–March 1776." *Journal of Southern History* 55 (1989): 21–48.

Olwell, Robert A. *Masters, Slaves and Subjects: The Culture of Power in the South Carolina Low Country, 1740–1790.* Ithaca, NY: Cornell University Press, 1998.

O'Shaughnessy, Andrew J. *An Empire Divided: The American Revolution and the British Caribbean.* Philadelphia: University of Pennsylvania Press, 2000.

Ousterhout, Anne M. *A State Divided: Opposition in Pennsylvania to the American Revolution.* Westport, CT: Greenwood, 1987.

Paine, Thomas. *Common Sense.* In *Thomas Paine: Collected Writings,* ed. Eric Foner. New York: Library of America, 1995.

Palmer, R. R. *The Age of Democratic Revolutions.* Princeton, NJ: Princeton University Press, 1959.

Pemberton, James. *The Life and Travels of John Pemberton, A Minister of the Gospel of Christ.* London: Gilpin, 1844.

Pencak, William. *War, Politics, and Revolution in Provincial Massachusetts.* Boston: Northeastern University Press, 1981.

Perica, Ester. *The American Woman: Her Role during the Revolutionary War.* Monroe, NY: Library Research Associates, 1981.

Piker, Joshua. *Okfuskee: A Creek Indian Town in Colonial America.* Cambridge, MA: Harvard University Press, 2004.

Potter, Janice. *The Liberty We Seek: Loyalist Ideology in Colonial New York and Massachusetts.* Cambridge, MA: Harvard University Press, 1983.

Potter-MacKinnon, Janice. *While the Women Only Wept: Loyalist Refugee Women.* Montreal: McGill-Queens University Press, 1993.

Potts, J. Manning, ed. *The Journal and Letters of Francis Asbury.* 3 vols. London: Epworth, 1958.

Purcell, Sarah. *Sealed with Blood: Sacrifice and Memory in Revolutionary America.* Philadelphia: University of Pennsylvania Press, 2002.

Pybus, Cassandra. *Epic Journeys of Freedom: Runaway Slaves of the American Revolution and Their Global Quest for Liberty.* Boston: Beacon Press, 2006.

Quarles, Benjamin. *The Negro in the American Revolution.* Chapel Hill: University of North Carolina Press, 1961.

Rack, Henry. *Reasonable Enthusiast: John Wesley and the Rise of Methodism.* London: Epworth, 1989.

Randall, Willard Sterne. *A Little Revenge: Benjamin Franklin and His Son.* Boston: Little, Brown, 1984.

Ranlet, Philip. *The New York Loyalists.* Knoxville: University of Tennessee Press, 1986.

Raphael, Ray. *The First American Revolution: Before Lexington and Concord*. New York: New Press, 2002.

Raphael, Ray. *A People's History of the American Revolution: How Common People Shaped the Fight for Independence*. New York: New Press, 2001.

Rediker, Marcus. *Between the Devil and the Deep Blue Sea: Merchant Seamen, Pirates, and the Anglo-American Maritime World, 1700–1750*. New York: Cambridge University Press, 1987.

Reinier, Jacqueline S. *From Virtue to Character: American Childhood, 1775–1850*. New York: Twayne, 1996.

Rhodehamel, John, comp. *George Washington: Writings*. New York: Library of America, 1997.

Richards, Leonard. *Shays's Rebellion: The American Revolution's Final Battle*. Philadelphia: University of Pennsylvania Press, 2002.

Richey, Russell E. *Early American Methodism*. Bloomington: Indiana University Press, 1991.

Richter, Daniel. *Beyond the Covenant Chain: The Iroquois and Their Neighbors in Indian North America, 1600–1800*. Syracuse, NY: Syracuse University Press, 1987.

Richter, Daniel. *Looking East from Indian Country: A Native History of Early America*. Cambridge, MA: Harvard University Press, 2001.

Ritcheson, Charles R. "Loyalist Influence on British Policy towards the United States after the American Revolution." *Eighteenth Century Studies* 7 (1973): 1–17.

Roberts, Cokie. *Founding Mothers: The Women Who Raised Our Nation*. New York: HarperCollins, 2004.

Roeber, A. G. "In German Ways? Problems and Potentials of Eighteenth-Century German Social and Emigration History." *William and Mary Quarterly*, 3rd ser., 44 (1987): 750–774.

Roeber, A. G. *Palatines, Liberty, and Property: German Lutherans in Colonial America*. Baltimore: Johns Hopkins University Press, 1993.

Rohrbough, Malcolm J. *The Trans-Appalachian Frontier: People, Societies, and Institutions, 1775–1850*. New York: Oxford University Press, 1978

Rohrer, S. Scott. "Searching for Land and God: The Pietist Migration to North Carolina in the Late Colonial Period." *North Carolina Historical Review* 79 (2002): 409–439.

Ronda, Jeanne, and James P. Ronda. "'As They Were Faithful': Chief Hendrick Aupaumut and the Struggle for Stockbridge Survival, 1757–1830." *American Indian Culture and Research Journal* 3 (1979): 43–55.

Rosswurm, Steven. *Arms, Country and Class: The Philadelphia Militia and the "Lower Sort" during the American Revolution, 1775–1783*. New Brunswick, NJ: Rutgers University Press, 1987.

Royster, Charles. *A Revolutionary People at War: The Continental Army and American Character, 1775–1783*. New York: Norton, 1979.

Russell, E. *The American Bloody Register.* Boston: Russell, 1784.

Ryan, Dennis P. "Landholding, Opportunity, and Mobility in Revolutionary New Jersey." *William and Mary Quarterly,* 3rd ser., 36 (1979): 571–592.

Ryerson, R. A. "Political Mobilization and the American Revolution: The Resistance Movement in Philadelphia, 1765 to 1776." *William and Mary Quarterly,* 3rd ser., 31 (1974): 565–588.

Sainsbury, John. *Disaffected Patriots: London Supporters of Revolutionary America, 1769–1782.* Kingston: McGill-Queen's University Press, 1987.

Salinger, Sharon. *"To Serve Well and Faithfully": Labor and Indentured Servants in Pennsylvania, 1682–1880.* New York: Cambridge University Press, 1987.

Salisbury, Neal. "Native People and European Settlers in Eastern North America, 1600–1783." In *The Cambridge History of the Native Peoples of the Americas,* 2 vols., ed. Bruce G. Trigger and Wilcomb E. Washburn, 1:399–460. New York: Cambridge University Press, 1996.

Saunt, Claudio. *A New Order of Things: Property, Power, and the Transformation of the Creek Indians, 1733–1816.* New York: Cambridge University Press, 1999.

Scholten, Catherine M. *Childbearing in American Society, 1650–1850.* New York: New York University Press, 1985.

Schultz, Constance B. "Children and Childhood in the Eighteenth Century." In *American Childhood: A Research Guide and Historical Handbook,* ed. Joseph M. Hawes and N. Ray Hiner, 57–109. Westport, CT: Greenwood, 1985.

Schultz, Constance B. "Daughters of Liberty: The History of Women in the Revolutionary War Pension Records." *Prologue: The Journal of the National Archives* 16 (1984): 139–153.

Schwartz, Sally. *"A Mixed Multitude": The Struggle for Toleration in Colonial Pennsylvania.* New York: New York University Press, 1987.

Selesky, Harold E. *War and Society in Colonial Connecticut.* New Haven, CT: Yale University Press, 1990.

Semmel, Bernard. *The Methodist Revolution.* New York: Basic Books, 1973.

Sensbach, Jon. *A Separate Canaan: The Making of an Afro-American World in North Carolina, 1763–1840.* Chapel Hill: University of North Carolina Press, 1998.

Shannon, Timothy J. *Indians and Colonists at the Crossroads of Empire: The Albany Congress of 1754.* Ithaca, NY: Cornell University Press, 2000.

Shy, John. *A People Numerous and Armed: Reflections on the Military Struggle for American Independence.* New York: Oxford University Press. 1976.

Sidbury, James. *Ploughshares into Swords: Race, Rebellion and Identity in Gabriel's Virginia, 1730–1810.* New York: Cambridge University Press, 1998.

Sidwell, Mark. "The Fruit of Freedom." *Christian History* 18 (1999): 38–41.

Simpson, Robert, ed. *American Methodist Pioneer: The Life and Journals of the Rev. Freeborn Garrettson, 1752–1827.* Rutland, VT: Academy, 1984.

Skemp, Sheila. *Benjamin and William Franklin: Father and Son, Patriot and Loyalist.* Boston: Bedford, 1994.

Skemp, Sheila. *William Franklin: Son of a Patriot, Servant of a King*. New York: Oxford University Press, 1990.

Smith, Barbara Clark. "Food Rioters and the American Revolution." *William and Mary Quarterly*, 3rd ser., 51 (1994): 3–38.

Smith, Billy G. *The Lower Sort: Philadelphia's Laboring People, 1750–1800*. Ithaca, NY: Cornell University Press, 1990.

Smith, Daniel Blake. *Inside the Great House: Planter Family Life in Eighteenth-Century Chesapeake Society*. Ithaca, NY: Cornell University Press, 1980.

Smith, Paul H. *Loyalists and Redcoats: A Study in British Revolutionary Policy*. Chapel Hill: University of North Carolina Press, 1964.

Snapp, J. Russell. *John Stuart and the Struggle for Empire on the Southern Frontier*. Baton Rouge: Louisiana State University Press, 1996.

Sobel, Mechal. *The World They Made Together: Black and White Values in Eighteenth-Century Virginia*. Princeton, NJ: Princeton University Press, 1987.

Sosin, Jack M. *The Revolutionary Frontier, 1763–1783*. New York: Holt, Rinehart and Winston, 1967.

Sosin, Jack M. "The Use of Indians in the War of the American Revolution: A Re-assessment of Responsibility." *Canadian Historical Review* 46 (1965): 101–121.

Steffen, Charles G. *The Mechanics of Baltimore: Walkers and Politics in the Age of Revolution, 1763–1812*. Urbana: University of Illinois Press, 1984.

Stegeman, John F., and Janet A. Stegeman. *Caty: A Biography of Catherine Littlefield Greene*. Athens: University of Georgia Press, 1977.

Taylor, Alan. *American Colonies*. New York: Viking Penguin, 2001.

Taylor, Alan. *The Divided Ground: Indians, Settlers, and the Northern Borderland of the American Revolution*. New York: Knopf, 2006.

Taylor, Alan. *Liberty Men and Great Proprietors: The Revolutionary Settlement on the Maine Frontier, 1760–1820*. Chapel Hill: University of North Carolina Press, 1990.

Tebbel, John. *Between Covers: The Rise and Transformation of American Book Publishing*. New York: Oxford University Press, 1987.

Tees, Francis, comp. "Journal of Thomas Rankin, 1773–1778." Drew University Library, Madison, NJ.

Telford, John, ed. *Letters of John Wesley*. 8 vols. London: Epworth, 1931.

Thompson, Peter. *Rum Punch and Revolution: Taverngoing and Public Life in Eighteenth-Century Philadelphia*. Philadelphia: University of Pennsylvania Press, 1999.

Thorne, Dorothy Gilbert. "North Carolina Friends and the Revolution." *North Carolina Historical Review* 38 (1961): 323–340.

Tiedemann, Joseph S. "Queens County, New York, Quakers in the American Revolution: Loyalists or Neutrals?" *Historical Magazine of the Protestant Episcopal Church* 52 (1983): 215–227.

Tiedemann, Joseph S. *Reluctant Revolutionaries: New York City and the Road to Independence, 1763–1776*. Ithaca, NY: Cornell University Press, 1997.

Tigert, Jonah. *A Constitutional History of American Episcopal Methodism [1894]*. Nashville, TN: Methodist Episcopal Church, 1908.

Titus, James. *The Old Dominion at War: Society, Politics, and Warfare in Late Colonial Virginia*. Columbia: University of South Carolina Press, 1991.

Tyerman, Luke. *The Life and Times of Rev. John Wesley, M.A., Founder of the Methodists*. New York: Harper and Brothers, 1872.

Tyler, John. *Connecticut Loyalists*. New Orleans: Polyanthus, 1977.

Ulrich, Laurel Thatcher. *A Midwife's Tale: The Life of Martha Ballard, Based on Her Diary, 1785–1812*. New York: Knopf, 1990.

Van Buskirk, Judith. *Generous Enemies: Patriots and Loyalists in Revolutionary New York*. Philadelphia: University of Pennsylvania Press, 2002.

Van der Zee, John. *Bound Over: Indentured Servitude and American Conscience*. New York: Simon and Schuster, 1985.

Van Tyne, Claude Halstead. *Loyalists in the American Revolution*. New York: Smith, 1929.

Waldstreicher, David. *In the Midst of Perpetual Fetes: The Making of American Nationalism, 1776–1820*. Chapel Hill: University of North Carolina Press, 1997.

Walker, James W. St. G. *The Black Loyalists: The Search for a Promised Land in Nova Scotia and Sierra Leone, 1783–1870*. New York: Dalhousie University Press, 1976.

Wallace, Anthony. *Death and Rebirth of the Seneca*. New York: Vintage, 1972.

Walsh, Richard. *Charleston's Sons of Liberty*. Columbia: University of South Carolina Press, 1959.

Walzer, John. "A Period of Ambivalence: Eighteenth-Century American Childhood." In *The History of Childhood*, ed. Lloyd DeMause, 351–382. New York: Psychohistory Press, 1975.

Watts, Michael R. *The Dissenters*. Oxford: Clarendon, 1978.

Weir, Robert M. "'The Violent Spirit': The Reestablishment of Order, and the Continuity of Leadership in Post-Revolutionary South Carolina." In *An Uncivil War: The Southern Backcountry during the American Revolution*, ed. Ronald Hoffman, Thad W. Tate, and Peter J. Albert. Charlottesville: University Press of Virginia, 1985.

Welderson, Paul. *Governor John Wentworth and the American Revolution: The English Connection*. Hanover, NH: University Press of New England, 1994.

Wesley, John. *A Calm Address to Our American Colonies*. London: R. Harris Hawes, 1775.

White, Alexander. *A Narrative of the Life and Conversion of Alexander White*. Boston: Powars and Willis, 1784.

White, Donald Wallace. *A Village at War: Chatham, New Jersey, and the American Revolution*. London: Associated University Presses, 1979.

White, Richard. *The Middle Ground: Indians, Empires, and Republics in the Great Lakes Region, 1650–1815.* New York: Cambridge University Press, 1991.

White, Shane. *Somewhat More Independent: The End of Slavery in New York City, 1770–1810.* Athens: University of Georgia Press, 1991.

Wigger, John H. *Taking Heaven by Storm: Methodism and the Rise of Popular Christianity in America.* New York: Oxford University Press, 1998.

Williams, William Henry. *The Garden of American Methodism: The Delmarva Peninsula, 1769–1820.* Wilmington, DE: Scholarly Resources, 1984.

Wilson, Ellen Gibson. *The Loyal Blacks.* New York: Putnam's, 1976.

Wokeck, Marianne S. *Trade in Strangers: The Beginnings of Mass Migration to North America.* University Park: Pennsylvania State University Press, 1999.

Wood, Gordon S. *The Creation of the American Republic, 1776–1787.* Chapel Hill: University of North Carolina Press, 1969.

Wood, Gordon S. *The Radicalism of the American Revolution.* New York: Knopf, 1992.

Wood, Peter H. "'The Dream Deferred': Black Freedom Struggles on the Eve of White Independence." In *Resistance: Studies in African, Caribbean, and Afro-American History,* ed. Gary Okihiro, 166–187. Amherst: University of Massachusetts Press, 1983.

Wood, Peter H. "'Taking Care of Business' in Revolutionary South Carolina: Republicanism and the Slave Society." In *The Southern Experience in the American Revolution,* ed. Jeffrey J. Crow and Larry E. Tise, 268–293. Chapel Hill: University of North Carolina Press, 1978.

Wright, Esmond, ed. *A Tug of Loyalties: Anglo-American Relations, 1765–1785.* London: Athlone, 1975.

Young, Alfred F. "George Robert Twelves Hewes (1742–1840): A Boston Shoemaker and the Memory of the American Revolution." *William and Mary Quarterly,* 3rd ser., 38 (1981): 561–623.

Young, Alfred F. *Masquerade: The Life and Times of Deborah Sampson, Continental Soldier.* New York: Vintage, 2005.

Young, Alfred F. *The Shoemaker and the Tea Party: Memory and the American Revolution.* Boston: Beacon, 1999.

Young, Alfred F., ed. *Beyond the American Revolution: Explorations in the History of American Radicalism.* De Kalb: Northern Illinois University Press, 1993.

Young, Philip. *Revolutionary Ladies.* New York: Knopf, 1977.

Zagarri, Rosemarie. *A Woman's Dilemma: Mercy Otis Warren and the American Revolution.* Wheeling, IL: Davidson, 1995.

Zimmer, Anne Y. *Jonathan Boucher: Loyalist in Exile.* Detroit: Wayne State University Press, 1978.

Zuckerman, Michael. "The Irrelevant Revolution: 1776 and Since." *American Quarterly* 79 (1992): 11–38.

Zuckerman, Michael. *Peaceable Kingdoms: New England Towns in the Eighteenth Century.* New York: Knopf, 1970.

Index

NOTE: italic page numbers indicate pictures.